FEMINIST
INTERPRETATIONS
OF
G. W. F. HEGEL

RE-READING THE CANON

NANCY TUANA, GENERAL EDITOR

This series consists of edited collections of essays, some original and some previously published, offering feminist reinterpretations of the writings of major figures in the Western philosophical tradition. Devoted to the work of a single philosopher, each volume contains essays covering the full range of the philosopher's thought and representing the diversity of approaches now being used by feminist critics.

Already published:

Feminist Interpretations of Plato, ed. Nancy Tuana (1994)

Feminist Interpretations of Simone de Beauvoir, ed. Margaret A. Simons (1995)

Feminist Interpretations of Hannah Arendt, ed. Bonnie Honig (1995)

FEMINIST INTERPRETATIONS OF G. W. F. HEGEL

EDITED BY
PATRICIA JAGENTOWICZ MILLS

THE PENNSYLVANIA STATE UNIVERSITY PRESS
UNIVERSITY PARK, PENNSYLVANIA

Library of Congress Cataloging-in-Publication Data

Feminist interpretations of G.W.F. Hegel / edited by Patricia
  Jagentowicz Mills.

     p. cm.—(Re-reading this canon)
    Includes bibliographical references and index.
    ISBN 0-271-01490-3 (cloth : alk. paper)
  ISBN 0-271-01491-1 (paper : alk. paper)
    1. Hegel, Georg Wilhelm Friedrich, 1770–1831. 2. Feminist theory.
  I. Mills, Patricia Jagentowicz. II. Series.
  B2948.F42   1996
  193—dc20   95-12708
                                            CIP

It is the policy of The Pennsylvania State University Press to use acid-free paper for the
first printing of all clothbound books. Publications on uncoated stock satisfy the
minimum requirements of American National Standard for Information Sciences—
Permanence of Paper for Printed Library Materials, ANSI Z39.48-1992.

For my son, Holland Mills,
in celebration of the love that binds our separate journeys.

And to the memory of E. Stuart Dalrymple,
gifted teacher, loving friend

Contents

Acknowledgments

Seyla Benhabib, "On Hegel, Women, and Irony," is reprinted by permission of the author and the publishers, Penn State Press and Polity Press, from *Feminist Interpretations and Political Theory*, ed. Mary Lyndon Shanley and Carole Pateman (University Park: The Pennsylvania State University Press, 1991), 129–45. Copyright © 1991 by Seyla Benhabib.

Luce Irigaray, "The Eternal Irony of the Community," is reprinted by permission of Cornell University Press from *Speculum of the Other Woman*, trans. Gillian C. Gill (Ithaca: Cornell University Press, 1985), 214–26. Copyright © 1985 by Cornell University.

Patricia Jagentowicz Mills, "Hegel's *Antigone*," is reprinted (with minor revisions) by permission of *The Owl of Minerva* from *The Owl of Minerva* 17, no. 2 (Spring 1986): 131–52. A slightly different version was incorporated into chapter 1 of her *Woman, Nature, and Psyche* (New Haven: Yale University Press, 1987).

David Farrell Krell, "Lucinde's Shame: Hegel, Sensuous Woman, and the Law," is a revised version of an article with the same title that appeared in *Cardozo Law Review* 10, nos. 5/6 (1989): 1673–86. Material from the original article is reprinted by permission of the author. Copyright © 1989 by David Farrell Krell.

Frances Olsen, "Hegel, Sexual Ethics, and the Oppression of Women: Comments on Krell's 'Lucinde's Shame,' " is a revised version of her "Comments on David Krell's 'Lucinde's Shame: Hegel, Sensuous Woman, and the Law.' " Material from the original article is reprinted by permission of *Cardozo Law Review* from *Cardozo Law Review* 10, nos. 5/6 (1989): 1687–93.

Naomi Schor, "Reading in Detail: Hegel's *Aesthetics* and the Feminine," reproduces material from her *Reading in Detail: Aesthetics and the Feminine* (New York: Routledge, 1987), which is reprinted with permission of the author and the publisher, Routledge, New York. Copyright © 1987 by Naomi Schor.

Eric O. Clarke, "Fetal Attraction: Hegel's An-aesthetics of Gender," is a revised version of an article with the same title that appeared in *differences: A Journal of Feminist Cultural Studies*, 3, no. 3 (1991): 69–93. Material from the original article is reprinted by permission of the author and *differences*.

Mary O'Brien, "Hegel: Man, Physiology, and Fate," is reprinted (with minor revisions) by permission of Westview Press, from Mary O'Brien, *Reproducing the World: Essays in Feminist Theory* (Boulder: Westview Press, 1989), 163–200.

Carole Pateman, "Hegel, Marriage, and the Standpoint of Contract," is derived from material in Carole Pateman, *The Sexual Contract* (Stanford: Stanford University Press, 1988) with the permission of the publishers, Polity Press and Stanford University Press. Copyright © 1988 by Carole Pateman.

Heidi M. Ravven, "Has Hegel Anything to Say to Feminists?" is reprinted by permission of *The Owl of Minerva* from *The Owl of Minerva* 19, no. 2 (Spring 1988): 149–68. Ravven's "Postscript" includes material excerpted from "A Response to 'Why Feminists Should Take the *Phenomenology of Spirit* Seriously,' " *The Owl of Minerva* 24, no. 1 (Fall 1992): 63–69. Material from the original response is reprinted by permission of *The Owl of Minerva*.

Carla Lonzi, "Let's Spit on Hegel," is a translation of an essay originally published in 1970 and reprinted in 1974. A third edition appeared in 1978 in a collection of the author's essays, *Sputiamo su Hegel: La donna clitoridea e la donna vaginale, e altri scritti*. All three versions were published in Milan, Italy, by Scritti di Rivolta Femminile. The translation by Giovanna Bellesia and Elaine Maclachlan is reprinted by permission of Scritti di Rivolta Femminile.

Preface

Nancy Tuana

Take into your hands any history of philosophy text. You will find compiled therein the "classics" of modern philosophy. Since these texts are often designed for use in undergraduate classes, the editor is likely to offer an introduction in which the reader is informed that these selections represent the perennial questions of philosophy. The student is to assume that she or he is about to explore the timeless wisdom of the greatest minds of Western philosophy. No one calls attention to the fact that the philosophers are all men.

Though women are omitted from the canon of philosophy, these texts inscribe the nature of woman. Sometimes the philosopher speaks directly about woman, delineating her proper role, her abilities and inabilities, her desires. Other times the message is indirect—a passing remark hinting at woman's emotionality, irrationality, unreliability.

This process of definition occurs in far more subtle ways when the central concepts of philosophy—reason and justice, those characteristics that are taken to define us as human—are associated with traits historically identified with masculinity. If the "man" of reason must learn to control or overcome traits identified as feminine—the body, the emotions, the passions—then the realm of rationality will be one reserved primarily for men,[1] with grudging entrance to those few women who are capable of transcending their femininity.

Feminist philosophers have begun to look critically at the canonized texts of philosophy and have concluded that the discourses of philosophy are not gender-neutral. Philosophical narratives do not offer a universal perspective, but rather privilege some experiences and beliefs over others. These experiences and beliefs permeate all philosophical theories whether they be aesthetic or epistemological, moral or metaphysical. Yet this fact has often been neglected by those studying the traditions of philosophy. Given the history of canon formation in Western philosophy, the perspective most likely to be privileged is that of upper-class, white males. Thus, to be fully aware of the impact of gender biases, it is imperative that we re-read the canon with attention to the ways in which philosophers' assumptions concerning gender are embedded within their theories.

This new series, *Re-Reading the Canon*, is designed to foster this process of reevaluation. Each volume will offer feminist analyses of the theories of a selected philosopher. Since feminist philosophy is not monolithic in method or content, the essays are also selected to illustrate the variety of perspectives within feminist criticism and highlight some of the controversies within feminist scholarship.

In this series, feminist lenses will be focused on the canonical texts of Western philosophy, both those authors who have been part of the traditional canon, as well as those philosophers whose writings have more recently gained attention within the philosophical community. A glance at the list of volumes in the series will reveal an immediate gender bias of the canon: Arendt, Aristotle, Beauvoir, Derrida, Descartes, Foucault, Hegel, Hume, Kant, Locke, Marx, Mill, Nietzsche, Plato, Rousseau, Wittgenstein, Wollstonecraft. There are all too few women included, and those few who do appear have been added only recently. In creating this series, it is not my intention to reify the current canon of philosophical thought. What is and is not included within the canon during a particular historical period is a result of many factors. Although no canonization of texts will include all philosophers, no canonization of texts that exclude all but a few women can offer an accurate representation of the history of the discipline as women have been philosophers since the ancient period.[2]

I share with many feminist philosophers and other philosophers writing from the margins of philosophy the concern that the current canonization of philosophy be transformed. Although I do not accept the position that the current canon has been formed exclusively by power relations, I do believe that this canon represents only a selective history of the tradition. I share the view of Michael Bérubé that "canons are at once the location, the index, and the record of the struggle for cultural representation; like any other hegemonic formation, they must be continually reproduced anew and are continually contested."[3]

The process of canon transformation will require the recovery of "lost" texts and a careful examination of the reasons such voices have been silenced. Along with the process of uncovering women's philosophical history, we must also begin to analyze the impact of gender ideologies upon the process of canonization. This process of recovery and examination must occur in conjunction with careful attention to the concept of a canon of authorized texts. Are we to dispense with the notion of a tradition of excellence embodied in a canon of authorized texts? Or, rather than abandon the whole idea of a canon, do we instead encourage a reconstruction of a canon of those texts that inform a common culture?

This series is designed to contribute to this process of canon transformation by offering a re-reading of the current philosophical canon. Such a re-reading shifts our attention to the ways in which woman and the role of the feminine is constructed within the texts of philosophy. A question we must keep in front of us during this process of re-reading is whether a philosopher's socially inherited prejudices concerning woman's nature and role are independent of her or his larger philosophical framework. In asking this question attention must be paid to the ways in which the definitions of central philosophical concepts implicitly include or exclude gendered traits.

This type of reading strategy is not limited to the canon, but can be applied to all texts. It is my desire that this series reveal the importance of this type of critical reading. Paying attention to the workings of gender within the texts of philosophy will make visible the complexities of the inscription of gender ideologies.

Notes

1. More properly, it is a realm reserved for a group of privileged males, since the texts also inscribe race and class biases that thereby omit certain males from participation.

2. Mary Ellen Waithe's multivolume series, *A History of Women Philosophers* (Boston: M. Nijhoff, 1987), attests to this presence of women.

3. Michael Bérubé, *Marginal Forces/Cultural Centers: Tolson, Pynchon, and the Politics of the Canon* (Ithaca: Cornell University Press, 1992), 4–5.

Introduction

Patricia Jagentowicz Mills

This anthology on Hegel, and the series of which it is a part, underscores not only the male bias of Western philosophy but one of the most significant issues in feminist theory today: feminist interpretation as contested ground. Single-volume anthologies on the canon done by feminists usually present only one interpretation of each thinker included: a feminist interpretation of Plato, followed by a feminist interpretation of Aristotle, and so on. Such an approach tends to elevate each feminist interpretation of a particular thinker to "the" feminist

My thanks to Nancy Tuana for her invitation to edit this volume and for her enthusiastic support and guidance during all stages of its development; to Peter Elbow who transformed my approach to writing at a crucial time; and to Sonia Kruks for her careful critical reading of the first draft of the Introduction. Finally, a special thanks to Larry Stepelevich for nurturing and encouraging my study of Hegel.

interpretation, obscuring the fact that there is not necessarily agreement among feminists about how to read any given philosopher. With the anthologies in this series the single interpretation approach is shattered, revealing a multiplicity of interpretations that mark the complexity of re-reading the canon through feminist eyes.[1]

The contemporary feminist concern with the German philosopher Georg Wilhelm Friedrich Hegel (1770–1831) began when the French feminist Simone de Beauvoir creatively appropriated parts of his philosophy for the development of her analysis of woman as Other in *The Second Sex* (1949). Beauvoir argued that the master-slave dialectic, the first moment of self-consciousness in Hegel's *Phenomenology of Spirit*, illuminates the relationship between man and woman: woman, if not literally man's slave, has nevertheless been condemned to a slave consciousness. Throughout history woman has neither lived on terms of full equality with man nor been conceptualized as his equal. In the dualistic metaphysics of Western patriarchal thought, man is the Subject, the Absolute, representing mind, transcendence, and spirit; woman is the object, the Other, the second sex, representing matter, immanence, and the flesh. Woman, understood as negativity, as all that is "not male," in this process of "othering"[2] is sentenced to a limited and dependent form of consciousness. Forced to serve as man's Other woman is alienated from her self.

The Second Sex is a monumental redefinition of what Marxism called "the woman question." As such it presents a feminist analysis in which Hegel's philosophy is embedded in an elaborate attempt to graft Marxist theory onto Sartrean existentialism. For Marx the master-slave dialectic gives a general description of the economic exploitation of the working class in capitalist society. This means that the working class, like the slave in Hegel's schema, represents the possibility of freedom through a dialectical overcoming. Within this analysis patriarchal domination, or the oppression of women by men, is seen as a consequence of economic exploitation.

Understanding heterosexual relations in terms of the master-slave dialectic complicates the Marxist project. Beauvoir contends that the sexual *oppression* of women by men revealed in her use of this dialectic is *significantly different* from the economic *exploitation* of the working class revealed by Marx's reliance on the same dialectic. Thus, where she believes a Marxist or socialist revolution is necessary to overcome class inequalities she does not believe that such an economic revolution is sufficient to break the chains of patriarchal domination.

Beauvoir maintains, with Hegel, that the heterosexual couple forms a "fundamental unity" made up of two halves that are necessary to one another (although she disagrees with the logical and ethical claims that Hegel makes based on the biological "fact" of heterosexual difference).[3] Women, therefore, as a group, can never achieve the solidarity of the working class or other oppressed groups. That is, the reproductive bond between men and women prevents women from organizing themselves into a single oppositional force against men, the group that oppresses them. Women, for Beauvoir, are a sex, not a class, and in their necessary relations with men, they are divided from one another.

This understanding of women as a sex-group should not, however, be seen as an "essentialist" position. Beauvoir does not hold that there is such a thing as "woman's nature," an innate, immutable or unchanging essence that is transcultural and transhistorical. Rather, she pulls apart the distinction between sex and gender in her famous statement that "one is not born, but rather becomes, a woman."[4] Through this conceptual separation of sex and gender the concept of "woman" is "de-essentialized" and "de-naturalized" as Beauvoir gives an account of how femininity is socially constructed to serve patriarchal interests.[5]

While Beauvoir argues that in patriarchy the subject is exclusively male, making woman merely an object, her own theory of subjectivity remains tied to the masculine, tied to Hegel's theory of the subject as actively moving out of "the dark cave of immanence 'into the light of transcendence.' "[6] Here, as many have noted, Beauvoir reduplicates the patriarchal formulations that link femininity to passivity and negativity, and masculinity to activity and positivity. At the same time, however, she challenges these formulations by arguing that women, too, can become subjects, can move out of immanence and achieve transcendence. But this is no easy task; it is a dangerous and risky project which requires that women embrace the terrifying freedom of Sartrean existentialism. What develops, according to Beauvoir, is a tension between women's struggle for freedom, for intellectual and economic autonomy, and the "bad faith" of women who accept their objectification, women who conspire to remain Other in order to avoid the dangers and risks of freedom.

With the emergence of the social and political struggles of the women's movement in the 1960s and 1970s, and the consequent development of feminist theory, Beauvoir's position came under attack. The politics of sisterhood, along with the emergence of lesbian separatism, combined to challenge Beauvoir's formulation of a necessary heterosexuality that precluded solidarity among women. And new feminist critiques of Hegel took her to task for (among other things) missing the crucial point that the master-slave dialectic is, for Hegel, a moment in the development of intersubjective relations between men that cannot be applied to relations between men and women. It was argued that woman does not, and cannot, have the consciousness of a slave because in Hegel's philosophy "woman" and "slave" are conceptualized as having radically different relationships to life, death, and work.[7]

Moving away from the master-slave dialectic to explain the oppression of women, feminists in the 1980s and 1990s began to focus critical attention on a more comprehensive analysis of Hegel's philosophical system. For the most part, it is this latest flowering of Hegel studies within feminist theory that is represented here. The authors in this volume think both with and against the grain of Hegel in their readings: some focus on prominent passages in his philosophy where he analyzes woman and the feminine; some search in the margins of his text for references to sexual difference; and some analyze aspects of his system that are only implicitly marked by sex/gender categories.

Included here are feminist readings by philosophers and theorists from many academic disciplines. Each article has its own way of reading Hegel and, together, the articles stress not only his phallogocentrism or "masculine rationality" (even when attempting to point beyond it), but the transgressive nature of feminist theory as it challenges disciplinary boundaries. It is important to note that this boundary dispute is not engaged in for the purpose of setting up new boundaries. That is, the contributions here are not to be seen as individual pieces in some attempt to create a unified feminist critical system; they are, rather, the articulation of the many different strategies and positions of the "vigorous debate" that is feminist theory.[8]

The volume is arranged so that articles with texts or themes in common are grouped together. We begin with four articles and a commentary (the chapters by Benhabib, Irigaray, Mills, Krell, and Olsen) that consider Hegel's conceptualization of woman in the *Phenomenology of Spirit* (1807) and the *Philosophy of Right* (1821). These two works contain Hegel's most conclusive and substantial comments on woman and heterosexual difference. The significance of these comments is, however, embedded in a philosophical system that is notoriously difficult, concerned as it is with saying everything in a totalizing system that is meant to make philosophy "speak German" as well as it "speaks Greek." Thus, there is no easy "introduction" to Hegel: one can only begin by thinking *with* him. This means thinking at a formidable level of opacity in which moments of philosophical brilliance sometimes eclipse patriarchal assumptions.

The *Phenomenology*, which Hegel describes as "the science of the experience *(Erfahrung)* which consciousness goes through" (para. 36), attempts to give an account of the progressive development of mind as it is realized in history. It begins with ordinary "natural" consciousness, and advances dialectically upward until it reaches the stage of consciousness in which truth is achieved as absolute knowledge. Consciousness is shown first in what appears as simple, unmediated sensation or "sense-certainty"; it then develops through perception and understanding *(Verstand)* to culminate in reason *(Vernunft)* as absolute mind. The successive stages of consciousness are said to be the unfolding of Spirit or *Geist,* defined as self-thinking thought or the self-knowledge of the universe.

In each stage of consciousness the same dialectical logic of becoming is at work in which a contradictory "moment" or negation emerges through Spirit's self-alienation or externalization *(Entaußerung);* a profound struggle between the two moments of opposition then takes place, from which emerges a third moment of "reconciliation" that simultaneously maintains, negates, and transcends the earlier moments. This third moment of dialectical overcoming, the *Aufhebung,* in which all dualisms, contradictions, and otherness are overcome or sublated, resists easy translation. The German word includes all three elements— preservation or maintenance, negation, and transcendence—and is a process that may occur instantaneously or over time.

Through dialectical logic the movement of thought is revealed as a process that overcomes the conceptual dualism or mutual exclusivity of the concepts of the understanding *(Verstand).* At the stage of reason *(Vernunft)* a higher unity or identity of concepts emerges that fuses concepts without canceling out their differences: reason can apprehend the concepts as an identity of identity and non-identity (identity-in-difference). Through this conceptualization of identity theory the *Phenomenology* sets out to challenge binary oppositions: the dualisms of mind and matter, universal and particular, history and nature, subject and object, self and Other, man and woman.

In the *Philosophy of Right*, Hegel continues the project of the *Phenomenology*, developing an explicit analysis of how Spirit or *Geist* objectifies itself in the modern world as law, social and political activity, and the state. The aim of this work is to resolve the relationship of desire to morality and ethical life. The analysis begins with a discussion of sexual desire within marriage, shifts to a focus on the generalized desire of civil society and the abstract morality of that sphere, and ends with a consideration of the concrete ethical life *(Sittlichkeit)* of the state. Where the *Phenomenology* describes the bifurcation of reason in the ancient world into the antagonisms of particular and universal, family and polis, woman and man, this bifurcation is shown to be dialectically overcome in the development of the modern Christian world into a triad consisting of family, civil society, and state.

The *Philosophy of Right*, as well as the *Phenomenology*, restricts the discussion of woman to the discussion of the ethical family. Thus, in the *Phenomenology* Hegel's reflections on woman are limited to the section on "Spirit" entitled "The ethical world. Human and Divine Law: Man and Woman" (BB.VI.A.a). In the *Philosophy of Right* they are confined to the section on "The Family" that begins the discussion of ethical life *(Sittlichkeit)*. It is important to note that in the ancient world described in the *Phenomenology* Hegel focuses only on the free woman, the woman who is, or will become, the wife of the male citizen, and ignores women who are slaves. In a similar manner, in the modern world described in the *Philosophy of Right*, his discussion focuses on the white European Christian bourgeois woman, the wife of the male citizen, and ignores all differences among women.

In his attempt to create a philosophical system that can recognize difference, Hegel holds to the complementary nature of the sexes, arguing for sexual difference in the context of a theory meant to be one of "separate but equal" spheres. He contends that each sex represents a different aspect of ethical consciousness that needs the other. This difference entails that woman and man occupy distinct arenas of life. Woman, and all she represents, remains outside the political community, confined to the private realm of the family. The development of human consciousness or subjectivity that takes place in the public spheres is therefore sex-specific, limited to man.

The first two articles in this anthology extrapolate from Hegel's representation of woman as "the eternal irony of the community" in the

Phenomenology. Womankind—representing the familial moment of particularity that is essential to the community but is suppressed by it—becomes a disruptive or subversive principle in the ancient pagan world, threatening the polis, the arena of male political life.

We begin with Seyla Benhabib's reading of Hegel done through the "doubled vision" of feminist theory, a vision in which one eye is on what the text explicitly says about women while the other eye is on what the text conceals about them.[9] As a prologue to her analysis of Hegel, Benhabib describes three different feminist ways of re-reading the canon: (1) the "teaching of the good father"; (2) "the cry of the rebellious daughter"; and (3) a "feminist discourse of empowerment."

The "teaching of the good father" describes readings by mainstream liberal feminists in which the sexism of their favorite Enlightenment male philosopher is seen as an unfortunate accident of history. This "father" is then reclaimed though a re-visioning of his work to aid in the struggle for women's equality. The second approach, "the cry of the rebellious daughter," describes those readings (influenced by Lacan) that search in the margins of a philosopher's text for female speech in order to subvert the binary oppositions of phallogocentric discourse. The third reading, a "feminist discourse of empowerment," is an approach that Benhabib develops in her essay on Hegel. While Benhabib does not name any feminist theorists in connection with the first two approaches, a few of the thinkers included in this anthology might, with varying degrees of qualification, be said to fit her schema. What is more significant, however, is that the readings of Hegel given here reveal Benhabib's framework as much too narrow: most of these readings are outside its boundaries.

The heart of Benhabib's critique of Hegel's political thought focuses on the development of his views on heterosexual relationships and the subordination of women as they emerge out of his dialectical "logic of oppositions." As a way to illuminate the conservative conceptions of love, marriage, and gender difference inscribed in Hegel's later work, Benhabib explores his earlier writings. She analyzes the romantic musings on sex and love in the "Fragment on Love" (1797–98) together with the condemnation of free love in the marginal notes on *Lucinde* (Friedrich Schlegel's utopian novel) in the *Philosophy of Right* (1821). This contrapositioning of texts leads to a consideration of Hegel's presentation of Antigone in the *Phenomenology* (1807). Benhabib concludes that women, along with irony, tragedy, and contingency, are the victims of the historical march of the Hegelian dialectic whose vision of reconciliation "has long ceased to convince."

Arguing that women need to "restore irony to the dialectic" by reclaiming the lives of its female victims, Benhabib situates Hegel's views on women within their historical context. She presents a sketch of several German women who were Hegel's contemporaries, women who were the foremothers of female emancipation. Thus, Caroline Schlegel Schelling and Karoline von Günderode, among others, are recalled to inspire a feminist discourse of empowerment.

The second article on woman and irony in the *Phenomenology* is a radical meditation done by the controversial French feminist Luce Irigaray. Readers may find the Irigaray chapter a troublesome piece, requiring as it does both a knowledge of the concept of woman developed in Hegel's text, and a familiarity with Irigaray's complex and convoluted philosophy. The difficulty is compounded by the fact that where Irigaray gives a close reading of Hegel's text, she nevertheless rejects traditional forms of argumentation, speaking instead "excessively" and "hysterically" from the place of woman as Other than "not male." For those unfamiliar with Irigaray's philosophy I offer in what follows some background information in order to clarify what she is attempting to do in her meditation on Hegel.

The significance for feminist theory of Irigaray's reading of Hegel lies not only in its fundamental challenge to the concept of woman in the *Phenomenology*, but also, as Naomi Schor has shown, in the relationship of Irigaray's theorizing to Beauvoir's philosophy. For both Beauvoir and Irigaray the central concern of feminism is "women's exile from subjectivity."[10] They share the conviction that within patriarchy the subject is exclusively male; and they share the belief that to challenge patriarchal domination woman must move into the position of the subject. But this commonality belies a deep disagreement: Beauvoir and Irigaray are not talking about the same subject.

The subject of Beauvoir's philosophy is, as noted earlier, a Hegelian (as well as a Sartrean) one. It is a sovereign, transcendent subject born out of the active struggle with all that is deemed Other. Woman in this account must move out of immanence in order to participate fully in the privileges of the "universal" subject. Irigaray's subject, on the other hand, is that of post-Sartrean/"postmodern" French thought; as such, its main attribute is language, not activity. Thus, for the female to achieve subjectivity in Irigaray's account she must "speak woman" (*parler-femme*).

And speaking woman, speaking a language of feminine specificity, subverts the notion of a universal Hegelian subject.

While Irigaray and Beauvoir present radically different theories of woman's subjectivity, it is important to note that they can also be understood as articulating two sides of the same problem. That is, where Beauvoir analyzes the process of "othering," the way woman is fixed in place as the Other, the second sex, Irigaray may be said to expose the process of "saming," a process in which woman as Other is not Other at all but only a defective male.

Saming is, for Irigaray, the logic of identity that permeates Western thought. It is a logic whose conceptualization of otherness allows only a pseudo-difference, a semblance of difference, to emerge. Woman as Other in identity logic is not truly Other, according to Irigaray, but merely the reverse or inferior copy of man; she is defined only in negative terms, in terms of absence, defect, and want. Woman not only "lacks" a penis, but because of this is said to have diminished rational capacities. The concept of "woman" in the metaphysical dualisms of patriarchal thought leaves all that is specific to woman unthought, unspoken, and unsymbolized.[11]

Where Beauvoir's analysis of othering "involves attributing to the objectified other a difference that serves to legitimate her oppression," the process of saming described by Irigaray "denies the objectified other the right to her difference."[12] The challenge for feminist theory here becomes that of thinking "woman" by thinking Beauvoir and Irigaray (othering and saming) together.[13]

In opposition to Beauvoir, Irigaray argues for feminine difference to be understood as positivity rather than negativity. This is an axial turn that redefines "the woman question," as "a question of woman," a question of self-understanding and self-creation posed by woman herself. In this context Irigaray claims that woman, because of her unique physiology, enjoys a special relationship to fluids/fluidity—with that which is in flux, non-identical. Her insistence on taking the female body into account in her philosophy of the feminine has led some postmodern theorists to charge Irigaray with "essentialism." They see in her work a return to an identity of sex and gender that had been so persuasively refuted by Beauvoir. In response to these charges several theorists have called for a more nuanced reading of Irigaray. While this is an important debate it is not one that can be resolved here.[14] Instead I simply want to underscore that in her reading of Hegel, Irigaray understands the relationship of woman to fluids/fluidity as part of the unsymbolized maternal-feminine that is the basis of all masculine philosophical constructions.[15]

For Irigaray the maternal-feminine-fluid that has been repressed or repudiated by phallogocentric metaphysics must be reclaimed in order to articulate sexual difference. Thus, when "speaking woman" in her meditation on the *Phenomenology* included here, Irigaray draws us into a psychoanalytic reading of Hegelian womanhood through blood imagery. Hegel's moment of "sublation," the *Aufhebung* or identity-in-difference of man and woman, is for Irigaray a mythical moment. It is a moment created out of the repression of sexual difference, the repression of woman as she represents "the power of red blood *(sang rouge)*."

Hegel's ideal relationship between man and woman is, in the *Phenomenology*, the (non-sexual, non-desiring) relationship of brother and sister found in the story of Antigone. What is important for Irigaray is that Antigone, the guardian of the (matriarchal) red-blood tie, is the sister who dies for her blood-brother, Polynices. Thus, the ideal relationship between man and woman is one that costs woman her life-blood, the rich, red fluid that links her originally to her mother. The loss of woman's blood in her menstrual flow recalls this sacrifice of the maternal-feminine, a sacrifice that Irigaray argues is required, but simultaneously repudiated, for the realization of male subjectivity in Hegel's philosophy.

But this male subjectivity, constituted by woman's bloodletting, becomes "bloodless." The assimilation of woman's life-blood in a process of "saming" that denies woman's specificity creates only an anemic, sickly male subject. Woman lives on, however, as the irony of the community, as the repressed, unconscious substance/fluid, erupting unexpectedly to express the power of the maternal-feminine red blood. In these moments of "the return of the repressed," woman's difference disrupts patriarchy, threatening the male community and the empty universality of male subjectivity.[16]

Irigaray has noted in *Speculum of the Other Woman* that woman's exile from subjectivity begins with her exile from the pre-Oedipal relation to her mother, a relationship nourished not only by red blood but by uterine fluids/fluidity. Therefore to speak woman into subjectivity is to invoke the plenitude of this fluid relationship. This entails no simple "identity" of mother and daughter, but rather, an "excessive" matriarchal identification where generations of females spiral through a genealogical ebb and flow.

Following Irigaray's meditation is my immanent critique of Hegel's philosophy, a critique that analyzes the contradictions in his elliptical discussion of Sophocles' *Antigone* in the *Phenomenology* and the *Philosophy of Right*. It is a reading of Hegel that is indebted to the work of T. W. Adorno, one of the critical theorists of the Frankfurt School. In my critique the previous concern with woman as "the irony of the community" is subsumed within an account of the relation between desire and recognition that excludes woman from subjectivity in Hegel's schema.

I argue that Hegel's interpretation of the *Antigone* is pivotal for understanding woman's role in his system. His fascination with this play emerges in both the *Phenomenology* and the *Philosophy of Right* where it serves to illustrate that the ethical life of the family is woman's unique responsibility in both the ancient and modern worlds. In the *Phenomenology* the tale of Antigone is told in the context of a historically specific account of the ancient pagan world as a world divided between universal and particular, man and woman. Here the relationship between Antigone and Polyneices, between *sister* and *brother*, is seen as the ideal relationship between woman and man because it is supposedly *free* from sexual desire. Then, surprisingly, in the *Philosophy of Right*, Antigone, the virgin sister of the ancient world, comes to represent a transhistorical and "wifely" ideal. She is invoked in this later work as the symbol of "family piety," the ethical purity of the relationship between *wife* and *husband* in the modern world, a relationship that is said to *transcend* sexual desire.

The omissions and discrepancies in Hegel's treatment of *Antigone* can be seen to emerge from his (mis)use of the play to serve the interests of his dialectical formulations. Two of the most telling omissions that I reclaim are Antigone's suicide and her relationship to her sister Ismene. Through a reinterpretation of the play I show that Antigone's actions move her beyond "woman's place" in the Hegelian system. My argument details how Antigone can be understood to subvert Hegel's concept of reconciliation, the *Aufhebung*, which denies the difference that woman represents and denies her access to self-consciousness. The limitations placed on woman by Hegel reveal not only woman's domination but the limitations of his dialectical philosophy as a closed system of identity logic. This impels us to reconceive dialectical thinking, pointing to Adorno's *negative* dialectic that remains open to the difference that woman represents.

In the next chapter David Krell, influenced by Derrida's deconstructive turn, searches in the margins of Hegel's *Philosophy of Right* for the "excess" or textual debris. Rethinking the margins, the marginalia or textual excess, is important for postmodern readings of the canon that emphasize the problem of (sexual) difference. This strategy puts into question the distinction between what is central to or "inside" a text and what is marginal or "outside." The margin as "the other" of a text, reveals the inability of any text to be totalizing, to incorporate all that is "other." What remains "outside" or in the margins (i.e., sexual difference) "decenters" the text, challenging not only the distinction between margin and center but all hierarchical dualisms. "Marginal" readings, therefore, are said to subvert Western phallogocentrism by "exceeding" all its binary oppositions.

Krell, like Benhabib, finds the literary figure of Lucinde in the margins of the *Philosophy of Right,* situated between the figures of the Venus *vaga* (the wandering or vagabond Venus/Aphrodite) and Antigone. His reading stays within the German text and focuses on several of Hegel's handwritten notes on *Lucinde* that have not been included in the English translation. Krell begins by recalling that Hegel wants Spirit "alive." Spirit alive is Spirit that is sensuous as well as rational; it is a notion of Spirit that Krell links to woman, the embodiment of "sentience, sensibility, and sensuality." But Lucinde, as sensual woman, disturbs Hegel according to Krell, causing him anxiety as he tries to "place" her in a philosophical system that both requires and attempts to control what she represents.

In order to tease out the significance of the margins Krell recounts the tale of *Lucinde,* Schlegel's "scandalous novel" of "free love" between a man and an older woman, published in 1799. Krell argues that in abandoning herself to her young lover, Lucinde, more than Antigone, represents the "law of woman," as the "law of the goddess," the law of Venus/Aphrodite. Woman as lover, giving in freely to her desire, refuses submission to the Hegelian system that tries to fix her in place. Unwilling to die like Antigone, Lucinde remains alive to haunt Hegel's system as the representative of the passionate surrender that subverts the rule of reason by undermining the laws of marriage and the family meant to contain desire.

In her commentary on Krell, Frances Olsen remarks that what he shows us is that Lucinde, as the representation of sensuous woman, "places the whole of Hegel's speculative system in jeopardy." But Olsen questions Krell's elevation of Lucinde to man's equal as passionate lover, giving "freely" of herself. She sees this representation of woman as a male fantasy, a dream of woman's equality that occludes the reality of patriarchal domination. Olsen puts the question of sexual equality into a contemporary perspective by referring back to Hegel's linkage of Lucinde with the female victims of male seducers: here "free love" is understood to be at woman's expense. In a society built on gender hierarchies of male domination, woman is never man's equal; a male lover never pays the social and/or emotional price that woman is required to pay for defying social conventions. Olsen concludes her reflections on Krell's reading with comments on the female literary characters created by Jane Austen and the Brontë sisters—characters that do not fit neatly into male fantasies about women.

We then turn to two different considerations of Hegel's *Aesthetics*, both of which are influenced by postmodern/poststructural theories. The first article, by Naomi Schor, focuses on "the detail" as an aesthetic category in Hegel's work as it relates to his conceptualization of "the feminine." The second piece, by Eric Clarke, looks at the relation between aesthetic creation and maternity in Hegel's philosophy.

A much-neglected but important work, the *Aesthetics* is a difficult text, compiled from notes for a series of lectures that Hegel gave in Berlin in the 1820s; the work was first published in 1835, after Hegel's death; a second and revised edition appeared in 1842. What Hegel was attempting to do in these lectures was to develop a philosophy of artistic beauty as an Ideal distinct from the beauty of nature. Surveying the history of art in terms of the dialectical development of aesthetic consciousness, Hegel delineates three forms of art: the symbolic, the classical, and the romantic. He then associates each of these three general forms of art with particular arts (i.e., architecture, sculpture, painting, music, and poetry).

Schor's close and careful reading of Hegel's *Aesthetics* is part of a larger work, her "feminist archaeology" of the detail as an aesthetic category in nineteenth-century art and literature.[17] It is a study born of the contemporary cultural legitimation of the detail, the privileging of the particular over the general or universal. Schor contends that the detail cannot be understood without reference to sexual difference—without reference to the complex and "overdetermined" process in which "the detail is gendered as feminine." Noting that there are few explicit references to sexual difference in the *Aesthetics*, Schor argues that this omission does not mean Hegel's Idealist aesthetic theory is sexually neutral. On the contrary, the implicit and recurring association of "the detail as negativity" with "the feminine" in this work marks Hegel's participation in a wider discourse of misogyny. Thus, Hegel's "dialectical sublation or sublimation of the detail" is exposed as a limiting move for woman and all that is linked to femininity.

Schor frames her reading of the *Aesthetics* with the question, Is the detail feminine? It is a question that foregrounds the problem of essentialism. That is, where the detail has been traditionally associated with the feminine and "devalorized," the question still remains as to whether it *is* feminine. (Are women more grounded than men in the everyday world of the particular, the world of immanence? Does women's art exhibit more attention to homey and/or ornamental details than art produced by men?) In the context of her answer to this question Schor begins to develop a feminist "aesthetics of difference" by critically appropriating Lukács's study of the detail in Hegel's *Logic* (1812–16).

While Schor's reading of the feminine is a feminist archaeology, a feminist reading influenced by postmodern strategies, it should be noted that where some feminists find the postmodern or linguistic turn important for the development of feminist theory, other feminists are suspicious of it. Some are concerned about the current hegemony of postmodern feminism because they see it creating an excessive intellectualism, a "pure" theory divorced from feminist practice. Some are wary of what they perceive to be the relativism of postmodernism. And some also see in this turn the development of a radical nominalism in which historical women are removed from postmodern discursive practices, thereby precluding any analysis of the lived reality of women's lives. Still others object to postmodern strategies as attempts by male theorists (writing after the "death of the [male] subject") to co-opt "the newly born woman," the subject conceived through woman's voice. This co-optation is possible because speaking the postmodern "feminine" requires no link to "woman's experience": sex and gender are categorically severed at the same time that "woman," "women," and "experience" are put under erasure as "essentialist" concepts. Postmodern theorists who contend that language constitutes experience dismiss feminist invocations of "woman's body" or "women's experience" as a naive essentialism thus creating a postfeminist postmodernism: a "feminism without women" that is seen to sabotage the social and political activity at the heart of feminist theory.[18] The issues raised in the contentious debate about the relation between feminism and postmodernism cannot be decided here; they must remain in abeyance as we move on to the second article on Hegel's *Aesthetics*. [19]

Eric Clarke's reading of the *Aesthetics* is done through the lens of what Hegel has written in his *Encyclopedia* (1817; 1827), especially in the *Philosophy of Nature* and the *Philosophy of Mind*. Clarke argues that to appreciate fully the connection between "woman" and artistic creation in the *Aesthetics* requires an examination of how Hegel creates a "sex/gender tautology" in the *Encyclopedia*. The influence of postmodern strategies can be seen in Clarke's assertion that the category of "woman" occupies a "centripetal marginality" in Hegel's philosophy: "woman" is "paradoxically central because so marginal."

Clarke begins by examining Hegel's conceptualization of human reproduction in the *Philosophy of Nature*, a conceptualization that recalls Aristotle's views: woman is said to be passive, to provide the "matter" of fetal development, while the male supplies "spirit" or "subjectivity." In the *Philosophy of Mind* these "natural" differences become logical determinations that link woman to Nature and man to Spirit. At the same time, however, Hegel argues for the significance of prenatal maternity. The mother-fetus relationship is seen as one of fluid identity in which the mother's physical/psychic influence is manifest on the body of the infant as "birthmarks." Clarke's reading of the *Encyclopedia* then recasts Hegel's analysis: the sundering of woman into two (mother-fetus) is aligned not with Nature but with Spirit's ability to undergo self-alienation.

When Hegel's understanding of maternity is set in the context of his discussion of aesthetic creation, Clarke finds that motherhood sustains and gives meaning to a masculine Ideal of art, the work of artistic genius, while the feminine and the maternal remain inferior elements in Hegel's grand schema. Thus there is, according to Clarke, a "doubling"—a splitting of the *Aesthetics* into two texts—through "the simultaneous denial and appropriation of women and their procreative abilities." Moreover, this "contradictory deployment" of the feminine-maternal is disruptive; it unsettles and undermines Hegel's notion of dialectical progression.

Following the two readings of the *Aesthetics*, we come to a series of articles (those by O'Brien, Pateman, Ravven, and Starret), each of which re-visions some aspect of Hegel's account of marriage, reproduction, and the family. The first article in this series, by the Canadian feminist Mary O'Brien, ties in with Clarke's reading insofar as it focuses on the dialectics of maternity and paternity in Hegel's philosophy.

O'Brien's reading of Hegel is, like mine, an immanent critique. But where I read Hegel through the lens of Adorno's critical theory, O'Brien reads him through the lens of Marx's materialism, arguing that Hegel's idealized and ahistorical account of human reproduction should be reconceived to become the foundation of a materialist epistemology. In a discussion of the master-slave dialectic as a paradigm of class struggle O'Brien finds it irrelevant to the analysis of male supremacy. She then attends to Hegel's conceptualization of reproductive relations in the *Early Theological Writings* (1795–c.1800) and the *Phenomenology*. Here she finds the process of reproduction dialectically structured: the child is seen as the embodied unity of the two separated parents. Hegel is excused by O'Brien for his limited understanding of human reproduction that describes conception as a merely "natural" phenomenon. She argues that it was not possible to see reproduction as part of history, as subject to rational ordering, before the development of sophisticated contraceptive technologies.

In developing a feminist philosophy of birth, O'Brien presents an analysis of the "reproductive consciousness" of the two sexes. For man, she argues, there is an "alienation of his seed" in copulation that causes a shadow to fall over paternity: "there is no paternal certainty." In Hegel's philosophy this leads to the development of paternity as a Concept: paternity is conceptualized because it is not immediately known. Woman, on the other hand, always knows her child: there is no uncertainty of maternity. But what is most significant for O'Brien is something that fails to find a place in Hegel's analysis. It is the fact that woman *overcomes* "the alienation of *her* seed," her separation from the child, through the mediation of her labor in childbirth.

Having considered maternity and paternity in Hegel we then turn to Carole Pateman's article on the marriage contract in the *Philosophy of Right*. Pateman begins by distinguishing marriage from the family in order to highlight the contractual origin of the family. She reveals that a "sexual contract" (the story of man's patriarchal rule over woman) is the foundation of the social contract and the marriage contract (a contract that implies that man and woman are "civil" equals). In her examination of Hegel's views on contract and marriage Pateman unearths a puzzle. On the one hand, Hegel is a harsh critic of social contract theories and he argues against Kant's presentation of marriage as a purely contractual agreement. Kant's position is seen to degrade an ethical/love relationship into a relationship of "reciprocal use." On the other hand, Hegel insists that marriage originates in contract, although it is "precisely a contract to transcend the standpoint of contract."

In order to work through this Hegelian conundrum Pateman first untangles Kant's confusing but influential account of marriage. Kant is shown to both presuppose and deny that women have the "civil personality" necessary for being party to a (marriage) contract. This muddle is ultimately resolved for Kant when he casts woman in the role of man's property, making her an object, a thing, rather than a person. According to Pateman, Hegel's criticism of Kant only serves to obscure the similarity of their positions. That is, Hegel's marriage contract, like Kant's, suffers from a concern to secure what Pateman terms "the patriarchal rights of husbands." This leads Hegel, in spite of his enlightened views on marriage and divorce, to create a story of the sexual contract that remains one of male superiority in which woman is seen as a "natural" subordinate.

Pateman ends with a brief discussion of the legal and social history of the marriage contract that encompasses the period from the early nineteenth century to the last few decades. She examines this history in the context of feminist arguments seeking marriage contract reform. Beyond the difficulties and male bias in Hegel's marriage contract, Pateman finds that he provides insights into contract theory that feminists would do well to heed.

Following Pateman's analysis we turn to an article by Heidi Ravven on Hegel's concept of the family. Ravven highlights Hegel's critical attitude toward the traditional bourgeois family as she explores a path toward its transcendence. Disapproving of feminist readings that suggest to her that Hegel's philosophy be abandoned, Ravven finds that Hegel has something important to say to feminists. She argues that despite the fact that women and the family are left behind in the historical march of the Hegelian dialectic, there are grounds within Hegel's philosophy to view them as "capable of inner development through a process of dialectical self-criticism."

Ravven's reading emphasizes Hegel's "radical tendencies and liberal intentions" instead of his conservative views on women and the family. According to Ravven, bringing Hegel into the twentieth century necessarily means assuming women are fully human and rational. This done, she endeavors to follow through the implications of such an assumption for a neo-Hegelian feminist theory of human, social, and familial liberation. She ends with a postscript that argues against those who attempt to place the relationship between man and woman in the context of Hegel's master-slave dialectic.

Shari Neller Starrett, like Ravven, takes issue with feminist readings of Hegel that discount what she holds to be his critical insights. In particular, Starrett disputes readings in which the confinement of woman to the family and divine law is understood *only* as a form of oppression. Instead, she re-reads Hegel's philosophy in the context of an analysis of the feminist-spirituality/ecofeminist movement, focusing on the work of Charlene Spretnak and Mary Daly. She argues that Hegel's story of the confinement of woman to the family circle and divine law is also a story of "critical relations" in which the concept of the family is radicalized to become multi-generational in "a dramatic way" through its ties to the dead.

In addition, Starrett argues for a difference feminism on Hegelian grounds by extracting from Hegel's philosophy a form of woman's subjectivity that she finds important for the development of feminist theory. That is, women are seen to embody not only family piety but also a familial relationship that is "co-active": it is a "connective (and spiritual) being-with-others." This conceptualization of woman's subjectivity, constituted through its ties to others, is the opposite of the being-for-self or atomic individualism of man. Starrett is, however, careful to sound a note of warning about Hegel's (and Daly's) essentialism. And she notes the treacherous character of any analysis that reinforces the confinement of women to the family circle. Nevertheless Starrett believes that the risks involved in her re-reading of Hegel are outweighed by the possibilities proffered for feminist politics.

The last two articles, by Carla Lonzi and Alison Brown, focus on the relation of Hegel's philosophy to the feminist political practice of consciousness-raising. But where they share similar concerns, Lonzi and Brown offer diametrically opposed readings: Lonzi invites us to "spit on Hegel" in order to put woman in the place of the subject, while Brown wants to reclaim for feminism what she calls Hegel's theory of communication.

The article by the Italian feminist Carla Lonzi is a new translation by Giovanna Bellesia and Elaine Maclachlan of an early (1970) polemical piece. This work is an important document of European feminism and retains the tone of the early days of the women's liberation movement:

it is direct, uncompromising, and filled with the urgency of a revolutionary spirit. Lonzi's celebrated pamphlet informed the Italian feminist practice of *autocoscienza*, a process similar to, but not identical with, feminist consciousness-raising in the United States. *Autocoscienza* emphasizes woman's difference and stresses the discovery and (re)creation of woman as subject, a subject understood as both individual and social.[20]

Lonzi's reading of Hegel resonates with Marx's *Communist Manifesto* but she is critical of Marx's theory of revolution insofar as it remains wedded to Hegel's master-slave dialectic. Since Marx conflates women's oppression with economic exploitation his theory of revolution requires that women enter into the process of commodity production as abstract "workers" rather than as concrete "women." This effectively denies the specificity of patriarchal domination. Lonzi, in a move that presages the work of Irigaray, re-visions Marx to offer a radical redefinition of "the woman question" as "in and of itself both the means and the end" of revolutionary transformation.

Since the problems in Marx concerning women's oppression are seen to come from his appropriation of Hegel, Hegel's philosophy is denounced for its sexism. Lonzi asserts that "the *Phenomenology of Spirit* is a phenomenology of the patriarchal spirit." Yet, beyond her vehement dismissal of Hegel, she finds in his work a formula for the destruction of patriarchal society: the revolutionary alliance of women and young males against the patriarchs. Freedom will be achieved when women reject the patriarchal family and young men refuse to participate in war.

Lonzi seeks a social and symbolic revolution in which woman puts herself in the position of the subject, the position denied her by what we today call phallogocentrism. This subject-woman is the subject "unexpected" by the master-slave dialectic, the subject who "claims her own transcendence." This is no mere mimicry of male (Hegelian) transcendence (as in Beauvoir) but a "new" transcendence through which woman (re)creates history.

In the final chapter, Alison Brown looks to Judith Butler's account of the "genesis of language" in Hegel in order to argue that what Hegel has to say to feminists has to do with silences and a politics of communication. Brown explores what she terms Hegel's "implicit theory of communication," a theory that encompasses the silence of *intra*subjective or internal communication, communication with oneself, and the silence of *inter*subjective or external communication, the communication between self and other. Beginning from the problem of how women readers respond to their exclusion from the canon of philosophy, Brown distinguishes readings that merely process information from those that internalize and "give meaning to" a text. Arguing for a reading that calls "marginalized entities to presence," she contends that Hegel can help women to "understand the exact point where communication excludes by gender." Such an understanding reveals where and how women need to speak out against their oppression.

According to Brown, Hegel theorizes a first internal silence that is "gender-neutral" because it occurs "prior to meaning." At the same time, this silence has implications for feminist consciousness-raising because, through it, we come to understand our possibilities, our capacity to change ourselves. Hegel's second silence, the intersubjective silence or "the silence between a subjectivity and all its others," is then explored in terms of the enforced silence of women, the silence of the oppressed. Through an extrapolation of Hegel's theory of communication Brown contends that attending to the first silence enables women to break the second silence, to refuse being silenced by, and in relation to, others. She ends her essay with a critique of heterosexist gender constructions, arguing instead for gender diversity, for an understanding of (gender) identity as performative and provisional.

Read together, the essays in this anthology raise a constellation of questions that spin and weave themselves into a tapestry of the contemporary feminist debates. The problem of woman's exile from subjectivity becomes complicated by differing feminist readings that try to put woman in the place of the subject. What we must now ask is not only *how* women attain subjectivity, but *what* subject position are women seeking? In addition, a complex of questions are raised about the relation between postmodernism and feminism: How and when is a "postmodern" reading feminist? Is it enough to deconstruct "woman," "the feminine," or "sexual difference"? Or enough to see these concepts as issues of the "margins" of philosophy? After "decentering" a text what then? What *is* the relation of feminist theory to feminist practice? Is it always or necessarily "essentialist" to speak about "women's experience," or to argue for a connection between sex and gender, between biology and the social construction of femininity? How do postmodern arguments about gender diversity or gender "identity" as performative/provisional relate to feminist concerns regarding women's bodily experience (e.g., maternity, objectification, rape, abortion, or forced sterilization)? Does the post-modern linguistic turn effectively eliminate any way to understand the infant's pre-verbal "experience"?[21] How do the feminism/postmodernism debates relate to issues of marriage, maternity, and the family as issues of contract theory and reproductive consciousness? Can the problem of women's equality in marriage be solved by rewriting the marriage con-tract? Do women have a unique connection to "spirituality"? And, if so, can women's spirituality provide an antidote to atomic individualism, despirited materialism, and religious fundamentalism? Is it necessary and/or possible to think through the logics of woman's "othering" and "saming" at the same time? And, finally, how does the displacement of consciousness-raising, from the small groups that characterized the inception of the women's movement to the more generalized social and cultural forms of today, affect our understanding of the process of consciousness-raising as feminist practice?[22]

These questions lead us back to our beginning: the question of Hegel's relation to feminist theory. Hegel *articulates* one of the central problems with which political feminists are concerned: how to conceptualize identity and difference.[23] While feminism began with an identity politics that often did not take differences among women into account, postmod-ernism leaves us with a multiplicity of "differences" that seems to abandon feminist politics for the "high road" of theory. What remains to be done is to conceptualize woman's subjectivity as a form of intersub-jective recognition (a relation between self and other) that allows for both identity and concrete differences. This is a search for a relation that does not construct a group identity ("women") by denying differ-ences among women (differences of class, race, ethnicity, religion, sexual preference (differences that have engendered their own identity politics); neither, however, does it want to allow these differences to rule out the possibility of solidarity among women.

The point of contention that becomes evident from the various readings included here is whether or not, beyond the essentialism of his concept of woman, Hegel's speculative system, with its attempt to "reconcile" identity and difference, points us toward "answers" to the problem he has so well articulated. Is Hegel a "good father" whose philosophy needs only to be re-visioned through feminist eyes to enable the project of women's freedom (as Ravven, Starrett, Brown, and O'Brien contend)? Or do his limitations make him a "father" who offers only some insights that should be heeded (as Pateman indicates)? Or, is he, rather, just another "deadbeat dad," one who fails to deliver on his promise of freedom for women and therefore deserves only our contempt—to be spat upon—as Lonzi declaims? Is it the case that Hegel's concept of reconciliation (the *Aufhebung*) is a "mythical moment" (as Irigaray asserts) that ultimately "fails to convince" (as Benhabib suggests) because (as Krell, Clarke, Schor, and I argue) this concept of reconciliation cannot contain "woman" except through her domination, a formulation that not only "defeats" "woman" but subverts his philosophical system?

Because of the multiplicity of approaches, evaluations, and conclusions about the relation of Hegel's philosophy to feminist theory we arrive at the end of the volume with questions where some readers might have expected definitive answers. I hope that these questions will provoke more re-readings of Hegel that both broaden and deepen our understanding of feminist theory and feminist practice. In support of this aim I have included a Select Bibliography at the end of the book.

Notes

1. See, for example, *Women in Western Thought*, ed. Martha Lee Osborne (New York: Random House, 1979); *The Sexism of Social and Political Theory: Women and Reproduction from Plato to Nietzsche*, ed. Lorenne M. G. Clark and Lynda Lange (Toronto: University of Toronto Press, 1979); *Women in Western Political Philosophy: Kant to Nietzsche*, ed. Ellen Kennedy and Susan Mendus (Brighton: Wheatsheaf Books, 1987); *Feminist Interpretations and Political Theory*, ed. Mary Lyndon Shanley and Carole Pateman (University Park: Pennsylvania State University Press, 1991). Obviously the single-interpretation approach also applies to volumes by a single author who attempts to re-read the canon. See Susan Moller Okin, *Women in Western Political Thought* (Princeton: Princeton University Press, 1979); Jean Bethke Elshtain, *Public Man, Private Woman: Women in Social and Political Thought* (Princeton: Princeton University Press, 1981); Genevieve Lloyd, *The Man of Reason: "Male" and "Female" in Western Philosophy* (Minneapolis: University of Minnesota Press, 1984); and Arlene W. Saxonhouse, *Women in the History of Political Thought: Ancient Greece to Machiavelli* (Westport, Conn.: Praeger, 1985).

A limited challenge to the single-interpretation approach can be found in the two volumes edited by Bat-Ami Bar On: *Engendering Origins: Critical Feminist Readings in Plato and Aristotle* (Albany: State University of New York Press, 1994) and *Modern Engenderings: Critical Feminist Readings in Modern Western Philosophy* (Albany: State University of New York Press, 1994).

2. The term "othering" was coined by Mary Louise Pratt in "Scratches on the Face of the Country; or, What Mr. Barrow Saw in the Land of the Bushmen" (139), in *"Race," Writing, and Difference*, ed. Henry Louis Gates Jr. (Chicago: University of Chicago Press, 1989), 138–63. Cited in Naomi Schor, "This Essentialism Which Is Not One: Coming To Grips With Irigaray" (45), *differences* 1, no. 2 (summer 1989): 38–58.

3. Simone de Beauvoir, *The Second Sex*. trans. and ed. H. M. Parshley (New York: Bantam Books, 1961), xix.

4. Ibid., 249. This is the opening line of Book 2, chap. 12, on childhood. Unfortunately, Parshley's translation of Beauvoir's work leaves much to be desired. His translation of the title of Book 2 (*L'Expérience vécue*) as "Woman's Life Today" obliterates the phenomenological element of Beauvoir's account. A better translation would be "(Woman's) Lived Experience." For a comprehensive critique of Parshley's translation, see Margaret A. Simons, "The Silencing of Simone de Beauvoir: Guess What's Missing from *The Second Sex?*" in *Women's Studies International Forum* 6, no. 5 (1983): 559–64.

5. Sonia Kruks, "Gender and Subjectivity: Simone de Beauvoir and Contemporary Feminism." *Signs: Journal of Women in Culture and Society* 18, no. 1 (autumn 1992): 91.

6. Schor, "This Essentialism," 43 (citing Beauvoir, *The Second Sex*, 675).

7. See especially Mary O'Brien, *The Politics of Reproduction* (Boston: Routledge and Kegan Paul, 1981), 67–73; and Patricia Jagentowicz Mills, " 'Feminist Sympathy' and Other Serious Crimes: A Reply to Swindle," *Owl of Minerva* 24, no. 1 (fall 1992): 55–62.

In contemporary feminist debates African-American women have objected to the association of women and slaves, arguing that when white women claim their experience is synonymous with slavery they ignore the brutal reality of slavery in order to appropriate slavery for their own purposes. See bell hooks, *Ain't I A Woman: Black Women and Feminism* (Boston: South End, 1981). For the difficulties entailed by separating the categories "woman" and "slave" (since some slaves were women), see Elizabeth Spelman, *Inessential Woman* (Boston: Beacon, 1988), chap. 2.

For recent interpretations of Beauvoir in relation to the development of feminist theory see *Re-Reading the Canon: Feminist Interpretations of Simone de Beauvoir*, ed. Margaret A. Simons (University Park: Pennsylvania State University Press, 1995).

8. Elaine Showalter, ed., *The New Feminist Criticism: Essays on Women, Literature and Theory* (London: Virago, 1986), 4.

9. Benhabib's understanding of the "doubled vision" of feminist theory elaborates a formulation first developed by Joan Kelly-Gadol; see Kelly-Gadol, "The Social Relation of the Sexes: Methodological Implications of Women's History," in *Signs: Journal of Women in Culture and Society* 1, no. 4 (summer 1976): 809–23; reprinted in *Women, History and Theory* (Chicago: University of Chicago Press, 1984), 1–18.

10. Schor, "This Essentialism," 45. My presentation of the relationship between Beauvoir and Irigaray is, for the most part, a recapitulation of Schor's compelling and important argument.

11. Margaret Whitford, *Luce Irigaray: Philosophy in the Feminine* (New York: Routledge, 1991), 5.

12. Schor, "This Essentialism," 45.

13. Ibid. While Schor argues that feminist theory needs to think together how othering and saming conspire to oppress women, she also notes that it remains an elusive, perhaps insuperable, task.

14. Schor's "This Essentialism" gives an excellent account of the debate.

15. Whitford, *Luce Irigaray*, 7.

16. Irigaray's meditation on woman in the *Phenomenology* has been interpreted as a recasting of the master-slave dialectic by Heidi Ravven (see Chapter 10, note 34). However, Margaret Whitford argues against this interpretation since, unlike the master-slave relationship, Irigaray sees the male-female relationship as *essentially* non-reversible. See Whitford's *Luce Irigaray*, 120, 183–84.

17. Schor's reading takes a cue from Michel Foucault insofar as he used the term *archaeology* to describe his early explorations of discourse formation; see Foucault, *The Archaeology of Knowledge* (New York: Harper, 1972). Foucault also calls for the writing of a history of the detail in *Discipline and Punish: The Birth of the Prison* (New York: Pantheon Books, 1977).

18. I would argue that experience both precedes and exceeds language but that we must name experience in order to understand it. Thus, while naming can never capture the immediacy of experience—what is articulated is never *the same as* experience—we name experience to comprehend it; without naming, experience is simply passed through or endured. When concepts are linked to experience so that experience is understood, not just undergone, we are led to a rediscovery of philosophy as critical theory.

It is important to remember at this juncture that the women's movement began by naming experiences that had been undergone but were either surrounded by silence or misnamed (e.g., abortion and marital rape): naming experience was, and is, central to the process of consciousness-raising.

For an insightful account of the relationship between experience and language, see Linda Alcoff's "Are 'Old Wives' Tales' Justified?" in *Feminist Epistemologies*, ed. Linda Alcoff and Elizabeth Potter (New York: Routledge, 1993), 217–44.

19. For the feminism/postmodernism debate see, for example, Seyla Benhabib, Judith Butler, Drucilla Cornell, and Nancy Fraser, *Feminist Contentions: A Philosophical Exchange* (New York: Routledge, 1995); the introduction to Linda Nicholson, ed., *Feminism/Postmodernism* (New York: Routledge, 1990); Tania Modleski, *Feminism Without Women* (New York: Routledge, 1991); Linda Alcoff, "Cultural Feminism versus Post-Structuralism: The Identity Crisis in Feminist Theory," *Signs: Journal of Women in Culture and Society* 13, no. 3 (1988): 405–36; Sonia Kruks, "Gender and Subjectivity"; Sandra Bartky, "Sympathy and Solidarity: On a Tightrope with Scheler," in *Feminists Rethink the Self*, ed. Diana Meyers (Westview Press, 1995); Linda Martín Alcoff, "The Politics of Postmodern Feminism, Revisited," unpublished manuscript (1995); and bell hooks, "Postmodern Blackness" in *Yearning: race, gender, and cultural politics* (Boston: South End, 1990).

The phrase "the newly born woman" is taken from the title of a book by Hélène Cixous and Catherine Clément (Minneapolis: University of Minnesota Press, 1986).

20. For a discussion of the Italian feminist movement and the concept of *autocoscienza*, see *Italian Feminist Thought: A Reader*, ed. Paola Bono and Sandra Kemp (Oxford: Basil Blackwell, 1991), 8–12, and *Sexual Difference* by the Milan Women's Bookstore Collective (Bloomington: Indiana University Press, 1990), chap. 1.

21. Some psychoanalytic theories argue that it is precisely because our early experiences are prelinguistic that they maintain a disturbing intensity that colors adult life.

22. It is important to notice here that outside the boundaries of the feminism/postmodernism debates in the academy, in which subjectivity is simultaneously emphasized and challenged, the feminist memoir has developed into a protean genre in which women are writing for their lives. Women who no longer have the small political consciousness-raising groups in which to re-create themselves as social subjects have turned to the act of writing to re-member themselves. See, for example, Mab Secrest, *Memoir of a Race Traitor* (Boston: South End Press, 1994); Nancy Mairs, *Remembering the Bone House* (New York: Harper & Row, 1989); Elaine Brown, *A Taste of Power* (New York: Pantheon Books, 1993). For a theoretical account of women's autobiographical writing, see Shoshana Felman, *What Does a Woman Want?* (Baltimore: Johns Hopkins University Press, 1993).

23. In the past, the tradition of philosophy has addressed the problem of identity by asking the question: How are we the same person from infancy to adulthood? In answer to this question of identity I would argue that we have a bodily integrity (maintained through our physiological changes) imbued with memory that "identifies" us as "one particular person." Identity is therefore a complex and changing sense of self in which memory establishes a temporal continuity (the past recaptured in the present) through reason and imagination. Just as memory is fundamental to identity or selfhood, it is also central to political feminism. That is, memory is the mediation between the psychological and political spheres of life, and critical re-membrance is the impetus for women's liberation. See Patricia Jagentowicz Mills, "Memory and Myth: Woman's Time Reconceived," in *Taking Our Time: Feminist Perspectives on Temporality*, edited by Frieda Johles Forman with Caoran Sowton (New York: Pergamon Press, 1989), 61–73.

1

On Hegel, Women, and Irony

Seyla Benhabib

Das Bekannte überhaupt ist darum, weil es bekannt ist, nicht erkannt.
(The well-known is unknown, precisely because it is well-known.)
G. W. F. Hegel, *Phänomenologie des Geistes*

Some Methodological Puzzles of a Feminist Approach to the History of Philosophy

The 1980s were named "the decades of the humanities" in the United States. In many institutions of higher learning this designation prompted a debate as to what constitutes the "tradition" and the "canon" in literary, artistic, and philosophical works worth transmitting to future generations in the last quarter of the twentieth century. At the center of

Some of the material in this essay formerly appeared as Seyla Benhabib and Linda Nicholson, "Politische Philosophie und die Frauenfrage," in Iring Fetscher and Herfried Münkler, eds., *Pipers Handbuch der politischen Ideen* (Munich and Zurich: Piper, 1987), 5:513–62. I thank Linda Nicholson for her agreement to let me use some of this material in the present essay.

this continuing debate is the question: If what had hitherto been considered the major works of the Western tradition are, almost uniformly, the product of a specific group of individuals, namely propertied, white, European and North American males, how universal and representative is their message, how inclusive is their scope, and how unbiased their vision?

Feminist theory has been at the forefront of this questioning, and under the impact of feminist scholarship the surface of the canon of Western "great works" has been forever fractured, its unity dispersed and its legitimacy challenged. Once the woman's question is raised, once we ask how a thinker conceptualizes the distinction between male and female, we experience a *Gestalt* shift: We begin to see the great thinkers of the past with a new eye, and in the words of Joan Kelly Gadol "each eye sees a different picture."[1] The vision of feminist theory is a "doubled" one: one eye sees what the tradition has trained it to see, the other searches for what the tradition has told her was not even worth looking for. How is a "feminist reading" of the tradition in fact possible? At the present, I see two dominant approaches, each with certain shortcomings.

I describe the first approach as "the teaching of the good father." Mainstream liberal feminist theory treats the tradition's views of women as a series of unfortunate, sometimes embarrassing, but essentially corrigible, misconceptions. Taking their inspiration from the example of a progressive thinker like John Stuart Mill, these theorists seek in the classical texts for those moments of insight into the equality and dignity of women. They are disappointed when their favorite philosopher utters inanities on the subject, but essentially hold that there is no incompatibility between the Enlightenment ideals of freedom, equality, and self-realization and women's aspirations.

The second view I would characterize as "the cry of the rebellious daughter." Agreeing with Lacan that language is the symbolic universe which represents the "law of the father," and accepting that all language has been a codification of the power of the father, these rebellious daughters seek female speech at the margins of the Western logocentric tradition. If it is impossible to think in the Western logocentric tradition without binary oppositions, then the task of feminist reading becomes the articulation not of a new set of categories but of the transcendence of categorical discourse altogether. One searches not for a new language but for a discourse at the margins of language.

Juxtaposed to these approaches, in this essay I outline a "feminist discourse of empowerment." With the second view, I agree that the feminist challenge to the tradition cannot leave its fundamental categories unchanged. Revealing the gender subtext of the ideals of reason and the Enlightenment compromises the assumed universality of these ideals. Nonetheless, they should not be thrown aside altogether. Instead we can ask what these categories have meant for the actual lives of women in certain historical periods, and how, if women are to be thought of as subjects and not just as fulfillers of certain functions, the semantic horizon of these categories is transformed. Once we approach the tradition to recover from it women's subjectivity and their lives and activities, we hear contradictory voices, competing claims, and see that so-called descriptive discourses about the sexes are but "legitimizations" of male power. The traditional view of gender differences is the discourse of those who have won out and who have codified history as we know it. But what would the history of ideas look like from the standpoint of the victims? What ideals, aspirations and utopias of the past ran into a dead end? Can we recapture their memory from the battleground of history? This essay applies such a "discourse of empowerment" to G. W. F. Hegel's views of women.

Hegel's treatment of women has received increased attention in recent years under the impact of the feminist questioning of the tradition.[2] This feminist challenge has led us to ask, Is Hegel's treatment of women merely a consequence of his conservative predilections? Was Hegel unable to see that he made the "dialectic" stop at women and condemned them to an ahistorical mode of existence, outside the realms of struggle, work, and diremption that in his eyes are characteristic of human consciousness as such?[3] Is the "woman question" in Hegel's thought one more instance of Hegel's uncritical endorsement of the institutions of his time, or is this issue an indication of a flaw in the very structure of the dialectic itself? Benjamin Barber, for example, siding with the second option has recently written:

> What this paradox reveals is that Hegel's position on women is neither a product of contingency nor an effect of ad hoc prejudice. Rather, it is the necessary consequence of his belief that the "Prejudices" of his age are in fact *the* actuality yielded by history in the epoch of liberation. Hegel does not have to rationalize them: because they *are*, they are already rational. They need only be encompassed and explained by philosophy.

Spirit may guide and direct history, but ultimately, history alone can tell us where spirit means it to go.[4]

Judging, however, where "history alone can tell . . . spirit" it means it to go, requires a more complicated and contradictory account of the family and women's position at the end of the eighteenth and the beginning of the nineteenth century in the German states than either Barber or other commentators who have looked at this issue so far have provided us with. I suggest that to judge whether or not the Hegelian dialectic has stopped at women, we must first attempt to define the "discursive horizon" of competing claims and visions within which Hegel articulated his position. To evaluate the historical options concerning gender relations in Hegel's time, we have to move beyond the methodology of traditional text analysis to the "doubled vision" of feminist theory. In practicing this doubled vision we do not remain satisfied with analyzing textual discourses about women, but we ask where the women themselves were at any given period in which a thinker lived. With one eye we see what stands in the text, and with the other, what the text conceals in footnotes and in the margins. What then emerges is a "discursive space" of competing power claims. The discursive horizon of Hegel's views of women and the family are defined on the one hand by the rejection of political patriarchy (which mixes the familial with the political, the private with the public), and on the other by disapproval of and antagonism toward efforts of early female emancipation.

This essay is divided into two parts: by using the traditional method of text analysis in the first part I explore *the logic of oppositions* according to which Hegel develops his views of gender relations and female subordination. In particular I focus on the complex relationship among reason, nature, gender, and history. Second, having outlined Hegel's views of women in his political philosophy, I situate his discourse within the context of historical views on women and the family at the turn of the eighteenth century. I read Hegel against the grain; proceeding from certain footnotes and marginalia in the texts, I move toward recovering the history of those which the dialectic leaves behind.

Women in G. W. F. Hegel's Political Thought

In many respects Hegel's political philosophy heralds the end of the traditional doctrine of politics, and signals its transformation into social science. *Geist*, which emerges from nature, transforms nature into a second world; this "second nature" comprises the human, historical world of tradition, institutions, laws, and practices *(objektiver Geist)*, as well as the self-reflection of knowing and acting subjects upon objective spirit, which is embodied in works of art, religion, and philosophy *(absoluter Geist)*. *Geist* is a transindividual principle that unfolds in history, and whose goal is to make externality into its "work." *Geist* externalizes itself in history by appropriating, changing, and shaping the given such as to make it correspond to itself, to make it embody its own subjectivity, that is, reason and freedom. The transformation of substance into subject is attained when freedom and rationality are embodied in the world such that "the realm of freedom" is actualized, and "the world of mind [is] brought forth out of itself like a second nature." The social world is *Substance*; that is, it has objective existence for all to see and to comprehend;[5] it is also *subject*, for what the social and ethical world is can only be known by understanding the subjectivity of the individuals who compose it.[6] With Hegel's concept of objective spirit, the object domain of modern social science, that is, individuality and society, make their appearance.

Does his concept of *Geist* permit Hegel to transcend the "naturalistic" basis of gender conceptions in the modern period, such as to place the relation between the sexes in the social, symbolic, historical, and cultural world? Hegel, on the one hand, views the development of subjectivity and individuality within the context of a human community; on the other hand, in assigning men and women to their traditional sex roles, he codifies gender-specific differences as aspects of a rational ontology that is said to reflect the deep structure of *Geist*. Women are viewed as representing the principles of particularity *(Besonderheit)*, immediacy *(Unmittelbarkeit)*, naturalness *(Natürlichkeit)*, and substantiality *(Substanzialität)*, while men stand for universality *(Allgemeinheit)*, mediacy *(Vermittlung)*, freedom *(Freiheit)*, and subjectivity *(Subjektivität)*. Hegel develops his rational ontology of gender within a logic of oppositions.

The Thesis of the "Natural Inequality" of the Sexes

On the basis of Hegel's observations on the family, women, and the rearing of children, scattered throughout the *Lectures on the Philosophy of*

History, I conclude that he was well aware that differences among the sexes were culturally, symbolically, and socially constituted. For example, in the section on Egypt, Hegel refers to Herodotus's observations "that the women urinate standing up, while men sit, that the men wear one dress, and the women two; the women were engaged in outdoor occupations, while the men remained at home to weave. In one part of Egypt polygamy prevailed; in another, monogamy. His general judgment on the matter is that the Egyptians do the exact opposite of all other peoples."[7]

Hegel's own reflections on the significance of the family among the Chinese, the great respect that is shown to women in this culture, and his comment on the Chinese practice of concubinage again indicate an acute awareness that the role of women is not naturally but culturally and socially defined.[8]

These passages show a clear awareness of the cultural, historical, and social variations in family and sexual relations. Nevertheless, although Hegel rejects that differences between "men" and "women" are naturally defined, and instead sees them as part of the spirit of a people (*Volksgeist*), he leaves no doubt that he considers only one set of family relations and one particular division of labor between the sexes as rational and normatively right. This is the monogamic sexual practice of the European nuclear family, in which the woman is confined to the private sphere and the man to the public. To justify this arrangement, Hegel explicitly invokes the superiority of the male to the female while acknowledging their *functional complementarity* in the modern state.

The "Superiority" of the Male

The most revealing passages in this respect are paragraphs 165 and 166 of the *Philosophy of Right* and the additions to them. In the Lasson edition of the *Rechtsphilosophie*, Hegel writes that "The natural determinacies of both sexes acquire through its reasonableness *intellectual* as well as *ethical* significance."[9] This explicit reference to the "natural determinacies of the sexes" is given an ontological significance in the next paragraph:

> Thus one sex is mind in its self-diremption into explicit self-subsistence and the knowledge and volition of free universality, i.e. the self-consciousness of conceptual thought and the volition

of the objective final end. The other sex is mind maintaining itself in unity as knowledge and volition in the form of concrete individuality and feeling. In relation to externality, the former is powerful and active, the latter passive and subjective. It follows that man has his actual substantive life in the state, in learning, and so forth, as well as in labour and struggle with the external world and with himself so that it is only out of his diremption that he fights his way to self-subsistent unity with himself. In the family he has a tranquil intuition of this unity, and there he lives a subjective ethical life on the plane of feeling. Woman, on the other hand, has her substantive destiny in the family, and to be imbued with family piety is her ethical frame of mind.[10]

For Hegel men's lives are concerned with the state, science, and work in the external world. Dividing himself (*sich entzweiend*) from the unity of the family, man objectifies the external world and conquers it through activity and freedom. The woman's "substantial determination," by contrast, is in the family, in the unity and piety (*Pietät*) characteristic of the private sphere. Hegel suggests that women are not *individuals*, at least, not in the same measure and to the same extent as men are. They are incapable of the spiritual struggle and diremption (*Entzweiung*) that characterize the lives of men. In a passage from the *Phänomenologie* concerned with the tragedy of Antigone, he indicates that for the woman "it is not *this* man, not *this* child, but *a man* and *children in general*" that is significant.[11] The man by contrast, individuates his desires, and "since he possesses as a citizen the self-conscious power of universality, he thereby acquires the right of desire and, at the same time, preserves his freedom in regard to it."[12]

Significantly, those respects in which Hegel considers men and women to be spiritually different are precisely those aspects that define women as "lesser" human beings. Like Plato and Aristotle, Hegel not only assigns particularity, intuitiveness, passivity to women, and universality, conceptual thought, and "the powerful and the active" to men, but sees in men the characteristics that define the species as human. Let us remember that Geist constitutes second nature by emerging out of its substantial unity into *bifurcation* (*Entzweiung*), where it sets itself over and against the world. The process through which nature is humanized and history constituted is this activity of *Entzweiung*, followed by *externalization* (*Entäusserung*), namely the *objectification* (*Vergegenständlichung*) of human purposes and institutions in a world such that the world becomes a home for human self-expression. Women, since they cannot overcome unity and emerge out of the life of the family into the world of *universality*, are excluded from history-constituting activity. Their activities in the private realm, namely, reproduction, the rearing of children, and the satisfaction of the emotional and sexual needs of men, place them outside the world of *work*. This means that women have no history, and are condemned to repeat the cycles of life.

The Family and Political Life

By including the family as the first stage of ethical life (*Sittlichkeit*), alongside "civil society" and "the state," Hegel reveals how crucial, in his view, this institution is to the constitution of the modern state. The family is significant in Hegel's political architectonic because it is the sphere in which the right of the modern individual to particularity (*Besonderheit*) and subjectivity (*Subjektivität*) is realized.[13] As Hegel often notes, the recognition of the "subjective moment" of the free individual is the chief strength of the modern state when compared to the ancient polis. In the family the right to particularity is exercised in love and in the choice of spouse, whereas the right to subjectivity is exercised in the concern for the welfare and moral well-being of other family members.

   The various additions to the section on the family, particularly in the Griesheim edition of the *Philosophy of Right*,[14] reveal that Hegel is concerned with this institution, not like Aristotle in order to discipline women, nor like Rousseau to prepare the true citizens of the future, but primarily from the standpoint of the freedom of the male subject in the modern state. Already in the *Philosophy of History*, Hegel had observed that the confusion of familial with political authority resulted in patriarchalism, and in China as well as in India this had as consequence the suppression of the freedom of the will through the legal regulation of family life and of relations within it. The decline of *political* patriarchy also means a strict separation between the private and the public, between the moral and intimate spheres, and the domain of public law. The legal system stands at the beginning and at the end of family; it circumscribes it but does not control its internal functioning or relations. It recognizes and administers, along with the church, the marriage contract as well as legally guaranteeing rights of inheritance when the family unit is dissolved. In this context, Hegel allows women certain significant legal rights.

He radically criticizes Kant for including women, children, and domestic servants under the category of *jura realiter personalia* or *Personen-Sachen-Recht*.[15] Women are persons, that is, legal-juridical subjects along with men. They are free to choose their spouse;[16] they can own property, although once married, the man represents the family "as the legal person against others."[17] Nevertheless, women are entitled to property inheritance in the case of death and even in the case of divorce.[18] Hegel is against all Roman and feudal elements of the law that would either revert family property back to the family clan (*die Sippe*), or that would place restrictions on its full inheritance and alienability.[19]

The legal issue besides property rights that most concerns Hegel is that of divorce. Divorce presents a particular problem because, as a phenomenon, it belongs under two categories at once. On the one hand, it is a legal matter just as the marriage contract is; on the other, it is an issue that belongs to the "ethical" sphere, and more specifically to the subjectivity of the individuals involved. Hegel admits that because the bodily-sensual as well as spiritual attraction and love of two particular individuals form the basis of the marriage contract, an alienation between them can take place that justifies divorce; but this is only to be determined by an impersonal third-party authority, for instance, a court.[20] Finally, Hegel justifies monogamy as the only form of marriage that is truly compatible with the *individuality* of personality, and the subjectivity of feeling. In an addition to this paragraph in the Griesheim lectures he notes that monogamy is the only marriage form truly compatible with the equality of men and women.[21]

Contrary to parroting the prejudices of his time, or ontologizing them, as Benjamin Barber suggests, with respect to the right of the free choice of spouse, women's property, and divorce rights, Hegel is an Enlightenment thinker, who upholds the transformations in the modern world initiated by the French Revolution and the spread of the revolutionary Code Civil. According to the Prussian *Das Allgemeine Landrecht* of 1794, the right of the free choice of spouse and in particular marriage among members of the various *Stände*—the feudal stratas of medieval society—was strictly forbidden. It was legally stipulated "that male persons from the nobility . . . could not enter into marriage . . . with female persons of peasant stock or the lesser bourgeoisie (geringerem Bürgerstand)."[22] If such marriages nonetheless occurred, they were declared "null" and the judges "were not empowered to accept their continuation."[23] To avoid social dilemmas, the lawgivers then distinguished between "the lesser" and "the higher bourgeoisie."

Hegel's position on this issue, by contrast, follows the revolutionary proclamations of the French assembly which, codified as the Code Civil in 1804, were also adopted in those parts of Germany conquered by Napoleon.[24] Social strata differences are irrelevant to the choice of spouse and must not be legally regulated: the free will and consent of two adults (as well as of their parents), as long as they are legally entitled to marriage (that is, have not been married before or otherwise have falsified their civil status), is the only relevant point of view.

Yet Hegel inserts an interesting detail in considering this issue, which is wholly characteristic of his general attitude toward modernity. Distinguishing between the extremes of arranged marriages and the wholly free choice of spouse, he argues that: "The more ethical way to matrimony may be taken to be the former extreme or any way at all whereby the decision to marry comes first and the inclination to do so follows, so that in the actual wedding both decision and inclination coalesce."[25] Presumably this decision can also involve such relevant "ethical" considerations as the social background and appropriateness of the spouses involved. Consideration of social origin and wealth are now no longer legal matters to be regulated, as they were in feudal society, but personal and ethical criteria to be kept in view by modern individuals, aware of the significance, as the British Hegelian Bradley named it, of "my station and its duties."

While Hegel certainly was ahead of the Prussian legal practices of his time, and endorsed the general transformations brought about by the French Revolutionary Code Civil, he was, as always, reluctant to follow modernity to its ultimate conclusion and view the choice of spouse as a wholly individual matter of love and inclination between two adults. Hegel's views on love and sexuality, when placed within the larger context of changes taking place at this point in history, in fact reveal him to be a counter-Enlightenment thinker. Hegel surreptitiously criticizes and denigrates attempts at early women's emancipation and seeks to imprison women once more within the confines of the monogamous, nuclear family which they threatened to leave.

The Question of Free Love and Sexuality:
The Thorn in Hegel's Side

Hegel's 1797–98 "Fragment on Love" reflects a more romantic conception of love and sexuality than the tame and domesticized view of
marriage in the *Rechtsphilosophie*. Here love is given the dialectical
structure of spirit; it is unity in unity and separateness; identity in
identity and difference. In love, lovers are a "living" as opposed to a
"dead" whole; the one aspect of dead matter that disrupts the unity of
love is property. Property separates lovers by making them aware of their
individuality as well as destroying their reciprocity. "True union or love
proper exists only between living beings who are alike in power and thus
in one another's eyes living beings from every point of view. . . . This
genuine love excludes all oppositions."[26]

Yet the discussion of the family in the *Philosophy of Right* is in general
more conservative and criticizes the emphasis on free love as leading to
libertinage and promiscuity. One of the objects of Hegel's greatest ire is
Friedrich von Schlegel's *Lucinde*, which Hegel names "Die romantische
Abwertung der Ehe" (the romantic denigration of love).[27] To demand
free sexuality as proof of freedom and "inwardness" is in Hegel's eyes
sophistry, serving the exploitation of women. Hegel, in smug bourgeois
fashion, observes:

> Friedrich v. Schlegel in his *Lucinde*, and a follower of his in the
> *Briefe eines Ungennanten*, have put forward the view that the
> wedding ceremony is superfluous and a formality which might
> be discarded. Their reason is that love is, so they say, the
> substance of marriage and that the celebration therefore detracts
> from its worth. Surrender to sensual impulse is here represented
> as necessary to prove the freedom and inwardness of love—an
> argument not unknown to seducers.

And he continues:

> It must be noticed in connexion with sex-relations that a girl in
> surrendering her body loses her honour. With a man, however,
> the case is otherwise, because he has a field for ethical activity
> outside the family. A girl is destined in essence for the marriage

tie and for that only; it is therefore demanded of her that love shall take the form of marriage and that the different moments in love shall attain their true rational relation to each other.[28]

Taking my cue from this footnote in the text, I ask what this aside reveals and conceals at once about Hegel's true attitudes toward female emancipation in this period. The seemingly insignificant reference to Friedrich Schlegel's *Lucinde* is extremely significant in the context of the struggles for early women's emancipation at this time.

Remarking on the transformations brought about by the Enlightenment and the French Revolution, Mary Hargrave has written:

> The close of the eighteenth and the beginning of the nineteenth centuries mark a period of Revolution for men and Evolution for women. The ideas of the French Revolution, that time of upheaval, of revaluing of values, of imperious assertion of the rights of the individual, swept over Europe like a quickening wind and everywhere there was talk of Liberty, Equality, Fraternity, realised (and perhaps only realisable) in that same order of precedence. . . .
>
> The minds of intellectual women were stirred, they became more conscious of themselves, more philosophic, more independent. . . . France produced a writer of the calibre of Madame de Stäel, England a Mary Sommerville, a Jane Austen; and Germany, although the stronghold of the domestic ideal, also had her brilliant intellectual women who, outside their own country, have perhaps not become as widely known as they deserve.[29]

In this work devoted to *Some German Women and their Salons*, Mary Hargrave discusses Henriette Herz (1764–1847) and Rahel Varnhagen (1771–1833), both Jewesses, Bettina von Arnim (1785–1859), and Caroline Schlegel (1763–1809), among others. Of particular importance in this context is also Karoline von Günderode (1780–1806), the most significant woman German poet of the Romantic era, in love with Hegel's high-school friend, Hölderlin. These women, through their lives and friendships, salons, and contacts, and in some cases through their letters, publications and translations, were not only forerunners of the early women's emancipation, but also represented a new model of gender relations, aspiring to equality, free love, and reciprocity.

Definitive for Hegel's own contact with these women and their ideals, was the so-called Jenaer Kreis, the Jena circle, of the German Romantics, Friedrich and August Wilhelm Schlegel, Novalis, Schleiermacher, and Schelling. The journal *Athenäum* (1798–1800) was the literary outlet of this circle, frequented by Goethe as well as Hegel after his arrival in Jena in 1801. The "Jena circle" had grown out of friendship and literary cooperation among men but counted Caroline Schlegel among its most influential members. She had extraordinary impact on the Schlegel brothers, and was the inspiration for many of Friedrich Schlegel's literary characters as well as for his views on women, marriage, and free love.[30] It is widely believed that Caroline Schlegel was the model for the heroine in the novel *Lucinde*.

Born as Caroline Albertina Michaelis, in Göttingen, as the daughter of a professor of Old Testament, Caroline was brought up in an intellectual household.[31] Following traditional patterns, in 1784 she married a young country doctor, Georg Böhmer, and moved from Göttingen to Clausthal, a mining village in the Hartz mountains. Although she suffered from the narrowness of her new surroundings and from the lack of intellectual stimulation, she remained there until her husband's sudden death in 1788. Caroline, who was then mother of three, lost two of her children after her husband's death. With her daughter Auguste Böhmer, she returned to the parental city. At Göttingen she met August Wilhelm Schlegel, six years her junior, who fell in love with her. In 1792 she left Göttingen for Mainz, the home now of her childhood friend Teresa Forster, born Heym. In December 1792 the city fell to the French under General Custine; the aristocrats fled and the republic was proclaimed. Teresa's husband, Forster, who was an ardent republican, was made president of the Jacobin Club. His wife, no longer in sympathy with his views, left him but Caroline stayed on and worked with revolutionary circles. In the spring of the following year, 1793, a German army mustered from Rheinisch principalities, retook Mainz. Caroline was arrested and with her little daughter Auguste was imprisoned in a fortress. After some months, her brother petitioned for her release, offering his services as an army surgeon in return, and August Wilhelm Schlegel exercised what influence he could to obtain her freedom.

Caroline was freed, but was banned from the Rheinisch provinces; even Göttingen, her home town, closed its doors to her. She was now pregnant, expecting the child of a French soldier, and August Wilhelm arranged for her to be put under the protection of his brother, Friedrich, then a young student in Leipzig. A lodging outside the city had to be found for her; here a child was born, but it did not live. In 1796, urged by her family and realizing the need for a protector, Caroline agreed to become August Schlegel's wife and settled with him in Jena. She never really loved Schlegel, and with the appearance of the young Schelling on the scene in 1798 a new love started in her life. Caroline's daughter, Auguste, died in July 1800. Schlegel settled in Berlin in 1802, and the increasing estrangement between them was resolved by a divorce in 1803. A few months later, she and Schelling were married by his father, a pastor, and they lived in Jena until her death in 1809.

Hegel lived in the same house with Caroline and Schelling from 1801 to 1803, and certainly the presence of this remarkable woman, an intellectual companion, a revolutionary, a mother, and a lover, provided Hegel with a flesh-and-blood example of what modernity, the Enlightenment and the French Revolution could mean for women. And Hegel did not like what he saw. Upon her death, he writes to Frau Niethammer: "I kiss a thousand times over the beautiful hands of the best woman. God may and shall preserve her as befits her merit ten times longer than the woman of whose death we recently learned here [Caroline Schelling], and of whom a few here have enunciated the hypothesis that the Devil had fetched her."[32] A damning and unkind remark, if there ever was one!

Whether Hegel should have liked or approved of Caroline, who certainly exercised a caustic and sharp power of judgment over people, making and remaking some reputations in her circle of friends—Schiller's, for example—is beside the point. The point is that Caroline's life and person provided an example, and a very close one at that, of the kinds of changes that were taking place in women's lives at the time, of the possibilities opening before them and also of the transformation of gender relations. In staunchly defending women's place in the family, and in arguing against women's education except by way of learning the necessary skills to run a household, Hegel was not just "falling prey to the prejudices of his time." "His time" was a revolutionary one, and in the circles closest to Hegel, that of his Romantic friends, he encountered brilliant, accomplished, and nonconformist women who certainly intimated to him what true gender equality might mean in the future. Hegel saw the future, and he did not like it. His eventual critique of Romantic conceptions of free love is also a critique of the early Romantics' aspirations to gender equality or maybe some form of androgyny.

Schlegel's novel *Lucinde* was written as a eulogy to love as a kind of union to be enjoyed both spiritually and physically. In need of neither religious sanction—Lucinde is Jewish—nor formal ceremony, such true love was reciprocal and complete.[33] In the Athäneums-Fragment 34, Schlegel had defined conventional marriages as "concubinages" to which a "marriage à quatre" would be preferable.[34] *Lucinde* is a critical text, juxtaposing to the subordination of women and the duplicitous sexual conduct of the times a utopian ideal of true love as completion between two independent beings. Most commentators agree, however, that *Lucinde,* despite all noble intentions, is not a text of female emancipation: Lucinde's artistic pursuits, once they have demonstrated the equality of the lovers, cease to be relevant. The letters document Julius's development as a man, his *Lehrjahre,* his movement from sexual desire dissociated from respect and equality to his attainment of the ultimate companionship in a spiritually and erotically satisfying relationship. Women are idealized journey-mates, accompanying the men on this spiritual highway. "Seen on the one hand as the complementary opposites of men, embodying the qualities their counterparts lack, they are on the other, complete beings idealized to perfection."[35] Although in a section of the novel called "A dithyrambic fantasy on the loveliest situation in the world,"[36] there is a brief moment of reversal of roles in sexual activity which Julius sees as "a wonderful . . . allegory of the development of male and female to full and complete humanity,"[37] in general in the *Lucinde,* the spiritual characteristics of the two genders are clearly distinguished.

In his earlier essays such as "Über die weiblichen Charaktere in den griechischen Dichtern" and "Über die Diotima" (1793–94), composed after meeting Caroline Schlegel Schelling, and being enormously influenced by her person, Friedrich Schlegel had developed the thesis—to be echoed later by Marx in the *1844 Manuscripts*—that Greek civilization decayed or flourished in proportion to the degree of equality it accorded to women. In particular, Schlegel emphasized that inequality between men and women, and the subordination of women, led to a bifurcation in the human personality, whereby men came to lack "innocence, grace and love," and women "independence." As opposed to the crudeness of male-female relations in Homer, Sophocles in Schlegel's eyes is the poet who conceives his male and female characters according to the same design and the same ideal. It is Antigone who combines the male and female personality into an androgynous ideal: she "desires only the true Good, and accomplishes it without strain," in contrast to her sister,

Ismene, the more traditional feminine, who "suffers in silence."[38] Antigone transcends these stereotypes and represents a blending of male and female characteristics; she "is the Divine."

Read against the background of Schlegel's views, Hegel's generally celebrated discussion of Antigone in the *Phenomenology of Spirit* reveals a different message. In Hegel's version of Antigone, she and Creon respectively stand for "female" and "male" virtues, and forms of ethical reality. Antigone represents the "hearth," the gods of the family, of kinship and of the "nether world."[39] Creon stands for the law, for the city, human law and the dictates of politics that are of "this world." Their clash is a clash between equal powers; although through her acknowledgment of guilt, Antigone presents that moment in the dialectic of action and fate which Hegel considers necessary, it is eventually through the decline of the family and the "nether world" that Spirit will progress to the Roman realm of law and further to the public light of the Enlightenment. Spiritually, Antigone is a higher figure than Creon, although even the most sympathetic commentators have to admit that what Hegel has accomplished here is "an apologia for Creon."[40]

Ironically, Hegel's discussion of the *Antigone* is more historically accurate in terms of the condition of Greek women than Schlegel's; for Hegel sees their confinement to the home, and the enormous clash between the newly emerging order of the polis and the laws of the extended family on which Greek society until the sixth and seventh centuries had rested.[41] But in his version of Antigone, Hegel was not simply being historically more accurate than Schlegel; he was robbing his romantic friends of an ideal, of a utopian vision. If Antigone's greatness derives precisely from the fact that she represents the ties of the "hearth and blood" over and against the polis, notwithstanding her grandeur, the dialectic will sweep away Antigone in its onward historical march, precisely because the law of the city is public as opposed to private, rational as opposed to corporal, promulgated as opposed to intuited, human as opposed to divine. Hegel's narrative envisages no future synthesis of these pairs of opposites as did Schlegel's; whether on a world-historical scale or on the individual scale, the female principle must eventually be expelled from public life, for "Womankind—the everlasting irony (in the life) of the community—changes by intrigue the universal end of the government into a private end."[42] Spirit may fall into irony for a brief historical moment, but eventually the serious transparency of reason will discipline women and eliminate irony from public life. Already in Hegel's discussion of Antigone, that strain of restorationist thought, which will celebrate the revolution while condemning the revolutionaries for their actions, is present. Hegel's Antigone is one without a future; her tragedy is also the grave of utopian, revolutionary thinking about gender relations. Hegel, it turns out, is women's gravedigger, confining them to a grand but ultimately doomed phase of the dialectic, which "befalls mind in its infancy."

What about the dialectic then, that locomotive of history rushing on its onward march? There is no way to disentangle the march of the dialectic in Hegel's system from the body of the victims on which it treads. Historical necessity requires its victims, and women have always been among the numerous victims of history. What remains of the dialectic is what Hegel precisely thought he could dispense with: irony, tragedy, and contingency. He was one of the first to observe the ironic dialectic of modernity: freedom that could become abstract legalism or selfish pursuit of economic satisfaction; wealth that could turn into its opposite and create extremes of poverty; moral choice that would end in a trivial project of self-aggrandizement; and an emancipated subjectivity that could find no fulfillment in its "other." Repeatedly, the Hegelian system expunges the irony of the dialectic: the subject posits its opposite and loses itself in its other, but is always restored to selfhood via the argument that the "other" is but an extension or an exteriorization of oneself. Spirit is infinitely generous, just like a woman; it gives of itself; but unlike women, it has the right to call what it has contributed "mine" and take it back into itself. The vision of Hegelian reconciliation has long ceased to convince: the otherness of the other is that moment of irony, reversal, and inversion with which we must live. What women can do today is to restore irony to the dialectic, by deflating the pompous march of historical necessity—a locomotive derailed, as Walter Benjamin observed—and by giving back to the victims of the dialectic like Caroline Schlegel Schelling their otherness, and this means, in true dialectical fashion, their selfhood.

Notes

1. Joan Kelly Gadol, "Some Methodological Implications of the Relations Between the Sexes," *Women, History and Theory* (Chicago: University of Chicago Press, 1984), 1ff.

2. Cf. Genevieve Lloyd, *The Man of Reason: "Male" and "Female" in Western Philosophy* (Minneapolis: University of Minnesota Press, 1984); Patricia J. Mills, *Woman, Nature, and*

Psyche (New Haven: Yale University Press, 1987); Benjamin Barber, "Spirit's Phoenix and History's Owl," *Political Theory* 16, no. 1 (1988): 5–29.

3. Cf. Heidi Ravven, "Has Hegel Anything to Say to Feminists?" *The Owl of Minerva* 19, no. 2 (1988):149–68. Reprinted with minor revisions as Chapter 10 of this volume.

4. Barber, "Spirit's Phoenix and History's Owl," 20; emphasis in original.

5. Hegel, *Hegel's Philosophy of Right*, trans. and ed. T. M. Knox (Oxford: Oxford University Press, 1973), para 144, 105.

6. Ibid., para 146, 105–6.

7. G. W. F. Hegel, *Vorlesungen über die Philosophie der Weltgeschichte*, in *Hegels Sämtliche Werke*, ed. G. Lasson (Leipzig, 1923), 8:471. English translation by J. Sibree, *The Philosophy of History* (New York: Dover, 1956), 205. Since Sibree's translation diverged from the original in this case, I have used my translation of this passage.

8. *Philosophy of History*, trans. Sibree, 121–22.

9. I have revised the Knox translation of this passage in *Hegel's Philosophy of Right*, para. 165, 114, in accordance with Hegel, *Grundlinien der Philosophie des Rechts*, ed. Lasson, para. 165, 144; emphasis in original.

10. *Hegel's Philosophy of Right*, ed. Knox, para. 166, 114.

11. G. W. F. Hegel, *Phänomenologie des Geistes*, ed. J. Hoffmeister, Philosophische Bibliothek (Hamburg, 1952), 114:326. English translation by A. V. Miller, *Hegel's Phenomenology of Spirit* (New York: Oxford University Press, 1977), 274; emphasis in the text.

12. Ibid.

13. *Hegel's Philosophy of Right*, ed. Knox, paras. 152 and 154, 109.

14. Cf. the excellent edition by K. H. Ilting, prepared from the lecture notes of K. G. v. Griesheim (1824–25), *Philosophie des Rechts* (Stuttgart: Klet-Cotta, 1974), vol. 6.

15. *Hegel's Philosophy of Right*, ed. Knox, para. 40 addition, 39; cf. also Griesheim edition, para. 40 Z, 180–81.

16. *Hegel's Philosophy of Right*, ed. Knox, para. 168, 115.

17. Ibid., para. 171, 116.

18. Ibid., para. 172, 117.

19. The one exception to this rule is the right of primogeniture, that is, that the oldest son among the landed nobility receives the family estate. It has long been observed that here Hegel indeed supported the historical interests of the landed Prussian gentry against the generally bourgeois ideology of free and unencumbered property and commodity transactions, which he defended in the rest of his system. However, on this issue as well Hegel is a modernist insofar as his defense of primogeniture among the members of the landed estate is justified not with reference to some family right but with reference to securing an independent income for the eldest son of the family, who is to function as a political representative of his class. Cf. *Hegel's Philosophy of Right*, ed. Knox, para. 306 and addition, 293.

20. Ibid., para. 176, 118.

21. *Philosophie des Rechts*, Griesheim ed., para. 167 Z, 446.

22. Hans Ulrich Wehler, *Deutsche Gesellsachftsgeschichte* (Darmstadt: C. H. Verlag, 1987), 1:147.

23. Ibid.

24. Emil Friedberg, *Das Recht der Eheschliessung* (Leipzig: Bernhard Tauchnitz, 1865), 593ff.

25. *Hegel's Philosophy of Right*, ed. Knox, para. 162, 111.

26. G. W. F. Hegel, "Love," in his *Early Theological Writings*, trans. T. M. Knox (Philadelphia: University of Pennsylvania Press, 1971, 304).

27. *Hegel's Philosophy of Right*, ed. Knox, para. 164 addition, 263; cf. Griesheim ed., 436.

28. *Hegel's Philosophy of Right*, ed. Knox, para. 164, 263.

29. Mary Hargrave, *Some German Women and their Salons* (New York: Brentano, n.d.), viii.

30. Cf. ibid., 259ff; Kurt Lüthi, *Feminismus und Romantik* (Vienna: Harmann Böhlaus Nachf., 1985), 56ff.

31. Cf. ibid., 251ff.

32. G. W. F. Hegel, *The Letters*, trans. Clark Butler and Christiane Seiler (Bloomington: Indiana University Press, 1984), 205.

33. Friedrich Schlegel, *Friedrich Schlegel's Lucinde and the Fragments*, trans. and intro. Peter Frichow (Minneapolis: University of Minnesota Press, 1971); cf. Sara Friedrichsmeyer, *The Androgyne in Early German Romanticism*, Stanford German Studies (New York: Peter Lang, 1983), 18:151ff.

34. Schlegel, *Lucinde and the Fragments*, 165.

35. Friedrichsmeyer, *Androgyne*, 160; cf. also, Lüthi, *Feminismus und Romantik*, 95ff.

36. Schlegel, *Lucinde and the Fragments*, 46ff.

37. Ibid., 49.

38. Cited in Friedrichsmeyer, *Androgyne*, 120.

39. Hegel, *Phenomenology of Spirit*, 276.

40. George Steiner, *Antigones* (New York: Oxford University Press, 1984), 41.

41. Hegel's reading of Antigone is more inspired by Aeschylus, who in his *Oresteia* exposed the clash between the early and the new orders as a clash between the female power of blood and the male power of the sword and the law. The decision to speak Orestes free of the guilt of matricide is signaled by an astonishingly powerful statement of the clash between the maternal power of birth and the paternal power of the law. Athena speaks on behalf of Orestes: "It is my task to render final judgment: / this vote which I possess / I will give on Orestes' side / For no mother had a part in my birth; / I am entirely male, with all my heart, / except in marriage; I am entirely my father's. / I will never give precedence in honor / to a woman who killed her man, the guardian of her house. / So if the votes are but equal, Orestes wins." Aeschylus, *The Oresteia*, trans. David Grene and Wendy O'Flaherty (Chicago: University of Chicago Press, 1989), 161–62.

42. Hegel, *Phenomenology of Spirit*, 288.

2

The Eternal Irony of the Community

Luce Irigaray

Translated by Gillian C. Gill

On the one hand, the uterus in the male is reduced to a mere gland, while on the other, the male testicle in the female remains enclosed within the ovary, fails to emerge into opposition, and does not become an independent and active cerebrality. The clitoris moreover, is inactive feeling in general; in the male on the other hand, it has its counterpart in active sensibility, the swelling vital, the effusion of blood into the corpora cavernosa and the meshes of the spongy tissue of the urethra. The female counterpart of this effusion of blood in the male consists of the menstrual discharges. Thus, the simple retention of the conception in the uterus, is differentiated in the male into productive cerebrality and the external vital. On account of this difference therefore, the male is the active principle; as the female remains in her undeveloped unity, she constitutes the principle of conception.

'In the case of the eye,' says *Sömmerring*, 'it seems that the arteries are continued in finer branches, which no longer contain red blood. These branches pass initially into a similar vein, but finally into veinlets carrying red blood.'

—G. W. F. Hegel, *Philosophy of Nature*

The purpose that moves blood relatives to action is the care of the *bloodless*. Their inherent duty is to ensure *burial for the dead*, thus changing a natural phenomenon into a spiritual act. One more step (into negation) and we see that it is the task of womankind, guardian of the blood tie, to gather man into his final figuration, beyond the turmoil of contingent life and the scattered moments of his Being-there. Man is thereby raised into the peace of simple universality. In essence, woman has to take it upon herself over and over again, regardless of circumstances, to bury this corpse that man becomes in his pure state. She has to enable man to sublate a universality that smacks too much of the natural, or so it would seem, by affirming—for this is pure truth restored—that death is merely the peace of/and universality of the conscious essence of self. Man is still subject to (natural) death, of course, but what matters is to make a movement of the mind out of this accident that befalls the single individual and, in its raw state, drives consciousness out of its own country, cutting off that return into the self which allows it to become self-consciousness. Just as man must strive to make this negativeness into an ethical action by sacrificing his life for the city—in war for example—so woman must be that external and effective mediation that reconciles the dead man with himself *by taking upon herself the operation of destruction* that the becoming of mind cannot manage without. Thus woman takes this dead being into her own place on his return into the self—a being that is universal, admittedly, but also singularly drained of strength, empty and yielded passively up to others. She must protect him both from all base and irrational individuality and from the forces of abstract matter, which are now more powerful than he. Shielding him from the dishonoring operation of unconscious desires and natural negativeness—*preserving him from her desire, perhaps?*—she places this kinsman back in *the womb of the earth* and thus reunites him with undying, elemental individuality. To do this is also to reassociate him with a—religious—community that controls the violent acts of singular matter and the base urges which, unleashed upon the dead man, might yet destroy him. This supreme duty constitutes the divine law, or *positive* ethical action, as it relates to the individual.

Yet, on the other hand, human law places a negative meaning upon this individualism. In fact each member of the city has a right both to a living and to Being-for-itself, wherein the mind finds its reality and its being-there. But the mind is at the same time the strength of the whole, and hence it gathers *these individual parts* into *one negative entity*. The mind reminds the parts that they are dependent upon this totality and that they owe their *life* to it entirely. Thus any associations—such as families—that one assumes have been founded primarily to serve individual ends, whether the acquisition of personal wealth or the search for sexual pleasures, invite a war that may disrupt their intimate life and violate their independence since these threaten to shatter the whole. All those who persist in following the dictates of individualism must be taught by the government to fear a master: death. They must be prevented from sinking into the neutral Being-there, from regressing into the inner world of the senses, from ecstatically entering a world beyond, lacking all predicates that can be appropriated by the self of consciousness. *The cult of the dead and the cult of death* would thus be the point where divine law and human law join. And also that point where, at least on the higher ethical level, the relationship between man and woman is possible.

This unsullied relationship takes place only *between brother and sister.* They are the same blood, but in them blood is at rest and in balance. Thus they do not desire each other, they have neither given nor received this Being-for-the-self from each other, they are free individualities vis-à-vis each other. What is it, then, that impels them to unite so that finally one passes into the other? What meaning does each have for the other that draws them thus into this exchange? Is it recognition of *blood?* Of their common allegiance to the power of the *same blood?* Could it be their complicity in the permanence, the continuance of blood that a matriarchal type of lineage ensures in its purest and most universal being? In this sense the family of Oedipus would be quite exemplary because the mother of the husband is also his wife, thus re-marking the blood tie between the children of that union—including Polynices and Antigone. Furthermore, the uncle—the mother's brother—will in this family be the representative of an already patriarchal power. Or is it rather that brother and sister share in the *same sperm,* thus giving consanguineity an (other) equilibrium, ridding it of its own magic passion but counterbalancing it with another? In fact, however, the sperm does not join with the blood (though it was long thought to do so) but with the ovum: had this copulation been given its full weight and "effectiveness," it would already have irremediably shattered the unity of mind and ethical substance. Moreover, copulation takes place only in the impure mingling of the marriage of husband and wife. Are we then to seek this pact between sister and brother in a *common name,* in the notion that their co-uterine attraction is matched by their submission—represented by the patronymic—to symbolic rules that might be supposed to carry the potency of blood one step further and already to raise the family community to the types of laws in force in the city?

Thus, for one instant, brother and sister would recognize each other in their single self, each able to affirm a right that is achieved through the power each has when balanced in/by the other; the power of red blood and of its reabsorption, its sublation into a process of denominating—i.e., of semblance. An ideal distribution would hypothetically occur in which the (ethical) substance of matriarchy and of patriarchy would coexist, contributing their own subsistence to each other, in a peace without alloy, a relationship without desire. The war of the sexes would not take place here. But this moment is mythical, of course, and the *Hegelian dream* outlined above is already the effect of a dialectic produced by the discourse of patriarchy. It is a consoling fancy, a truce in the struggle between uneven foes, a denial of the guilt already weighing heavily upon the development of the subject; it is the delusion of a *bisexuality* assured for each in the connection and passage, one into the other, of each sex. Yet both sexes, male and female, have already yielded to a destiny that is different for each. This is so even if rape, murder, breaking and entering, injury, were still, in appearance at least, in general at least, suspended between brother and sister. But in fact such is not the case, as Hegel admits when he affirms that the brother is for the sister that possibility of recognition of which she is deprived as mother and wife, but does not state that the situation is reciprocal. This means that the brother has already been invested with a value for the sister that she cannot offer in return, except by devoting herself to his cult after death.

Certainly, in the work of Sophocles, which marks the historical bridge between matriarchy and patriarchy, things are not yet that clear. No decision has yet been made about what has more value. On the one hand, *blood is no longer pure* in Sophocles: the father, at least for a time, was king; the king thereby affirms his rights as father, as well as the complicity between family (patriarchal) power and that of the State. And tragedy enacts the punishment that is incurred by a taste for blood. On the other hand, *the privilege of the proper name is not yet pure*: the power of the father's name, had its right already been in force, should have prevented Oedipus from committing murder and incest. But this is not what happens. Moreover, the fact that each sister and brother has a double also indicates that this is still a transition in which the extremes—which will later be defined as being more masculine or more feminine: i.e., Eteocles and Ismene—seem almost like caricatures. Now, whereas Ismene is termed a sister because she shares *the same blood* as Antigone, and whereas Polynices is termed a brother because he was born of *the same mother*, Eteocles is brother because he is the son of *the same father and the same mother*.

These things can be stated in other ways. *Ismene* seems indisputably a "woman" in her weakness, her fear, her submissive obedience, her tears, madness, hysteria—all of which in fact are met with condescending scorn on the part of the king. Ismene is subsequently shut up, as a punishment, in the palace, the house, with the other women, who are all thus deprived of their freedom of action for fear they may sap the courage of the most valiant warriors. For *Antigone* things are less simple, and the king himself fears she may usurp his manhood—"Better be beaten, if need be, by a man, than let a woman get the better of us."[1]—if she does not pay for her insolence with death. Antigone does not yield to the law of the city, of its sovereign, of the man of the family: Creon. And she will choose to die a virgin, unwedded to any man, rather than sacrifice the ties of blood, rather than abandon her mother's son to the dogs and vultures, leaving his double to roam in eternal torment. Better to die than to refuse service to the divine law and to the attraction she feels for the gods below. There her *jouissance* finds easier recognition, no doubt, since her allegiance to them frees her from the inventions of men. She defies them all by/in her relationship to Hades. In her nocturnal passion she acts with a perversity which has nothing in common with the wretched crimes that men stoop to in their love for money, or so the king says. Indeed she boasts of this, stating publicly that she had rather die than give up such practices. And that, moreover, *between her and the king, nothing can be said.* She alone among the Cadmeans, *the literates,* reasons thus. At least out loud. In this way, she becomes the voice, the accomplice of the people, the slaves, those who only whisper their revolt against their masters secretly. Without friends, without husband, without tears, she is led along that *forgotten path* and there is *walled up* alive in *a hole* in the rock, shut off forever from the light of the sun. Alone in her crypt, her cave, her den, her womb, she is given just enough food by those who hold power to ensure that the city is not soiled and shamed by her decay. She is alone in confronting the underground god in order to see—again—if she will survive that solitary ritual.[2] But love, for her, has far too many fatal representations for her desire to recover from such punishments. However guiltless, she feels she bears the burden of her mother's fatal marriage, feels guilty for being born of such terrible embraces. Thus she is damned, and by consenting to a punishment she has not merited and yet cannot escape, at the least she accepts on her own account the death knell of her *jouissance—or is mourning itself her jouissance?*—by killing herself. Does she thus anticipate the decree of death formulated by those in power?

Does she duplicate it? Has she given in? Or is she still in revolt? She repeats, in any case, upon herself the murderous, but not bloody, deed of her mother. Whatever her current arguments with the laws of the city may have been, another law is still drawing her along her path: identification with her mother. *But how are mother and wife to be distinguished?* This is the dreadful paradigm of a mother who is both wife and mother to her husband. Thus the sister will strangle herself in order to save at least the mother's son. She will cut off her breath—her voice, her air, blood, life—with the veil of her belt, returning into the shadow (of a) tomb, the night (of) death, so that her brother, *her mother's desire,* may have eternal life. She never becomes a woman. But she is not as masculine as she might seem if seen from an exclusively phallic viewpoint—for it is tenderness and pity that have motivated her. Rather, she is a captive of a desire whose path has reached a dead end, has never been blazed. And did she seek the relationship with the mother in *Polynices* because he was the more feminine of the brothers? The younger? Or at any rate the weaker, the one who is rejected. The more irritable and impulsive one, who in his anger will seek to open the veins of his blood again. He who is armed for/by the love of a woman, married, unlike his siblings, and through that foreign match condemning his sister to die buried alive. At least in his passion for blood he has annulled the right of his brother—*Eteocles*—to command, has destroyed his brother's—his elder's?—relation to power, reason, property, the paternal succession. And has, with the same blow, killed himself.

Yet the government's mode of action remains unchanged. Another man was ready to take up the challenge: *Creon.* He also is alone—like Antigone—but he has the instrument of the law. Desperate he is, no doubt, but he yet claims that all power is his alone. Though he has brought son and wife to utter destruction, he climbs back onto the throne, without love, and the scepter remains in his hands. Death-stricken he is, and/but regulating his practice rigidly. Inflexible in his severity. Implacable in his reasons. His fragile strength, as apt to be broken as to break, demands that he fear pleasure, domination by women, the passion of youth represented by his son, the plots of the people, the slaves' revolt, even the gods (who are still controlled and divided by desires), soothsayers, therefore, and finally the "elders." He defends his privilege of being the sole safeguard of speech, truth, intelligence, reason—the fairest of all possessions—though at the same time he raves a little wildly in his relations with the gods and with women, for example. And in this mass grave of all the members of his family—Ismene is set aside in a golden prison which a change of ruler in fact risks transforming into a simple private home—in this general outflowing of blood, he thus (thereby) remains *one*. But nonetheless, he is *broken* between a self-sureness that is now only misfortune—is he not a superfluous man, weighed down by unbearable destiny, for whom everything and everybody has become equally contingent?—and the rigid sovereignty of a Being-for-the-self empty of content (of the substance of blood), an omnipotence alien to itself. A man who receives his personal power only by exercising a right that has resolved all (blood) ties between individuals into abstract universality. Soon a God, but a god without any desire but that of submitting everyone to the law of blood congealed in the status of semblance: the Ego.

This is a necessary moment in the development of the mind, but Hegel expresses almost melancholic regret of/in this passage, and the dream of going back to that attraction to the/his sister which is unmingled (by blood). Back to the time when the species and genus had, it seems, not yet come into being, and when that unity, that individuality, *that still living, blood subject* simply took place. And in the nostalgia aroused by this return into the past. Hegel reveals his desire for a relationship that is certainly sexuate but does not need to pass through the realization of sexual desire. Desire intervenes to break the harmony unified in its blood cycle, in which brother and sister are theoretically between the phases—still relatively undifferentiated in their animality—of blood's circulation: inspiration/expiration, fluidity/hardening, apprehension/resorption of an outside. Thus one (male or female) would breathe out while the other would begin to breathe in, he/she would be becoming red blood while the other would return to self in his/her veins, he/she would affirm atomic individuality as cell(s) while the other would remain lymph, he/she would return to the earth in the form of carbon at the very moment when the other is rousing from torpor and taking fire, etc. But perhaps they are already irremediably separated throughout that process called *digestion*. For if the female one can recognize herself in the male one, who has therefore supposedly assimilated her, the reverse is not necessarily true. And if Antigone gives proof of a bravery, a tenderness, and an anger that free her energies and motivate her to resist that *outside* which the city represents for her, this is certainly because she had digested the masculine. At least partially, at least for a moment.

But perhaps this will have been possible only at the time when she is mourning for her brother, just long enough to give him back the manhood he had lost in death and to feed his soul therewith. And to die in the act.

Already, then, the balance of blood has been upset, changed, dissolved. And the unadulterated happiness that is to be had from digesting one's own substance, from giving oneself fluidity, from breaking into one's own movement, from giving birth to oneself, is not shared equally between male and female, brother and sister. But, as long as the sister goes on in her living unity she can be the self-representative basis of that substance—the blood—that the brother assimilates in order to return to the self. She can guarantee that the son develops for himself (pour soi), independently of the couple that made him: she is the living mirror, the source reflecting the growing autonomy of the self-same. She is the privileged place in which red blood and its semblance harmoniously (con)fuse with each other, though she herself has no right to benefit from this process. And the different recognition that the city pays to their auto-speculation, the one in the other, has always already perverted their union, although sometimes a public remark is needed to make it obvious that the one must eliminate the other.

Thus male and female will be split further and further apart. The wife-mother will henceforward become more and more associated with nourishing and liquefying lymph, almost white while she loses her blood in cyclic hemorrhages, neuter and passive enough in her matter for various members and organs of society to incorporate her and use her for their own subsistence. The man (father) will persevere in developing his individualization by assimilating the external other into and for the self, thus re-enforcing his vitality, his irritability, and his activity; a particular triumph is experienced when man absorbs the other into himself in his intestine. The Father-king will repeat the rupture of (living) exchange between man and woman by sublating it into his discourse. Blood is burned to cinders in the writing of the text of law whereby man produces (himself) at the same time (as) the double—differently in him, in his son, and in his wife—and the color of blood fades as more and more semblances are produced, more atoms of individual egos, all bloodless in different ways. In this process some substance is lost: blood in its constitution of a living, autonomous subjectivity.

At the heart of the dialectic is hypochondria, melancholia. It can be linked to a clot of blood, cruor, reminiscent of the bloody Calvary that set it on high, or else to the last froth left by an in(de)finite liquid which opens up the cup of its chalice even in Absolute Mind. Such clots and lymph, had they been able to close up wounds without weeping fluids, would have left the mind (only) to stony solitude and innocence. Assuming that the stone referred to serves to close off and mark the space in which femininity dies.

Thus we must go back to the decisive ethical moment which saw the blow struck producing a wound that no discourse has closed simply. The harmonious relationship of brother and sister involved a (so-called) equal recognition and nonviolent co-penetration of two essences, in which femininity and masculinity achieve universality in human and divine law. But this mutual agreement was possible only for as long as *adolescence* lasted and neither was impelled to act. A prolongation of childhood, a kind of Eden shielded from war and blessed by the household gods. But these idyllic and/because *immaculate* loves of childhood could not last. And each will soon realize that his or her equal is also his or her worst enemy, negation, and death. For the rule of law is impossible in a situation of mutual sharing in which one has as much value as the other, is equitably the same. In such circumstances consciousness could not recognize its simplicity or that wholeness which is the pathos of its duty. It must therefore make up its mind to act in accordance with that part of the ethical essence which has become apparent to it—that is, to the part which would correspond to its natural allegiance to one sex. Thus, without realizing it, consciousness finds itself embroiled willy-nilly in the rape of the other, who is henceforward injured by the partial character of such an operation. It is immediately clear, however, that the particular individual is not guilty or at fault. He is but the ineffective shadow acting on behalf of a universal self. And in fact, whatever his lack of personal responsibility, he will pay for his crime by finding that, subsequently, he is cut off from/in himself. In any event, he becomes conscious of that scission whereby the other side is now revealed to him in opposition and enmity. A dark potentiality that has always been on the watch comes suddenly into play when the deed is done: it catches the consciousness of self in the act—the act of also being, or having, that *unconsciousness* which remains alien to it but yet plays a major role in the decision consciousness takes. Thus the public offender who has been killed turns out to be the father, and the queen who has been wedded is the mother. But the purest fault is that committed by the ethical consciousness, which knew in advance what law and power it was disobeying—that is to say, necessarily, the fault committed by femininity. For if the ethical essence in its divine, unconscious, feminine side, remains obscure, its prescriptions on the human, masculine, communal side are exposed to full light. *And nothing here can excuse the crime, or minimize the punishment.* And in its burial, in its decline into ineffectiveness and pure pathos, the feminine must recognize the full measure of its guilt.

What an amazing vicious circle in a single syllogistic system. Whereby the unconscious, while remaining unconscious, is yet supposed to know the laws of a consciousness—which is permitted to remain ignorant of it—and will become even more repressed as a result of failing to respect those laws. But the stratification, on top/underneath, of the two ethical laws, of the two beings-there of sexual difference—which in fact have to disappear as such after the death of brother and sister—comes from Self, of itself. The movement by which the mind ceaselessly sublates necessity, climbing to the top of its pyramid more easily if the other is thrust deeper down into the well. Thus the male one copulates with the other so as to draw new strength from her, a new form, whereas the other sinks further and further into a ground that harbors a substance which expends itself without the mark of any individualism. And it is by no means sure that the rape to which she continues to be subjected is visible in broad daylight, for the rape may equally well result in her retreating down into a crypt where she is sealed off. Or else in the resurgence of an "essence" so different, so other, that even to expect it to "work on the outside" reduces it to sameness, to an unconscious that has never been anything but the unconscious of someone conscious of human law alone. Which is as much as to say that the crime can easily occur unnoticed and that the operation may never be translated into a fact. Unless each of these/its terms is doubled so radically that *a single dialectic is no longer sufficient to articulate their copulation.* For if it is asserted that the one character and the other are split into a conscious and an unconscious, with each character itself giving rise to that opposition, there remains the question of how it will be possible to *translate* the laws of the unconscious into those of the conscious, the so-called laws of God into the laws of philosophy, the laws of the female into those of the male.

What will be the passage of their *difference* in the subsequent movement of the mind? Or rather, how will that difference be resolved? How does the mind acquire, in a variation of deferred action (*après-coup*), the right to make laws and official statements about (the) matter, when a certain process of statement has already excluded difference in its desire to return to sameness? This problem can be approached in another way: the masculine will be able to retrace the path of his discursive law, but it is also the role of the masculine to prescribe the law for the female, since she can have no knowledge (of it) for herself. And the fact that, ideally, each is both unconscious and conscious does not in practice prevent the conscious from being identified as masculine, whereas the unconscious remains fixed on the female side, repressed as a result of the impossibility of differentiating the maternal. This implies that masculinity—in man and possibly in woman—will to some extent be able to dialecticize its relationships and identificatory allegiance to the maternal, including a negativization of female singularity, but this would not be true for femininity, which is aware of no difference between itself and the maternal, or even the masculine, except one that is mediated by the abstract immediacy of *the* being (as) or by the rejection of *one* (as) being. The female lacks the operation of affirming its singular and universalizable link to one as self.

Woman has no gaze, no discourse for her specific specularization that would allow her to identify with herself (as same)—to return into the self—or break free of the natural specular process that now holds her—to get out of the self. Hence, woman does not take an active part in the development of history, for she is never anything but the still undifferentiated opaqueness of sensible matter, the store (of) substance for the sublation of self, or being as what is, or what he is (or was), here and now. There is a doubling of a present of utterance in which present is already no more, has already passed into the universal, when woman appears in that *quasi-subjectivity* that is supposedly hers. And that cannot be possessed as consciousness of self. In her case "I" never equals "I," and she is only that individual will that the master takes possession of, that resisting remainder of a corporeality to which his passion for sameness is still sensitive, or again his double, the lining of his coat. Being as she is, she does not achieve the enunciatory process of the discourse of History, but remains its servant, deprived of self (as same), alienated in this system of discourse as in her master and finding some hint of her own self, her own ego, only in another, a You—or a He—who speaks. Her own will is shattered so afraid is she of the master, so aware of her inner nothingness. And her work in the service of another, of that male Other, ensures the ineffectiveness of any desire that is specifically hers.

But, when woman renounces her claim to desire, external things are positively molded, their forms are determined by a self that is not re-marked by any individual pathos or by any contingent arbitrariness, things in which the mind might intuit itself as objective reality. This would be the final meaning of the obedience demanded of woman. She is merely the passage that serves to transform the inessential whims of a still sensible and material nature into universal will.

Woman is the guardian of the blood. But as both she and it have had to use their substance to nourish the universal consciousness of self, it is in the form of *bloodless shadows*—of unconscious fantasies—that they maintain an underground subsistence. Powerless on earth, she remains the very ground in which manifest mind secretly sets its roots and draws its strength. And self-certainty—in masculinity, in community, in government—owes the truth of its word and of the oath that binds men together to that substance common to all, repressed, unconscious and dumb, washed in the waters of oblivion. This enables us to understand why femininity consists essentially in laying the dead man back in the womb of the earth, and giving him eternal life. For the *bloodless one is the mediation that she knows in her being,* whereby a being-there that has given up being as a self here passes from something living and singular and deeply buried to essence at its most general. Woman can, therefore, by remembering this intermediary moment, preserve at least the soul of man and of community from being lost and forgotten. *She ensures the Erinnerung* (remembrance/memory) *of the consciousness of self by forgetting herself.*

But at times the forces of the world below become hostile because they have been denied the right to live in daylight. These forces rise up and threaten to lay waste the community. To turn it upside down. Refusing to be that unconscious ground that nourishes nature, womanhood would then demand the right to pleasure, to *jouissance,* even to effective action, thus betraying her universal destiny. What is more, she would pervert the property/propriety of the State by making fun of the adult male who no longer thinks of anything but the universal, subjecting him to derision and to the scorn of a callow adolescence. In opposition to the adult male, she would set up the strength of youth possessed by the *son*, the *brother*, the *young man*, for in them, much more than in the power of government, she recognizes a *master*, an *equal*, a *lover*. The community can protect itself from such demands only by repressing them as elements of *corruption* that threaten to destroy the State. In fact these *seeds* of revolt, in principle, are quite powerless, are already reduced to nothing by being *separated from the universal goal* pursued by the citizens. Any community has a duty to transform these too immediately natural forces into its own defenders by inciting the young men—in whom the woman's desire takes pleasure—to make war upon each other and slaughter one another in bloody fights. It is through them that the still living substance of nature will sacrifice her last resources to a formal and empty universality, scattering her last drops of *blood* at a multitude of points which it will no longer be possible to gather up in the intimacy of the familiar cave.

And if, in those *points*, the *sperm*, the *name*, the *whole individual* can find a representing basis that allows them to rise up again and recover, blood in its autonomous flow will never re-unite again. But the eye—at least in the absolute—would have no need of blood to see with, anymore perhaps than the Mind to think with.

Notes

1. Sophocles, *Antigone*, in *The Theban Plays*, trans. E. F. Watling (Harmondsworth: Penguin, 1947), 144.
   2. Ibid., 147:

> I'll have her taken to a desert place
> Where no man ever walked, and there walled up
> Inside a cave alive, with food enough
> To acquit ourselves of the blood guiltiness
> That would else lie upon our commonwealth.
> There she may pray to Death, the god she loves
> And ask release from death or learn at last
> What hope there is for those who worship death.

3

Hegel's *Antigone*

Patricia Jagentowicz Mills

The *Antigone* [is] one of the most sublime and in every respect most excellent
works of art of all time.

—G. W. F. Hegel, *Aesthetics*

Hegel's interpretation of Sophocles' play *Antigone* is central to an
understanding of woman's role in the Hegelian system. Hegel is fasci-
nated by this play and uses it in both the *Phenomenology* and the
Philosophy of Right to demonstrate that familial ethical life is woman's
unique responsibility. Antigone is revealed as the paradigmatic figure of
womanhood and family life in both the ancient and modern worlds
although there are fundamental differences between these two worlds for
Hegel. In order to situate the interpretation of this play within its wider
context I use Seyla Benhabib's understanding of the "doubled vision" of
feminist theory, a method that takes traditional issues into account but
does so by simultaneously focusing on gender issues that have been
"traditionally" marginalized.[1] Thus, my analysis of Hegel's *Antigone* pro-

ceeds through an internal or immanent critique of the *Phenomenology*, then turns to an immanent critique of the *Philosophy of Right*.

In the *Phenomenology* we learn that history can be understood as a dialectic of particular and universal: man seeks recognition of his own particular self from all men; he seeks universal recognition of his particularity.[2] And universality, as the overcoming, reconciliation, or *Aufhebung* of the opposition between particular and universal, is "concrete" or universal individuality. However, in the pagan world, which is a specific historical moment in the movement of Spirit toward self-realization, the dialectical opposition between the particular and the universal cannot be overcome in life because the polis or city-state only recognizes or realizes the universal aspect of human action and risk while the particular remains embedded in the family.

Man is necessarily a member of a family and the family is the sphere of the particularity of the pagan male's existence. Within the family, man is *this* particular father, *this* husband, *this* son, and not simply *a* father, *a* husband, *a* son. But the family is the sphere of "merely natural existence," "mere particularity"; as such its supreme value is essentially inactive biological existence or animal life. While man has particularity inside the family circle, it is an unconscious particularity because, within this circle, there is no negating action—no risk of life for recognition. Within the family man cannot achieve self-consciousness or truly human satisfaction because, according to Hegel, in the pagan world the truly human demands the conscious risk of life.[3]

While neither male nor female can achieve self-consciousness within the family in Hegel's schema, the pagan male moves out to become a citizen. He does so "because it is only as a citizen that he is actual and substantial, the individual, so far as he is not a citizen but belongs to the Family, is only an unreal insubstantial shadow."[4] Hegel writes that within the polis "the community is that substance conscious of what it actually does," which is in opposition to the family as "the other side" whose form is that of "immediate substance or substance that simply is" (PS, para. 450, 268). The community draws man away from the family: By subduing his "merely natural existence," and his "mere particularity," it induces him to live "in and for the universal." What is achieved in the polis, through action and risk, is "the manhood of the community." But while the universal aspect of a man's existence is recognized here, this existence is not truly *his*: It is not *he* as a particular who is recognized by the polis. Acting on behalf of the polis man achieves universality at the expense of his particularity. The *Aufhebung* of the familial particular and the political universal that results in concrete or universal individuality is possible only in death in the pagan world.[5]

In that world the transcendence of death in and by historical memory is achieved through the family. The ethical relation between the members of the family is not that of sentiment or love but duty in connection with burying and remembering the dead—as well as avenging them if need be. Through these obligations to the dead the "powerless, simply isolated individual has been raised to universal individuality" (*PS*, para. 452, 271). Since familial life does not depend on the activity of the members but simply on their being—their inaction—death changes nothing in the value attributed to and by the family.[6] And by burying and remembering the family members, the family maintains the continuity of the human community through time.

In the pagan world the family and the polis, the particular and universal spheres of man's existence, are mutually exclusive: The family represents life and the polis represents the risk of life. The conflict between these two spheres is inescapable and unalterable. Man cannot renounce the family, since he cannot renounce the particularity of his existence, nor can he renounce the universality of his action in and for the polis. This conflict between the familial and the political makes for the tragic character of pagan life and creates a fundamental antinomy between family life, as the natural ground of ethical life, and ethical life in its social universality, or "second nature," in the polis.[7]

For Hegel the conflict between family and polis, particular and universal, is also a conflict between divine law and human law as represented in the conflict between woman and man. Nature, according to Hegel, assigns woman to divine law and man to human law. Thus while the political life of the city-state represents the manhood of the community, the family is the sphere of womanhood. The two are opposed such that when they come into open conflict woman, as the representative of divine law, sees human law as "only the violence of human caprice" while man, as the representative of human law, sees only "the self-will and disobedience of the individual" in obedience to the divine (*PS*, para. 466, 280).

In the section on the pagan or Greek ethical world in the *Phenomenology* where the interpretation of the *Antigone* appears, and where we find the only discussion of woman, Hegel is in search of the ideal relationship between a man and a woman as a relation of identity-in-difference. He begins with an analysis of heterosexual marriage and says that there is reciprocal recognition between husband and wife in the pagan world, but that this recognition is "natural self-knowledge," not realized ethical life. That is, it is a process of recognition rooted in the immediacy of desire or affective understanding, not in conscious ethical intention.

Hegel claims that the wife's desire for the husband always has a universal significance while for the husband desire and universality are separate. Here Hegel accepts the traditional view that there is a separation of morality and desire in man's relation to woman, but that morality and desire are united in woman's relation to man, and, therefore, that woman is ethically "purer" in her love relations. That is, a wife's ethical relation to her husband is not to feeling or the sentiment of love but, rather, is a relation to the universal (PS, para. 457, 274–75). What creates the separation of morality or universality and desire or particularity in man is the bifurcation of his life into the public and private spheres. While woman remains confined to, and defined by, the family, man lives within the polis as well as within the family. In this way Hegel distinguishes the family for-itself from the family in-itself. That is, woman represents the family as immediately universal for-itself while, from the perspective of the man, she represents the family in-itself as the sphere of particularity. Thus, central to the relationship between particularity and universality in the family is the split between desire and morality in the pagan male's existence.

For Hegel, the husband acquires the *rights* of desire over his wife precisely because he has the rights of a citizen. The husband's authority and position in the polis allow him to have sexual domination over the wife in the family and simultaneously keep him "detached" from his desire for her: Man rules woman in the private sphere because he rules in the public world. And as he rules in the public world and in the family he rules himself.

What is most significant in this analysis of desire in marriage is that for Hegel it is *male* desire that taints the purity of the male-female relationship: The husband's desire for the wife is expressed as merely particular desire such that a moment of indifference and ethical contingency is introduced into the relationship. However, insofar as this relationship *is* ethical, the wife is without the moment of knowing herself as *this* particular self in and through an other.[8] Thus, in the ethical family of the pagan world the husband gains an unconscious particularity, as *this* husband, through the wife's exercise of universal recognition of him as *a* husband, while his recognition of her is such that she never achieves particularity. He is particularized but she is not. Man, says Hegel, achieves particularity in the pagan family, through the wife's recognition of him, precisely because he leaves this sphere to attain universal recognition in the political sphere. But woman never enters the political sphere; she is caught and bound within the immediacy of the family circle.

For Hegel, the relationship between husband and wife in the pagan world is a mixed and transitive one in which male desire infects the process of recognition between a man and a woman so that each maintains a knowledge of dissimilarity or "independent being-for self." Husband and wife are separated as male and female. Because the husband and the wife each retain a moment of independence—a being-for-self—the "return-into-itself" of the relationship cannot take place. Rather, the relationship is necessarily externalized through the child. Thus, the husband-wife relationship is not complete in itself; it needs the child to complete it, and the child changes the relationship (*PS*, para. 456, 273). Given this, the husband-wife relationship is not the ideal relationship of identity-in-difference between man and woman.

However, Hegel believes he has found this ideal in the relationship between a brother and a sister because he believes that this relationship is without desire and therefore without the separation and ethical uncertainty that male desire entails. He writes:

> The relationship [between man and woman] in its unmixed form is found, however, in that between brother and sister. They are the same blood which has, however, in them reached a state of rest and equilibrium. Therefore, they do not desire one another, nor have they given to, or received from, one another this independent being-for-self; on the contrary, they are free individualities in regard to each other. (*PS*, para. 457, 274)

Brother and sister are not independent of one another because they are united through the blood tie. Thus, the brother-sister relationship is a unity of male and female that is not recognition as separation, distinctiveness or dissimilarity: It is a relationship of identity-in-difference. Their recognition is that of "free individualities in regard to each other" which transcends the indifference or ethical contingency characteristic of the husband-wife relationship. Whereas mere particularity is impli-

cated in the husband-wife relationship through male desire, "The
brother . . . is for the sister a passive similar being" and the recognition
of the sister in the brother "is pure and unmixed with any natural
desire" (*PS*, para. 457, 275). The brother's nature is ethically like the
sister's—that is, directly universal—which allows for the realization of
self in and through an other. The sister's recognition of herself in the
brother is therefore pure and complete, as is his recognition of himself
in her, and "the moment of the individual self, recognizing and being
recognized, can here assert its right" (*PS*, para. 457, 275). Thus, Hegel
makes a distinction between, on the one hand, the process of recognition
between man and woman based on an immediate unity (an immediate
universality grounded in blood) that is transcended through the process
of recognition into a unity or identity-in-difference (brother-sister); and,
on the other hand, recognition grounded in desire, the mere particularity
of male desire, that necessarily retains separation and dissimilarity in
such a way that a unity of male and female cannot be fully realized
(husband-wife).

While Freud's theories and anthropological studies of incest taboos
would seem to make the assertion that "brother and sister . . . do not
desire one another" at least dubious if not altogether untenable, it is
significant that Hegel believes that this lack of desire offers woman, as
sister, the possibility of truly mutual recognition. The death of a brother
thus becomes an irreparable loss for the sister since with his death she
loses the ideal relationship with a man. And, the nature of this
relationship is such that the sister's familial duty to the brother is the
highest in terms of honoring and remembering him after his death.

Woman as sister in the pagan world is the paradigmatic foreshadowing
of ethical life, precisely because she represents familial duty to man
which is "purely" spiritual. But the brother-sister relationship is not one
of *conscious* ethical life; rather, the law of the family is the sister's
immediate, unconscious nature. The sister in the pagan world cannot
realize or actualize this life completely because, according to Hegel, the
dualism of the pagan world resists the possibility of transcendence or the
realization in consciousness of ethical life. Hegel writes:

> The feminine, in the form of the sister, has the highest *intuitive*
> awareness of what is ethical. She does not attain to *consciousness*
> of it, or to the objective existence of it, because the law of the
> Family is an implicit, inner essence which is not exposed to the

daylight of consciousness, but remains an inner feeling and the divine element that is exempt from an existence in the real world. The woman is associated with these household gods [Penates] and beholds in them both her universal substance and her particular individuality, yet in such a way that this relation of her individuality to them is at the same time not the natural one of desire. (*PS*, para. 457, 274)

Hegel retains his understanding of the ethical purity of the brother-sister relationship being tied to sexual purity in his *Philosophy of History* where he describes Apollo as "pure" precisely because "he has no wife, but only a sister [Artemis, the virgin goddess of the hunt], and is not involved in various disgusting adventures, like Zeus."[9]

The unity of the brother-sister relationship necessarily "passes beyond itself" when the brother "leaves this immediate, elemental, and there-fore, strictly speaking, negative ethical life of the Family, in order to acquire and produce the ethical life that is conscious of itself and actual" (*PS*, para. 458, 275). The sister merely moves into another family situation by marrying and becoming a wife: She moves from the family of origin to the family of procreation. Thus, the brother passes from divine to human law while the sister continues to maintain divine law as wife. In this way, according to Hegel, natural sexual difference comes to have an ethical determination.

At this point it is important to note several problems in the brother-sister relationship that Hegel does not address. In the first place, this relationship takes place *within* the family of origin before the brother has entered the sphere of the city-state and accepted the claims made on him by that sphere. Woman is said to realize herself within the family, but insofar as the brother is still only part of the family, he is an adolescent, not part of the manhood of the community and therefore not an adult male in Hegelian terms. The fact that the brother is in this way only a *potential* man, not a realized one, undermines Hegel's claim that brother and sister represent the ideal relationship between man and woman. Certainly such a relationship requires, at the very least, that there *be* a man and a woman. Second, the brother-sister relationship does not entail equal responsibility. Since the brother's vocation is to accept the bifurcation of life, and with it the separation of desire and morality, he leaves the family of origin and does not look back. The sister assumes the familial obligations of divine law, which require that she bury and remember her brother when he dies, but there is no mention of any responsibility the brother has to his sister in terms of human or political law. Thus woman, as sister, assumes a responsibility for the brother as a member of the family of origin that the brother does not reciprocate. This unequal responsibility mitigates the sense in which the brother-sister relationship can be seen as ideal. And third, Hegel is in search of the self-complete relationship between man and woman that is an identity-in-difference: It must be a "natural" relationship that is dialectically transcended through consciousness (recognition/history). But there is no guarantee that a woman will *have* a brother. Insofar as Hegel attempts to institutionalize forms of consciousness this means that a woman without a brother can never achieve even a glimmer of an unconscious self that might be the equal of man's.

Setting aside these objections for the moment we find that in Sophocles' *Antigone* Hegel finds the superiority of the sister-brother relationship demonstrated in a way that reveals the profound ethical conflict inherent in the pagan world between family and polis, woman and man, particular and universal, divine law and human law. Thus, while the central *conflict* for Hegel is between Antigone and Creon (as woman and man who represent the conflict between the family, as the natural ground of ethical life, and ethical life itself in its social universality in the polis) the central *relationship* in this drama is, for him, that between Antigone and Polyneices: Antigone's enduring sense of duty to her dead brother is explained in terms of the ideal male-female relationship of mutual recognition.[10] Antigone "premonizes and foreshadows" most completely the nature of familial ethical life precisely because she represents the relation between man and woman not as wife but as sister. She is the paradigm of the law of the family as she carries out her "highest duty" toward her brother in attempting to bury and honor him.

While it is true that Antigone's burial of Polyneices represents familial duty (and in particular that between sister and brother), Hegel does not consider the play in its entirety. His references to the *Antigone* are scattered throughout his discussion of the ethical world and ethical action in the *Phenomenology* as "evidence" for his claims regarding the relationship between male/human law and female/divine law in the Greek pagan world. But Hegel's interpretation of this play, and in particular the conflict between Creon and Antigone, is an oversimplication made to fit his view of the tragic character of pagan life as a conflict between equal and contrary values.

Hegel considers the situation that precedes the action in the *Antigone*: the struggle between the two brothers, Eteocles and Polyneices, for control of the city of Thebes. "Nature" has provided two potential rulers where only one can rule. In the pagan world the ruler is the community as individual soul: Two cannot share power. Hegel claims that the two brothers each have an equal right to rule and that the inequality of the natural order of birth can have no importance when they enter the ethical community of the polis. Thus, the right of primogeniture is denied here. However, the equal right of the brothers to rule destroys them both, since in their conflict over power they are both wrong.

In human law or political terms, it is the right of possession that is most important. Thus, because Eteocles was in power when Polyneices attacked the city, Eteocles is given a formal burial by Creon, who has become the ruler of the war-torn city-state. But Creon's edict, which forbids anyone to bury Polyneices on pain of death, is a denial of sacred claims: Without burial Polyneices' soul cannot safely enter Hades. By honoring one brother and dishonoring the other, human law and divine law are set in opposition. And the "right" of human law is revealed as "wrong" through the vengeance of war waged on Thebes by Argos (*PS*, paras. 473–74, 285–87).

Through his elliptical discussion of the *Antigone*, Hegel reveals the way in which the tragic conflict in pagan society between the universalistic polis and the particularistic family ends in the destruction of the pagan world such that it becomes one "soulless and dead" bare universal community. But, according to Hegel, it is not only external forces that destroy the community. Rather, there is within the community the seeds of its own destruction in the family. The family, for Hegel, is "the rebellious principle of pure individuality" (*PS*, para. 474, 286), which, in its universality, is inner divine law; and this law, as he claims again and again, is the law of woman. Here, woman is the agent of destruction of the pagan world. Since particularity is not *included* in the polis, it destroys the polis. Woman, as the representative of the family principle, the principle of particularity which the polis represses, is the internal cause of the downfall of the pagan world:

> Since the community only gets an existence through its interference with the happiness of the Family, and by dissolving [individ-

ual] self-consciousness into the universal, it creates for itself in
what it suppresses and what is at the same time essential to it
an internal enemy—womankind in general. Womankind—the
everlasting irony [in the life] of the community—changes by
intrigue the universal end of the government into a private end,
transforms its universal activity into a work of some particular
individual, and perverts the universal property of the state into a
possession and ornament for the Family. (PS, para. 475, 288)

Woman, as the representative of both the immediacy of family life and
the principle of particularity, represents the spirit of individualism as
subversive. She revolts and destroys the community in the pagan world
by acting on the young man who has not yet completely detached
himself from the family of origin and therefore has not yet subordinated
his particular existence to the universality of the polis. She persuades
him to exercise his power for the family dynasty rather than for public
welfare. According to Hegel, woman does this by asserting the power of
youthful male authority, as the power of the son, the brother, or
the husband.[11]

The question of exactly how woman can represent the sphere of
particularity while never knowing herself as this particular self is a
question never addressed by Hegel. In Negative Dialectics T. W. Adorno
challenges Hegel on precisely this transformation of the particular into
particularity. For Adorno, "the particular would not be definable without
the universal that identifies it, according to current logic; but neither is
it identical with the universal."[12] Thus, for Adorno the concept of the
particular is a concept of the dialectics of non-identity whereas the
concept of particularity eliminates the particular as particular in order to
absorb it into a philosophy of identity dominated by the universal. The
transformation of the analysis away from a concern with the particular
to a concern with particularity in relation to woman is the paradigm
case of what Adorno points to. That is, Adorno shows that Hegel's
identity philosophy necessarily excludes forms of human experience, and
it is my contention that it is primarily forms of female experience, which
Antigone symbolizes, that are excluded.[13]

While Antigone, as the paradigm of the ethical family, does not, in
the Phenomenology, represent woman as the principle of particularity
destroying the polis through intrigue and perversion, nevertheless Hegel
misses what is most significant: that Antigone must enter the political

realm, the realm of second nature, in order to defy it on behalf of the realm of the family, the realm of first nature. In doing this, as we shall see, Antigone transcends Hegel's analysis of "the law of woman" as "natural ethical life," and becomes *this* particular self.

Sophocles presents a situation in which Antigone must reconcile her obligations to the family and its gods with the demands of the political sphere represented by Creon. Her tragedy is that no matter which course of action she chooses she cannot be saved. If she defies the law of the polis and buries Polyneices, she will die; if she fails in her familial duty to her brother she will suffer divine retribution and loss of honor. She defies Creon and in so doing brings divine law into the human community in opposition to the authority of the polis.

According to Hegel, in the pagan world the two forms of law, human and divine, as represented by man and woman, exclude and oppose each other; their separation means the loss of certainty of immediate truth and creates the possibility of crime and guilt. Crime is defined here as the adherence to one of the two laws over and against the other. Thus, there is no *Aufhebung* of the two laws, but only opposition. For Hegel, "essential reality" is the unity or identity-in-difference of both human law and divine law; that is, there can be no justice without revelation (PS, para. 460, 276). But such an *Aufhebung* is only possible in the *modern* world, after the advent of Christianity. It is the revelation of God in Christ that allows man to acquire the knowledge necessary to make the transition to an ethical life that is self-conscious and therefore truly universal. In the pagan world conflict is always "resolved" on one side or the other, but the two laws are inextricably bound up with each other such that the fulfillment of one calls forth the other's revenge. The purer ethical consciousness acknowledges the other law but interprets it as wrong and acts as it deems necessary because "what is *ethical* must be *actual*" (PS, para. 460, 276). In this sense Antigone wittingly commits a "crime," according to Hegel. However, by acknowledging the other law, ethical consciousness must acknowledge that it has committed a crime against this law, and it must admit guilt. It is here, in the analysis of the relation between crime and guilt, that we begin to see the inadequacy of Hegel's interpretation of the *Antigone*.

Against Hegel's interpretation, Sophocles does not create Antigone and Creon as ethical equals. Antigone alone is the ultimate defender of the good; one sees this revealed in the fate meted out to Creon and in Antigone's *refusal* to admit guilt. In Hegel's attempt to fit the *Antigone* into his view of the tragic character of pagan life in terms of crime and guilt he has to "interpret" this play in the *Phenomenology* to the extent of changing Antigone's final words. In the section on ethical action Hegel makes it seem as if she acknowledges her "guilt" for the "crime" of burying her brother. What she actually says is:

> . . . I have done no wrong,
> I have not sinned before the gods. Or if I have,
> I shall know the truth in death. But if the guilt
> Lies upon Creon who judged me, then, I pray,
> May his punishment equal my own.[14]

With her death she believes that she will enter the world of the gods and that *they* will determine whether her act was right or wrong. In a dialectical turn, Creon ends up living the fate he has tried to inflict on Antigone by entombing her alive: He must endure the solitude of a "living death," for his actions lead to the suicides of his son, Haemon, and his wife, Eurydice. In the end he declares: "I alone am guilty" (32).

While Antigone chooses to obey the gods, or divine law, nevertheless she does not admit guilt concerning human law.[15] From Hegel's point of view Antigone's admission of guilt is necessary for her ethical consciousness to be equal to that of Creon and for the play to represent the tragic conflict of pagan life. When we adhere to what actually happens in the play and put it within Hegel's interpretative framework we find that Creon's admission of guilt actually makes *him* the hero of the play since it gives him a *higher* ethical consciousness. Thus, there are not two equal and contrary values in opposition in the conflict between Antigone and Creon, as Hegel tries to claim, but rather a "higher" political consciousness of the male and a "lower" familial consciousness of the female. From this perspective the play should have been called *Creon* since only Creon has the self-recognition made possible through the admission of guilt. While the action of the play transforms Creon from a criminal to a tragic figure for both Sophocles and Hegel, within Hegel's framework Antigone remains "criminal" in that she upholds only the law of the family and does not recognize the law of the polis as legitimate. Thus, Hegel *wants* Antigone to be a tragic character but he cannot show her as such without misrepresenting and "adapting" what she says to make it look as if she admits guilt.

In his interpretation of the *Antigone,* with its emphasis on crime and guilt, Hegel misses several critical components that are central to an understanding of female experience. To begin with, Antigone retains a steadfast devotion to what is noble and just that goes far beyond the mere intuition of natural ethical life and the consciousness that comes from burying and remembering the dead. Antigone has a moral courage that allows her to *choose* a course of action even though it condemns her to death. Whereas Hegel claims that the sister's intuition of ethical life is not open to the daylight of consciousness, the chorus in Sophocles' play cries out to Antigone: "Your death is the doing of your conscious hand" (21). Sophocles shows Antigone choosing to carry out her duty to her brother and choosing to disobey Creon's edict. While she claims to owe a stronger allegiance to the dead, to her brother and to the gods, it is not an unreflective position she takes. It is not an unconscious intuition of her ethical duty as Hegel would have us believe. Rather, it is a noble stance, consciously taken.[16]

According to Hegel, the woman who remained in her place never felt the tragic character of pagan life, never felt the conflict between particular and universal because she never entered the polis, the sphere of universality. Thus, it is Ismene, Antigone's sister, rather than Antigone herself, who maintains the traditional place of woman. Curiously, Hegel fails even to mention Ismene in his references to the play. This is probably because Ismene's "instinctive" reaction is contrary to her supposed "natural ethical orientation": She explicitly sides with the political authority of the polis over the divine law. And in siding with the law of the polis Ismene bows to "the law of woman" as male domination. When Antigone asks Ismene if she wishes to help bury their brother Ismene cries out:

> Think how much more terrible than these
> Our own death would be if we should go against Creon
> And do what he has forbidden! We are only women,
> We cannot fight with men, Antigone!
> The law is strong, we must give in to the law
> In this thing, and in worse.
>
> (2)

However, Ismene, motivated by feelings of sisterhood, overcomes her initial fears and attempts to share the responsibility for burying Polyneices. Antigone protests that there is no need for both of them to die for something she alone has done. To this Ismene replies:

> What do I care for life when you are dead?
>   (14)

While Antigone rejects Ismene's offer of sisterly solidarity, what we see here in Ismene is a second, more traditional woman, a woman representing conventional womanhood, created in human rather than heroic proportions, choosing an honorable death over the continuation of an ignoble life.[17] Thus, Ismene wavers in her commitment to the good but her decision to do what is right is rooted in the familial devotion between sisters, not in the sister-brother relationship. Hegel completely disregards this aspect of the play.

Unlike Ismene, Antigone *acts* on behalf of the family, the sphere of inaction. She moves outside the sphere of the family and as a consequence becomes different *within* the family. As we saw earlier, the brother-sister relationship of mutual recognition, in which the sister is said to realize herself, necessarily ends when the brother leaves the family of origin. And Hegel asserts that it makes no difference to woman that she is not *this* particular self within the family of procreation. He claims that there is reciprocal recognition between husband and wife, but when we examine this claim carefully we find that it contradicts his claim concerning what one is to *gain* from the process of recognition within the family of procreation, i.e., particularity. Thus, man gains an unconscious particularity through woman's relation to the universal, but man's relation to the universal is separate from his relation to woman so that she is never *this* particular self. While the husband cannot renounce the particularity of his being in the pagan world, the wife never achieves it. She cannot achieve an unconscious particularity as *this* wife within the immediacy of the ethical family and she is not allowed out into any other sphere of life.

In the Hegelian schema woman cannot even achieve the self-consciousness of the slave since she does not experience the two central elements of slave consciousness. That is, she experiences neither the ubiquitous personal fear of death as "the absolute Lord," nor the "service" or work on nature as thinghood, the work of objectification that re-creates the world to create history.[18] Woman's response to death is said to be resignation while her primary responsibility is to memorialize the dead in order to raise them to living memory (*PS*, para. 457, 274–75). And, woman is represented as someone that does not *do* anything and therefore can have no universal recognition of her action or humanity in the polis; she is not seen as someone who *acts* but merely as someone who *is*.

Since woman remains confined inside the family she must remain the walking dead of "unreal insubstantial shadow." Thus, if Antigone were to proceed as a "normal" woman she would marry Haemon, her be-trothed and Creon's son, move from the family of origin to the family of procreation, and never know herself as *this* particular self. But Antigone, like the male, leaves the family to risk her life in the polis. While it is true that she is in the polis on behalf of the family, nevertheless she experiences the duality of pagan life and has the potential to become *this* particular self. Through the conscious risk of life in the sphere of the polis, Antigone transcends the limitations of womanhood set down by Hegel.

If we accept Hegel's interpretation of pagan life as a tragic conflict between the familial particular and the political universal that cannot be overcome in life, then Antigone's decision to commit suicide, which Hegel does not discuss, is of paramount importance. That is, unlike the male, Antigone cannot *live* out the contradiction of pagan life. Man is able to endure the duality of pagan life through his relation to woman— she maintains the family as the sphere of his particularity while he acts in the polis, the sphere of universality. But woman's relation to man does not offer her a way to make this duality tolerable. His desire for her is such that she is never a particular self in relation to him nor does she experience the universality of the polis through him. When woman leaves the family to experience the universality of the polis and to achieve particularity her relation to man cannot sustain her. Thus, man lives the tragic conflict of pagan life but woman dies from it. By violating the norms of womanhood set down by Hegel, Antigone comes to embody the tragic conflict that he finds inherent in Greek life. Her suicide expresses the inability to be both particular and universal in the pagan world. It expresses the fact that there can be no reconciliation, no *Aufhebung*, of particular and universal in that world. Against Hegel's focus on crime and guilt, which misrepresents Antigone, a consideration of the play itself, and most notably, a consideration of Antigone's *actions* on behalf of the sphere of inaction, reveals her tragedy as the tragedy of Greek life in Hegelian terms.

In addition, we can see Antigone's suicide as a form of defiance against patriarchal domination. By choosing to kill herself Antigone does not allow Creon to have the ultimate power over her fate which he seeks: She takes her own life to refute the power of the male, as the power of the universal, over her. In Greek society death was seen as preferable to slavery: It was more noble to kill oneself than to have one's fate controlled by another. Hegel himself writes of the liberating aspects of suicide, although not in regard to Antigone's tragedy. In his essay on "Natural Law" (Naturrecht) Hegel claims that voluntary death is a manifestation of freedom because it reveals one's independence from the life situation. He qualifies this by saying that this is not a realization of freedom, since it ends in nothingness rather than in free existence.[19] However, in Antigone's situation a manifestation of freedom is all that is possible since her choices are only death or submission to the male principle as the principle of universality, which decrees that she remain confined to the family in subjugation to man. If we extrapolate from Hegel's theory of desire we can also see Antigone's suicide as maintaining her purity since she never marries and therefore never has a husband whose desire can overreach her ability to become this particular self. Antigone's suicide is an honorable alternative which shows that she prefers honor and arete to male domination.

In the Phenomenology "action is the principle by which distinction in unity is carried out in social life. Therefore the consideration of its significance is an essential problem of the social mind."[20] Yet Hegel chooses to emphasize only Antigone's burial of Polyneices and misrepresents her "confession." When one considers all of Antigone's actions we see first that her burial of Polyneices was a moral imperative that goes beyond the mere intuition of ethical life and that she confesses no guilt in terms of the human law; second, that her action in the sphere of the polis allows her to transcend the Hegelian framework (which confines her to the family) so that she becomes a particular self; and third, that her suicide may be seen as the ultimate expression of the tragic character of pagan life as well as a refutation of male domination. Thus, through her actions Antigone goes far beyond what Hegel attributes to her.

For Sophocles it is because Antigone and Creon come upon the limits of their respective spheres that they both are transformed from criminal to tragic figures. Hegel also wants to show this but he misrepresents Antigone and Creon. That is, where Hegel does not consider the consequences that result from the fact that Antigone must leave the family in order to protect it, must *act* on behalf of the sphere of inaction, he also does not consider that Creon's behavior must *necessarily* be unjust. Hegel's interpretation of Creon as the just representative of the law of the polis is as radical a departure from Sophocles' tragedy as is his portrayal of Antigone. The conflict between the just moral law and the unjust political law that is central to Sophocles' *Antigone* is muted in Hegel's interpretation. For Sophocles, Creon's rule is *not* that of reasoned arguments and the rational order of the city-state; nor is Creon the community as an individual soul. Rather, Sophocles shows Creon to be a misogynist and a tyrant who requires unquestioned obedience.

Creon is forever fearful that man shall be "done in" by woman, yet he expects a man to bury Polyneices; he finds it unthinkable that a woman, even as the necessary defender of the divine law, would act in the public realm to transgress the laws of the polis. When he finds out that Antigone has committed the "crime," he exclaims: "If we must lose, let's lose to a man, at least! Is a woman stronger than we?" (17). And when Haemon challenges Creon's decision condemning Antigone to death, Creon rebukes him saying "Fool, adolescent fool! Taken in by a woman!"[21] Finally, when the polis, in the form of the chorus, sides with Antigone, Creon declares:

> Whoever is chosen to govern should be obeyed—
> Must be obeyed, in all things, great and small,
> Just and unjust! . . .
> My voice is the one voice giving orders in this City! . . .
> The State is the King!
>
> (16, 18)

Confronted with the inexorable force of Antigone acting on behalf of the family, Creon becomes irrational precisely because he cannot incorporate the claims of the family within the political sphere that he rules. In a world divided between family and polis, particular and universal, Antigone becomes tragic when she must leave the family to protect it, and Creon becomes tragic when, to protect the polis, he must become an irrational and unjust ruler.

In summary, what we find are four aspects of Sophocles' *Antigone* that are overlooked by Hegel in the *Phenomenology* in his attempt to use the play to reveal the pagan world as a world defined by tragic conflict between particular and universal, family and polis, divine law and human law, woman and man. First, Hegel completely disregards the sister-sister relationship in his search for the ideal relationship as a male-female relationship of identity-in-difference. Thus, Hegel describes the family as the sphere of womankind without showing any curiosity about the relations *between* women. This is like describing the sphere of pagan political life as "the manhood of the community" without ever discussing the relations between men! While Antigone rejects Ismene's show of solidarity, nevertheless, it is important to note the attempt at sisterhood and to recognize that Ismene does not display the "natural ethical orientation" required of her sex: She instinctively sides with male political authority rather than with the divine law of the family.

Second, Hegel disregards the conscious choice involved in Antigone's actions. Sophocles creates a conflict in which Antigone represents not only eternal familial values but individual moral choice, in opposition to Creon who represents not only temporal legal authority but dictatorial rule.[22] Hegel fails to see Antigone's action as anything more than the result of her intuition of the natural ethical law of the family, just as Creon fails to see it as anything more than the result of female rebellion against his absolute, patriarchal authority. But Antigone's tragedy is the result of strength and moral courage—the so-called "masculine" virtues—not simply a response to "feminine" intuition. (One wonders if Hegel would have "reduced" Socrates' "daimon"—which is a private intuition unrecognized and persecuted by the polis—to the level of "feminine intuition" if Socrates had been a woman.)[23]

Third, Antigone transcends woman's place in Hegel's framework because she breaks out of the limitation to the familial, which he requires of her sex. She represents the ethical family and as such she must relate to the universal as immediate, but, according to Hegel, she is not to know herself as this particular self. When we look carefully we find that woman is bound to immediacy as wife within the family through male desire, which overreaches her ability to become this particular self in and through her relationship with her brother. The brother-sister relationship as a relationship of mutual recognition, is transitory and ends when he enters the polis. The sister does not act in the polis but merely moves into another family to become the wife—the object of male desire. And, the husband's life in the pagan city-state overreaches the wife's familial life as she remains confined to first nature. Woman has no contradiction to negate between herself and "first nature"; she lacks negativity because she remains confined within the sphere of "mere animal life" and thus remains "unreal insubstantial shadow." But Antigone moves into the political sphere on behalf of the sphere of the family and becomes, like man, a participant in both spheres. She does not represent "the irony of the community," the principle of particularity that changes the community through intrigue, but openly insists on the rights of the family, the rights of "first nature," within the polis.[24] Unlike other women, it becomes possible for Antigone, subordinating herself to the universal, to know herself as *this* particular self and thus to epitomize the tragic conflict between particular and universal which Hegel claims characterizes the ancient Greek, pagan world.

And finally, Hegel fails to discuss Antigone's suicide. When the chorus declares: "What woman has ever found your way to death?" (20) it reveals Antigone as unique, as the exception to female behavior, and therefore as a transitional character, not the paradigm of pagan divine law as represented by woman. While embodying the tragic conflict between particular and universal, Antigone represents the history of the revolt of women who act in the public sphere on behalf of the private sphere, the sphere of inaction. She is the precursor of the women who, in the recent past, proclaimed the personal as political.[25] Antigone rebels against Creon's claim to the right of the universal *over* the particular; in so doing she refuses to fit neatly into the Hegelian enterprise in which universality ultimately dominates. In criticizing Hegel's interpretation of the *Antigone* we begin to see another story in Western philosophy, one other than that of Hegelian reconciliation—the revolt of the particular against subsumption under a universal schema.

In the analysis of Hegel's interpretation of the *Antigone* in the *Phenomenology* I have focused on Hegel's understanding of the pagan world as suffering from a dualism in which particularity, as represented by woman in the family, is in conflict with universality, as represented by man in the polis. I have shown that his understanding of this conflict causes him to systematically misrepresent or ignore critical aspects of female experience that Sophocles' play actually reveals.[26] Given the inadequacy of the account of the *Antigone* in the *Phenomenology*, it is not surprising to find that Hegel's use of the play in the *Philosophy of Right* is also partial, and therefore "false." This indicates that Hegel's own philosophy of the modern world cannot reconcile the opposition between particular and universal in the context of sexual difference any more than the ancient world could. I will argue in the following pages that the modern world described by Hegel, like the pagan world, is made at woman's expense and that Antigone is misused to represent woman in the family in transhistorical terms.

In the *Philosophy of Right* we learn that the bifurcation of reason in the pagan world is *aufgehoben* in Spirit's movement toward universal self-knowledge with the development of the modern Christian world into a triad consisting of the family, civil society, and the state. The bourgeois family is the sphere of the universal as undifferentiated unity or immediacy;[27] civil society represents the moment of particularity; and the state is the sphere of universality in which the universal and particular are reconciled. The aim of the *Philosophy of Right* is to resolve the relationship of desire to morality and ethical life; the analysis begins with a discussion of sexual desire within marriage, shifts to a focus on the generalized desire of civil society and the abstract morality of that sphere, and ends with a consideration of the concrete ethical life or *Sittlichkeit* of the state.

The reference to the *Antigone* and the only discussion of woman in the *Philosophy of Right*, as in the *Phenomenology*, appears within the discussion of the ethical life of the family. And, as in the *Phenomenology*, the *Antigone* is used as a paradigm to justify woman's confinement to the family. But, significantly, here the play does not represent the relationship between brother and sister as a relationship untainted by male desire; nor does the play represent the relationship between crime and guilt. Rather, it represents the opposition between man and woman as the opposition between divine law and human law within the context of a discussion of the relationship between husband and wife. In the *Philosophy of Right* Hegel is not concerned with finding the ideal relationship between man and woman that is *free* from desire, but with showing how the relation *of* desire itself can be transcended.

Hegel claims that the husband-wife relationship is the ideal ethical relationship between man and woman in the modern world because the secret moment of desire, the moment of physical passion, is transformed into self-conscious love through marriage. Physical desire is a moment that vanishes when satisfied, while the spiritual bond of Christian marriage is above the contingency of desire. Here Hegel distinguishes the marriage ceremony from the marriage contract. The ceremony, as a public proclamation of the ethical intention to take responsibility for family life, puts sensual desire into the background while the marriage contract is said to be a contract to transcend the standpoint of contract.[28] That is, a contract is a relation of civil society between atomic individuals while the ethical family is a unity bound together by love in such a way that one exists in it not as an atomic individual but as a member of the group. Through a relation of civil society the family transcends the familial problem of desire: The marriage contract eliminates the capricious subjectivism of love as sentiment, an "immediate form of reason," and makes love the ethical or self-conscious moment in marriage.

This is quite a different situation from the one we encountered in the *Phenomenology*, where love in the pagan world was not self-conscious and where male desire infected the relationship between husband and wife so that it could not be the ideal relationship between man and woman. The bifurcation of man's life in the pagan world into public and private spheres caused a split between desire and morality that introduced a moment of ethical contingency into the marriage. Only the brother-sister relationship, which was supposedly free from desire and took place before the brother entered the polis and experienced the bifurcation of his life, could be seen as ideal. According to Hegel, the modern Christian world has radically transformed the situation so that male desire is no longer a problem. The tripartite structure of this world is seen as overcoming the dualism of the pagan world and allowing for the reconciliation of desire and morality through the marriage ceremony, which is both a contractual relation (a relation of civil society) and a religious (familial) one.

Thus, in the *Philosophy of Right* there is a significant shift away from the brother-sister relationship as the ideal relation of recognition between man and woman, as a relationship *free* from desire, to a consideration of the husband-wife relationship as a relationship that *transcends* desire. This shift is characteristic of the claim of the Hegelian philosophy as a whole to overcome the externality of Greek philosophy and society with the realization of philosophy in historical life. Significantly, the shift changes the site of the paradigm of male-female relations from the family of origin to the family of procreation. Here Hegel wants to distinguish the "natural" feeling of love, which binds family members through an original blood tie, from a later, deeper, self-conscious tie of love in marriage.[29] He defends the nuclear family against the rights of the extended family of origin. In the modern world any conflict of claims regarding duties and obligations between the family of origin and the family of procreation is always resolved in favor of the higher ethical family, the family of procreation; that which comes later is a more mature form of reason. The shift to the focus on the family of procreation also replaces the contingency we noted earlier. That is, while only some women may have brothers in the family of origin all women may potentially have husbands.

In the *Philosophy of Right* love is subordinated to the claims of marriage and reproduction, which in turn are subordinated to the claims of property. Thus, the relation of husband and wife in the modern world is no more inherently self-complete than it was in the pagan world. The husband and wife still need the child as an externalization of the unity of their love (*PR*, addition to para. 173, 264–65). Marriage is for procreation and woman must remain confined to the family as "mother" so that the family may achieve its objective, explicit unity. As I have argued more comprehensively elsewhere, it is not really a question of man and woman coming together in love that is at issue here, but rather the inheritance of family property.[30] For Hegel, property is the manifestation of ethical self-consciousness in the material and public world. Man expresses his freedom and gains historical continuity by effectively appropriating and transmitting property through his family. Woman, on the other hand, is allowed to own property in her lifetime, but she cannot bequeath it to others. Thus, woman's relation to the family property leaves her deprived of the experiences of freedom and historical continuity. Hegel's complicated schema, which attempts to give woman, as person, equal rights in terms of the family property, is ultimately overreached by his conception of woman as mother, tied to immediacy.

According to Hegel, woman, as wife and mother in the modern world, like her sister in the pagan world, is a passive and subjective being who has knowledge only as feeling or intuition. She never leaves the family but "has her substantive destiny in the family, and to be imbued with family piety is her ethical frame of mind." Here Hegel refers to the *Antigone* as "one of the most sublime presentations" of family piety as the law of woman (*PR*, para. 166, 114). However, the reference to the *Antigone* in the *Philosophy of Right* is within a context that puts the claims of the family of procreation over and above the claims of the family of origin, whereas Hegel's interpretation of the *Antigone* in the *Phenomenology* concerns the highest claim of duty and obligation within the family of origin: the duty of the sister to bury and honor her brother. Given Hegel's original interpretation of Antigone as the paradigm of ethical family life *precisely because* she represents the relationship be-tween man and woman, *not* as wife but as *sister*, this new appropriation of the play within the context of a discussion of marriage in the modern world seems quite untenable. While Hegel believes that the modern world has transformed the relation of desire between man and woman through the Christian marriage tie, and consequently has solved the problem of male desire, nevertheless, since Antigone represents "holy sisterly love" (a love free from desire according to the *Phenomenology*) *and* since she never marries, it is hard to see how she can serve as a model for wifely piety in the modern world. Hegel's attempt to use the play to reinforce his assumption that woman must remain confined to the family in the modern world is without a historical or conceptual analysis that would justify such a use. Most significant, Hegel posits Antigone as a *transhistorical* paradigm of ethical family life and the role of woman: The play has lost its historical reference to the pagan world in the *Philosophy of Right* in order to justify the confinement of woman within the family in the modern world. While Hegel's system is meant to be a historical account of the development of humanity, woman is presented as outside history.

For Hegel, as we have seen, particularity must necessarily be incorpo-rated into political life in order for that life to be truly rather than abstractly universal. But this does not mean that woman *qua* woman needs incorporation into the political sphere. Rather, Hegel develops a philosophical system in the *Philosophy of Right* in which he conceives of particularity without the impediment of immediacy. Where woman was confined to the family in the pagan world as the representative of particularity, in the modern world she is confined to the family as the representative of immediacy; particularity and immediacy are separated, and particularity is taken up into the male realm of civil society while woman remains trapped in the ahistorical immediacy of the family. Thus, the *Philosophy of Right* details man's progressive movement into a world that reconciles particular and universal, but woman is forced to take a step backward: she now represents immediacy—a moment that *precedes* particularity and is therefore a less developed form of reason.

Hegel wants to claim that freedom is realized in the modern world; at the same time, he excludes woman from the spheres of civil society and the state, the spheres in which man manifests his freedom. Woman's exclusion from these spheres is made necessary by the dialectical struc-ture that requires that the sphere of the family be maintained or preserved as well as negated in the process of development toward the universality of the state. Modern man leaves the family in order to move into the realm of civil society, where he emerges as a particular; but the sphere of undifferentiated universality or immediacy must be maintained. Therefore, modern woman is forced to do the family "maintenance" work required by the Hegelian dialectic: Woman stays home to preserve the family. Only man "dirempts" himself; only he struggles for recognition in the universal sense. Fortunately, he can come home after a hard day of self-diremption to the wife who offers him "a tranquil intuition of . . . unity" (PR, para. 166, 114). In this way man achieves a wholeness through woman while woman remains confined to the family where only an abstract or undifferentiated identity can be achieved. Confined to the family as the sphere of immediacy in the modern world, woman still lacks the negativity that results from the initial sundering from nature; therefore she never achieves an independent self-consciousness. In preserving the sphere of the family woman is again forced to sacrifice her claim to self-consciousness. Thus, modern man's realization of himself and the dialectical structure are at modern woman's expense.

Given Hegel's schema, in which woman must necessarily remain confined to the family, he must systematically misrepresent Antigone, especially her movement out of the family. His failure in the *Phenomenology* to analyze Antigone's actions comprehensively means that he cannot bring an analysis of these actions into the discussion of Antigone in the *Philosophy of Right*. Rather, he misuses her as a transhistorical ideal of woman as wife confined to the family as the sphere of animal life, the sphere of inaction.

Examining the *Philosophy of Right* via Hegel's discussion of Antigone raises two crucial issues: the problem of female desire and the question of whether or not the sphere to which woman has been assigned *can be* taken up and dialectically *aufgehoben* in Hegel's sense if woman is to be allowed her freedom.

In the *Philosophy of Right*, as in the *Phenomenology*, Hegel tries to solve the problem of the division of man's life by leaving woman in the position of not experiencing the division. Marriage to woman is said to resolve the bifurcation of modern man's life between family and civil society by mediating two forms of desire: (1) desire as familial, heterosexual union and (2) desire as general and differentiated in civil society. Woman remains confined to one sphere, the sphere of the family, precisely for the purpose of giving man an intuition of unity. In Hegel's schema, if woman lived in two spheres she could not offer man the access to wholeness he seeks. However, Hegel does not address the fact that *because* she lives in only one sphere woman has no internal motive for seeking marriage as mediation. That is, there is no necessity for the institutional mediation of two forms of desire in woman's life since she does not experience two forms. Therefore, woman does not need marriage as ceremony and contract. From her perspective, marriage is the result of external coercion: Out of *his* need for marriage man forces her to accept it. Given this conceptual framework, what emerges is that woman's confinement to the family as the sphere of immediacy indicates that she can represent desire only as capricious and contingent. Just as woman has no internal motive for marriage, she also has no internal motive for desiring one man over another. Female desire itself, if it is to focus on a stable object (one husband rather than many lovers), must be coerced. Thus, when we look carefully, we find that in Hegel's schema of the modern world the problem of male desire is "solved" only by creating a problem of female desire.

In terms of the dialectical structure, Antigone can be seen as the representative of woman as actor who refuses to fit neatly into Hegel's system, a system that requires her to stay home to preserve the family. Her move out of the family transforms her so that she has the potential to be a particular self. However, when woman in the modern world follows in Antigone's footsteps by participating in civil society and the state, the spheres of particularity and universality, then the family is not preserved or maintained as well as transcended in the Hegelian sense. Once woman lives in more than one sphere she cannot offer man the intuition of unity he seeks and the dialectical structure necessarily breaks down.[31]

Hegel's philosophic formulation of the relation between woman and man in the modern world is important because it reveals the problem of how to achieve unity in a world in which each one seeks satisfaction of particular needs and desires. But through an examination of Antigone in the *Philosophy of Right* we find that his solution, which separates particularity and immediacy so that the family remains the sphere of immediacy in which woman is confined and coerced, is not an adequate formulation of the required mediation. And, for Hegel, it is precisely the *Aufhebung* or reconciliation of the modern world that reveals the dualistic conflict of the ancient world. Given the inadequacy of Hegel's formulation of the modern reconciliation in the context of sexual difference he must necessarily misrepresent this conflict in his interpretation of the *Antigone* in the *Phenomenology*.

By confining woman to the family in the *Phenomenology* and the *Philosophy of Right* Hegel prevents the progressive movement of Spirit toward universal self-consciousness from being recapitulated in woman. The development of human consciousness outside the family is sex-specific, limited to man. Woman can never aspire to "concrete" universality or individuality; she cannot attain particularity much less universality.

With the limitation of woman there is a limitation of the Hegelian system. Hegel's universal is necessarily male and male is *not* universal. Humanity is both male and female and the claim to encompass the universality of human experience must allow for woman's experience and participation outside the sphere of the family; it must allow for a more comprehensive account of the *Antigone* than Hegel can provide.

My analysis of Hegel's *Antigone,* done through a doubled feminist vision, reveals that Hegel's attempt to include dialectically all oppositional "moments" presents us with an abstract negation in which woman, defined as an ontological principle of otherness, represents the "difference" that cannot be fully comprehended in the logical Idea. As a result, Hegel's dialectical theory becomes a closed system, a system that is the quintessential form of identity logic in which difference is ultimately dominated and denied rather than reconciled. Hegel's concept of reconciliation—the idea that latent in contradictions is an ultimate unity or identity-in-difference of subject and object, mind and matter, universal and particular, history and nature, man and woman—has always meant domination: of the subject over the object, mind over matter, universal over particular, history over nature, man over woman.[32]

My critique, however, should not be understood as a dismissive stance that claims that Hegel has "nothing to say to feminists." Rather, I believe Hegel's philosophy is significant because the Hegelian problem of the relation between identity and difference that is central to his phenomenology is at the heart of the feminist project to create a free and equal society. That is, Hegel *articulates* the fundamental problem of contemporary society with which feminists are concerned even though his analysis fails when sexual difference is "essentialized" and all that woman represents is confined to the family and "overreached." But it is precisely this "failure" to "overcome" or "reconcile" sexual difference that moves us to reconceive dialectical thinking, pointing to Adorno's critique of Hegel where *negative* dialectics prevents the closure of identity logic.

For Adorno it is the *non*-identity of nature and history, subject and object, particular and universal, that is required of a dialectical theory motivated by a concern for freedom. Thus, negative dialectics seeks to realize the goal of Hegel's philosophy, the goal of intersubjective recognition without recourse to domination, by refuting the moment of Hegelian reconciliation in which the negation of the negation becomes a positive moment of domination. Adorno writes: "The reconciled condition would not be the philosophical imperialism of annexing the alien [the Other]. Instead, its happiness would lie in the fact that the alien, in the proximity it is granted, remains what is distant and different, beyond the heterogeneous and beyond that which is one's own."[33] Adorno's critique of Hegel keeps dialectical thought open to the negativity that motivates it and in so doing allows for the emergence of Antigone as the particular, the representation of difference, beyond the domination of a logic of identity.

Notes

1. Seyla Benhabib, "On Contemporary Feminist Theory," in *Dissent*, no. 36 (summer 1989): 366–70. Joan Kelly-Gadol was the first to formulate a concept of a feminist "doubled vision." See Introduction, note 9.

2. Throughout this chapter the term *man* is used to refer to adult males and never as a generic or universal term. This is done to illuminate the problems of sexual difference and sexual domination that are obscured by the use of "man" and "mankind" to refer to the human species.

3. Alexandre Kojève, *Introduction to the Reading of Hegel*, trans. James H. Nichols Jr. (New York: Basic Books, 1969), 58–61.

4. G. W. F. Hegel, *Phenomenology of Spirit*, trans. A. V. Miller (Oxford: Clarendon, 1977), para. 451, 270 (amended translation); hereafter cited as *PS*, with paragraph number followed by page number. Miller's translation of *marklose* as "impotent" is not to be confused with Hegel's term *Ohnmacht*, used to describe nature as "impotent" or "unconscious." Many of Hegel's ontological insights are rooted in Aristotle's philosophy. The bifurcation between familial and political life to which Hegel here subscribes can be found in Aristotle's *Politics*.

5. J. N. Findlay, *Hegel: A Re-Examination* (London: Allen and Unwin, 1958), 116–17; Kojève, *Introduction*, 60–61, 296–98; Charles Taylor, *Hegel* (Cambridge: Cambridge University Press, 1975), 172–77.

6. Kojève, *Introduction*, 61.

7. Ibid., 61, 298.

8. *PS*, para. 457, 274–75; cf. G. W. F. Hegel, *The Phenomenology of Mind*, trans. J. B.

Baillie (New York: Harper Torchbooks, 1967), 477; hereafter cited as *PM*. In both the Miller and the [1910, 1931] Baillie translations of this passage the word "particular" is added in several places to reveal Hegel's meaning. Hegel sometimes underscores the word for "this" *(dieser)* instead of using the word *Einzelheit* to refer to the "particular" individual.

9. G. W. F. Hegel, *The Philosophy of History*, trans. J. Sibree (New York: Dover, 1956), 245–46.

10. The speech in which Antigone defends her decision to bury her brother, saying she would not make the same sacrifice for a husband or son, is omitted from many modern translations. This speech is reprinted in *Ten Greek Plays in Contemporary Translations*, edited by L. R. Lind (Boston: Riverside, 1957), 100. For a discussion of the history of inclusion/ exclusion of this speech, see Costas Douzinas, "Law's Birth and Antigone's Death: On Ontological and Psychoanalytical Ethics," *Cardozo Law Review* 16, nos. 3–4 (January 1995): 1353–54.

It is worth noting that this paradigm of mutual recognition between sister and brother, which is supposed to be devoid of desire, is rooted in the incestuous origins of the house of Thebes. Antigone's father, Oedipus, is also her brother making Polyneices her uncle as well as her brother and she his aunt as well as his sister. In choosing this seemingly atypical family to represent the family as natural ethical life, Hegel gives significance to the Oedipus myth long before Freud.

It is also important to note here that the figure of Antigone in the ancient Greek tragedy is not quintessentially European or Aryan. As Martin Bernal has persuasively argued, the culture of ancient Greece emerged out of the colonization of Europeans by Egyptians and Phoenicians (Africans and Semites). See his *Black Athena: The Afroasiatic Roots of Classical Civilization*, vol. 1 (New Brunswick: Rutgers University Press, 1987).

11. *PS*, para. 475, 288. By claiming that woman shows man the power of his authority, especially that as son he is master of his mother, Hegel suggests that woman conspires to realize male domination.

12. Theodor W. Adorno, *Negative Dialectics*, trans. E. B. Ashton (New York: Seabury, 1973), 173.

13. I understand experience not as something fixed and unalterable, grounding an "essentialism," but rather as a continuous process of engagement with and in the world through which subjectivity is created, re-created, and understood.

14. Sophocles, *Antigone*, in *Drama: An Introductory Anthology*, alternate edition, ed. Otto R. Reinhert (Boston: Little Brown, 1964), p. 22 (amended translation); all subsequent references to *Antigone* are to this edition. See also *PS*, para. 470, 284; and *PM*, 491.

15. One might want to argue that these gods are the divine representatives of male authority to which Antigone bows. Nevertheless, she does not accept male domination in its more obvious human guise.

16. Later, in his *Aesthetics*, Hegel himself describes Antigone as choosing her course of action: Insofar as she has pathos, she has free will. Here, Hegel describes Antigone's pathos as less than that of Creon's because she worships the underworld gods of Hades while Creon worships the daylight gods of self-conscious political life. However, the argument concerning the conscious, deliberate choice involved in Antigone's actions undermines the claim in the *Phenomenology* that the sister's ethical life is not conscious or actualized. See *Aesthetics: Lectures on Fine Art*, trans. T. M. Knox (Oxford: Clarendon, 1975), 232, 464.

17. Joyce Nower, "A Feminist View of Antigone," in *The Longest Revolution* (February– March 1983), 6. Why Antigone rejects Ismene's offer of sisterly solidarity is an enigma that can perhaps be illuminated by the fact that patriarchal society attempts to set women against each other so that they learn to see themselves primarily in relation to men.

18. It is important to note the fact that in Hegel's analysis of the master-slave dialectic there is no mention of woman: master and slave are both seen as males even though

historically many slaves were women. This means that the difference between "free" and slave women is necessarily overlooked. For an important discussion of how the man-woman distinction ignores class and race divisions in the ancient world, see Elizabeth V. Spelman's discussion of Aristotle in "Who's Who in the *Polis*," chap. 2 of *Inessential Woman* (Boston: Beacon, 1988).

Several authors have attempted to present gender relations as an instance of the Hegelian master-slave dialectic in which woman's consciousness is equated with slave consciousness. One of the earliest feminist attempts was that done by Simone de Beauvoir in *The Second Sex*, trans. and ed. H. M. Parshley (New York: Vintage Books, 1974), 73. The inadequacy of Beauvoir's account is examined by Mary O'Brien in her book *The Politics of Reproduction* (Boston: Routledge and Kegan Paul, 1981), 67–73.

More recently Stuart Swindle has tried to make the case in a rhetorical attack on my own analysis of Hegel. In a detailed response to Swindle I show that it is delusive to argue that we can simply "recall" the master-slave dialectic to explain gender relations. There is no textual evidence in the *Phenomenology* for such a claim. To argue as Swindle does is to misconstrue Hegel's analysis of the master-slave dialectic while subverting the analysis of woman's unique consciousness. See Stuart Swindle, "Why Feminists Should Take the *Phenomenology of Spirit* Seriously" and my response, " 'Feminist' Sympathy and Other Serious Crimes: A Reply to Swindle" (*The Owl of Minerva* 24, no. 1 [fall 1992]: 41–62).

19. G. W. F. Hegel, *Natural Law*, trans. T. M. Knox (Philadelphia: University of Pennsylvania Press, 1975), 90–92. See also Kojève, *Introduction*, 247–48.

20. *PM*, 483. These are Baillie's words, not Hegel's.

21. P. 18. Creon's reproach to Haemon underscores Hegel's contention that woman acts on the adolescent male in her effort to destroy the pagan world. In *Let's Spit on Hegel* Carla Lonzi extrapolates from this relation to argue for the revolutionary potential of political solidarity between women and young men in bringing down the modern world of the patriarchs; see Chapter 12, this volume. The psychological basis of Creon's fear of womankind is explored by Eli Sagan in *The Lust to Annihilate: A Psychoanalytic Study of Violence in Ancient Greek Culture* (New York: Psychohistory Press, 1979), 95–101.

22. In their play *The Island*, Athol Fugard, John Kani, and Winston Ntshona present the *Antigone* as a play within a play to reveal the ancient drama's relevance to the situation of South African prisoners. In both plays moral laws are juxtaposed to state laws to demonstrate that justice and the law are not necessarily the same thing. This point, as we have seen, is lost in Hegel's interpretation.

23. My intent is not to demean "feminine intuition" but rather to reveal the sexist implications in Hegel's account, which does demean it.

24. According to Hegel it is because Polyneices offered Antigone the ideal relationship of mutual recognition between woman and man in life that Polyneices makes the greatest claim on Antigone with his death. I have argued that within the family of origin Polyneices was only a *potential* man and becomes a man at the same time that he severs his relationship to his sister, thus challenging the sense in which this relationship can be seen as the ideal one between woman and man. According to Sophocles, it is not the relationship of recognition based on blood ties, but the *uterine* relationship, that exerts the primary claim on Antigone: It is the fact that Polyneices and Antigone are of the same womb, the same mother, that is most significant. Antigone says: "if I had suffered him who was born of my mother to lie in death an unburied corpse, in that case I would have sorrowed . . . it is nothing shameful to revere those . . . from the same womb" (lines 465–511). Here the ancient womb/tomb imagery, the association of women with life and death, is revealed as an integral part of the play. Creon shifts the discussion away from the uterine relationship to a discussion of the more general concept of blood ties (lines 512–13). This shift and the emphasis on the uterine relationship in the Greek text are revealed in the Oxford translation of the *Antigone* (1880).

25. Antigone may also be seen as the precursor of the suffragists of the late nineteenth and early twentieth centuries and the women involved in the temperance movement insofar as those women were trying to achieve familial goals in the public realm. For an interesting analysis of this process see Jean Bethke Elshtain, "Moral Woman and Immoral Man: A Consideration of the Public-Private Split and Its Political Ramifications," *Politics and Society* 4, no. 4 (1974): 453–73.

26. To be sure, Hegel believes that the real historical conflict of the pagan world would be visible only after the Christian revelation had introduced the possibility of its *Aufhebung*. Nevertheless, since Hegel sees the tragic conflict of the pagan world revealed through the great Greek tragedians, all significant aspects of the plays of these ancient authors would have to be taken up in the *Aufhebung*.

27. Hegel's philosophy is ideological in its lack of analysis of the difference between the working class and the bourgeois family as well as in its patriarchal assumptions. It is difficult to know how the working-class woman, confined to a subsistence level of existence within her own family that is *not* based on property and capital, or confined to the bourgeois family as a domestic servant, fits Hegel's schema. The working-class woman produced and reproduced laborers, not heirs to the family property.

28. G. W. F. Hegel, *Philosophy of Right*, trans. T. M. Knox (London: Oxford University Press, 1967), paras. 161–64, 111–14; hereafter cited as *PR*, with paragraph number followed by page number.

29. *PR*, para. 172, 116; Hegel also maintains this understanding of the relation between the family of origin and the family of procreation in the *Aesthetics*, 463–64.

30. Patricia Jagentowicz Mills, "Hegel and 'The Woman Question': Recognition and Intersubjectivity," in *The Sexism of Social and Political Theory: Women and Reproduction from Plato to Nietzsche*, edited by Lorenne M. G. Clark and Lynda Lange (Toronto: University of Toronto Press, 1979): 74–98; see also chap. 1 of my *Woman, Nature, and Psyche* (New Haven: Yale University Press, 1987), 39–43.

31. My analysis of Hegel is part of a larger project that focuses on the relation between the domination of nature and the domination of woman in the dialectical tradition that includes Hegel, Marx, Marcuse, Horkheimer, and Adorno. See Mills, *Woman, Nature, and Psyche*.

32. Adorno, *Negative Dialectics*, 3–8.

33. Ibid., 191.

4

Lucinde's Shame:
Hegel, Sensuous Woman, and the Law

David Farrell Krell

In honor of the fifth and final movement of Johann Sebastian Bach, "Overture No. 4," BWV 1069, designated "Rejouissance."

Ethicality turned somewhat pale, and her eyes welled with tears. "But only yesterday I was so virtuous. . . . It's all I can do to deal with my own reproofs; why must I hear still more of them from you?"
—Friedrich von Schlegel, "Allegory of Impudence," *Lucinde*

Hegel wants spirit *alive*. Spirit alive is not only rational, not only thinking and willing spirit, not only the spirit of logic, but also spirit sentient, sensible, and sensuous. This essay is about sentience, sensibility, and sensuality, so essential to life yet so difficult to control, so mobile and prolific. A tradition as old as that of "spirit" identifies sentience and the sensuous with various figures of woman—as though spirit alive were *of woman*. Hegel's philosophical system confronts the following predicament: If woman were purged from his system, the system of spirit, spirit would die; remaining within the system, however, woman condemns spirit and its system to a fate worse than death.

In the handwritten notes and the addendum to §164 of Hegel's *Philosophy of Right* we find two explicit references to Friedrich von

Schlegel's novel *Lucinde*, first published in 1799.[1] "Lucinde" is the second of three major figures of woman dominating the first part of the first division of "Ethicality" (§§142–360), treating the family (§§158–81) and marriage (§§161–69). The first figure is *Venus vaga* (mentioned in the handwritten notes to §161), the wandering, vagrant, or vagabond Venus, whom the Greeks called Pandemian or "Common" Aphrodite; the third is of course the heroine of Sophocles' *Antigone* (§166). Hegel's dialectical account of marriage and the family reacts most intensely to these three figures of woman: the goddess of sensual love and beauty is quickly abandoned for the infinitely free personality of the romantic beloved, the free personality symbolized by and portrayed in *Lucinde*, while the figure of Lucinde in turn is abjured for Antigone, at which point the law of woman succumbs to the law of the State.

I do not have the leisure to survey the entire process, familiar, at any rate, in its general outlines. I shall focus instead on the middle figure, Lucinde, and ask what it is about her that so unnerves Hegel. For whenever Lucinde is invoked in his text, Hegel's irritability and even anxiety or sense of jeopardy wax strong. What has the system to fear from her? Nothing—if we trust Hegel's account of her pitiable position, forever on the brink of shame. Everything—if Philippe Lacoue-Labarthe is right to see in her poetry, literature, and aesthetics as such, the troublesome parts of the system, the rejected and dejected materials that inevitably return to haunt the speculative.[2]

Taking my cue from Lacoue-Labarthe, I ask about those troublesome parts of literature and life. I shall examine some of the predicates that cling to Lucinde in Hegel's text, comparing them to passages in Friedrich Schlegel's *Lucinde*; I shall then shamelessly examine Hegel's Jena lectures on the pudenda, the "shameful parts"; and I shall close with some speculations concerning sensuous woman (if one can write such a phrase in the singular, as though she were one) and the law. But first a word about Friedrich Schlegel's scandalous novel, *Lucinde*.

Throughout Jacques Derrida's *Glas* much is made of the fact that when the French pronounce the name "Hegel" it comes out sounding like their word for eagle.[3] And there is some truth in saying that Hegel himself identified with the heraldic Prussian eagle, the high-flying, sharp-taloned bird of philosophy, at least when philosophy flies by day. Friedrich Schlegel, in his impudent prologue to *Lucinde*, citing the examples of Petrarch, Boccaccio, and Cervantes, identifies himself by contrast with the swan: while the eagle expends its energies lording it over the lowly crow, the swan only dreams of how it can ingratiate itself with a beautiful woman, how it can "cleave to the bosom of Leda, without doing any harm" (6).

It is not easy to describe this "smiling, touching" book of Schlegel's, though it is easy to imagine a sober reader's indignation over it. A brief novel of about one hundred pages, Schlegel's *Lucinde* (Part 1 is all Schlegel ever completed) consists of thirteen unnumbered sections. Some of the more insolent section titles communicate the peculiar humor of the book's "smiling" visage: "Dithyrambic Fantasy Concerning the Loveliest Situation," "Allegory of Impudence," "Idyll of Idleness," "Fidelity and Frolic," "Apprenticeship to Manliness," "Metamorphoses," "Languor and Repose," "Baubles of Fantasy," and in the midst of all this, "A Reflection." In these ironic and overdetermined "arabesques," as Schlegel liked to call them, Schlegel elaborates a theory of love, marriage, and the status of women that can only be called revolutionary for its time. The two leading characters, Lucinde and Julius, embrace one another with as much religiosity as sensuous abandon; what others would regard as obscenity they celebrate as their system; voluptuousness is their virtuosity and their virtue; their carnival of love and lust builds cathedrals, and when they weary of cathedrals, they laugh and tear them down, like children at play. In their sensuous passivity, a passivity they seem to cultivate actively, Lucinde and Julius scorn Prometheus and worship Hyacinth.

Lucinde is an artist, a painter. She is a mature woman, and in giving herself over to young Julius, she seems to be adopting an orphan. She mixes her colors well, swirling the sacred blues of motherhood into the roses of profane and passionate love. All her works, all their works together, consist of baubles, bangles, and bright shiny rosary beads: they act like happy beasts, with the intention of transforming humanity into divinity. Hegel has to take an interest in this, for the spirited lovers claim to be the agents of spirit as such—agents of a spirit born out of wedlock.

For Hegel, by way of contrast, love-and-marriage is all a matter of proper sequence, succession, and consequence. It is essentially a matter of reversing a *natural* chronology or sequence of events by grace of a spiritual anachronism. If nature brings together a particular "this" (who happens to be a male) with a second particular "this" (who happens to be a female), as it must do if the species is to perpetuate itself; and if natural passion causes all the "chords" of one self-consciousness "to reverberate only in this other one, only in the possession of this one *contingent* person"; then spirit will have to elevate the merely accidental conjunction of these persons by reversing the order of dependence that is established in the course of events. For Hegel the proper order, the order of spirit, will be: Marriage and (only then) love. Meeting and mating will not lead to marriage but will be consequent upon marriage and subsequent to it. Love and marriage will go together like a horse and carriage only if the carriage is not placed before the horse. Only in this way will the particularity and contingency of passionate sensibility dissolve in the universality of bonded spiritual love. Only in this way will the high necessity of spiritual progression to family, civil society, and the State occur. Only in this way will love slough off its natural integument and rise on the divine afflatus of spirit proper.

Yet the stakes are hardly the same for the two "thises" destined to be elevated by the spiritual anachronism of matrimony. Hegel sets the stakes high, infinitely high, for woman, inasmuch as her honor (*Ehre*) is won solely on the field of marriage (*Ehe*). Honor and matrimony are in fact one for woman, and could be written as *Eh(r)e*. That becomes clear in the otherwise elliptical notes that Hegel jotted into his copy of the *Grundlinien*. Let us examine extracts from two sets of these notes, those to §162 and §164. First, those from §162: "What does the man want, what does the girl [*Mädchen*] want? The girl wants a man; the man wants a woman [*eine Frau*]."

The exchange of desires seems fair enough. And yet the difference in the stakes is already clear. Twice the word *Mann* (man, husband) asserts itself, serving as both the subject and the object of desire: the girl wants a man (or husband), the man wants a woman. As the subject of desire,[4] the girl is apparently equal to herself (although even here the self-sufficiency is illusory), whereas as an object of desire she will have to be transmogrified from girl into woman. How will this happen? Hegel continues: "She loves him. Why? Because he is to become her husband."

It is still the same word, *Mann*, that serves for male, man, and husband alike. But to continue: "He is to make her into a woman [*Frau*]. She is to receive from him as the man [or husband] her dignity, value, joy, and happiness as a *wife* [*Ehefrau*], insofar as she becomes woman [*Frau*]. Love—she recognizes the basis of her interest in the man; this is preeminently *the girl's sensibility.*"

At least two kinds of appropriation are going on here. We are by now accustomed to one of them: appropriation of the names *girl, woman,* and *wife* as tokens of masculine desire. Yet the second appropriation, albeit every bit as traditional, is far more difficult to descry and less calculable in its effects: the first stage of ethicality as a whole, namely, the stage of love as the nonmediated substantiality of spirit; the family as a unit of sensibility (§158), is in effect surrendered to the girl. Without sensibility, Hegel himself stresses, the life of spirit would be dry and brittle (addendum to §33); indeed, without sensibility in the Kantian sense, the processes of intelligence and cognition would not have their start.[5]

However, sensibility and receptivity are appropriated to and by a young girl, neither a goddess nor a mortal woman, but a mere maid. Antigone, perhaps, at least if we think of the Antigone in the play that bears her name, and not the Antigone of *Oedipus at Colonos,* who ought to be younger than *Antigone's* Antigone, but who seems much older. Antigone, we recall, is a girl who is under arrest. And, because she will die as a *Mädchen* rather than as the *Frau* of the king's own son, she is and remains a case of arrested development. Is Hegel therefore on the side of Creon, the king and patriarch?

On the one hand, Hegel holds no truck with patriarchy, which makes slaves of its children and even arranges their marriages, as though love were a matter of contract (as it apparently was for bachelor Kant). Hegel does not wish to reproduce the monkish mistake of vilifying natural vitality and mortifying sensuality as negative in themselves. On the other hand, sensibility and sensitivity are clearly of woman. The problem is that in the transition from girlhood to womanhood tender sensitivity can readily become what novelists like Schlegel call "the sensibility of the flesh" (26). Sentience, sensibility, sensitivity, and sensuality will thus have to be a passing moment for Hegel and for spirit, if not for Lucinde and Julius. It is no accident that all the predicates of sensibility, the life's blood of spirit and an essential component of the system, assemble in one place in *The Philosophy of Right:* these predicates—naturalness, contingency, accident, particularity, inclination, drive, and desire—loom at and as the origins of evil (§139).

The second set of handwritten notes (those to §164) takes up the seducer's sophism, Prove That You Love Me Darling, and the stakes for an O-Please-Don't-Make-Me-Prove-It maid. Of course, the notes become compelling only in the context of §164 viewed as a whole. Herewith, then, a brief résumé.

Only when solemnization of the lovers' union through matrimony takes place, in the presence of the family and community, does natural love receive its spiritual bond. Hegel emphasizes the importance of the "antecedence" of the ceremony, this antecedence alone reversing the natural sequence of events in such a way that "the sensuous moment pertaining to natural vitality is posited in its ethical relationship as a consequence and mere accident." True, some romantic moderns take solemnization itself to be accidental and superfluous, an extrinsic formality, a mere civil instance that interrupts the intimacy of the lovers' union. These persons do not accept that the formal ceremony is "the antecedent condition of their mutual and total abandon." (The word rendered here by "abandon" is *Hingebung*, and it will soon return to haunt the spiritual bond.) They even believe that love is disunited[6] by such ceremonial intrusion. Modern, romantic love is no doubt superior to the "Platonic love" of popular conceit, for it is closely tied up with the essential individualism of modernity and of Protestant Christianity as such. Nevertheless, romantic love does raise the "pretension" (cf §162, "Remark") of being purer than purity itself. It denies the ethicality of love, rejects "the more elevated inhibition and suppression of the mere physical drive," an inhibition and suppression that occur naturally through "shame" and spiritually through the inculcation of "chastity" and "decency." (Why natural shame is insufficient and needs the supplement of inculcated "decency" would be an arresting question.) The natural and sensuous moment is thus to be subordinated or demoted (§163); else all is insolence, impudence, and even impudicity, for we are already talking about Lucinde and her paramour Julius. Insolence or impudence is the very allegory played out so shamelessly by the author of *Lucinde*, an author possessed of intellect and wit but blind to the speculative nature of love and marriage—which is acknowledged, on the contrary, by the "legislation of all Christian peoples."[7]

Perhaps now we are in a position to work our way through the handwritten notes to the "Remark" of §164, and to cite verbatim that section's addendum. Sophistry, the seducer's art, as Schlegel all but admits ("A stream of importunities, flatteries, and sophisms flowed from his lips" [47]), demands sensuous abandon as proof of love *before* marriage, whereas love believes, and spiritual consciousness has faith.[8] The girl, victimized by such sophistry, surrenders her honor. Not so the man. For the man still has another field for his ethical efficacy; for example, in the corporations of the State (cf. §255, "Remark"). Not so the girl. For her, ethicality subsists essentially in the relation of marriage. Here there is no parity. On the part of the man, sensuous abandon is no proof of love and no threat to honor. Love, Hegel notes laconically, can make demands that are different from those of marriage. For love is the substantial unity of spirit in sensibility (§158), but also "the most monstrous contradiction, one which the intellect cannot resolve" (addendum to §158). With love, all is one and undivided, both sensuous and ethical. However, only the supplement of solemnization in the presence of representatives of the family and the larger community, the public exchange of spoken words and stipulated promises, establishes the relation in such a way that sensuous abandon is not its cause but a consequence (indeed, a consequence that is essentially inconsequential for marriage, in which sensuality is effectively suppressed, in order that connubial equanimity not be disturbed by passion; see the addendum to §163). In agreeing to the marriage, concludes Hegel cryptically, "the girl concedes this too."

Hegel's note is unclear. What does the girl concede? Does she concede that sensuous abandon will now follow? Or does she concede that sensuality is merely a supplement, indeed a bothersome appendage to the ethical bond? What does the girl concede in marriage? We do not know, even if Hegel's remarks on the role of the housewife (addendum to §167) certainly give us some indication of the concessions involved on her part. What we do know is that at the end of these handwritten notes appears the underlined word *Lucinde*. The juxtaposition of the title of Schlegel's novel with these notes on a victimized girl is nothing short of bizarre, as we shall soon see. But let me now cite and discuss the addendum to §164:

> *Addendum.* That the ceremony which sets the seal on the marriage is superfluous, a mere formality that can be set aside inasmuch as love is what is substantial, and that love even loses some of its value through this solemnization—this has been argued by Friedrich von Schlegel in *Lucinde* and by an anonymous supporter in a series of letters.[9] Here sensuous abandon [*Hingebung*] is represented as though it were demanded as a proof of the freedom and intense ardor of love, an argumentation not foreign to seducers. Furthermore, one must note concerning the relation of man and woman that the girl surrenders her honor in sensuous abandon, which is not the case with the man, who has yet another field for his ethical activity than the family. The girl is defined essentially only in the relation of marriage; what is called for is that love receive the form of marriage and that the sundry

moments of love assume their truly rational relationship to one another.

We know that the truly rational relationship enjoined by Hegel is the inversion, not to say perversion, of the natural order or sequence, whereby sensuous abandon follows upon matrimony rather than inducing it. Let us now examine more closely the scene of sensibility. The girl's honor is at risk; she is being asked to surrender herself, to give herself over to utter abandon and erotic transport, or else to sheer degradation and enslavement; the man's honor will not be at risk in this transaction, inasmuch as he performs his ethical activity not only in marriage and the family but also in civil society and the State. Honor, abandon, and activity: let me focus on these three aspects of the scene of sensibility.

Honor is ubiquitous in Hegel's *Philosophy of Right*. This is surprising, since it belongs more to the bygone era of chivalry, to the age of heroes and patriarchs (§71, handwritten notes), or even to the age of oriental potentates (§§348–49, 355) than to the modern world. For the girl, the meaning of honor is exhausted in her resisting sensuous abandon prior to marriage. (That claim is true of course—if it is ever true—only if we forget for the moment that Antigone too is a girl, one who pays her brother "the ultimate honor" [§118, handwritten notes], confronting the State with the stubbornness of a Cassandra.) For a man, honor is more a matter of involvement in the corporations of the State, or of his class and status in civil society (§§244, 253, 255), than of the family. Even a criminal has his honor (§132), namely, the honor that consists in reaping punishment for his deeds (see the "Remarks" to §§100 and 120). Honor is also a matter of right, thought, and the concepts themselves, inasmuch as in a philosophical system all these must "come to honor" (see §§140a, 140e, 211 addendum, and 189 addendum).

One matter of honor to which Hegel attaches great importance is that of "spiritual production," for example, in the authorship of books (§69, "Remark"). Such honor is threatened by overt plagiarism and covert scholarly pilfering. Yet no legal code can protect an author from such pilferage, just as no act of law can protect neophytes from the sophistry of seducers. How well does honor function in the law's stead? Given the fact that we no longer hear about plagiarism in the learned world, says Hegel, one must assume that honor has thoroughly "suppressed" such dishonor. Either that, or we have come to accept that adding a little windfall of one's own to someone else's work, a touch-up here, a touch-up there, suffices for originality. Ah, yes, the precarious honor of all spiritual production, of the fragile flowers of spirit! Some two hundred pages before he mentions Schlegel's *Lucinde*, Hegel complains bitterly about the fact that "the most wretched novel can have a higher [financial] value than the most thoroughly researched book" (handwritten notes to the "Remark" of §64). That *Lucinde* should outsell *The Philosophy of Right*—is the cruelest irony of ironies![10]

Sensuous abandon is essentially the girl's capitulation to the man, in order to attain womanhood through the man or husband she desires. In the "Remark" to §164 Hegel speaks of abandon as mutual; in §168 he emphasizes that "unconstrained abandon" proceeds from the infinitely proper personality of the two sexes bonded or bound to one another in marriage, though never in incest (always the afterthought of incest, which poses the gravest danger to civil society . . .). In another context, Hegel speaks (only once, as far as I know, and we shall return to it below) of sensuous abandon as the activity of the *man*; otherwise, such devotion, surrender, and sensual transport or ecstasy are markedly feminine, female, or—in a sense that is very difficult to determine—"of" woman. She gives herself. One must try to prevent her from giving up her frangible honor too soon. Such prevention is no doubt a burden and a nuisance. She gives herself wholly. And it is an infinite invitation to a conscientious thinking man's guilt and chagrin. One hears it in Hegel's wry, doleful phrase, "an argumentation not foreign to seducers." The Voice of Experience. The Voice of Hegel. She gives herself actively, with no thought to herself. For the love of spirit, who can stop her? Useless, Leopold Bloom says, might as well try and stop the sea. And it is much more than a mere nuisance. She gives herself. She? Milly? Or is it Molly? And where is the *Moly* that will prevent a man from turning into a pig and a girl into worse? Useless. She actively gives herself somewhere on that shifting scene of sentient sensibility and sensuality, somewhere between act 1, Girlhood, and act 2, Womanhood.

In Schlegel's novel, sensuous abandon is likewise of woman, but of woman inextricably entangled with man. "I begged you," remembers Julius, "to abandon yourself for once utterly to furious passion, and I implored you to be insatiable" (10; cf. 28, 47, and 58). In his "Dithyrambic Fantasy Concerning the Loveliest Situation," which culminates in a childlike ring-around-the-rosy of male-female roles, his (now Lucinde's) role is "the protective vehemence of the man," while her (now Julius's) role is "the inviting abandon of woman, the charming, attractive giving-over that draws the other toward itself" (16). The ultimate oxymoron: a giving-over that draws toward and takes in. Julius accounts it an "allegory of the consummation of male and female in humanity whole and entire," and he concludes impudently: "A lot lies in this—and what lies there certainly will not rise as quickly as I do when I lie under you" (16). An impudent translation, no doubt, of the more ambiguous German: *wenn ich Dir unterliege,* "whenever I am inferior to you." Sensuous abandon is Julius's happy defeat, his glorious infirmity, his situated and saturated inferiority. He gives himself. Hegel would agree at least with this: Julius's "foolhardy enthusiasm," "divine to the point of vulgarity," his identification of freedom and impudicity, can prevail only "at the cost of manliness itself" (17). He gives himself wholly. For while she gives herself, she also takes him. He gives himself, and he is taken. "She was not a little surprised, although she sensed it all along, that after the surrender he would be more loving and more faithful than before. . . . They were altogether devoted and one, and yet each was altogether himself, or herself, more than they had ever been" (66–67). However, there is one more reference to sensuous abandon, in another text of Hegel's, to which we now turn in search of *activity.*

Activity. Doing the deed. Or, as Hegel calls it in §166, "the mighty and the activating." In Hegel's 1805–6 lectures at Jena on human genitality and the mating process, activity is attributed to the bifurcated part, the self-differentiating part that belongs exclusively to the male: it is not the testicle, which though twofold is "closed in," like the ovary of the female, "which does not emerge into its opposite, does not become for-itself, does not become an active brain."[11] Hegel does not specify this bifurcated, self-differentiating, diaphoric/metaphoric male organ that moves across space toward its opposite, although he cites its passive homologue in the female: "And the clitoris is inactive feeling in general; in contrast to it, we have in the male active feeling, the upswelling heart." "Thus," Hegel can conclude, or believes he can conclude, although we will have to return to all this in a moment, "the man is the active one, by the fact that his activity possesses this distinction."

Active feeling, the upswelling heart, is of course the penis in something like diastole. Whose heart? And where is it located? The handwritten notes to §165 invoke "the hearts of men." Oddly, the metaphoric or metonymic hearts of men—so powerful and all-activating—fall under the spell of another power. Among the exceedingly rare words of poetry that appear in *The Philosophy of Right* are some verses extracted from that great epic poem of honor and chivalry, *El Cid*:

> The mystery is—the power of
> Women over the hearts of us men.
> This mystery hides in them,
> Deeply concealed; the Lord God,
> I believe, cannot plumb such depths.　　　(Now you've gone too far!)
>
> When on that Great Day
> The sins of all are brought to light,
> God will look into women's hearts:
> *Either he will find them all*
> Culpable, or all equally innocent,
> So interwoven is their heart.
> 　　　　　(7:318; Hegel's emphasis)

The hearts of us men, the upswelling hearts of us men, are defenseless under the power of the tightly interwoven hearts of woman. Like Julius under Lucinde, the male heart remains under the power of the singular and single heart of woman, a heart so close to God that He cannot see it (no matter how bravely Hegel's marginal exclamation tries to restore orthodoxy.) The undifferentiated and undifferentiating heart of woman, as tightly woven as a wreath of rush, is closer in its undeveloped unity to the spirit of origins and the origins of spirit than My Lord Cid will ever be. For, as long as sensibility prevails, all individuality surrenders, abandons itself, and gives itself over to *her*. Thus, for all the talk about activity, we find ourselves tossed back to sensuous abandon. She gives, she takes. She receives, harbors, and conceives:

> Conception is the contraction of the whole individual into simple self-surrendering unity; contraction into the representation of the individual; semen [or, the seed; *der Samen*] the simple physical representation—altogether one point, like the name, and the whole self. —Conception nothing else than the becoming-one of these abstract representations. (*Jenaer Systementwürfe* 3:174)

The simple physical representation, the simple seed of semen, Simple Semen, contracting in self-abandoning unity, now becomes the unit that serves as the congenital mark of woman, the fertilized egg in the womb; contracting in spasmodic waves, the foaming waves of Aphrodite and the shuddering waves of *Venus vaga*, she gives, she takes, she harbors, and she conceives. She conceives the creature, if not the concept. Let us see if the hearts of us men can escape the implication that if spirit is alive, (s)he is in some vital sense of woman, and that to conceive the creature is to do the work of the concept. Can our male hearts escape the ties that bind, the ties that bond, in life, love, and logic? Can an essentially phallocentric and phallocratic system spill over into something gynocentric and gynocratic? Can it do anything other than this?

Jacques Derrida is very much interested in working out an answer to these questions. In his remarkable account of Hegel's "Holy Family," that is, the scene in which spirit and its concept are formed in the family, even though the family is ostensibly merely one passing moment for spirit, Derrida pays particular heed to Hegel's account of woman. Derrida's account appears about a third of the way through his treatment of the "remains" of absolute knowing in Hegel's phenomenology and philosophy of spirit (G, 126–35; 110–17). It follows his treatment of Hegel's early theological text on the "spirit of Christianity," the first part of which deals with the spirit of Judaism, and leads to his detailed treatment of Hegel's early text on "natural law," his mature *Philosophy of Right*, and the figure of Antigone in *Phenomenology of Spirit*.

Derrida begins by noting the importance for Hegel of sexual union (copulation) as the sublation that cancels the particularity of the two sexes and raises men and women to the level of species-identity proper. To be sure, it raises them only in a bestial way; that is, in a way that humanity shares with animals and even plants. In both sexual difference and the difference between humanity and other life forms, Derrida sees Hegel's desire to establish a dissymmetry between the opposites man/woman, human/beast. It is a desire that mirrors a fundamental yet undiscussed hierarchy in Hegel's dialectic. For example, it is not merely a matter of one element prevailing in male genitality, another in female genitality. The passive, "indifferent" part that defines the essence of the female for Hegel (in opposition to the "active difference" that defines the male) mirrors the hierarchy by which spirit prevails over matter generally: activity over passivity, light over darkness, transparency over opacity. If the male embodies difference in the phallus and paired testicles, then in some sense he embodies difference *as such,* and hence *is* the sexual difference as such. If the indifferent part (the uterus) in woman lowers itself in man and becomes a mere gland (the prostate), the male's hovering testicle, only a pace behind the erect penis, has as its counterpart the female ovary, which "remains enveloped." The development, the unfolding of the inside to a free and autonomous outside, is hindered in the female parts, which "remain" indifferent and lag far behind those of the male. The ovary does not activate itself, does not rise to meet its opposite; neither the uterus nor the ovary "steps out" into the world of opposition. Nowhere in the female genitalia is there an "active brain"; everywhere we find instead a fundamental lethargy, receptive but passive. Even the clitoris, which has an active-sounding name (the German word *der Kitzler,* masculine in gender, means "the tickler"), does not share the action of its morphological paradigm: it is "inactive feeling in general."

"In general?" asks Derrida. Who or what pronounces this "in general"? What hierarchy, derived from where, and applied by whom? Every answer to questions like these betrays the fact that Hegel's onto-theo-teleo-logy, in a word, his *system,* "articulates the most traditional phallocentrism." The male possesses "active feeling." His "upswelling heart," despite the euphemism, travels like a winged metaphor through space (dependably? predictably? on schedule? autonomously? at will?), thanks to the fact that it retains its blood and does not expend it in a debilitating menstruation. The turgescent, tumescent "heart" of the glans guides the active brain and its contents to its passive opposite, its fulfillment.

Yet what about that object of its fulfillment, over there, so pitiably passive but so undeniably alluring, which does not need to budge in order to move? Derrida helps us to see the strange reversal that awaits all spiritualist hierarchies, the reversal by which phallocentrism erects willy-nilly a feminism:

> Man's superiority costs him an inner division. In passively receiv-ing, woman remains One (close) by herself [*une auprés d'elle-même,* which is the very earmark of *spirit*—my interpolation]; she works less but lets herself be worked (over) less by negativity. "The receiving [*Das Empfangen:* this is also the conceiving of childbirth—Derrida] of the uterus, as simple behavior, is accordingly in the male divided in two (*entzweit*), into the

productive brain and the external heart (*in das produzierende Gehirn und das äußerliche Herz*). The man, then, through this difference, is the active one (*Der Mann ist also durch diesen Unterschied das Tätige*); but the woman is the receptacle (*das Empfangende*), because she remains in her undeveloped unity (*weil sie in ihrer unentwickelten Einheit bleibt*).

Remaining enveloped in undifferentiated unity, the woman keeps herself nearer to the origin. The man is secondary, as the difference that causes his passing into opposition. Paradoxical consequences of all phallocentrism: the hardworking and determining male sex enjoys mastery only in losing it, in subjugating itself to the feminine slave. The phallocentric hierarchy is a feminism; it submits dialectically to Femininity and Truth, both writ large, making man the *subject* of woman.[12]

In genitality as everywhere else, woman remains the cryptic figure of the family, eluding conceptuality as the very one who conceives, as the very concept of conception.

The opposition of active organs and passive receptivity brings us back one more time to sensuous abandon, surrender, and erotic devotion. In the margin of the Jena lectures, just above the paragraph on conception, at the point where woman is designated as the one who conceives, Hegel enters a marginal note about the breast: "Digestion turned to the outside—woman, milk of the breast." Next to this, as marginalia to marginalia, Hegel writes: "The metaphorical surrender of heart and soul to the woman."

As one confronts the necessity of translating *metaphorisches Hingeben des Herzens und Seele an das Weib*, one puzzles long and hard. It should be the *woman* who gives her heart and soul. The marginal note should read: *an dem Weibe, am Weibe, beim Weibe*, in the dative case. Yet Hegel's accusative clearly points the finger: *he* gives, the man gives, *to her*, his heart and soul; *to her*, his upswelling heart and even his active brain. Or, without the commas: he gives to her heart and soul, to her upswelling heart and active brain, to her conceiving—as though none of these things were any longer "his," as though in the history of spirit they were only "his" for a fleeting moment.

However, let me not abandon the margin too quickly, but linger on the breast. For it too, according to Julius, is engorged and magnificently swollen, though not with blood. Lucinde's body, bathed in the glimmer of twilight, is luxuriant, uxorious (67), and the very vision of her goads his love to fury. These are not the breasts of a girl, Schlegel's Julius tells us; this is not a maidenly body trembling on the brink of maturity, a tremulous body stammering its O-Please-Don't-Make-Me-Prove-It. Her swelling outlines, which he is mad to touch, tell him and us once again—even if we are untouched by the extraordinary force and heat of her embrace—that Lucinde is not a girl at all. Lucinde is a woman. We remember that some time ago she has had a son, who is now dead (65). Mourning marks her past. Because she is an accomplished painter, her eye, hand, and brain are markedly active. She too is a human being who produces spirituality, like those who write books on spirit or deliver lectures in the university. She thus bears an uncanny resemblance to Hegel. Except perhaps for those swellings, although even in those swellings she is not *altogether* different from Hegel or from other male members of her species. Julius, watching waves of ebon hair flow over the snowfields of those white breasts murmurs, Magnificent woman! Masterly woman! Lordly woman! *Herrliche Frau!* (66).

Lucinde, a helpless girl ripe for the blandishments of seduction? Friedrich Schleiermacher never took her as that. When young "Karoline," advocating "the honor of maidens," complains that Julius should never have left his younger and more innocent beloved for Lucinde, Schleiermacher's epistolary hero replies that "a kiss from a woman who has already seen love face-to-face is undeniably more significant and more decisive than a maiden's very best approximation" (*Intimate Letters*, 87). The Voice of Experience. The voice of Schleiermacher, here peeping under all the veils that are woven in his name. In the face of Hegel's juxtaposition of the seduction story and Schlegel's *Lucinde*, one must ask: Can Hegel have *read* Friedrich Schlegel's epoch-making *Lucinde*?[13]

Of course he read it. That is why the third figure has to be conjured once again. An adolescent girl who accompanies her honor into the tomb, joining her brother and lover in Death. The law of the State seals her tomb with a granite boulder, the granite of spiritual fate, as Nietzsche says. In the same way, her lips are sealed: no further impudence against the substantial spirit of the State. She will contract into simple unity one last time. In the nick of time: no swelling profile, no uxoriousness. For Lucinde's is the law that unsettles every law and deranges all positing. Lucinde undercuts religion with sensuous transport; Julius adores her (10, 15, 29, 71, 81). She undercuts matrimony with what he calls "the elevated lightheadedness of our marriage" (14, 63, 75–76). Homely ethicality pales before her (23), and all wisdom is baffled (28). She is a spirited woman. And she absorbs his activity utterly, thus undercutting society, law, and the State: "You feel everything entirely and infinitely, you allow nothing to be separated off, your being is one and indivisible. That is why you are so serious and so joyful; that is why you take everything to heart and are so careless of it; and that is why you also love me wholly, leaving no part of me to the State, to posterity, or to my men friends. Everything belongs to you" (14).

That is why Hegel must stop her, for the sake of Julius and all men of the State. In order that the work of spirit be done. In order, for example, that the possibility of warfare be assured. Seal Lucinde's lips, then, and seal her fate, as though she were Antigone. Useless, counters Bloom: might as well try and stop the sea. In the dark cavern of her heart, her many hearts, unstoppable diastole, upswelling, engorgement of the lips with blood and the breast with milk. And Lucinde's words, Lucinde's tears and laughter, Lucinde's give and take, her shame supplemented not by chastity but by sensuous abandon. The law of woman will be heralded not by Antigone, the interred adolescent, and not as the law of the ancient gods, as Hegel has it. Hers is the law of the goddess, Venus vaga, Lucinde's glory, the contracting waves of subterranean power, "eternal law of which no one knows from what dawn it appeared."[14]

Has Hegel successfully sealed off and fully interiorized the law of woman? Can he step over the threshold of the house into the State and civil society? Has he forgotten nothing? And would we remember him at all if he claimed to be so perfectly memorious?

In the preface to the Phenomenology of Spirit, Hegel depicts the moment at which extraneous preoccupation with results, conclusions, and generalities ends and thinking begins, not as remembrance but as self-forgetting. Like Lucinde giving herself over to Julius's mouth and ardor, or Julius's surrendering himself to Lucinde's snowscape and tropics, the phenomenologist remembers when to give himself or herself over to the "matter," the "sake" of thinking (die Sache, which is feminine in gender): "to linger with the matter in question and to forget himself in her, . . . abandoning himself to her."[15]

Notes

1. G. W. F. Hegel, Grundlinien der Philosophie des Rechts, in Werke in zwanzig Bänden, Theorie Werkausgabe, ed. Eva Moldenhauer and Karl Markus Michel (Frankfurt am Main:

Suhrkamp, 1970), 7:317. I shall cite Hegel's *Rechtsphilosophie* principally by section number in the body of my text. Hegel's other works, except for those listed in notes 4 and 9, I shall cite by volume and page in this edition, e.g.: 13:93–95. Friedrich von Schlegel's *Lucinde: Ein Roman* was first published in 1799 by Heinrich Froelich in Berlin. I have used the text edited by Wolfgang Hecht, Friedrich von Schlegel, *Werke in zwei Bänden* (Berlin and Weimar: Aufbau-Verlag, 1980), 2:5–99. After completing this I discovered a fine English translation of *Lucinde and the Fragments*, trans. Peter Firchow (Minneapolis: University of Minnesota Press, 1971), containing Schlegel's novel, the *Athenaeum Fragments*, and other writings. I shall cite the German edition of *Lucinde* simply by page number in the body of my text. As for English translations of Hegel's *Philosophy of Right*, they omit Hegel's handwritten notes, which are essential to my topic; thus I will refer to the German edition only; translations are my own.

2. Philippe Lacoue-Labarthe, "L'imprésentable," in *Poétique*, no. 21 (1975): 53–95. Lacoue-Labarthe discusses Hegel's references to *Lucinde* in *The Philosophy of Right*, but focuses principally on the *Lectures on Aesthetics*. His thesis concerns the uneasy presence of poetry (and art and literature generally) in Hegel's system of speculative philosophy; it is a thesis that cannot be reduced to a few words here. Suffice it to say that Lacoue-Labarthe's preoccupation is with Hegel's moral accusation against Schlegel's *Lucinde*, an artwork that establishes the epoch not of romantic art proper but of moral turpitude and dissipation. Even though Schlegel's novel does mark an epoch in the history of art and literature, it is nonetheless Schiller's more edifying poesy to which Hegel constantly reverts. Unlike Schiller, Schlegel is (as Creon says to his son Haeman) "weaker than woman." Yet behind the contempt in which Hegel holds Friedrich Schlegel, Lacoue-Labarthe senses a certain anxiety—indeed, an anxiety for the whole of the speculative system. In the context of *The Philosophy of Right*, see especially part 3 of Lacoue-Labarthe's fine essay, the part entitled "Impudicity: The Veil and the Figure," 64–75. The clearest and most succinct statement of his thesis appears in part 4, "The Subornation of Aphrodite: Poesy and Philosophy," 78, 85–86. (My warm thanks to Rodolphe Gasché, who first presented me with Lacoue-Labarthe's "L'imprésentable.") Hegel's references to Friedrich Schlegel in his *Lectures on Aesthetics* and in other works would have to occupy a separate study. In a nutshell, they relate Schlegel's moral lassitude to his poor poetry, bad prose, and contemptible pathos. See 13:93–95, 348, 383, 404–5, and 513; 14:116, 180, and 305; 15:497. Other references to Schlegel in Hegel's works will be noted as my paper proceeds.

3. *Hégel, aigle*. Perhaps in English we could say "Heagle." Jacques Derrida, *Glas* (Paris: Galilée, 1974), 7a, 22a (insert), 46a, 65a, 68b (insert), 106a, 117a, 138b (insert), 206–7a (insert), 217–18b (insert), 234a (insert); English translation by John P. Leavey Jr. and Richard Rand (Lincoln: University of Nebraska Press, 1986), 1a, 15a (insert), 37a, 54–55a, 57b (insert), 91a, 102a, 120b (insert), 184a (insert), 194b (insert), 209a (insert). I am grateful to John Leavey for these references; see his remarkable Glossary to *Glassary* (Lincoln: University of Nebraska Press, 1986), 213. Henceforth I shall cite *Glas* in the body of my text as *G*, with page numbers from first the French, then the English editions.

4. I am of course using the phrase that serves as the title of Judith P. Butler's study, *Subjects of Desire: Hegelian Reflections in Twentieth-Century France* (New York: Columbia University Press, 1987). Butler concentrates on Hegel's *Phenomenology of Spirit*, especially chap. 4, on the "ontology of desire" and on lordship and bondage, all of which I shall have to leave out of account here. See Krell, "Pitch: Genitality/Excrementality from Hegel to Crazy Jane," in *boundary 2*, special issue, "On Feminine Writing," 12, no. 2 (1984): 113–41, which takes its point of departure from a passage in Hegel's remarks on "Observational Reason" in the *Phenomenology*.

5. See G. W. F. Hegel, *Enzyklopädie der philosophischen Wissenschaften 1830*, ed. Friedhelm Nicolin and Otto Pöggeler (Hamburg: F. Meiner, "Philosophische Bibliothek," no. 33, 1969),

§§ 399–402, and 445–47. On sensibility and intelligence in the context of "interiorizing remembrance" (*Erinnerung*), see chap. 5 of D. F. Krell, *Of Memory, Reminiscence, and Writing: On the Verge* (Bloomington: Indiana University Press, 1990).

6. "Disunited" renders the word *veruneinige*. George Lasson reads it as *verunreinige* (to pollute), as though pollution could be due to the altar or the civil registry rather than to the order of nature. Even Friedrich Schlegel did not dare go so far.

7. A letter written in October 1824 reveals that Hegel never crossed Schlegel's path until that date, and even then it did not come to a meeting between the two men. Schlegel's conversion to Catholicism and his support of the House of Habsburg against Napoleon no doubt displeased Hegel. See *Briefe von und an Hegel*, ed. Johannes Hoffmeister, 4 vols. (Hamburg: F. Meiner, 1952), 1:283 and 2:165; cf. *Werke*, 7:284. Yet surely it is Schlegel's liaison with Dorothea Veit (taken by virtually every early reader of *Lucinde* to be the heroine-in-real-life of that scandalous work) that most disturbs him. When Schlegel seduces Dr. Veit's wife, he duplicates the crime committed by Schelling against Schlegel's own brother, August Wilhelm: just as Schelling inveigles himself with Caroline Schlegel, so Schlegel insinuates himself with Dorothea Veit. Thus Friedrich Schlegel becomes something of a fratricide, committing the very crime that has been perpetrated against his own flesh. Reason enough to raise Hegel's ire. . . . Yet this is all speculation on my part; we are no doubt better advised to seek the reasons within *Lucinde* itself, and in "Lucinde" herself.

8. In his foreword to Hermann Friedrich Wilhelm Hinrichs' *Philosophy of Religion* (11:61; cf. 18:81), Hegel identifies Schlegel as an advocate of everything that is wrong with the times: the accidental and fortuitous quality of subjective feeling and opinion, bound up with the particular "formation of reflection" (cf. 7:311 and 383) that betrays that (Schlegel's) spirit is incapable of knowing the truth—which incapacity the ancients called *sophistry*. Schlegel's sophistry is "worldly wisdom," for he is expert in the contingent, untrue, and temporal; he elevates vanity and the accidents of feeling to the Absolute. Sophistry shares with philosophy the "formation of reflection," yet does so in a merely formal way. And because it rejects the truths of revelation, Schlegel's sophistry has no other ground to stand on than its own vanity.

9. That anonymous supporter was Schlegel's "roommate," or host, Friedrich Schleiermacher, *Vertraute Briefe über* [Intimate letters on] *Friedrich Schlegels "Lucinde,"* first published in 1800. I have used the edition by Karl Gutzkow (Hamburg: Hoffmann und Campe, 1835). No doubt Schleiermacher is an ally of Schlegel's: "And now we have this work, which stands there like a vision from a future world—God alone knows how far in the future!" (2). And: "Love must be resurrected, a new life must unify and ensoul its fragmented members, so that it can prevail joyously and freely in the hearts of mankind and in all its works, driving out the lifeless shadows of once-vaunted virtues" (9). How difficult such an alliance is for Schleiermacher becomes clear in the sixth letter, "To Eduard," in which the divine advocate tries rather desperately to condemn Wieland's erotic writings while blessing Schlegel's; see esp. 94.

10. With regard to irony: in his review of Karl Wilhelm Ferdinand Solger's *Posthumous Writings and Letters* (11:215, 234, and 255), Hegel refers to the "most audacious and luxuriant period of irony" in German letters, mentioning by name *Lucinde* and the *Athenaeum Fragments*. He endorses Solger's view that Schlegel's notion of irony is "one-sided" and "dogmatic." Schlegel will not condescend to make arguments, to give reasons and grounds; his high perch on "divine impudence" is therefore also "satanic," "diabolical" impudicity. Claiming to straddle the peak of philosophic wisdom, Schlegel never penetrates the valleys of science. When in 1816 he offers a course on "transcendental philosophy" at Jena, he runs out of things to say after only six weeks, thus defrauding his listeners. (See *Hegels Briefe*, 2:98; cf. *Werke*, 4:420–21.) Though clever and doubtless well-read, Schlegel remains utterly uninitiated in "thinking reason." Schlegelian irony is Fichtean subjectivism without the saving grace of Fichte's practical, ethical philosophy: that is the gist of Hegel's judgment on Schlegel in

the *Lectures on the History of Philosophy* (20:415–17). In the Solger review (11:256–57), Hegel refers us to his discussion of irony in *The Philosophy of Right*, §140, which treats of evil as it appears in modern philosophy itself. (See also the addendum to §140; 7:284–86.) As significant as the polemic no doubt is for Hegel's critique of romanticism as a whole, let the following suffice: whereas Plato's Socrates ironizes the pretense of the sophists, he never ironizes the ideas themselves—whereas this is precisely what Schlegel does (see also 18: 460–61). Finally, Solger's own views on tragic irony and downgoing may well strike us as more radical than Hegel's, and as pointing forward to Nietzsche. Precisely for that reason, they resist reduction to a note.

11. G. W. F. Hegel, *Gesammelte Werke*, vol. 8, *Jenaer Systementwürfe III*, ed. Rolf-Peter Horstmann (Hamburg: F. Meiner, 1976), 173–74. (In the paperback edition of 1987 ["Philosophische Bibliothek," no. 333], 160–61.) I have discussed these materials at greater length in "Pitch," cited in note 4.

12. G, 130/113. The slight discrepancies in the wording of the quotations from Hegel result from the fact that Derrida used the only edition of the *Jenenser Realphilosophie II* that was available until 1976, namely, that of Johannes Hoffmeister for the "Philosophische Bibliothek," no. 67, published by Felix Meiner in 1931. One ought to complement Derrida's analysis by the remarkable pages of Luce Irigaray, "The Eternal Irony of the Community," in *Speculum de l'autre femme* (Paris: Minuit, 1974), 214–26; trans. Gillian C. Gill as *Speculum of the Other Woman* (Ithaca: Cornell University Press, 1985); see Chapter 2, this volume. I hope to work further on the complex dialectic of genitality in a book now under way: "Eggs and Lips: Toward a Philosophy of Genitality."

13. My colleague Stephen Houlgate poses this question quite seriously: we have no definitive evidence that Hegel actually *read* the novel; he may be reacting merely to the brouhaha that surrounded its publication. In which case, of course, the avatar of spirit is condemning something of which he is ignorant, something concerning which he remains in the indifference of an undivided unity, but without reception, without conception.

14. Sophocles' *Antigone*, lines 456–57, cited by Hegel in both *The Phenomenology of Spirit* and *The Philosophy of Right* (see the "Remark" to §166). Cf. *Phänomenologie des Geistes*, ed. Johannes Hoffmeister (Hamburg: F. Meiner, "Philosophische Bibliothek," no. 114, 1952), 311.

15. ". . . in ihr (der Sache) zu verweilen und sich in ihr zu vergessen, . . . sich ihr (hingeben)." Hegel, *Phänomenologie*, 11.

5

Hegel, Sexual Ethics, and the Oppression of Women: Comments on Krell's "Lucinde's Shame"

Frances Olsen

G. W. F. Hegel and David Krell's essay on Hegel (see Chapter 4) raise the question of how men and women can relate to one another as equals—or at all. How is it possible to have intimate relations between men and women in a society in which men as a group dominate women as a group? Women are systematically subordinated to men; by just about any measure we devise, women are treated as unequal. Women are paid less—about three fifths of men's salary[1]—and battered more.[2] Men's needs set the standard and men's viewpoint is the privileged perspective.[3] Men's voices are heard.[4]

This gender hierarchy creates a problem for men of goodwill who wish to behave ethically, reproducing, in a sense, a problem encountered by feminist theorists. We seem to be faced with a choice between two strategies. First, we can acknowledge the present inequality of women and deal with it as well as we can. Unfortunately, this strategy seems to accept as tolerable the present inequality of women, and it may encourage us to advocate policies that are not ideal—policies that are *based* on the inequality that we wish to end. These policies would not be ideal or appropriate for the equal society that we hope to build.

The second strategy is to pretend that equality already exists.[5] This strategy focuses attention on a few exceptional women who are subject to less domination, and tries to build on these exceptions. A weakness in this strategy is that pretending an equality exists or building on rare exceptions is unlikely to change the condition of gender inequality. Indeed, we may advocate policies that would be fine in an equal society, but these policies will not be appropriate to our actual situation and will not advance the interests of women or of society.

Men of goodwill who wish to relate intimately to women are faced with a similar dilemma in our society. The choices available seem similar to those just discussed. First, men can recognize the present inequality of women and deal with it as best they can. The practices in which these men engage and the relationships they can establish will not be ideal and would not be ideal in the equal society that we hope to build. Additionally, to recognize the present inequality may appear to represent an *acceptance* of women's inequality.

Alternatively, men can pretend that equality already exists—or focus on a few exceptional women who are subject to less domination and try to build on these exceptions. But again, the pretense of equality does not bring about equality. The practices in which these men engage and the relationships that they try to establish might be fine in an equal society, but the practices will not be appropriate to our actual situation and will not advance the interests of women or society.[6] Moreover, I am skeptical about the relationships these men will establish in our actual world and skeptical about the few rare exceptional women they find—or think they find—and the exceptional relationships they think they establish when they pretend or imagine an equality that does not exist. The actual effect of the pretense of equality may be to reinforce or aggravate the subordination of women.

A familiar figure is the misogynist man who claims to love an individual woman because she is an exception, unlike the standard run-of-the-mill inferior women. The "you're different from other women" line has come to seem as insulting to women as the "I don't think of you as a Negro" line has become to African-Americans. The more subtle versions of such patronizing exceptionalism are more difficult for many to recognize and oppose.

However, men of goodwill *are* faced with a quandary. If Friedrich von Schlegel's *Lucinde*[7] represents the second of the two choices I have proposed, G. W. F. Hegel may represent the first. When Hegel suggests that the stakes regarding sensuous abandon are higher for women than men and that men have another field for ethical efficacy,[8] is he not basically correct in describing his society? What if it is not Hegel who "sets the stakes high . . . for woman,"[9] but society. If we take Hegel's statements as description and not endorsements, they take on a different significance. Although I do not want to make insupportable claims about Hegel's intentions, or to label him a feminist, I also think it is too simple to be appalled by his comments about women. I hope that in another generation readers will be appalled by the sexism that we glide over today. Perhaps we should read Hegel as approaching the world as it actually was—recognizing the radical subordination of women—and making the best he could of it all within that context.

Hegel draws an analogy between Lucinde and the victims of seducers—an analogy that David Krell sharply criticizes. Lucinde, according to Krell, is a free woman, strong and equal. Here, I would argue, Krell is adopting a form of the second strategy: focus on an exceptional woman and try to build on the exceptions.

Krell raises the suggestion that Lucinde places the whole of Hegel's speculative system in jeopardy. Hegel does not want to mortify sensuality as negative in itself; without sensibility the life of the spirit would be dry and brittle.[10] Hegel's system attempts to embrace sensibility but to avoid the death, suicide, and madness that Hegel saw resulting from romanticism. Lucinde is this threat, says Krell. Thus the *outrageous* linkage by Hegel of Lucinde and the victims of seducers! (Krell calls this linkage "bizarre.") Lucinde, the sexy woman who has a passionate love affair with a married man is shameless about it.

But do not most seducers try to make a woman feel like Lucinde—to think of herself as Lucinde? And what if Lucinde is a male fantasy? An escape fantasy?

Now, almost any woman would rather be Lucinde than the other chief alternative that men offer: the castrating, moralizing woman Nietzsche presents and despises.[11] No woman wants to be the embittered feminist who identifies with the victim's suffering rather than with the lover's *jouissance,* the feminist who warns the woman of great soul against her own grandeur, who urges Lucinde to embrace the ideology of lesser expectations and accept the lukewarm discontent of the castrated woman.[12]

Hegel might say that to romantics anything short of insanity may seem dull. Hegel does offer an alternative to Lucinde—but that alternative is to be a plant. Hegel tells us: "The difference between men and women is like that between animals and plants. Men correspond to animals, while women correspond to plants because their development is more placid."[13]

Nietzsche suggests that the choice is between Lucinde and the castrating, moralizing woman. Hegel seems to offer us the choice of Lucinde or plants; that is, objects that may be moved by others but do not move themselves. Krell chooses Lucinde over plants; and given these choices, it is not too difficult to support his preference, even if Krell correctly asserts that Lucinde jeopardizes the whole of Hegel's speculative system. It is easy to balk at plants. But again, I would hope that in another generation we will balk at many of the aspects of Hegel that we glide over at present as unproblematic.

What if women reject all the choices offered by men—or reject their characterizations? We can choose, perhaps with Hegel, to approach the world as it actually is and to recognize and take into account the present radical subordination of women. To minimize the possible negative effects of this strategy we should criticize the inequality we acknowledge and seek to change the conditions of inequality.

Jane Austen offers another alternative to Lucinde. Austen approaches the world as it is—recognizing the present inequality—and in *Pride and Prejudice* offers us Elizabeth.[14] The choice between Lucinde and Elizabeth is surely a better choice than that offered by Krell or by our other male authors. Elizabeth is neither Hegel's plant nor Nietzsche's castrating, moralizing woman. Jane Austen can be viewed as carrying out the same project as Hegel: creating a world alive with sensibility and yet safe from the death, suicide, and madness of excess romanticism, or romanticism run amok. While Elizabeth is a remarkable and appealing young woman, she is not the rare exception of a woman who is subject to less domination. Elizabeth exists as a woman in a world in which women are oppressed. Austen's irony saves her from apologetics and allows her to criticize the inequality she recognizes. Elizabeth's behavior deals with the world that existed at that time as well as one could.

Austen creates another character in this novel, Lydia, who embodies much of what Hegel feared in romanticism.[15] Lydia might be viewed as a failed Lucinde. Lydia considered herself a romantic heroine and gave herself over to grand passion. Had it not been for the pervasive subordination of women to men, Lydia might have salvaged a tolerable life. Lydia's attempt to be the exceptional woman failed, as I believe Lucinde's attempt also failed, except on the level of male fantasy.

Obviously a powerful response for a critic to make to me at this point would be to raise the Brontë sisters.[16] Some of the Brontë heroines appear to share the romantic intensity of Lucinde. Catherine Earnshaw, the heroine of Emily Brontë's *Wuthering Heights*, certainly expressed grand passion toward Heathcliff, whether or not everyone would agree that she gave herself over to it. It has been suggested that Charlotte Brontë, "forty or fifty years before the beginnings of a full revolt against Victorian sexual reticence" expressed in her writing "humans' hunger for sexual fulfillment" and that she dreamed of "the terms on which fulfillment might possibly be allowed and attained."[17] Surely, the critic might argue, I could not dismiss the Brontë sisters' heroines as male fantasies.

Nevertheless, the Brontë heroines may have elements of male fantasy. Subordinate groups in society always to some extent participate in dominant culture; often the most read and respected members of a subordinate group will be those who most effectively reproduce dominant fantasies.

Certainly one possible interpretation is that the Brontë sisters are the pathetic outcome of a male-dominated household, well suited to a male dominated world. Their father has been characterized as "a half-crazy tyrant."[18] "Like many another Victorian patriarch, Patrick Brontë bound his children to him by the strength of a fiercely dominating personality balanced by an undeniable capacity for love."[19] Their brother, Branwell Brontë, received all the preferential treatment Victorian families tended to afford to sons. He was his father's "main purpose, . . . fond hope and pride."[20] The bleak, lonely parsonage where the sisters were brought up "was a household where men could indulge any caprice or despotism."[21]

Branwell's adult life illustrates Hegel's worst fears of romanticism run amok. Branwell remained fiercely attached to the romantic aspirations of his childhood as he threw himself into an adulterous affair, only to return home to lead a dissipated life. When the interfering husband had the good grace to die conveniently, Branwell's lover rejected Branwell and married a wealthy suitor. Branwell declined further into alcoholism and opium, and succumbed to a very early death.

Helene Moglen, in *Charlotte Brontë*, has argued that Branwell's disintegration was Charlotte Brontë's salvation (75). She writes: "It is not inappropriate that this woman, whose masochistic dependence and passivity had evolved within the strictures of a patriarchal Victorian family, should find the sources of freedom in the moral and physical disintegration of her brother" (78). Moglen supports her analysis, in part, by showing the development that takes place between Charlotte Brontë's early and later works. The early heroines, in her juvenilia, are unhappy.

> They suffer, all of them, because their lovers are unfaithful and capricious. They suffer because they are deserted. But they suffer most of all in their dependence upon . . . a male who . . . must define and affirm them. Rejection fulfills their expectations, confirms their doubts. Deprived of a sense of self, they cannot accept responsibility: moral choice is impossible. . . . Love for them cannot be completion. It is a means of self-abnegation, a rationalization of self-denial. (51)

Her later heroines struggle for independent self-realization, against their "need to be submerged in the powerful, masculine 'other' " (225). Brontë is concerned with both the "oppressive society" (195) and the "repressed individual" (195).

Interestingly, most of Charlotte Brontë's heroines were in positions of clear hierarchical inferiority to the males toward whom they felt passionate. Jane Eyre was the governess while Rochester the master; in *The Professor*, the heroine was a pupil who loved her teacher. As John Maynard expresses it, in his *Charlotte Brontë and Sexuality*, with no hint of critique, such hierarchies "obviously" create "an implicit sexual relationship" (174). While a number of feminists might well agree with him that our society eroticizes domination and subordination, they generally see this eroticization as a problem for women and for men of goodwill.[22] They would agree with Maynard that these relationships "bring with them the problems . . . of love under terms unequal to the female" (174). When Charlotte Brontë adds a status hierarchy to the sexual hierarchy, it becomes difficult to maintain that she is unaware of the reality of women being in a subordinate position. In *Jane Eyre*, the status switches by the end of the book when Jane has inherited wealth and her former master has become blind. At that point, she marries him.

The Brontës may also be read in a wide variety of other ways. Charlotte Brontë is said to have had a "deeply-held belief that adversity does people good" and that "for women to be exploited . . . was not an entirely bad state of affairs."[23] She criticized John Stuart Mill because he, as she put it, "forgets that there is such a thing as self-sacrificing love and disinherited devotion,"[24] and she charged that he "would make a hard, dry, dismal world of it."[25] Others read Brontë as expressing "rage at her role as a woman in a patriarchal society."[26] These various readings present interesting and difficult questions. Perhaps Charlotte Brontë supports the unequal status quo. Perhaps here is an effort to create a more effective version of the strategy of finding a rare, exceptional woman and trying to build on the exception. Alternatively and more likely, she, like Jane Austen, recognizes women's inequality and tries to make the best she can of life within those constraints, expanding them as much as possible.

Questions about how man and women can relate in our unequal society are interesting and difficult. Here I simply highlight the way in which David Krell's discussion of Hegel raises these questions; I do not resolve them at this time.

Notes

1. As well as doing vast quantities of essential but unpaid work, women who work full-time in paid employment are paid considerably less than men, in spite of the Equal Pay Act of 1963, Pub. Law No. 88-38, 77 Stat. 56 (codified as amended at 29 U.S.C. §206 [d] [1983]), and the federal law against sex discrimination in hiring, Civil Rights Act of 1964, Pub. Law No. 88-352, 78 Stat. 253-66 (codified as amended at 42 U.S.C. §§2000e to e-17 [1982 and Supp. IV 1986]). A frequently cited statistic compares the median income of the sexes from twenty-five to fifty-four years of age, from 1975 to 1983. In 1975, men's median income was $14,105.00 while women's was $8,155.00; in 1983, men's was $24,458.33 to women's $15,349.66; U.S. Department of Labor, Women's Bureau, Time of Change: 1983 Handbook of Women Workers, Bulletin 298, 456 (1983). In 1981, men's overall earnings exceeded women's by 68.8 percent; see Time of Change, 93. Nor has there been great improvement. For year-round, full-time work in 1991, women's medium income was $21,245 while men's was $30,332. Statistical Abstract of the United States 1993, 113th ed., U.S. Department of Commerce.

2. On the incidence of wife battery, see H. Lentzner and M. DeBerry, Intimate Victims: A Study of Violence Among Friends and Relatives (1980) (prepared for the U.S. Department of Justice); R. Dobash and R. Dobash, Violence Against Wives: A Case Against the Patriarchy (New York: Free Press, 1979), 14–20; and L. Walker, The Battered Woman Syndrome (New

York: Springer, 1984), 19–20. See also John M. Dawson and Patrick A. Langan, *Murder in Families* (Washington, D.C.: U.S. Department of Justice, 1994).

3. See C. MacKinnon, *Sexual Harassment of Working Women: A Case of Sex Discrimination* (New Haven: Yale University Press, 1979), 144–46.

4. The metaphoric use of "voice" became widespread with the popularity of Carol Gilligan's *In a Different Voice* (Cambridge: Harvard University Press, 1982). On the question of women's silencing, see A. Dworkin, *Pornography: Men Possessing Women* (New York: Perigee, 1981); S. Griffin, *Woman and Nature: The Roaring Inside Her* (New York: Harper and Row, 1978); C. MacKinnon, *Feminism Unmodified: Discourses on Life and Law* (Cambridge: Harvard University Press, 1987). For a popular presentation of the ways that men and women speak and hear one another differently, see Deborah Tannen, *You Just Don't Understand* (New York: Ballantine, 1990); see also John Gray, *Men are from Mars, Women are from Venus: A Practical Guide for Improving Communication and Getting What You Want in Your Relationships* (New York: HarperCollins, 1992). For a more academic treatment, see Cheris Kramarae, *Women and Men Speaking* (Rowley, Mass.: Newberry House, 1981).

5. For a vehement, though unreflective, defense of this strategy, see DuBois, Dunlap, Gilligan, MacKinnon and Menkel-Meadow, "Feminist Discourse, Moral Values, and the Law—A Conversation," *Buffalo Law Review* 34 (1985): 75–76 (comments by Mary Dunlap interrupting conversation between Gilligan and MacKinnon).

6. Professor Catharine MacKinnon criticizes the notion that one can "imagine the future you want, construct actions or legal rules or social practices *as if* we were already there, and that will get you from here to there." C. MacKinnon, *Feminism Unmodified*, 219. She maintains that "this magical approach to social change . . . lives entirely in the head, a head that is . . . determined by present reality . . . yet it is not sufficiently grounded in that reality to do anything about it. . . . As a strategy for social change . . . the 'let's pretend' strategy is [both] idealist and elitist" (219).

7. See F. Schlegel, *Lucinde and the Fragments*, trans. P. Firchow (Minneapolis: University of Minnesota Press, 1971). *Lucinde* is a short novel in which Schlegel proposed a theory of love, marriage, and the role of women that scandalized a record number of readers. Lucinde is a mature woman who enters into a love affair with a younger, and already married, man. Writing on a topic touchy to begin with, Schlegel described love scenes and expressed his own sympathies in a manner that was bound to offend many and to result in masses of free publicity and in large sales.

8. See G. Hegel, *Philosophy of Right*, para. 166, trans. T. Knox (Oxford: Clarendon Press, 1952); hereinafter *Philosophy of Right*.

9. Krell, "Lucinde's Shame," Chapter 4, this volume. Earlier versions of Krell's article and my comments appeared in *Cardozo Law Review* 10 (1989): 1673–93.

10. Krell is citing Hegel, *Werke in Zwanzig Bänden*, vol. 7, *Grundlinien der Philosophie des Rechts*, ed. E. Moldenhauer and K. Michel (Frankfurt am Main: Suhrkamp, 1970), para. 33A.

11. See J. Derrida, *Spurs: Nietzsche's Styles*, trans. B. Harlow (Chicago: University of Chicago Press, 1979), 95–101. For a more complex presentation of Nietzsche's view of women, see Christine Garside Allen, "Nietzsche's Ambivalence about Women," in *The Sexism of Social and Political Theory: Women and Reproduction from Plato to Nietzsche*, ed. L. Clark and L. Lange (Toronto: University of Toronto Press, 1979), 117–33.

12. On the "ideology of lesser expectations," see D. Cornell, *Beyond Accommodation* (New York: Routledge, 1991), 3–37; *The Philosophy of the Limit* (New York: Routledge, 1992); and "The Ethical Message of Negative Dialectics," *Social Concept* 4, no. 3 (1987).

13. Hegel, *Philosophy of Right*, para. 166A. It may seem that Hegel offers women a very definite and more attractive alternative to Lucinde, namely Antigone. According to Krell, with Antigone "the law of woman succumbs to the law of the State." He suggests that in

Hegel's *Philosophy of Right* (§166) "sensibility and receptivity are appropriated to and by" Antigone. Although Antigone herself may be an attractive figure to women, Hegel's Antigone has little of the appeal for women that Sophocles' has. See Patricia Jagentowicz Mills, "Hegel's *Antigone*," Chapter 3, this volume. In terms of her sexual life, Hegel's Antigone may be closer to a plant than most depictions. Antigone appears also in Hegel's *Phenomenology of Spirit*. For further discussion, see J. Derrida, *Glas* (Lincoln: University of Nebraska Press, 1986), 126–35, 110–17.

14. See J. Austen, *Pride and Prejudice* (London: T. Egerton, 1813). Elizabeth is the bright and charming but prejudiced heroine of the book who avoids falling passionately in love with the handsome villain Mr. Wickham and eventually marries the bright and wealthy but proud hero Mr. Darcy.

15. Lydia is the youngest sister of Elizabeth, flighty, self-important, and silly. She romantically and foolishly elopes with Mr. Wickham, who has no intention of marrying her. Mr. Darcy, for love of Elizabeth and from concern that pride may have contributed to his failure to expose Wickham's true villainy to the community, pressures and bribes Wickham into a loveless and barely respectable marriage with Lydia in order to "save" her.

16. J. Maynard, *Charlotte Brontë and Sexuality* (Cambridge: Cambridge University Press, 1984).

17. Ibid., 5. Charlotte Brontë "found ways to present the complexity of her understanding of sexual experience" (3).

18. P. Beer, *Reader, I Married Him* (London: Macmillan, 1974), 27.

19. H. Moglen, *Charlotte Brontë: The Self Conceived* (New York: Norton, 1976), 24.

20. W. Gerin, *Branwell Brontë* (London: T. Nelson, 1961), 2.

21. Beer, *Reader*, 27.

22. See F. Olsen, "Statutory Rape: A Feminist Critique of Rights Analysis," *Texas Law Review* 63 (1984): 431–32; and C. MacKinnon, *Feminism Unmodified*, 46–62.

23. Beer, *Reader*, 29.

24. Ibid., 30 (quoting a letter to Mrs. Gaskell, 20 September 1851).

25. Ibid., 31.

26. See J. Maynard, *Charlotte Brontë and Sexuality*, ix (characterizing views of others, to which he does not subscribe).

6

Reading in Detail: Hegel's *Aesthetics* and the Feminine

Naomi Schor

Let us not take it for granted that life exists more fully in what is commonly thought big than in what is commonly thought small.
                                        —Virginia Woolf

                    Hegel, still, always . . .
                                        —Jacques Derrida

We live in an age when the detail enjoys a rare prominence. Responding to a questionnaire entitled "The Adventures of Reason in Contemporary Thought and Science," Jürgen Habermas sketches some of the recent trends and tendencies that have contributed to the widespread legitimation of the detail: "Contextualism is heretofore spelled with a capital C; the living world appears only in the plural; ethics has taken the place of morality, the everyday that of theory, the particular that of the general."[1] Nowhere have these tendencies been more spectacularly in evidence than in the writings of some of the major figures of poststructuralist France. Himself a historian of the detail, Michel Foucault, writing in *Discipline and Punish*, called for the writing of a "History of the Detail"

My thanks and gratitude to Patricia J. Mills for her creative and patient editing of my text.

that would chart its passage from a theological category in the Age of Classicism to its present role as an instrument of both knowledge and power. Reflecting on his own painting technique, Roland Barthes confessed: "I have the (initial) taste for the detail." And, last, but not least, Jacques Derrida has elaborated a textual approach characterized by a strategic revaluation of neglected textual details: notes, epigraphs, post-scriptums and all manner of *parerga*.

The pervasive valorization of the minute, the partial, and the marginal runs the risk of inducing a form of amnesia that in turn threatens to diminish the import of the current privileging of the detail. For, as any historian of ideas knows, the detail has until very recently been viewed in the West with suspicion if not downright hostility. The censure of the particular was one of the enabling gestures of neoclassicism, which recycled into the modern age the classical equation of the Ideal with the absence of all particularity. The normative aesthetics of neoclassicism did not, however, simply fade away upon the advent of Romanticism; constantly reinscribed throughout the nineteenth century they continue to resurface well into the twentieth, constituting the indelible marker of nostalgics of the Ideal (e.g. Lukács and Baudrillard). Viewed in a historical perspective, the ongoing valorization of the detail appears to be an essential aspect of that dismantling of Idealist metaphysics which looms so large on the agenda of modernity.

Is the detail feminine? This question frames my feminist archaeology of the detail in Hegel's *Aesthetics*, a text in which explicit references to sexual difference are largely absent although there is an implicit and persistent association of his Idealist aesthetics with the discourse of misogyny. Hegel bears witness to the first great turning point in the modern history of the detail, its secularization, and deplores the invasion of the aesthetic realm, a realm he sees as the domain of the sacred, by the profane "prose of life." In the *Aesthetics* he argues for the dialectical sublation or sublimation of the detail that spiritualizes or sanctifies the everyday by denying the quotidian any significance outside of this *Aufhebung*.

The story of the rise of the detail is inseparable from the story of the demise of classicism and the birth of realism but it should not be reduced to that story: to retell the story from the perspective of the detail is inevitably to tell *another* story. To focus on the detail in traditional aesthetic theory, and more particularly on the *detail as negativity*, is to become aware of its participation in a larger semantic network, bounded on the one side by the *ornamental*, with its conventional connotations of effeminacy and decadence, and on the other, by the *everyday*, whose "prosiness" is rooted in the domestic sphere of social life presided over by women. In other words, to focus on the place and function of the detail since the mid-eighteenth century is to become aware that the normative aesthetics elaborated and disseminated by the Academy and its members has not been sexually neutral; it is an axiology carrying into the field of representation the sexual hierarchies of the phallocentric cultural order. The detail in this context does not occupy a conceptual space beyond the laws of sexual difference: the detail is gendered as feminine in a complex operation that is, in Freudian terms, overdetermined.

Traditional aesthetic theory viewed the history of the detail as sexually unmarked, placing it as a footnote to the history of realism. But so long as the history of the detail was viewed this way, a crucial factor in its current hegemony was overlooked: the breakdown of sexual difference. If today the detail and the wider semantic field it commands enjoys an undisputed legitimacy it is because the dominant paradigms of patriarchy have been largely eroded. Eroded, but not eradicated.

Throughout the history of Western philosophy woman has been associated with (devalorized) nature. Both as social being and as individual she is seen as more embedded in the concrete and the particular than man.[2] Thus, where phallocentric categories are unchallenged *masculinity* is associated with *transcendence,* the *universal,* the *general* or *mass,* and *femininity* is associated with *immanence,* the *particular,* the *concrete,* or the *detail.* If, however, we merely reverse the terms of the oppositions and the values of the hierarchies, we remain, or course, prisoners of the paradigms, only just barely able to dream a universe where these categories would no longer order our thinking and seeing.

Having raised the question of the feminization of the detail I shall now set it aside as I work through Hegel's analysis. I shall pick the question up again in my concluding remarks on feminism and an aesthetics of difference.

Sublimation in Hegel's *Aesthetics*

Hegel's *Lectures on Aesthetics* is a notoriously underread text, but it is also one of the most influential treatises on aesthetics in our Western heritage. The paradoxical status of Hegel's *Aesthetics* is wittily summed up by Paul de Man: "Few thinkers have so many disciples who have never read a word of their master's writings."[3] The neglect of Hegel's monumental work surely is due in part to its unwieldy form. The *Aesthetics* is a posthumous composite of manuscripts and student lecture notes that, while heavily edited by Hegel's pupil Heinrich Gustave Hotho, appears both repetitive and digressive, awash in a hodgepodge of empirical details drawn from an encyclopedic range of sources. The following attempts to extract from this mass of details what is in fact a remarkably consistent and coherent discourse *on* the detail; the detail as aesthetic category undergirds the entire edifice of the *Aesthetics*, serving as a means of distinguishing both between periods of art (Symbolism, Classicism, Romanticism) and between major artistic modes of representation (e.g. sculpture, poetry, painting).

The detail ordains both the diachronic and the synchronic axes of the *Aesthetics*, enabling generic distinctions as well as periodization. Synchronically the detail serves to distinguish among the arts, for Hegel does not assign the same role to the detail in the different artistic media:

> It is true that there is an essential distinction between the different arts according to the medium in which they are expressed. The fullness and detailing of external fact [*Ausführlichkeit und Partikularitäten des Äusseren*] lies further away from sculpture because of the peace and universality of its figures. . . . Epic, on the other hand, says *what* is there, *where* and *how* deeds have been done, and therefore, of all kinds of poetry needs the greatest breadth and definiteness of the external locality. So too painting by its nature enters especially in this respect upon detail [*Partikuläre*] more than any other art does.[4]

Diachronically the detail operates as an essential discriminant between the successive artistic epochs. It is the passage from a quasi-total absence of details to an excess thereof that allows Hegel to distinguish earlier from later epochs of art, as well as early from later moments of a single epoch. As Stephen Bungay writes: "Hegel accepted a model of stylistic development which goes back to Vasari, was adopted by Winckelmann, and had become a commonplace in the early nineteenth century, the model of growth, flowering, and withering. Arts, epochs, and styles have a period of groping imperfection, reach a peak, and decline into decadence, and Hegel uses the terms 'streng,' 'ideal,' and 'angenehm' or 'gefällig' for these periods, which he introduces as a perfectly usual set of distinctions."[5] Thus whereas Symbolic art forms and/or classical Greek sculpture in its "*streng*" or "ideal" phases eschew "the fullness and de-tailing of external fact," Romantic art forms and/or Classical sculpture of the decadent Hellenistic age embrace particularization.

Hegel is here reinscribing the traditional association between details and decadence constantly at work in academic aesthetic discourse, but this does not in any way diminish the interest of his model of periodiza-tion. To quote de Man once again, "the name 'Hegel' stands here for an all-encompassing vessel in which [so] many currents have gathered and been preserved."[6] In other words, what makes Hegel's discourse so very precious to us is that the *Aesthetics* is, in René Wellek's congruent for-mulation, "the culmination of the whole astonishing development of German speculation on art."[7]

But Hegel's *Aesthetics* claims our attention for yet another reason. Not only does Hegel chart the passage of one aesthetic age to another, his own writings are themselves situated at a moment of aesthetic crisis, on the cusp between neoclassicism and romanticism, in its conventional, un-Hegelian meaning. (Hegel, it will be recalled, collects under the rubric "Romanticism" all art since the Middle Ages.) Fredric Jameson has eloquently described the extraordinary "transitional period" that both produced and was memorialized by Hegel (and Beethoven): "it is to such a moment of possibility, such a moment of suspension between two worlds, that the philosophy of Hegel is the most ambitious and profoundly characteristic monument."[8] The *Aesthetics* bear the stamp of what we might call Hegel's double aesthetic allegiance: Hegel refuses to choose between the perfections of the Classical and the seductions of the Modern; and, further, between the assertion that art is dead and the rival claim that "the wide Pantheon of art is rising." This double split is what leads Sir T. M. Knox, the translator of the *Aesthetics* into English, to qualify them as a puzzle.[9] Hegel's fetishistic refusal to decide explains why the *Aesthetics* is not infrequently described as a split text, "a double and possibly duplicitous text" in de Man's words.[10] Wellek, for his part, concludes: "Hegel thus presents a curious double face, a Janus head, one side looking back into the past, yearning for the Greek ideal of serenity and ideal art . . . and the other side turned toward the future, looking with unconcern and even satisfaction at the death of art as a past stage of humanity."[11] If we consider the prominence of the detail in the writings of some of those who name pivotal moments in the history of modern aesthetics—Reynolds, Hegel, and Barthes—it would appear that at moments of aesthetic mutation the detail becomes a means not only of effecting change, but of understanding it.

As more than one of Hegel's critics has noted, his systematic aesthetics are flawed by the awkward mapping of his system onto history, of the triadic art forms (Symbolism, Classicism, Romanticism) onto the five particular arts: architecture, sculpture, painting, music, and literature, in that order. And yet, for all their misgivings, Hegel's critical commentators have respected his organization and espoused his chronologies. In what follows I do neither. Guided by the fate of particularization in the *Aesthetics*, a kind of Ariadne's thread, I have adopted a circular rather than a linear mode of exposition: my dis-ordered discussion of the arts is framed by Hegel's considerations on portraiture and those on Dutch genre painting.

Hegel's *Aesthetics* is based on and tends toward the Ideal, which is to say the Idea of Beauty. The total adequation of form and content that is Beauty consigns to the realm of the un-beautiful any superfluous sensuous element not fully invested by the soul. Accordingly, the Ideal implies "the negation of everything particular" (1:157); for Hegel, the Ideal is that which escapes the contamination of "chance and externality" (1:155). The Ideal is always bound up with the divine, since only God avoids completely the impure universe of the contingent: "The ideal work of art confronts us like a blessed god" (1:157). By making the quasi-divine Ideal the telos of all artistic endeavor, Hegel forecloses any access by women to the higher spheres of art. Elaborating on his theory of sexual difference in the *Philosophy of Right,* Hegel writes: "Women are capable of education, but they are not made for activities which demand a universal faculty such as the more advanced sciences, philosophy and certain forms of artistic production. Women may have happy ideals, taste and elegance, but they cannot attain to the ideal."[12]

It follows from this ideal of the Ideal that Hegel condemns any art—and especially any representation of the human figure—that remains mired in the material and the contingent. Thus, like Sir Joshua Reynolds, he condemns particularly the portrait painters who are content merely to imitate their models with improving on them, without raising them up to the Ideal. But whereas Reynolds banishes particularities in the name of general effect, Hegel displaces the question, shaking by the same gesture the foundations of the very neoclassical aesthetic he appears to be reinscribing. In Hegel the censure of the detail is motivated not by a concern with the *general,* but rather with the *spiritual,* which is not at all the same thing. That is what emerges from two similar but not identical passages spaced a few pages apart, demonstrating that Hegel's repetitions are not always on the order of repetitiousness, but on occasion of insistence:

> But even the portrait-painter, who has least of all to do with the Ideal of art, *must* flatter, in the sense that all the externals in shape and expression, form, colour, features, the purely natural side of imperfect existence, *little hairs, pores, little scars, warts,* all these he must let go, and grasp and reproduce the subject in his universal character and enduring personality. It is one thing for the artist simply to imitate the face of the sitter, its surface and external form, confronting him in repose, and quite another to be able to portray the true features which express the inmost soul of the subject. For it is throughout necessary for the Ideal that the outer form should explicitly correspond with the soul. (1:155–56; my emphasis)

> In the case of the human form, for instance, the artist does not proceed, as may be supposed, like a restorer of old paintings who even in the newly painted places reproduces the cracks which, owing to the splitting of the varnish and the paint, have covered all the other older parts of the canvas with a sort of network. On the contrary, the portrait painter will omit *folds of skin* and, still more, *freckles, pimples, pock-marks, warts,* etc., and the famous Denner, in his so-called "truth to nature," is not to be taken as an example. Similarly, muscles and veins are indicated indeed, but they should not appear in the distinctness and completeness which they have in reality. For in all this there is nothing of the spirit, and the expression of the spiritual is the essential thing in the human form. (1:164–65; my emphasis)

To single out Denner—known as *Poren-Denner* to critics scornful of the extreme of slavishly mimetic portraiture his work represents—is by Hegel's time a topos of German neoclassical aesthetics. What is nonetheless striking about these two passages is the extraordinary fascination exerted over Hegel by the very details that must be suppressed. In contrast to the very general and abstract terms in which Reynolds's condemnation of the particular is couched, Hegel's normative vocabulary exhibits a spectacular specificity. By means of a sort of preteritio—a rhetorical figure particularly apt to take over the oscillations of the fetishist Hegel is—Hegel succeeds in embodying the most natural, not to say naturalistic details, even as he consigns them to erasure. It is as though in Hegel's text details are, to borrow Derrida's expression, "under erasure": both absent and present at the same time.

But that is not all: equally striking in these passages is the choice of details Hegel makes. They are not just *any* details, but dermal details. Nor are these passages unique; in a passage on the human body, Hegel locates in the human skin's capacity to reveal at every point humanity's "ensouldness," humanity's superiority to animals. But, he adds, "however far the human, in distinction from the animal, body makes its life appear outwardly, still nevertheless the poverty of nature equally finds expression on this surface by the non-uniformity of the skin, in *indentations, wrinkles, pores, small hairs, little veins*, etc." (1:146; my emphasis). Hegel's obsession with human skin is in itself not remarkable; ever since Ulysses's scar, fleshly marks and mimesis have been closely linked. No, what arrests the attention of the reader is the manner both perfectly predictable and yet somehow unexpected (considering Hegel's strictures against particularity) in which the dermal details progress from the natural to the pathological. The notoriously unreliable French translation of the *Aesthetics* presents an interesting and, so far as I can make out, totally fanciful interpolation in the series of dermal blemishes, adding to the list "des cicatrices consécutives à la vaccination, taches produites par une maladie de foie."[13] Now, it is consonant with the metaphorics of neoclassicism to imagine that any natural detail is in constant danger of a morbid mutation; indeed, that the natural is finally indistinguishable from the pathological.

The question then becomes, How can the spiritual be made manifest without the intervention of the mutant detail since the work of art exists only from the moment the Idea is given sensuous form. Or, to phrase the question otherwise: *Can there be representation without particularization?* In order to answer this question, let us consider the exemplary case of sculpture, which in the Hegelian system—just as in Reynolds's, who writes: "sculpture is formal, regular, austere"[14]—functions as the degree zero of the detail.

Degree zero of the detail, certainly—but providing one distinguishes, as Hegel does not always do, detail and *detail*. For, as Hegel will repeat tirelessly, if sculpture—art of the classical ideal carried to perfection by the Greeks—is, by definition, "incompatible" with the figuration of natural details, it can in no way do without a certain degree of particularization; thus an art of "abstract generality," such as Egyptian sculpture, is an art of death. In fact, Hegel's sculptural ideal is informed by a pneumatic metaphysics, and highly individualized details secure the lifelike animation of carved stones:

> In looking at such works the eye cannot at first make out a mass of differences and they become evident only under a certain illumination where there is a stronger contrast of light and shade, or they may be recognizable only by touch. Nevertheless although these fine nuances are not noticed at a first glance, the general impression which they produce is not for this reason lost. They may appear when the spectator changes his position or we may essentially derive from them a sense of the organic fluidity of all the limbs and their forms. This breath of life, this soul of material forms, rests entirely on the fact that each part is completely there independently and in its own particular character, while, all the same, owing to the fullest richness of the transitions, it remains in firm connection not only with its immediate neighbour but with the whole. Consequently the shape is perfectly animated at every point; even the minutest detail [*das Einzelnste*] has its purpose; everything has its own particular character, its own difference, its own distinguishing mark, and yet it remains in continual flux, counts and lives only in the whole. The result is that the whole can be recognized in fragments, and such a separated part affords the contemplation and enjoyment of an unbroken whole. (2:725–26/669)

The lifelike effect produced by the sculptors of the fifth century is due to the proliferation of minute details, "fine nuances" situated just beneath the range of immediate perception or outside the field of perception altogether, in the shadowy, corporeal realm of the tactile. And yet it is from their very subliminal situation that these details derive their illusionistic power. Hegel insists on the impossibility for the spectator of taking in in the same glance both the details and the lifelike impression they produce; the spectator is condemned to an alternative mode of perception, seeing now the illusion, now its mainsprings. It is by arresting perception in its second stage, the stage of disillusionment, that Hegel gives us his ideal of the detail. Abandoning the neoclassical framework in favor of the aesthetic of the part object elaborated by German Romanticism,[15] Hegel links the fate of the detail to that of the fragment, lending to the humble detail some of the prestige of the noble fragment, all the while stressing their mutual dependence.

In Hegel's modulation of organicist theory there exists a relationship of "double synecdoche"—to borrow a term from the μ Group's *Rhétorique générale*—between detail and fragment. In other words, to the extent that both are distinct parts referring to the same totality, they are equivalent. At the same time, however, detail and fragment are in a hierarchical relationship, because it is the equal distribution and high density of purposeful details that ensures the integrity of the fragment. If each fragment is a microcosm of and acceptable aesthetic substitute for the whole, it is due to the animation of every inch of the sculpture in its entirety by the play of differential nuances. Put another way: it is in the virtuality of the fragment that the detail finds its finality, gains some measure of its legitimacy. In an aesthetic of an essentially archaeological order, where any totality is but a temporary assemblage of potential fragments, the detail is the guarantor of perennity.

We have in a few short pages moved away from our point of departure, the expulsion of natural details in the name of spirituality. The more closely one reads the *Aesthetics*, the more one realizes that in Hegel the problematic of the detail is in large measure divorced from that of representation. Thus it is that architecture—the fundamental art in Hegel's system—provides the most fully realized model of an organic whole. The Gothic cathedral—always enlisted as a foil for the Parthenon in neoclassical aesthetics—functions as the equivalent of Greek sculpture in the Romantic aesthetic Hegel undertakes to present.

> No one thing completely exhausts a building like this; everything is lost in the greatness of the whole. It has and displays a definite purpose; but in its grandeur and sublime peace it is lifted above anything purely utilitarian into an infinity in itself. This elevation above the finite, and this simple solidity, is its *one* characteristic aspect. In its other it is precisely where particularization [*Partikularisation*], diversity, and variety gain the fullest scope, but without letting the whole fall apart into mere trifles [*Besonderheiten*]

and accidental details [*Einzelheiten*]. On the contrary, here the majesty of art brings back into simple unity everything thus divided up and partitioned. The substance of the whole is dismembered and shattered into the endless divisions of a world of individual variegations, but this incalculable multiplicity is divided in a simple way, articulated regularly, dispersed symmetrically, both moved and firmly set in the most satisfying eurhythmy, and this length and breadth of varied details [*Einzelheiten*] is gripped together unhindered into the most secure unity and clearest independence. (2:635/635)

Whatever the art form considered, the stake of synecdoche remains the same; whether one goes from the detail to the fragment (centrifugal movement of Greek statuary), or from the detail to the whole (centripetal movement of the Gothic cathedral), it is always a question of ensuring the delicate balance between the autonomy of the part and the unity of the whole. Autonomy, unity . . . the choice of these words testifies to the profound complicity of the aesthetic and the political, as both are informed by the corporeal metaphor: thus the cathedral presents itself as a confederation of *definalized* details. By definalized I mean not having a finality, a goal, a telos. Sublimated by the totality into which they are absorbed, the ornamental details of the Gothic cathedral become, to borrow from Kant's aesthetic vocabulary, purposeless. It is as though under the aegis of Christianity, the ornamental can rise. In short, as long as the clauses of a certain *aesthetic contract* are respected— avoidance of the contingent, maintenance of the guarantors of classical order (simplicity, regularity, symmetry)—the proliferation of details is authorized, even encouraged. Even if by his reinscription of a certain number of rules and constraints Hegel remains the prisoner of aesthetic principles of a bygone era (though neoclassicism never really dies) by his praise of dispersion and recognition of the beauty of the parcellary (the particular in the etymological sense of the word) he announces the dawn of a new aesthetic age.

It would seem then that once one has eliminated the problem of the naturalistic detail, the no less troublesome problem of the degree of freedom and autonomy to be granted the detail remains. Nowhere is this difficulty more apparent than in Hegel's remarks on music, the second Romantic art. Music, as Hegel candidly admits, is not his strong suit: "I am little versed in this sphere" (2:893) he writes at the outset. Whereas in the fields of painting and literature, for example, Hegel could claim expertise and a substantial degree of firsthand knowledge, in the field of music he is a rank amateur or dilettante and according to him there is a major difference in the music appreciation of the amateur and the connoisseur: "What the layman likes most in music is the intelligible expression of feelings and ideas, something tangible, a topic, and therefore turns in preference to music as an accompaniment: whereas the expert who has at his fingers' ends the inner music relations between notes and instruments, loves instrumental music in its artistic use of harmonies and melodious interactings and changing forms: he is entirely satisfied by the music itself" (2:953–54).

The layman eagerly clutching at the content a text lends to music is Hegel, Hegel whose logocentrism[16] leads him to center his chapter on music on the relationship of words and music, on music as accompaniment and not on instrumental music, on music itself. Unlike its sister arts, music, a nonobjective art of memory, is deficient in regard to content: "This object-free inwardness in respect of music's content and mode of expression constitutes its formal aspect. It does have a content too but not in the sense that the visual arts and poetry have one; for what it lacks is giving to itself an objective configuration whether in the forms of actual external phenomena or in the objectivity of spiritual views and ideas" (2:892). A text acts as a sort of substitute for music's missing objective correlative; "the determinate sphere of words" (2:952) supplies or supplements the content music lacks: "The details of the content are precisely what the *libretto* provides" (2:941). The specific lack of unaccompanied music is then specificity itself. Why does music need specificity? Because in the listener—Hegel's concern here is reception—decontextualized melody, however moving, produces a specular "self-apprehension" that is "in the last resort merely a mood" (2:940) and thus at risk of trivialization. In the interpenetration of text and melody, the text gains the particularization necessary to heighten the affective response of the auditor: "But if grief, joy, longing, etc. are to resound in the melody, the actual concrete soul in the seriousness of actual life has such moods only in an actual context, in specific circumstances, particular situations, events, and actions . . . the more the heart flings itself with all its might into some particular experience, the more are its emotions intensified" (2:940–41).

There is then an inner necessity in music that calls for the supplement of the text and its wealth of details. But Hegel would not be Hegel if he were content to leave matters there. For, at the same time as the libretto grounds the melody in the particular, enhancing the listener's emotional response, it introduces a dangerous scissura between the *melody* and *characterization,* reproducing *within* music the differences that oppose the Italian (melodic) and the German (characteristic) schools of music on the one hand, sculpture and painting on the other.

Hegel is then in turn both the layman and the expert. Having first argued the case for the combination of words and music, he proceeds to warn against the great risk inherent in this alliance: the overpowering of the melody by the characterization and the ensuing loss of musicality itself: "So soon as music commits itself to the abstraction of characterization in detail, it is inevitably led almost astray into sharpness and harshness, into what is thoroughly unmelodious and unmusical" (2:948). So grave is the threat posed by the dispersive forces of characterization, that Hegel avows: "In this matter the chief demand seems to me to be that the victory shall always be given to the melody as the all-embracing unity and not to the disunion of characteristic passages scattered and separated individually from one another" (2:947).

Finally, music is the locus of the emergence of the tension always present throughout the *Aesthetics* between a drive toward unity, articulation, and wholeness and an equally strong countervailing drive toward fragmentation, disjunction, and particularization. Where architecture succeeds, one might say, music fails:

> [T]ruly musical beauty lies in the fact that, while an advance is made from pure melody to characterization, still within this particularization melody is always preserved as the carrying and unifying soul just as, for example, within the characteristic detail of a Raphael painting the note of beauty is always still retained. Further, melody is meaningful, but in all definition of its meaning it is the animation which permeates and holds together the whole, and the characteristic particulars appear only as emergence of specific aspects which are always led back by the inner life to this unity and animation. But in this matter to hit the happy medium is of greater difficulty in music than in the other arts because music more easily breaks up into these opposed modes of expression. (2:948)

If music is particularly prone to the conflicting pulls of melody and characterization, because of the successivity of reading, poetry and especially the descriptive poetry that would emulate painting, the art of simultaneity, is at constant risk of disintegration: "it can bring before our minds only in isolated traits one after another what we can see at one glance in the real world, and therefore in its treatment of an individual occurrence it cannot so far spread itself that the total view of it is necessarily disturbed, confused, or altogether lost" (2:982). And yet, according to Hegel, unlike lyric poetry which by virtue of its inwardness is by definition antidescriptive, epic poetry can and even must indulge in minute descriptions; it constitutes, then, an exception to the rule. To what is this exceptional status of the detail under the epic regime due? There is first what one might call the "psychological realism" of epic, that is of Homeric epic, which enjoys paradigmatic status in the *Aesthetics:* "Homer's circumstantial descriptions of things of this sort must not seem to us to be a poetic addition to rather dry material; on the contrary, this detailed [*ausführlicher*] attention is the very spirit of the men and situations described" (2:1055/950). Hence, to cite the most celebrated example of epic ekphrasis, "the shield of Achilles" is, according to Hegel's very Kantian formulation, "a description not to be regarded as an external parergon" (2:1055). The habilitation of the detail is always bound up with a breakdown of hierarchies; whereas in our day, Hegel writes, "we have an extensive hierarchy of grades of distinction in clothing, furnishings, etc. . . . the world of the heroes was not like this . . . it was possible to linger over their descriptions because all things rank alike" (2:1054). There is further what one might call the "argument according to Lessing": that in epic poetry there is no break between description and diegesis. Not only, as Lessing demonstrates, are epic descriptions active, but, as Hegel insists, the action is in turn informed by the descriptive details. What makes the epic detail so special is that, as both these arguments suggest, it is the product of a human praxis. In contradistinction to the natural detail, embodied by the dermal blemishes to be expunged from portraiture, the epic detail, typified by the crafted embellishments of homely objects, attests to the power of human agency to transform the brute given of nature and to inspirit the inert facticity of matter. Finally, and most surprising, there is the fact that epic poetry being—unlike dramatic poetry, which is entirely oriented by a telos, a crisis to resolve—a poetry with a slow and regular tempo, there is no reason to hurry through it.

On the contrary. The epic is a text that by virtue of its definalization offers the reader the leisure to take pleasure in the grain of the text that is the detail. It is quite literally in Hegel a text of pleasure, if not of *jouissance:* "such a total world, which nevertheless is concentrated into individual lives, must proceed tranquilly in the course of its realization, without hurrying on practically and dramatically towards some mark and the result of aiming at it, so that we can linger by what goes on, immerse ourselves in the individual pictures in the story and enjoy [*geniessen*] them in all their details [*Ausführlichkeit*]" (2:1044/941).

Let us not hasten to conclude this deliberately anachronistic reading of the *Aesthetics* on the triumphant note that often accompanies modernist appropriations of classical texts. Even if there is as much Barthes in Hegel as there is Hegel in Barthes (and that at least is the hypothesis that has guided me in this study), there is no question that a chasm separates the author of the *Aesthetics* from the author of *Mythologies*, that aesthetic of everyday life. The contempt Hegel flaunts for "the little stories of everyday domestic existence" and the "multiform particularities of everyday life"—in short, for all that he lumps under the dismissive heading "the prose of the world" (1:150)—goes along with his famously limited interest in the art of his time. Thus at the very moment when Balzac undertakes to write what was to become the *Comédie humaine,* Hegel elaborates an aesthetic where the novel is not recognized as a major genre.[17] Is this absence or displacement? If one reads Hegel on painting—the Romantic art par excellence, in Hegel's idiosyncratic use of that word—it would appear that one has but to transpose (with all the precautions and adjustments necessary) Hegel's analysis of the origins of romantic painting, and especially of the beauties of Dutch painting, to the field of writing in order to find the "theory of the novel" one seeks in vain under the rubric of poetry, even epic. There is nothing particularly surprising about this displacement when one considers the "preeminence of the pictorial code over literary *mimesis,*" which characterizes representation in the nineteenth century and from which Barthes, in a section of *S/Z,* entitled precisely, "Painting as a Model," derives the following consequences:

> Thus, realism (badly named, at any rate often badly interpreted) consists not in copying the real but in copying a (depicted) copy of the real: this famous *reality,* as though suffering from a fear-

fulness which keeps it from being touched directly, is *set farther away*, postponed, or at least captured through the pictorial matrix in which it has been steeped before being put into words: code upon code, known as realism.[18]

Let us note that Barthes's Platonic analysis of the painting-novel relationship in the nineteenth century does not go far enough in its demystification of the referential illusion; it seems to suggest that, unlike mediated fiction, painting enjoys an immediate proximity to the real, whereas, as E. H. Gombrich has shown, painting itself is never directly in touch with the real: it too is always already a copy of a copy.[19] But in the end what matters is not the degree of difference that separates painting and literature from the real: for anyone who wants to understand anything about the controversies provoked by the French realist novel—which are to a large extent controversies of the detail—the principal consequence of the primacy of *pictoria* over *poesis* in nineteenth-century representation is the primacy of the *theory of painting* over the *theory of the novel.* Whereas from the Renaissance up to the late eighteenth century, literature and its rhetoric held sway over painting, nineteenth-century fictional prose was governed by aesthetic norms derived from painting, and from Academic painting at that. It is then in the light of this relationship of the pictorial and the literary that one must read Hegel's remarks on painting.

The question arises: How does painting—the art of the detail—succeed in smuggling particularities, even naturalistic details, into the field of representation? Let us return, however briefly, to the "myth of origins" of Romantic art, to Hegel's conception of the evolution of Classical into Romantic art. This passage, it would appear, constitutes a chapter in the history of religions, in particular of the advent of Christianity, the religion of the human God. The humanization of the divine, which is the achievement of classical art, is replaced by the divinization of the human, which defines Christianity and the art it produced. This reversal entails the irresistible return of what classical art repressed:

But in so far as in this appearance the accent is laid on the fact that God is essentially an individual person, exclusive of others, and displays the unity of divine and human subjectivity not simply in general but as *this* man, there enter here again, in art, on account of the subject-matter itself, all the aspects of the contingency and particularity of external finite existence from which beauty at the height of the classical Ideal had been purified. (1:536)

In fact it is a question of more than the return of the repressed; what is involved is the promotion of the circumstantial, a radical rearrangement of the hierarchical ordering that underpins the composition of the classical painting: "painting must go beyond this immersion in the rich content of subjectivity and its infinity. On the contrary it must free, and release into independence, particular detail [*Besonderheit*], i.e. what constitutes as it were something otherwise incidental, i.e. the environment and the background" (2:812/741). The content of romantic painting—for unlike classical art, romantic art is characterized by the inadequation of form and content—would then be the refuse of the Ideal, that collection of insignificant materials left by the wayside in classical art:

> Thereby art becomes not only what romantic art is more or less throughout, i.e. portrait-like, but it completely dissolves into the presentation of a portrait, whether in plastic art, painting, or descriptive poetry; and it reverts to the imitation of nature, i.e. to an intentional approach to the contingency of immediate existence which, taken by itself, is unbeautiful and prosaic. (1:596) In the presentations of romantic art, therefore, everything has a place, every sphere of life, all phenomena, the greatest and the least, the supreme and the trivial. (1:594)

"If heart and thought remain dissatisfied," Hegel says, "close inspection reconciles us to them" (1:598). Where then does the pleasure those works provide come from? Such is the question posed most urgently by Dutch genre painting, a *locus criticus* in the history of the detail as aesthetic category.[20] Entirely devoted to the representation of the hidden side of the classic ideal, hyperbole of painting, Dutch art seems a priori to go against Hegel's stated preferences. How then does Hegel go about reconciling his ideal of the Ideal with his very favorable appreciation of this school of art, a school generally looked down upon by Reynolds and other Academic aestheticians, notably Hegel's most illustrious predecessors and contemporaries, Winckelmann, A. W. Schlegel, Schelling?

The myth of origins of painting we have just rehearsed in highly schematic fashion provides the elements of an answer in the form of an already familiar scenario:

> In general terms, the essence of painting's progress is this: a start is made with *religious* subjects, still *typically* treated. . . . Next there enter more and more into the religious situations the present, the individual, the living beauty of the figures . . . until painting turns towards the world; it takes possession of nature, the everyday experiences of human life, or historically important national events, whether past or present, portraits and the like, all down to the tiniest and most insignificant detail [*Unbedeutend-sten*], and it does this with the same love that had been lavished on the ideal content of religion. And in this sphere above all it attains not only the supreme perfection of painting but also the greatest liveliness of conception and the greatest individuality in the mode of execution. (2:870–71/790)

There is then according to Hegel a sort of *transference* onto profane subjects of the love initially lavished exclusively on sacred subjects.[21] If we admit that the detail is, as it were, sponsored by the religious, it follows that whatever the degree of secularization attained by a given civilization, the detail will never completely liquidate its debt to the sacred. In other words: to the extent that the profane detail (with its cluster of negative connotations: the everyday, naturalism, prosiness, smallness, insignificance) is shaped in the mold of the sacred detail, it will forever bear the stamp of its religious origins. Even camouflaged by the fetishism peculiar to our dechristianized consumer society, the detail entertains a relationship—however degraded—to the sacred. God, as Mies van der Rohe, Aby Warburg, and others are credited with saying, dwells in details.

But there is more. There is in Hegel—and it is in this sense that his conception of Romantic art can be qualified as romantic (in the restricted sense)—the possibility of conceiving of a *sublimation* of the detail, a new transcendence that would sublate "what is itself without significance" (1:596).[22] This *Aufhebung* of the prosaic detail is bodied forth in Dutch painting:

> Here the subject-matter may be quite indifferent to us or may interest us, apart from the artistic presentation, only incidentally,

for example, or momentarily. In this way Dutch painting, for example, has recreated, in thousands and thousands of effects, the existent and fleeting appearance of nature as something generated afresh by man. Velvet, metallic lustre, light, horses, servants, old women, peasants blowing smoke from cutty pipes, the glitter of wine in a transparent glass, chaps in dirty jackets playing with old cards—these and hundreds of other things are brought before our eyes in these pictures, things that we scarcely bother about in our daily life, for even if we play cards, drink wine, and chat about this and that, we are still engrossed by quite different interests. But what at once claims our attention in matter of this kind, when art displays it to us, is precisely this pure shining and appearing of objects as something produced by the *spirit* which transforms in its inmost being the external and sensuous side of all this material. For instead of real wool and silk, instead of real hair, glass, flesh, and metal, we see only colours; instead of all the dimensions requisite for appearance in nature, we have just a surface, and yet we get the same impression which reality affords. (1:162–63)

How is this "marvel of ideality" (1:163) produced; how is this "artistic phenomenalization" that succeeds in spiritualizing an initially vulgar matter arrived at? How are scenes and objects of everyday life—and in this perspective the shiny and the slimy are equivalent—invested with a transcendent aesthetic value? Hegel provides two answers: answers of a purely local sort, which take into account the specificities (ecological, economic, historical, and religious) of the Dutch situation, and philosophical answers that engage the very foundations of the *Aesthetics*. From the first series of explanations I shall retain only the religious argument that Hegel privileges, writing: "the Dutch were Protestants, an important matter, and to Protestantism alone the important thing is to get a sure footing in the prose of life, to make it absolutely valid in itself independently of religious associations, and to let it develop in unrestricted freedom" (1:598). If, as Hegel would have it, Protestantism is singularly receptive to profane details, that would explain the early rise of realism in Protestant countries such as Holland (painting) and England (novel). This hypothesis also raises a difficult question: Is there any difference between Protestant and Catholic varieties of realism?

It would not be exaggerated to claim that the transformation of the so-called insignificant object into an art-object engages the entire *Aesthetics*, in that this transformation relies on the superiority of the spiritual to the natural, which serves as the axiom of Hegel's lectures, and, more generally, his philosophical writings. Announcing from the start the differences between his approach and Kant's, Hegel excludes natural beauty from his field of inquiry, by virtue of the following principle: "spirit and its artistic beauty stands *higher* than natural beauty" (1:2). The insignificant object is then but an extreme example of the object in its natural state, before it has been informed and transformed by the creative spirit. What Dutch genre paintings make manifest— hence their exemplary status in the *Aesthetics*—is the equivalence, not to say the irrelevance, of the content, and by extension, of the faithful imitation of the real. What is finally at stake in the sublimation of the prosaic (which covers both "insignificant objects" and "the scenes of life which may seem to us not only contingent, but vulgar and common"), is the subject-object relationship. In order for the "sum of insignificances" that constitute the decor of everyday life to have access to the world of art, they must acquire "the look of independent and total life and freedom which lies at the root of the essence of beauty" (1:149); by the same token, for us to derive pleasure from their representation, "we must pull ourselves together and concentrate" (2:835). In other words, the subject-object relation must be characterized on both sides by independence and autonomy: a *double detachment* is required. In order for this relationship of mutual independence to be instituted, there must be a passage from a subject-object relationship of *appropriation* to one of *identification*. A complex process. This passage can be broken down into two stages: first, there must be what Hegel calls a "withdrawal" of the "desire" that links humans to their environment, for the indifference or repulsion inspired in us by the prosaic result from our tendency to view objects in a purposive fashion, in short, from our egocentrism:

> Further, if we allow our pleasure to be trivialized by accepting the supercilious intellectual reflection that we should regard such objects as vulgar and unworthy of our loftier consideration, we are taking the subject-matter of painting in a way quite different from that in which art really presents it to us. For in that case we are bringing with us only the relation we take up to such objects when we need them or take pleasure in them or regard them

from the point of view of the rest of our culture and our other aims; i.e. we are treating them only according to their external purpose, with the result that it is our needs which become the chief thing, a living end in itself. (2:834)

The withdrawal of desire corresponds to a definalization of the disdained object or scene, a *definalization* that cannot but provoke a *defamiliarization*: once the object or the other is freed from the practical bonds tying it to what we might call, borrowing from Freud, "his Majesty the Ego," they appear in a new and altogether different light.

At the second stage, the complementary movement of withdrawal of the object is accomplished, paradoxically favored by the interest that the subject bears or attributes to it:

> Man always lives in the immediate present; what he does at every moment is something particular, and the right thing is simply to fulfill every task, no matter how trivial, with heart and soul. In that event the man is at one with such an individual matter for which alone he seems to exists, because he has put his whole self and all his energy into it. This cohesion [between the man and his work] produces that harmony between the subject and the particular character of his activity in his nearest circumstances which is also a spiritual depth and which is the attractiveness of the independence of an explicitly total, rounded, and perfect existence. Consequently, the interest we may take in pictures of objects like those mentioned does not lie in the objects themselves but in this soul of life which in itself, apart altogether from the thing in which it proves to be living, speaks to every uncorrupt mind and free heart and is to it an object in which it participates and takes joy. (2:833)

This somewhat difficult passage is illuminated by another in which Hegel attempts to lay bare the mechanism of the "irresistible attraction" exerted on the spectator by the representation of vulgar subjects. It emerges that pushed to the limit, the deconstruction of the insignificant (vulgar)/ significant (noble) paradigm calls into question the very notion of insignificance-vulgarity. It is then that the concept of independence takes on its full meaning, for the independence of the subject represented confers upon the most vulgar scenes and characters a title to nobility that likens them to the gods of Olympus, those paradigms of the classical ideal. Here is Hegel at the moment when he is expanding on his praise of Dutch painting by praising Murillo's canvases:

> In the like sense the beggar boys of Murillo . . . are excellent too . . . the mother picks lice out of the head of one of the boys while he quietly munches his bread; on a similar picture two other boys, ragged and poor, are eating melon and grapes. But in this poverty and seminakedness what precisely shines forth within and without is nothing but complete absence of care and concern—a Dervish could not have less—in the full feeling of their well-being and delight in life. This freedom from care for external things and the inner freedom made visible outwardly is what the Concept of the Ideal requires. . . . We see that they [the boys of Murillo] have no wider interests and aims, yet not at all because of stupidity; rather do they squat on the ground content and serene, almost like the gods of Olympus. (1:170)

What does this all mean? It seems to me that Hegel is not far from proposing here the same analysis of the "irresistible attraction" exerted by the representation of inner freedom that Freud will propose nearly a century later to account for the magnetic effects of narcissism: "It seems very evident that another person's narcissism has a great attraction for those who have renounced part of their own narcissism and are in search of object-love. The charm of a child lies to a great extent in his narcissism, his self-contentment and inaccessibility, just as does the charm of certain animals which seem not to concern themselves about us, such as cats and the large beasts of prey."[23] Juxtaposed, these passages from Hegel's *Aesthetics* and Freud's "On Narcissism: An Introduction" (1913) disclose the aesthetics of narcissim, if not the narcissism of aesthetics. The fascinating freedom of Murillo's beggar boys and the seductive autarchy of Freud's children, animals (and, of course, women) display the same mechanism, as evidenced by the centrality of the child in both texts. In both instances, desire is mediated by the object's sui-referentiality. What is perceived as beautiful in Hegel's example is what Freud refers to as the object's "blissful state of mind" and the "unassailable libidinal position" it constitutes and with which the subject identifies.

But, finally, the reason why the subject-matter is indifferent and the

significant/insignificant paradigm impertinent, is that in their representation the formal aspect overrides the content to the point where it
becomes an end in itself. As the profane invades the universe of
representation, form is sacralized: "apart from the things depicted, the
means of the portrayal also becomes an end in itself, so that the artist's
subjective skill and his application of the means of artistic production
are raised to the status of an objective matter in works of art" (1:599).
Now the "illusion of reality" is closely bound up with the representation
of the/in detail:

> In supreme art we see fixed the most fleeting appearance of the
> sky, the time of day, the lighting of the trees; the appearances
> and reflections of clouds, waves, lochs, streams; the shimmering
> and glittering of wine in a glass, a flash of the eye, a momentary
> look or smile, etc. Here painting leaves the ideal for the reality
> of life; the effect of appearance it achieves here especially by the
> exactitude with which every tiniest individual part is executed.
> (2:812)

Artistic phenomenalization constitutes in some sense the *apotheosis of
the detail*, so much so that as long as the imperatives of the organicist
model are respected, realist art defies the ideal:

> Yet this is achieved by no mere assiduity of composition but by a
> spiritually rich industry which perfects each detail [*Besonderheit*]
> independently and yet retains the whole connected and flowing
> together; to achieve this, supreme skill is required. (2:812–13/
> 741)

Seen close up, pictorial details turn out to be insignificant signs that
become meaningful only in the differential play which opposes light and
darkness; the "reality-effect" (Barthes) depends then on maintaining a
"proper distance": if a spectator comes up too close to a painting, the
mimetic detail dissolves into a swirl of points and incoherent strokes:

> If we look closely at the play of colour, which glints like gold and
> glitters like braid under the light, we see perhaps only white or
> yellow strokes, points of colour, coloured surfaces; the single
> colour as such does not have this gleam which it produces; it is

the juxtaposition *alone* which makes this glistening and gleaming. (1:600)

This pulverulence is the final stage in the sublimation of the prosaic detail; it is as though the prosaic could not make its debut on the scene of representation except reduced to pure facticity, filtered through Hegel's myopic gaze for which all things resolve themselves into a haze of indistinct and dull color.

An Aesthetics of Difference and Feminism

In what is to my mind a most inspired appropriation of Hegel in the realm of aesthetics, Georg Lukács brings to bear on the problematic of the detail (*Einzelheit*, 'individuality') the full force of Hegel's *Logic*. Hegel's concept of particularity (*Besonderheit*), translated by Lukács as speciality, becomes the keystone of Lukács's system. Speciality or particularity, it will be recalled, is the mediating term in the triadic "Concept-structure" Hegel elaborates in the final section of his *Logic*, the other two being universality (*Allgemeinheit*) and individuality (*Einzelheit*). The concept is *at once* universal, particular, and individual for, as Hegel takes great pains to emphasize, the three categories are indissolubly linked. The Augustan distinction between the general and the particular is in a Hegelian perspective inconceivable; the universal is no "abstract generality": "the universal of the notion is not a mere sum of features common to several things, confronted by a particular which enjoys an existence of its own. It is, on the contrary, self-particularizing or self-specifying, and with undimmed clearness finds itself at home in its antithesis."[24] Hegel's triad informs the *Aesthetics*, of course, but only at the level of the overarching design. Overriding certain linguistic inconsistencies that seem to present "the art forms as particular and the arts as individual"—when it is not precisely the opposite—Stephen Bungay proposes the following tripartite division of the *Aesthetics:*

universality: the Ideal, the determination of art
particularity: the arts, as spatio-temporally different
individuality: the socio-historical factors involved in the actual works of
art, with real examples[25]

For Lukács, speciality or particularity is the middle or meeting point (*Sammelpunkt*) where all the centrifugal forces innervating the work of art are reconciled: "There is then . . . a movement going from speciality to universality (and back), and, at the same time, a movement going from speciality to individuality (and back); in both cases, it is the movement toward speciality that brings the process to closure."[26]

Lukács goes on to say: "the individual on the one hand, the universal on the other always appear both abolished and preserved (*aufgehoben*) in the special" (79/210). The promotion of speciality to a position of centrality rests on the *Aufhebung* or sublation of the universal and above all the individual. As Lukács emphasizes: "The relationship of particularity to individuality consists in an eternal process of cancellation (*Aufhebung*) wherein the moment of preservation (*Aufbewahrung*) is in a certain sense more strongly emphasized" (82/213). The notion of the *Aufhebung* of the individual constitutes without a doubt Lukács's most promising contribution to a theory of the detail; it allows us to begin to detect the presence of the detail even there where it appears absent; indeed, to find the *trace* of the detail in the totality with which it has been merged, into which it has vanished, been absorbed, rather than remaining obsessively fixated on the manifest detail, in its intractable thereness. Unfortunately, the theory of the phantom detail that we have teased out of Lukács's text is, in context, placed in service of a reflection theory long since discredited. However, the tendency of the detail to persist and to inform in absence is precisely what that other great neo-Hegelian aesthetician of the twentieth century so critical of Lukács, T. W. Adorno, describes when he writes: "In major art works the details do not just vanish in the totality."[27]

In short, the sublation of the individual in the special or particular signifies a vertiginous extension of the field of the detail, which no longer needs to be made manifest to produce its effects. The vaunted "reality-effect" is not necessarily produced by details duly inscribed in the text; it may spring from a set of cancelled particularities whose non-representation subliminally conditions one's response to a work of art. Thus, for example, during the genesis of *Madame Bovary*, Flaubert writes to Taine: "there are many details I don't write. Thus, Homais is slightly pockmarked."[28] The trace of a trace, Homais's pockmarks are for Flaubert essential details that would continue to haunt the text of *Madame Bovary*, ensuring its verisimilitude even while unwritten. My point remains, despite the fact that reversing himself, Flaubert did finally choose to write out this detail. In the definitive text of the novel the initial description of Homais reads: "A slightly pockmarked man in green leather slippers."[29] Invisible to the naked eye, inscribed in relief, the detail sublated both by and in the special/particular is a phantom detail. Detail of the trace, trace of the detail, the phantom detail is in some sense the modern or postmodern detail par excellence, to the extent that it participates in what, based on the foregoing analysis, we are now in a position to call an *aesthetics of difference*. That is, an aesthetics grounded in deferral rather than immediacy, absence rather than plenitude, erasure rather than expansion.

The modern fascination with the trivial, the playground of fetishism, constitutes a deliberate undoing of the romantic sublimation of the detail. It appears as a sort of happy end, spelling the demise or retreat of Idealist aesthetics. But from a feminist perspective a new and nagging question emerges: Does the triumph of the detail signify a triumph of the feminine with which it has so long been linked? Or has the detail achieved its new prestige by being taken over as masculine, triumphing at the very moment when it ceases to be associated with the feminine, or ceasing to be connoted as feminine at the very moment when it is taken up by the male-dominated cultural establishment?

Appearances notwithstanding, my initial question as to the detail's femininity was not rhetorical; it remains open. The detail has been traditionally connoted as feminine and devalorized; further, the modern age has witnessed a remarkable transvaluation of the detail accompanied by its no less significant degendering. Whether or not the detail *is* feminine—and I shall come to this much deferred point in a moment— given Western culture's long-standing association of the order of the small, and finely wrought, the *heimlich*, with the feminine sphere, the need to affirm the power and positivity of the *feminine particular* cannot for the moment be denied. Whether or not the "feminine" is a male construct, a product of a phallocentric culture destined to disappear, in the present order of things, we cannot afford not to press its claims even as we dismantle the conceptual systems that support it.

So again: Is the detail feminine? Are women—that is, females social-ized as women—as so many thinkers both male and female assert, more firmly grounded than men in the world of immanence? Do the works produced by women artists exhibit a higher density of homey and/or ornamental details than those produced by their male counterparts?

Doubtless my answer will disappoint. Despite the extensive and highly sophisticated work carried out in recent years by feminist critics committed to uncovering the specificities of women's artistic productions, there exists no reliable body of evidence to show that women's art is either more or less particularistic than men's. Indeed, further investigation of this question may lead us to formulate a surprising hypothesis, namely that feminine specificity lies in the direction of a specifically feminine form of idealism, one that seeks to transcend not the sticky feminine world of prosaic details, but rather the deadly asperities of male violence and destruction.

Notes

1. Jürgen Habermas, "Remettre le mobile en mouvement," *Le monde d'aujourd'hui*, August 6, 1984, xiii. All translations are mine except where otherwise noted.
2. Sherry Ortner, "Is Female to Male as Nature is to Culture?" in *Woman, Culture and Society*, ed. Michelle Zimbalist Rosaldo and Louise Lamphere (Stanford: Stanford University Press, 1974), 67–87. The relationship of woman and nature is, Ortner emphasizes, one of proximity rather than identity.
3. Paul de Man, "Sign and Symbol in Hegel's *Aesthetics*," *Critical Inquiry* 8 (summer 1982): 763. Also pertinent is Paul de Man, "Hegel on the Sublime," in *Displacement: Derrida and After*, ed. Mark Krupnik (Bloomington: Indiana University Press, 1983), 139–53.
4. Hegel, *Aesthetics: Lectures on Fine Art*, trans. T. M. Knox, 2 vols. (Oxford: Clarendon Press, 1975), 1:254–55. All subsequent references will be included in the text. *Aesthetik*, intro. Georg Lukács (Berlin: Aufbau-Verlag, 1955), 267. All German quotations are drawn from this edition and references will be included in the text.
5. Stephen Bungay, *Beauty and Truth: A Study of Hegel's Aesthetics* (Oxford: Clarendon Press, 1984), 115. Bungay's study, which appeared after the drafting of this chapter, is easily the best introduction to Hegel's *Aesthetics* currently available in English. See also Jack Kaminsky, *Hegel on Art* (New York: State University of New York Press, 1962) and Charles Karelis, "Hegel's Concept of Art: An Interpretive Essay," in *Hegel's Introduction to Aesthetics*, trans. T. M. Knox (Oxford: Oxford University Press, 1979), xi–xxvi.
6. De Man, "Sign and Symbol in Hegel's *Aesthetics*," 763.
7. René Wellek, *A History of Modern Criticism*, 4 vols. (New Haven: Yale University Press, 1955), 2:318.
8. Fredric Jameson, *Marxism and Form: Twentieth-Century Dialectical Theories of Literature* (Princeton: Princeton University Press, 1971), 44.
9. Sir T. M. Knox, "The Puzzle of Hegel's *Aesthetics*," in *Art and Logic in Hegel's Philolsophy*, ed. Warren E. Steinkraus and Kenneth I. Schmitz (New Jersey: Humanities Press, 1980), 1–10. This volume also contains a fairly comprehensive bibliography, "Studies of Hegel's Aesthetics" (239–49).
10. De Man, "Sign and Symbol in Hegel's *Aesthetics*," 773.
11. Wellek, *A History of Modern Criticism*, 334.
12. G. W. F. Hegel, *Hegel's Philosophy of Right* as quoted by Patricia Jagentowicz Mills, "Hegel and 'The Woman Question': Recognition and Intersubjectivity," in *The Sexism of*

Social and Political Theory: Women and Reproduction from Plato to Nietzsche, ed. L. Clarke and L. Lange (Toronto: University of Toronto Press, 1979), 94.

13. G. W. F. Hegel, *Esthétique*, trans. S. Jankélévitch, 4 vols. (Paris: Garnier-Flammarion, 1979), 1:222. *Se non e vero e ben trovato.* The vaccination scar can only allude to the smallpox vaccination discovered by Jenner in 1801. The beauty of this made-up detail is that it further specifies Hegel's detailing, inscribing it in time, at the same time as it extends its progression from the pathological to the prophylactic.

14. Sir Joshua Reynolds, *Discourses on Art*, ed. Robert R. Wark (New Haven: Yale University Press, 1975), 187.

15. On German Romanticism as an aesthetics of the fragment, see Philippe Lacoue-Labarthe and Jean-Luc Nancy, *L'absolu littéraire* (Paris: Seuil, 1978), especially 55–80.

16. Bungay, *Beauty and Truth*, 137.

17. Lukács, as we shall see later, will attempt to correct this oversight by writing what is virtually a supplement to the *Aesthetics*, his *Theory of the Novel* (Cambridge: MIT Press, 1977). But no belated supplement can mask this striking absence.

18. Roland Barthes, *S/Z*, trans. Richard Miller (New York: Hill and Wang, 1974), 55.

19. E. H. Gombrich, *The Sense of Order: A Study in the Psychology of Decorative Art* (Ithaca: Cornell University Press, 1979).

20. See, for example, Mario Praz's very Hegelian introductory chapter, "Genre Painting and the Novel," in *The Hero in Eclipse in Victorian Fiction*, trans. Angus Davidson (London: Oxford University Press, 1957), 1–33. Cf. in my *Reading in Detail* (New York: Routledge, 1987), chapter 1, the association of Dutch and genre painting with the lower order of taste displayed by women, 11–22.

21. If this reconstruction sounds very familiar to the literary critic, it is because the preeminent twentieth-century writings on realism—I am thinking, of course, of Auerbach's *Mimesis* (Princeton: Princeton University Press, 1953) and Ian Watt's *The Rise of the Novel* (Berkeley and Los Angeles: University of California Press, 1957)—are shot through with Hegelianism.

22. When I speak of sublimation in Hegel I shall not be referring to his writings on the sublime. The tendency to occlude the significance of Dutch art in Hegel's *Aesthetics* persists in the high deconstructionist tendency to focus almost exclusively on Hegel's writings on sublime Egyptian art.

23. Sigmund Freud, *The Standard Edition of the Complete Psychological Works of Sigmund Freud*, ed. James Strachey, trans. James Strachey et al., 24 vols. (London: Hogarth, 1953–74), 14:89.

24. G. W. F. Hegel, *The Logic of Hegel*, trans. William Wallace (Oxford: Clarendon Press, 1874), 252.

25. Bungay, *Beauty and Truth*, 55. One of the most recent avatars of Hegel's triad occurs in the opening pages of Barthes's *Writing Degree Zero*. Crossbred with Saussurean linguistics, the universal, the particular, and the individual produce *langue, parole*, and *écriture*. For more on Barthes and Hegel, see chap. 5 of my *Reading in Detail*.

26. Georg Lukács, "Das Besondere als zentrale Kategorie der Ästhetik," in his *Über die Besonderheit als Kategorie der Ästhetik* (Neuwied: Luchterhand, 1967), 209. I have relied heavily in what follows on the French translation of this text, "Le particulier comme catégorie centrale de l'esthétique," trans. Georges Kassai and Gérard Spitzer, *Les Lettres nouvelles*, special issue on "Ecrivains hongrois d'aujourd'hui" (September–October 1964): 76–99. The references included in the text are first to the French, then to the German. On Lukács's late aesthetics, see Bela Királyfalvi, *The Aesthetics of Gyorgy Lukács* (Princeton: Princeton University Press, 1975); G. H. R. Parkinson, *Georg Lukács* (London: Routledge and Kegan Paul, 1977), 125–44.

27. T. W. Adorno, *Aesthetic Theory*, trans. C. Lenhardt, ed., Gretel Adorno and Rolf Tiedemann (London: Routledge and Kegan Paul, 1984), 420. "Independent details" (420), argues Adorno in his characteristically dense reflection on the part-whole relationship, are an essential component of the work of art, which for him (as for Hegel and Lukács) is a "resultant of centripetal and centrifugal forces" (420). The "instant . . . of being touched" particularity provides makes possible the aesthetic experience, for "aesthetic experience can never grasp the whole in its immediacy, yet immediacy is constitutive of aesthetic experience" (420). Modern art, notably uninspired constructivist modern music, is threatened by a traceless disappearance of the detail into the whole, a particularly unfortunate development because in the detail resides a possible point of resistance to the oppression of the individual by society. Particularization in art "undoes the enduring injustice that society perpetrates against the individual" (422).

28. Charles Carlut, *La correspondance de Flaubert: Etude et répertoire critique* (Columbus: Ohio State University Press, 1968), 408.

29. Gustave Flaubert, *Madame Bovary* (New York: Norton, 1965), 52.

7

Fetal Attraction:
Hegel's An-aesthetics of Gender

Eric O. Clarke

After the meal had ended and the guest departed, Goethe asked his daughter:
"Now how did you like that man?" "Strange," she replied, "I cannot tell
whether he is brilliant or mad. He seems to me to be an unclear thinker."
Goethe smiled ironically. "Well, well, we just ate with the most famous of
modern philosophers—Georg Wilhelm Friedrich Hegel."

—Ottilie von Goethe

In its playful calculation, Goethe's question to his daughter evokes a
double-edged irony. Her response can indicate either quaint innocence
or irreverent insight. What sustains both ironic turns, however, is the
daughter's exclusion from Western philosophy, potently represented by
Hegel at this after-dinner scenario. The double irony available in Ottilie
von Goethe's comment is symptomatic of the ironies of exclusion that
Hegel's texts themselves construct around the category "woman." This
category occupies a kind of centripetal marginality for Hegel; paradoxi-

I thank Henry Abelove, Gerry Clarke Johnson, William Keach, Ellen Rooney, Patricia J. Mills,
and Robert Scholes for their helpful comments and suggestions.

cally central because so marginal, the Hegelian construction of "woman" continually threatens to spin into unexpected ironies and contradictions. This centripetal movement gains momentum through the convergence in Hegel's texts of his understanding of "literal" women, and their seclusion within the ethical life of the family, and figural "woman," whose explanatory power exceeds domesticity and disruptively seeps into the very texture of Hegelian dialectics.[1]

I shall explore the pervasive power of "woman" in Hegel by examining his conceptualization of sexed bodies and its purchase for his aesthetic theory. As Terry Eagleton has observed, aesthetics was "born as a discourse of the body" (13); however, contrary to its eighteenth-century predecessors, which sought to define the physiological effects of art ranging from the delicacies of taste to the rigors of judgment, Hegel's aesthetic theory is more concerned with the production and historical development of "the beautiful." Such human productivity occupies a central role in Hegel's philosophy; it embodies the process of "negating the negation," of overcoming the originary alienation of Spirit (Geist) from itself. For Hegel this self-alienation of Spirit is the origin of all oppositions in the world, giving rise to a morphology of difference that includes what Hegel terms the "sex-relation" (das Geschlechtsverhältnis). My inquiry will examine the extent to which Hegel's understanding of the "sex-relation" informs his theory of artistic production, the work of the "genius," as a central mode by which humans work toward achieving self-consciousness and advance the dialectical progression toward Absolute Spirit. While the physiological effects of art are not on Hegel's agenda, his understanding of sexed bodies informs the hierarchies structuring the stunning dialectical progressions in his aesthetic theory. What we will find in the Aesthetics is, as Paul de Man has noted, a "double and possibly duplicitous text" (773), but not only because of an assumed disjunction between theorizing and experiencing literature. The doubleness of Hegel's aesthetic theory betrays a disruptive reliance on "woman," a category Hegel conflates with and reifies into maternity. Hegel uses his conceptualization of maternity to sustain and give meaning to the work of artistic genius, while placing the feminine and maternal as inferior, though necessary, elements in his philosophical schema. Rather than confirming the progression of dialectics, this contradictory deployment of maternity reveals a radical inability of Hegelian dialectics to maintain its own subsumptive hierarchies.

Homology and Hierarchy

Structuring this contradictory deployment is the lack of rigorous, sustained distinctions between "woman," "female," and "mother" in Hegel's texts.[2] As Irigaray notes, femininity in Hegel is "aware of no difference between itself and the maternal, or even the masculine, except one that is mediated by the abstract immediacy of *the* being (as) or by the rejection of *one* (as) being. The female lacks the operation of affirming its singular and universalizable link to one as self" (*Speculum* 224). Hegel's conflation of sexual anatomy and socialized gender is of a piece with a systemic hierarchy subsuming the "literal" under the regime of the "ideal," creating a sex/gender tautology: women are determined by their anatomy, an anatomy that in turn derives from the idea of "woman." Because this sex/gender tautology stands, with his aesthetics, within the "encyclopedic development of the whole of philosophy," I begin my investigation by looking to the *Encyclopedia of the Philosophical Sciences* for an indication of how sex/gender functions in his system. Specifically, I interrogate Hegel's theorizations of human reproduction for its physiological, psychological, and philosophical significance. This will serve as a foundation for understanding the "encyclopedic" links between sexed bodies, gender hierarchies, and aesthetic production.

In part 2 of the *Encyclopedia*, the *Philosophy of Nature*,[3] Hegel denies women any active or constitutive role in reproduction, a view based on the assumed homology between male and female reproductive organs. Late eighteenth- and early nineteenth-century European studies of human anatomy and physiology were shifting from such sexual homologies between males and females, to absolute sexual differences; Hegel relies on an older model of a male-defined homology to construct a hierarchical complementarity.[4] While "the same type underlies both the male and female genitals, in one or the other, one or the other part predominates: in the female it is necessarily the passivity [*das Indifferente*], in the male, the duality [*das Entzweite*] of opposition" (*Nature* 412–13). This is not a homology of equity. Hegelian opposition here requires a passive and an active dichotomy. This anatomical homology establishes the inferiority of the female in general: "Just as in the male, the uterus is reduced to a mere gland [the prostate], so, on the other hand, the male testicle remains enclosed in the ovary in the female, does not emerge into opposition, does not develop on its own account into active brain [*zum tätigen Gehirn*]; and the clitoris is inactive feeling [*das untätige Gefühl*] in general" (*Nature* 413). While female organs remain undeveloped in the male, this is of no great consequence to him, because (and perhaps for this very reason) he embodies duality and division. In the female, however, the simple, passive retention of the testicle in the ovary does not "split [*entzweit*] into the productive brain [the testicles] and the active heart [the penis] [*in das produzierende Gehirn und das äußerliche Herz*]" as it does in the male. "Through this difference, therefore, the male is the active principle [*das Tätige*], and the female is the receptive [*das Empfangende*], because she remains in her undeveloped unity" (*Nature* 413).

This complementary differentiation between male and female organs is an isomorph of the relationship between Spirit and its self-externalization into materiality. Anatomically the female (material) is implicit in the male (spiritual) as an extension of the man. However, he is implicit in her only for the sake of recognizing himself in her, self-recognition being, for Hegel, the route toward self-consciousness. The biological equivalent of this self-recognition and concomitant overcoming (*Aufhebung*) of difference between self and other is procreation. At this moment the hierarchized sexes become one, and this unity is materially manifested in their child; parents see in their children "the entirety of their union objectified" (*Right* 264). Yet procreation as sublation does not *equalize* the opposing genders; their respective roles in conception correspond to the dichotomy established in their anatomical differences:

> Procreation must not be reduced to the ovary and the male semen, as if the new product were merely a composition of the forms or parts of both sides; the truth is that the *material element is contained in the female*, but the *subjectivity is contained in the male*. Conception [*Die Empfängniß*—reception] is the contraction of the whole individual into the simple self-surrendering unity, into its representation [*in seine Vorstellung*]; the seed [*der Same*] is this simple representation itself—simply a single point, like the name and the entire self. Conception therefore, is nothing else but this, that the opposite moments, these abstract representations, become one. (*Nature* 413–14; my emphasis)

In this schema, women supply only the material element of the fetus, while men supply the "entire self." Women do not give subjectivity to their children; they merely "keep" the fetus, like an oven, until it is born. [5]

In the *Philosophy of Right* Hegel elevates these biological principles into social paradigms, arguing that the "natural determination of the two sexes obtains, through its rationality [*durch ihre Vernünftigkeit*], an intellectual and ethical significance" (*Right* 114). This tautological synthesis of anatomical sex and socialized gender reveals a number of cultural assumptions about women current among the German middle classes at the end of the eighteenth and beginning of the nineteenth centuries. Bourgeois ideals of family life as a safe haven of affective and intimate bonds, beyond the competitive and public world of men and their work, led to what Ute Frevert calls "the differentiation of a mother-role" (16). This "mother-role" became the paradigm of femininity for many middle-class households, Frevert argues, such that the female body's reproductive capacities defined the sphere of a woman's activities. The middle-class "mother-role" retained some of the functions of the feudal *Hausmutter*, while emphasizing more of an affective, nurturing, and thoroughly "maternal" femininity. This new type of middle-class femininity saw women exclusively as wives and mothers, demanding careful attentiveness to the needs of their husbands and children. "Motherhood was a lifelong duty," Frevert writes, "which became all the more important and character-moulding as the bourgeois family and sexual ideology of the late eighteenth century turned it into a profession with high socio-cultural status. The biologically and socially defined role of the mother was virtually tailored to her body: tight-fitting and impossible to cast off" (45). For Hegel the biological and social status of women were inseparable. In each, women were the inferior complements of men, from their pure "receptivity" during sexual intercourse, to their "natural" suitability for the ethical life of the family.

Hegel's particular way of incorporating historically contingent conceptualizations of anatomy displays a remarkable mediation between the "natural" and the "logical," underscoring the relative ease with which the two can be synthesized. Within Hegel's philosophy generally, "natural" sex/gender distinctions embody the type of "logical" opposition requisite in the material world for sublation (*Aufhebung*) and self-consciousness to occur. As he states in the *Philosophy of Mind*, part 3 of the *Encyclopedia*, "It is however in the sex-relationship that difference becomes actual and particular, exposing the real nature of the individual's opposition to itself" (*Spirit* 2:23). The priorities within a hierarchized homology of sex/gender complements is conceptually congruent to Hegel's larger dialectical scheme. We can see this congruence, for example, in the relationship between Spirit and Nature in the *Philosophy of Nature:* "God," claims Hegel, "is subjectivity, activity [*Tätigkeit*], infinite actuosity, in which otherness is only a moment" (*Nature* 15). The transience, materiality, the radical otherness of Nature must be sublated (*aufgehoben*) in order to progress toward self-consciousness and the unity of Absolute Spirit:

> The goal of Nature is to destroy itself and to break through its husk of immediacy and sensuousness, to consume itself like the phoenix in order to come forth [*hervorzutreten*] from this external-ity rejuvenated as Spirit. . . . True, Nature is the immediate—but even so, as the other of Spirit, its existence is a relativity: and so, as the negative, is only *posited, derivative* [*nur ein Gesetztes*] . . . Spirit, because it is the goal of Nature, is *prior* to it, Nature has proceeded from Spirit [*aus ihn hervorgegangen*]. Spirit, therefore, itself proceeding, in the first instance, from the imme-diate, but then abstractly apprehending itself, wills to achieve its own liberation by fashioning [*herausbildend*] Nature out of itself; this action of Spirit is philosophy. (*Nature* 444; my emphasis)

The hierarchically divided roles of Spirit and Nature echo the anatomical roles defining male and female. Each side of the relation is necessary to the other, but in the movement of Hegel's systemic logic the unity of these related terms merely reestablishes the value of one over and above the other. Females and Nature are necessary derivatives of males and Spirit, that is, necessary for the latter's progression. As "others," females and Nature are derivative copies of a male and masculinized origin. They seem to exist only for the sake of Spirit's movement toward self-consciousness, a redemptive vision of a return to a more complex unity through the vehicle of the other. As Hegel states quite clearly in his *System of Ethical Life,* "The sexes are plainly in a relation to one another, one the universal, the other the particular; they are not absolutely equal" (110).

Spiritual Illness

However, Hegel does not always characterize women as passive comple-ments in procreation. Whereas the *Philosophy of Nature* claims that women do not give subjectivity to the fetus, the *Philosophy of Mind* establishes a more determinative maternal influence. This discussion of the prenatal occurs in the context of outlining the stages in the determinate life of the soul, and here we require a slight digression into Hegel's "Anthropology," the inquiry into the first stages of the soul's progression toward consciousness. Hegel delineates three principal stages: the natural soul (*die natürliche Seele*), the feeling soul (*die fühlende Seele*), and the actual soul (*die wirkliche Seele*). The natural soul is the first form of determinateness that soul, as being, develops into: a naturality that is at the same time a "totality," and as such is a bodily simulacrum or "likeness of the Concept [*Abbild des Begriff*]" (*Spirit* 2:230). Since this totality includes both physical and spiritual determinations, the natural soul for Hegel is "the place for the racial varieties of mankind and the spiritual differences between nations" (*Spirit* 2:23).[6]

The next stage, the feeling soul, occupies a rather contestive place in the anthropological *Bildung* of the soul. At this juncture the soul is midway between the totality of natural determinations, and the singular freedom of self-consciousness achieved by the actual soul under the rubric of the individual ego (*das Ich*). Thus the stage of the feeling soul is marked by the "singularization" of universals; the clearest example of this is sex/gender. The complementary differences of sex/gender exemplify the appearance of "universal" qualities "taken back into the unity of the human soul" (*Spirit* 2:23). Within the feeling soul "differences cease to be external," and become manifested within the individual soul itself, so that it becomes self-divided. This self-division reveals the "struggle for liberation which the soul has to wage against the immediacy of its substantial content in order to complete its self-mastery and become adequate to its Concept, in order to make itself into what it is implicitly or in accordance with its Concept, i.e., the simple self-relating subjectivity existing within the ego" (*Spirit* 2:213).

This struggle to develop the ego from within the prisonhouse of bodily, sentient existence occurs itself through three stages. The first involves the "dreaming through" (*Durchträumen*) and "divining" (*Ahnen*) of the soul's "natural life." The second stage is "the standpoint of derangement [*Verrücktheit*], that is to say of the soul at variance with itself" (*Spirit* 2:215). "In the third stage," Hegel argues, "the soul finally becomes master of its natural individuality, its corporeity, reducing it to a *subservient means* and projecting out of itself, as an objective world, the content of its substantial totality *not belonging to its corporeity*. Having reached this goal, the soul emerges into the abstract freedom of the ego and so becomes consciousness" (*Spirit* 2:215; my emphasis). As the feeling soul progresses beyond the mere naturality of one's body, the actual soul posits, through the agency of the ego, the feeling soul itself as an other to sublate and progress beyond:[7]

> Ego, the universal, the being-for-self of the soul [*die Seele für sich*], proceeds from nowhere but the sphere of feeling [*Gefühls-sphäre*]. It is by this that it is conditioned [*bedingt*], this is the ego's other, only its feeling is its other, and it determines itself as such, it being only through *the negation of the form or mode of feeling* that the ego is for itself. . . . It *is* only in that it relates to an object, and this object is the feeling it contains. . . . [The ego] expels the determinations of its feeling from out of itself and has them before itself as an object, a world. (*Spirit* 3:285; my emphasis)

The feeling soul helps to pave the path toward consciousness by becoming itself an "other" for the actual soul to objectify, sublate, and overcome. Just as feeling opposed itself to bodily determinations, so the ego must oppose itself to feeling and in this way progress dialectically beyond it.

The feeling soul as a point of mediation between determination and freedom, Nature and Spirit, resembles the position that "beautiful art" occupies, which for Hegel can mediate (in the context of Spirit's development toward self-consciousness in Absolute Spirit) between "immediate sensuousness and ideal thought"; but this point will be taken up later. More important for my purposes here, in this stage of feeling "the soul opposes itself to its substantiality, stands over against itself [*sich selber gegenübertritt*], and in its determinate sensations at the same time attains to the consciousness of its totality, but a consciousness which is not yet objective but only subjective" (*Spirit* 2:205). This self-division characteristic of the feeling soul necessitates considering it as a "diseased state" (*Krankheit*). "In this sphere," Hegel explains,

> there prevails a conflict between the freedom and unfreedom of the soul; for, on the one hand, soul is still fettered to its substantiality, conditioned by its naturalness, while, on the other hand, it is beginning to separate itself from its substance, from its naturalness, and is thus raising itself to the intermediate

stage between its immediate, natural life and objective, free consciousness [*sich somit auf die Mittelstuffe zwischen ihren unmittelbare Natürleben und dem objektiven freien Bewußtsein erhebt*]. (*Spirit* 2:205)

Far from a smooth transition to the Ideal and universal, "this stage of mind is the stage of its darkness [*Dunkelheit* 'obscurity']" (*Spirit* 2:219). It represents a state of mind "to which the soul, which has already advanced to consciousness and intelligence, may again sink down. It is the *incongruity* involved in the truer form of Spirit in a *subordinate* abstract existence that constitutes the diseased state [*Krankheit*]" (*Spirit* 2:221; my emphasis). We must both pass through and subsequently avoid this "life of feeling," for it represents a plague of the soul, a spiritual illness. As the very definition of disease, this stage can potentially reverse the hierarchy between Spirit and Nature and allow the *Geist* within us to be subdued, ruled, lorded over, either by an internal or an external agent. In the *Fragment on the Philosophy of Spirit*, Hegel says directly that the characteristics of the feeling soul "belong . . . only to a state and stage of spiritual disease, of Spirit's having sunk beneath the power of its true dignity to a lower determinate being [*Dasein*]" (*Spirit* 1:99). While sentience and feeling allow the subject to relate to itself, it is still "generally determined and limited" because it "is not in control of itself [*ist sie ihrer selbst nicht mächtig*]" (*Spirit* 1:35).

At this point Hegel's description of the state of the feeling soul represents a curious moment within the soul's dialectical development. On the one hand, the feeling soul emerges out of the simple self-unity characterizing the natural soul, and begins to manifest self-division. This self-division involves an opposition between the "freedom" and "unfreedom" of the soul, an intermediate state between its "immediate natural life" and "objective free consciousness." Yet because the implicit consciousness or germ of *Geist* can occupy a *subordinate* position in the feeling soul, this state does not *necessarily* embody *dialectical* opposition. Rather, it can disrupt the teleology of proper opposition because it involves the domination of the soul by that which either does not directly represent Spirit, or eschews opposition altogether. "The life of feeling," Hegel argues, "as a form or state of the self-conscious, cultured [*gebildeten*], self-possessed human being, is a disease, in which the individual relates itself *without mediation* to the concrete content of itself" (*Spirit* 2:243; my emphasis). In this state the subject has not yet attained self-reflection, and therefore is "passive" (*Spirit* 2:221). While this stage seems to inaugurate the subject's self-division, which enables dialectical progression, it also involves the absence of properly teleological mediation or opposition. The feeling soul embodies a self-division curiously characterized by the absence of *dialectical* duality. It embodies a paradoxically oppositionless division between materiality, its "concrete content," and consciousness. The feeling soul possesses a content in which "the universal and the singular, the subjective and the objective, have not yet become separated. At this stage, what I feel, I am, and what I am, I feel" (*Spirit* 2:207). The life of feeling represents the very essence of disease, a "passive" state that consciousness must continually objectify, or else "sink down" once again into a dehierarchized hyper-aesthesia. True self-consciousness, it would seem, the "truer form of Spirit," must be continually anaesthetized.

The predominance of feeling, the determinant of the soul's identity and being at this stage, can involve not just an internal passivity, but also the subject's domination by and merging with another soul—a phenomenon found in "magic relationships." Examples of such "magic relationships," Hegel writes, include instances of "animal magnetism" and close relationships "between friends, especially neuraesthenic female friends [*zwischen . . . nervenschwachen Freundinnen*]—a relationship which may go so far as to show magnetic phenomena—between husband and wife, and between members of a family" (*Spirit* 2:223). Yet it is the mother-fetus relationship that for Hegel most exemplifies such "magic relationships" of the feeling soul.[8] It is at this point that Hegel outlines a more powerful maternal influence than that described in the *Philosophy of Nature*. While the soul of a mother "dominates" that of a fetus, this domination involves fluidity rather than an absolute division and opposition. The prenatal represents "the condition of life in which *opposition is completely absent*" (*Spirit* 2:105; my emphasis). Moreover, Hegel argues that "the unborn child . . . is identical with the mother" (*Spirit* 2:103). We must progress beyond this state through birth and subsequently achieve self-consciousness so as to advance the self-adequation of Spirit.

Yet at the same time, Hegel explains how a subject carries the mark of its mother's determinative prenatal influence, the mark of this diseased, nonmediated, oppositionless, and fluid state. In the second section of the *Encyclopedia* a mother only gives a child its material, physical existence, but in the third section this influence incorporates and hovers between the physical and the psychic, suspended in an ambiguous relationship between them. This influence of a mother on a fetus

> manifests itself in the phenomena that go by the name of birthmarks [*Muttermale*]. Much that has been included under this heading may well have simply an organic cause. There are however many physiological phenomena which, since they have quite evidently been brought about through the sensation of the mother, undoubtedly have a *fundamentally psychic origination* [*eine psychische Ursache*]. (*Spirit* 2:237; my emphasis)[9]

Moles, blotches, discolorations, birth defects, and other such physiological "accidents" are the physical traces of a mother's psychic prenatal influence. The *mal* of *Muttermal* means sign, mark, stigma, stain, spot; it also can mean a point or duration of time. It is related to the word *malen*, to paint, portray, represent; *Maler* means "painter," and *Malerei* is "painting." The birthmark is thus the sign of a mother's psychic relation to a fetus "painted" onto its body. Does this psychic relation entail only the marking of a fetal body, or does the birthmark function, beyond wordplay, as a sign for something deeper, more detailed and determinative?

Genial Bodies

In the *Philosophy of Mind* Hegel deploys the mother-fetus relation both to explain the concept of Genius, and to delineate a determinative maternal function in shaping a subject's identity. This occurs first through comparing the Genius to a mother, and second through explicitly identifying the mother herself as a Genius. This is not the artistic genius, *das Genie*, but *der Genius*, meaning spirit or guardian angel (like the "Genius" of a certain locale in mythology; I have capitalized *der Genius* [Genius] in translation to distinguish it from *das Genie* [genius]). *Der Genius* signifies, in a general sense, one's individuality and uniqueness as a subject, while *das Genie* more closely approximates the contemporary connotations of the English word "genius." However, both words originate in the Latin *gen-*, root of *gignere*, meaning to beget. And the

Latin ultimately derives from the Greek *gignesthai*, to be born, to come into being. Both words in the German carry the root of conception and birth, but are assigned different, gendered functions in Hegel's system. Genius, *der Genius*, denotes a mother's *active* prenatal influence, an influence that paradoxically defines the *passivity* of spiritual disease because it curiously embodies the absence of mediation and teleological opposition. Moreover, one's Genius after birth is the trace one carries of this maternal domination, the Genius itself ruling over the subject who has not shed individuality for the freedom of self-conscious universality. A subject continues to be dominated by Genius (its own or someone else's), the psychic trace of its mother, in the passivity of the "magic relationships" of the feeling soul. In this respect, Genius represents the threat not only of improperly subordinating one (gendered) element of the psyche over another, but also of allowing this element to disperse hierarchy, to confuse and intermingle one's mental life in a diseased stew of nonmediation. At the same time, Hegel reserves genius, *das Genie*, for the active, "masculine" production of art. In the *Philosophy of Right* Hegel claims that

> Women are capable of education, but they are not made for activities which demand a universal faculty such as the more advanced sciences [*für die höheren Wissenschaften*], philosophy, and certain forms of artistic production. Women may have flights of fancy [*Einfälle*], taste, and elegance, but cannot attain to the Ideal [*aber das Ideale haben sie nicht*]. (*Right* 263)[10]

Hegel's *Aesthetics* is an attempt to delimit precisely a "masculine," Ideal, universal aspect of art that will justify aesthetics as a proper science. To understand how Hegel's conceptualization of maternity is simultaneously necessary to and erased within this endeavor, we need to explore the network of logic tying together the work of the "womb" and the masculine realm of artistic production: how maternity is figured as both active and passive.[11]

The focal point for uncovering this network, this matrix, is the subject's Genius, *der Genius*. The Genius is the "determining particularity of man, that which, in all situations and relationships, decides his action and his fate." It is what an individual is "*inwardly*, determined in a particular manner" (*Spirit* 2:239). In essence it signifies the subject's uniqueness and individuality, as opposed to its universality. Hegel explains the determinative relationship between a subject and its Genius in this way:

> Even consciousness, which consists of an alert understanding moving in universal determinations, is determined by its Genius in such an overpowering [übermächtige] manner, that the individual's relationship here appears to be that of a dependence [unselbständigkeit—helplessness, lack of originality] which might be compared with the reliance of the fetus upon the soul of the mother, or the passive manner in which the soul acquires a representation [Vorstellung] of its individual world in dreaming. (Spirit 2:241)

Here Hegel relies on a psychologized relationship between mother and fetus, as well as on the dream state, to explain the determinative force of the Genius on the individual's life. This force "draws together into one both the moment of the soul's simple unity with itself contained in natural dreaming, and that of the *duality in the life of the soul* present in the relationship of the fetus to the mother" (Spirit 2:241; my emphasis). Significantly, a woman's ability to bear a child gives her a "duality of soul" usually reserved solely for men (anatomically, socially, and politically), and for the movement of Spirit.

However, when Hegel directly outlines a maternal influence on a fetus, this relationship is no longer just a metaphor for the Genius–self duality; a mother is not only like a Genius, she is a Genius:

> The mother is the child's Genius, a Genius being understood here in the usual way as the selfhood and totality of spirit in so far as it exists for itself and constitutes the subjective substantiality of another which is only posited externally as an individual, and which has only a formal being-for-self [ein formelles Fürsichsein]. The substantial being of Genius is the entire totality of determinate being, life and character, not merely as a possibility, aptitude, or implicitness, but as effectiveness and activation, as concrete subjectivity. (Spirit 2:221–23)

A fetus is "permeable and resistant," dependent on its mother for its "subjective substantiality," for the "selfhood of its individuality." A mother gives her child more than moles and blotches; she gives it character, endows its subjectivity with substance. This individualization, far from a mere possibility, actually constitutes the active, effective, concrete life of subjectivity. This aspect of the subject, its Genius or individuality, is thus the *psychic* birthmark given by its mother.

How do mothers achieve this psychic shaping of their children? In a suggestive passage, Hegel states that this shaping cannot be reduced to the physiological relationship between mother and fetus; this would be "nothing more than a sensuous and reflective consideration of an external, anatomical and physiological existence" (*Spirit* 2:223). The physical and the psychic birthmark, the blotch and the Genius, signify more than "violent dispositional disturbances and injuries" experienced by a pregnant woman. They point toward the "entire psychic originary-differentiation [*Urteil* 'judgment'] of substance, in which the female nature, like the monocotyledons in the vegetable world, can split itself in two [*in sich entzweibrechen kann*]" (*Spirit* 2:223). *Urteil* here is ambiguous; its usual meaning of "judgment" does not immediately make sense in this context. The etymology of the German word implies an originary (*Ur-*) act of division (*-teil*) between two or more things. This understands judgment as a primary mode of discrimination and differentiation. Thus *Urteil* here draws our attention to the "originary," *psychic* nature of this ability to sunder oneself, the ability of a woman to "split herself in two," to sustain a "duality in the life of the soul." It is not just a determinate, biological fact of female anatomy; it is also "psychic," an act of judgment.[12]

This psychic ability of a woman to sunder herself in the act of conception comes dangerously close to the very essence of Spirit: the capability, indeed the necessity, to sunder itself, to undergo a self-alienation, and thus to manifest itself otherwise and yet leave its own mark. This proximity seems both to originate in and yet also to motivate Hegel's system of dialectical oppositions and progressions. The congruence between maternity and Spirit would seem to threaten the very distinction between that which is "prior" and that which is "derivative," a distinction central to the logical movement of Hegelian dialectics. Hegel's *Aesthetics* betrays a certain anxiety about the threat of such a conceptual congruity, especially in his use of maternity as a model for artistic production.[13] As we shall see, however, Hegel's philosophical conceptualization of the maternal body sustains the very birth of aesthetics as a properly philosophical discourse.

Artistic Conceptions

Hegel's understanding of art depends in the first instance upon articulating key oppositions: Spirit, Ideal, content, and universality stand against Nature, materiality, form, feeling, and contingency. These oppositions recall the general formulation of male as universal and female as particular. For Hegel an understanding of art relies on recognizing the hierarchized opposition between form (particularity, materiality) and content (universality, spirituality) working through both generic typologies and historical periods (divided by Hegel into Symbolic, Classical, and Romantic art). "[T]he work of art," he claims, "brings before us the eternal powers that govern history without this appendage of the immediate sensuous present and its unstable appearance" (*Aesthetics* 1:9). This transparency, through which the universal in art appears, enables a kind of spiritual liberation: "Art liberates the true content of phenomena from the pure appearance and deception of this bad, transitory world, and gives them a higher actuality, born of the spirit" (*Aesthetics* 1:8–9). Yet art needs materiality to exist, to come into being, to effect this liberation. For this reason art mediates between the materiality of form and the pure spirituality of content:

> What [Spirit] wants is sensuous presence which indeed should remain sensuous, but liberated from the scaffolding of its purely material nature. Thereby the sensuous aspect of a work of art, in comparison with the immediate existence of things in nature, is elevated to a pure appearance, and the work of art stands in the middle between immediate sensuousness and ideal thought. (*Aesthetics* 1:38)

"In this way," writes Hegel, "the sensuous aspect of art is spiritualized." Yet this pure appearance is still not what truly concerns a science of art. "[T]he external appearance [of art] has no immediate value for us; we assume behind it something inward, a meaning whereby the external appearance is endowed with the spirit [*begeistet* 'inspired']" (*Aesthetics* 1:19). The inspired status of true art is congruent to the human subject; both are "spiritualized sensuousness," mediations between Spirit and Nature: "Similarly [to the work of art], the spirit and the soul shine through the human eye, through a man's face, flesh, skin, through his whole figure, and here the meaning is always something wider than what shows itself in the immediate appearance" (*Aesthetics* 1:20).[14] This congruence between the work of art and the human subject would seem to necessitate similar conceptions: Who begets art? Where is the "womb" out of which art is born?

These questions do not have simple answers, for it appears there are at least two points of origin. Art's ultimate origin, as of everything, is Spirit. But Spirit needs "a subjective productive activity as its cause. . . . This activity [*Tätigkeit*] is the imagination of the artist" (*Aesthetics* 1:280). Spirit needs an artist's creative imagination in a similar way that males and females need each other to conceive. According to Hegel, in conception a man gives a child its subjective universality, the seed of Spirit in each human contracted into the sperm, while a woman provides its substance and Genius, the determined and particular aspect of its material, physical form and its inner, psychic life. In this sense a man "inspires" a child, while a woman gives form to this inspiration, determines it, gives it shape and personality. This form-giving function of maternity is precisely the function of imaginative activity, *Tätigkeit*, a word used by Hegel to refer usually to "masculine" activity alone. In the *Philosophy of Nature* the male reproductive role was the active (*das Tätige*), while the female was the passive/receptive (*das Empfangende*). The testicles represented active brain (*das tätige Gehirn*), while the clitoris represented inactive feeling (*das untätige Gefühl*). The congruence between the work of the "womb" and the imaginative activity of the artistic genius indicates that "conceptual activity" oscillates between a "paternal" and a "maternal" resonance. Hegel further emphasizes the congruence between his understanding of the imagination and the "womb" by restricting the place of artistic conception to the "subjective inner consciousness"; this inner consciousness shapes and forms art before it is "born into actuality [*herausgeboren*]." While Hegel seems to adopt a kind of "womb envy," such envy at the same time seems to motivate an exclusion, an assigned irrelevance. This "maternal" or "womblike" geography and activity of artistic production is mentioned "only to say that it is to be excluded from the area of scientific discussion, or at least that it permits of a few generalities only—although a question often raised is, from where does the artist derive this gift and ability of conception and execution, and how does he create a work of art?" (*Aesthetics* 1:280). Hegel sees nothing beyond this question but the spurious need for a recipe or formula for genius, a decidedly unscientific topic. But this is precisely the question raised by the incommensurability between Hegel's oppositional hierarchies and his conceptual congruities. Hegel's aesthetic theory opposes everything coded feminine to Spirit and true art while appropriating maternity, the true calling of Hegelian womanhood, as the enabling figure and identity for the *conception* (in both senses) of imaginative genius.

Yet an artist's productive imagination is linked not just metaphorically to the "womb," for Hegel's true artistic genius *by definition* occupies a maternal position. In the *Philosophy of Mind* a mother is the Genius of a fetus; not only does she undergo a psychic self-sundering of substance in the act of conception, but also she gives a child its determinate, particular character, its own Genius, the psychic birthmark of its mother. In the *Aesthetics* artistic genius of necessity functions similarly in relation to the work of art:

> Just as beauty is the Idea [*Idee*] made real in the sensuous and actual world, and the work of art takes what is spiritual and sets it out into the immediacy of existence for apprehension by eye and ear, so too the artist must fashion his work not in the exclusively spiritual form of thought, but within the sphere of intuition [*Anschauung*] and feeling [*Empfindung*], and, more precisely, in connection with sensuous material and in a sensuous medium. Therefore this artistic creation, like art throughout, includes in itself the aspect of immediacy and naturalness, and it is this aspect which the subject cannot generate [*hervorbringen*] in himself, but must find in himself as *immediately given*. This alone is the sense in which we may say that genius and talent must be inborn [*angeboren*]. (*Aesthetics* 1:284; my emphasis)

The ability to give immediacy and naturalness to a work of art, to realize it in its sensuousness, its material form and external appearance, cannot arise sui generis in an artist. This ability comes from his birth, what he is born with, and works through the spheres of intuition and feeling. This would suggest that creativity is a kind of regression into the "magic relationships" of the feeling soul, epitomized by the mother-fetus relation. Thus an artist cannot procreate (*hervorbringen*) art independent of his prenatal past. This inborn ability aligns with an artist's "natural impulse and immediate need to give form [*gestalten*] to everything he feels and imagines" (*Aesthetics* 1:286). In this sense artistic imagination and its productive activity originate in the prenatal state (are inborn), and retain the mark of maternity precisely because they duplicate both its physical and psychic procreative abilities.

However, the hierarchized terms by which Hegel's science of art functions logically denies such congruences, creating what Irigaray has termed "an isomorphism which must remain vigorously masked" ("Subject" 73). We see this operating in Hegel's theory of artistic inspiration, which attempts to redistribute a hierarchized difference between universal and particular, but in the process succeeds only in radically undermining such distinctions. For Hegel inspiration introduces the universal (spiritual) into the work of art. But for this to happen an artist himself must undergo a curious self-negation. Inspiration is "nothing but being completely filled with the theme, being entirely present in the theme, and not resting until the theme has been stamped and polished into artistic shape" (*Aesthetics* 1:288). Lest the particularity (the Genius) of a genius overpower or somehow dilute the universality of his theme, he must entirely forget himself as a particular individual, efface his *Muttermal* and his *Genius*: "But if the artist has made the subject matter into something entirely his own, he must on the other hand be able to forget his subjective particularity and its accidental particularities and immerse himself, for his part, entirely in his material, so that, as subject, he is only as it were *the form for the formation of the theme* which has taken hold of him" (*Aesthetics* 1:288; my emphasis). By forgetting that which was maternally given to him, his "subjective particularity," an artist paradoxically becomes more explicitly like a Hegelian mother, the "form for the formation of the theme." In order to be a genius, one must both have and not have Genius. In order to give birth to the universal in art, an artist must erase his maternal legacy. The logic of universality, dependent on both the inspiration and the exclusion of the self, must in the end rely on the maternal function it seeks to go beyond.

Formulating the feminine/maternal as an alterity to be overcome seems only to ensure a disruptive return of the repressed. In the *Aesthetics* Hegel utilizes maternity as the vehicle for understanding artistic creativity, yet at the same time excludes women as participants in such creativity. The enabling presence of maternity, in turn, forces the revelation of a birth that the *Aesthetics* both denies and duplicates. Through the activity of creative genius, maternity engenders the very object of study in the *Aesthetics*, and constitutes the alterior, excluded other of aesthetics *as a science* (*Wissenschaft* 'knowledge-creation'); indeed, it is this very exclusion that enables the conception of both art and philosophical aesthetics. Hegel associates the realm of subjective feeling, so central to most eighteenth-century European aesthetics, with the spiritually "diseased" state of the feeling soul, a state exemplified by, and originating in, the dominion of maternity. Hegel's own aesthetic theory must therefore excise this realm of maternal domination to ensure a properly dialectical, philosophical aesthetic theory. When justifying his philosophical enterprise, Hegel acknowledges that it "may look as if it would be inappropriate and pedantic to treat with scientific seriousness what is not itself of a serious nature. In any case, in this view, art appears as a superfluity, even if the softening of the heart which preoccupation with beauty can produce does not altogether become detrimental as effeminacy [*Verweichlichung*]" (*Aesthetics* 1:3–4). Hegel responds to this view by claiming that the justification for his science of a supposedly "effeminate" subject originates in and is presupposed by philosophy in general. He claims that it is "the task of an encyclopedic development of the whole of philosophy . . . to prove the Idea of the beautiful" (*Aesthetics* 1:25). The "effeminacy" of art as an object of philosophical scrutiny is displaced onto the philosophical task of the *Encyclopedia*, and yet returns through the metaphorics of maternity, for the Idea of the beautiful must be derived "necessarily from the presuppositions which antecede it in philosophy, out of whose womb it is born [*aus deren Schoße sie geboren wird*]" (*Aesthetics* 1:25). Philosophy thus has the "womb" that gives birth to the very possibility of the *Aesthetics*, a science that attempts both to appropriate and to efface Hegel's own conceptualization of a maternal femininity.

Philosophy's Belly-Button

In the section on "Absolute Mind" in the *Philosophy of Mind*, Hegel began to formulate aesthetics as a particular branch of philosophy, one that grasps and understands the essence of art.[15] Philosophy itself, as a science, is "the unity of Art and Religion. . . . Philosophy not only keeps them together in a totality, but also unifies them into the simple spiritual intuition [*Anschauung*], and then is raised [*erhoben ist*] to self-conscious thought" (*Mind* 302). The ontological identity of philosophy thus depends upon grasping its objects, art and religion, and raising them to their Ideality. Philosophy as such arises consequently out of the dialectical movement between Spirit and Nature occurring in each of these two realms of human activity. Out of this logical movement comes the "Idea of philosophy," a syllogism that has "self-knowing reason, the absolutely universal, for its middle [Mitte], which divides itself into Mind and Nature. . . . The self-judging [das Sich-Urteilen] of the Idea into its two appearances (secs. 575, 576) characterizes both as its [self-knowing reason's] manifestations" (Mind 314). The "womb" of philosophy that gives birth to aesthetics is itself the product of a peculiar birth. The Idea of philosophy is a syllogism hinged by die Mitte, the middle, the mean, the navel. What would the logical middle as navel signify? What would following such a paradigmatic possibility of language entail without subordinating it to a cancellation within a teleological hierarchy, a strict dialectical logic? I want to exploit this possibility, to see Mitte not just as "middle" but also as "navel," and thus to pull this hidden thread and untangle the effacements woven into the fabric of Hegel's philosophical enterprise.

While philosophy in its ideality epitomizes logical thought (the syllogism), such logic carries the mark of its birth, its Mitte or navel, a birth out of the "fetal" state of the feeling soul. For only after we have progressed beyond this "diseased" condition can we even begin to think of or to do philosophy, to realize its ideality. The dialectical progression to philosophy is marked by a literal and metaphoric birth of Spirit and the human subject out of the nonmediated, diseased prenatal state, where Geist is dominated by the form and the soul of the mother. It has escaped the magic relationship of fluid identity within the "womb," where subject and object cannot be properly discerned in the obscurity and darkness of the soul's illness. In the preface to the Phenomenology of Spirit, Hegel describes the "sunburst" that "in one flash" heralds a new epoch of philosophico-scientific thought and activity: "But just as the first breath drawn by a child after its long, quiet nourishment breaks the gradualness of merely quantitative growth—there is a qualitative leap, and the child is born—so likewise the Spirit in its formation matures slowly and quietly into its new shape" (Phenomenology 6). The Hegelian enterprise itself supposedly signified this "birth-time" and "period of transition to a new era." At the center of this new era's "infinite" spiraling is "Self-knowing reason," "the absolutely universal," the Mitte or navel of the syllogism forming the Idea of philosophy; as such, it signals the "maternal" function of philosophy itself. This syllogistic navel, self-knowing reason, marks the division of the Idea of Philosophy "into Mind and Nature" through the process of "self-judging" (*Sich-Urteilen*). "Self-judging," the ability to effect an "originary differentiation" that distinguishes "judgment" (*Urteil*) as a particular mode, characterizes not only the division of philosophy, but also that of the Hegelian mother, her psychic ability to divide herself in two at conception. Philosophy has escaped the spiritual illness of the "womb" through birth, only to have the mark of its birth, its syllogistic navel, render philosophy as the/a mother science.

Hegel's conceptualization of women as beings constituted through a maternal femininity occupies what Irigaray calls the "mute outside that sustains all systematicity; as a maternal and still silent ground that nourishes all foundations" (*Speculum* 365). It is in this sense that the *Aesthetics* is double, as is Hegel's conceptualization of philosophy, sundering themselves in two. The very dependence on this doubling, the simultaneous denial and appropriation of women and their procreative abilities within Hegel's corpus, *as well as* the need for (literal and metaphoric) birth to *conceive* of these texts, betrays the sustaining metaphoricity of Hegelian maternity, the continual infection of Hegelian dialectics with a spiritual "disease." Like the creative genius who must efface his maternal legacy in order to give birth to inspired art, the "effeminacy" of the Ideal of beauty must be denied and suppressed in order for philosophy to give birth to a proper science of art. The *Aesthetics*, as both the "child" of philosophy and the "mother" of its own particular subject, marks and is marked by this continual return of maternity, the begetter and birthmark of this discursive birth. This paradoxical relation to maternity in the science of art perhaps stems from the reluctant maternity of its own "mother," philosophy itself. This master discourse turns upon the syllogistic navel marking its escape from the fluid, unmediated, diseased illogic of the "womb." Yet this "birthmark" or navel structuring logic itself, ensures that philosophy will duplicate the mother's "judgment" as it divides itself (*Sich-Urteilen*) and engenders the aesthetic conception.

Sustaining such radical dissymmetries is a network of contradictions that is not easily reconciled within the Hegelian system: Do these contradictory effacements and retentions threaten to destructure what Irigaray (*Speculum* 217) has termed the "dialectic produced by the discourse of patriarchy"? Or can they be absorbed into the structuring movement of Hegelian dialectics itself? Rather than a dialectical sub-sumption, these returns of the repressed seem more of a piece with resistant moments in the Hegelian text, where the ideological presuppositions of a historically contingent logic of sex/gender produce disruptions against the speculative hegemony of Hegelian dialectics. This hegemony involves not only the transformation of the "natural" into the "logical," but also the conceptual appropriation of human productive activity, human *labor*, as a theoretical groundwork, as the very fuel of conceptual activity. As Marx noted, this appropriation is symptomatic of the basic contradiction within German philosophy at the time: the "opposition inside thought itself of abstract thought and sensuous reality or real sensuous experience" (100). Hegel's theorizations of sex/gender are central to this opposition, and reveal the appropriation (and erasure) of reproductive activity, of maternal labor as a fundamental condition of possibility for the idealist conceptualization of artistic labor, if not labor in general.[16] The primacy placed on (physical, conceptual, philosophical) birth in these texts suggests that the movement of Hegelian dialectics is continually intercepted by a reliance on and duplication of that which it seeks to go beyond. If dialectics is to retain a critical utility, as Althusser remarks, there can be no nostalgia for Hegel, no "yearning after the simplicity of the Hegelian 'womb' " (217 n. 50).

Notes

1. My inquiry owes a great deal to a number of feminist analyses of Hegel, especially those by Irigaray (*Speculum* 214–26; see also Chapter 2, this volume) and Schor (23–41; see also Chapter 6, this volume). More generally, my investigation takes as one of its points of departure Gayatri Spivak's comment that "the discourse of man is in the metaphor of woman" ("Displacement" 169). See also Jardine for an excellent analysis of the metaphoric function of "woman" in twentieth-century French thought.

2. The possible exception would be the sororal function of Antigone in the *Phenomenology* (see Irigaray, *Speculum* 214–26; see also Chapter 2, this volume). Throughout this article I shall generally use the term "sex/gender," when referring to either Hegel's theory of anatomical sex or his theory of gender roles, to indicate the mutual reliance of these two spheres in Hegel's thought. For Hegel, a woman's sex defines her gender; at the same time historically contingent constructions of gender inform his theory of anatomical sex. Moreover, as I shall discuss below, Hegel relied on both anatomical homologies *and* absolute differences to define what he saw as the anatomical and social relation between men and women; the relations between male and female sex/gender were characterized by hierarchical complementarities. While contemporary distinctions between sex and gender may seem anachronistic, fore-grounding Hegel's lack of such a distinction can help throw into relief his naturalization of gender hierarchies. This naturalization is especially apparent in Hegel's conflation of maternity

and femininity. Joan Scott has convincingly shown how meanings attached to maternity fluctuate historically, revealing the often regressive gender politics, based on the regulation of female sexuality, that can attend a universalized valorization of "the maternal." Other analyses of the difficulties of conflating "feminine" and "maternal," and of employing an ahistorical and/or totalizing conceptualization of maternity, include those by Butler (*Gender* 66), Friedman, Goux (146–48), Grimshaw (227–53), Spivak ("French"), and Stanton.

3. All quotations from the *Philosophy of Nature* are based on Miller's translation with some modifications of my own; all page numbers refer to this edition. Unless otherwise noted, all quotations from the third section of the *Encyclopedia*, the *Philosophy of Mind*, are from Petry's translation (in a dual-language edition entitled *Hegel's Philosophy of Subjective Spirit*) with some modifications of my own, modifications drawn in part from Wallace and Miller's complete translation of the *Philosophy of Mind*; all page numbers for this section refer to the Petry translation. (I should note that whereas Petry translates *Begriff* as "Notion," I have preferred to use "Concept.") All quotations from the *Philosophy of Right* and the *Aesthetics* are from Knox's translations, with some modifications of my own; all page numbers refer to these editions. The German edition used throughout is Moldenhauer and Michel's edition of Hegel's *Werke*. Generally I have quoted the English translations as they stand, except where they seem to obscure a particular feature of a passage (its logic, syntax, or vocabulary) that I want to emphasize.

4. For an excellent analysis of this shift in European anatomy and physiology, see Laqueur (149–92). Because he relies both on complementarity and incommensurability between men and women, Hegel seems to stand on either side of this shift. Other analyses of the gender politics of biology and reproductive theories that have been helpful for me include those by Jordanova, Schiebinger, and Tuana.

5. Derrida discusses these passages and others from the *Philosophy of Nature*, as well as Hegel's analysis of *Antigone*, in *Glas* (see especially 110–17), with regard to gender and the family in Hegel's philosophy. Irigaray also introduces her chapter on Hegel in *Speculum* with a quotation from this section of the *Philosophy of Nature*.

6. Sander Gilman has usefully explored some of the ways racial categories influenced Hegel's thought; see also Gasché's essay on Hegel and Orientalism.

7. This explanation occurs in the appendix: "The Phenomenology of Spirit (Summer Term, 1825)."

8. For an investigation of the impact of mesmerism, or animal magnetism, on late eighteenth- and early nineteenth-century German medicine and natural philosophy (including those of Fichte and Hegel), see Engelhardt. Goethe's *Elective Affinities* similarly understands close affective, as well as romantic, relationships according to a quasi-chemical paradigm like animal magnetism. In 1811 the German physician Friedrich Hufeland had also metaphorically linked the mother-fetus relationship and animal magnetism; see Bernoulli and Kern. The fact that such "magic relationships" for Hegel seem to originate in and in some ways to duplicate the mother-fetus relationship brings to mind, perhaps obliquely, Lacan's notion of the Imaginary and Kristeva's notion of the Semiotic as pre-Oedipal and prelinguistic stages the infant experiences before a stable individual identity is established: before, that is, the child can clearly distinguish itself from others, particularly from the mother; see Lacan (1–7), and Kristeva (19–106). For an excellent treatment of Hegel's influence on modern French thought, see Butler's *Subjects of Desire*.

9. The etymology of "birthmark" in other languages reveals similar beliefs. In Italian, birthmark is *il voglio*, meaning wish or desire. In French it is *la tache*, meaning stain, spot, or blemish, or *l'envie*, meaning desire, longing, or envy. Thus if a mother had cravings for carrots during her pregnancy, her child would be born with a carrot-shaped birthmark. The seventeenth-century French philosopher Nicholas Malebranche claimed that a mother's desire

could not only leave marks on the child's body, but also could cause women to give birth to "fruits they have wanted to eat, such as apples, pears, grapes, and other similar things" (117). Descartes makes similar, though less remarkable, claims; see his *Description du corps humain* (11:218–86) and *Passion de l'âme* (11:310–488). (No complete edition of Descartes was available to me in translation.) Malebranche and Descartes were perhaps influenced by Renaissance teratology, the study of "monsters." Teratology maintained that all birth defects were induced either by the mother's imagination, or by extraordinary or shocking sensory perceptions experienced by the mother during pregnancy; see Park and Daston. For an examination of the issue during the eighteenth century, see Boucé and Huet. Hegel himself was quite willing to believe the anecdotes used to confirm the mother's mind as the origin of birth defects—those used, for example, in great detail by Malebranche. Hegel states in the "Anthropology" section of the *Philosophy of Mind* that there are "reports of children being born with an injured arm because the mother had actually broken an arm or at least had knocked it so severely that she feared it was broken, or, again, because she had been frightened by the sight of someone else's broken arm. Similar examples are too familiar to require mention here" (*Spirit* 2:237).

10. This passage, one of Hegel's most infamous, continues: "The difference between men and women is like that between animals and plants. Men correspond to animals, while women correspond to plants because their development is more placid [*mehr ruhiges*] and the principle that underlies it is the rather vague [*unbestimmtere*] unity of feeling. When women hold the helm of government, the state is at once in jeopardy, because women regulate their actions not by the demands of universality but by arbitrary inclinations and opinions. The education of women takes place, no one knows how, as it were by breathing in ideas [*durch die Atmosphäre der Vorstellung*], more by living than acquiring knowledge. The status of manhood, on the other hand, is attained only by the stress of thought and much technical exertion" (*Right* 263–64).

11. Derrida has argued that for Hegel productive imagination [*die Phantasie*], like Kant's transcendental imagination, "carries along with it the contradictory predicates of receptive passivity and productive spontaneity" ("Pit" 79). It is part of my purpose in this essay to locate this contradiction within, and dispersed through, Hegel's theorizations and deployments of sex/gender.

12. Hegel describes judgment in general as an intermediary stage in "pure thought." It represents not just the *separation*, but also the *relation* between divided or separated elements. For an explanation of Hegel's various uses of the word *Urteil*, see Petry's "Introduction" (*Spirit* 1:cxliii–cxliv).

13. See Friedman's essay on the different uses of and responses to this metaphoric use of childbirth.

14. Hegel claims in the *Encyclopedia* that the body is an (imperfect) sign of Spirit: "It is because this shape [the body] is something immediate and natural in its externality and can therefore only signify Spirit in an indefinite and wholly imperfect manner [*und darum nur ein unbestimmtes und ganz unvollkommenes Zeichen für den Geist sein kann*], being capable of presenting it as the universal it is for itself, that this tone [*Ton*] [of spirituality] is such a delicate [*leichte*], and elusive [*unsagbare*] modification" (*Spirit* 2:411). Interestingly, it is precisely the development of the ego as the "abyss of presentation" necessary for the mind to manufacture signs that allows Spirit its "direct and more perfect expression" in language; see Derrida ("Pit" 76–77).

15. This section does not appear in Petry's translation; all page numbers from this section of the *Philosophy of Mind* will be to Wallace and Miller's translation, with some modifications of my own.

16. Judith Butler has persuasively argued that the Hegelian deployment of *Aufhebung* does

not always signal an appropriative subject, as Derrida has argued, but rather emphasizes that "assimilation is simultaneous with a radical revision of the subject itself" ("Commentary" 176). I agree, but with the qualification that while Hegel's *Aufhebung* implies a radical fluidity of the appropriative subject's identity, this fluidity does not necessarily disperse Hegel's hierarchies of appropriator/appropriated. As I have argued, however, we might locate such a dispersal in the continual return of maternity, that which effects a spiritual "disease" of oppositionless duality, throughout Hegel's texts.

Works Cited

Althusser, Louis. "On the Materialist Dialectic." In *For Marx*, translated by Ben Brewster, 161–218. London: Verso, 1990.

Bernoulli, Christoph, and Hans Kern, eds. "Friedrich Hufeland." In *Romantische Naturphilosophie*, 32–98. Jena: Eugen Diedrichs, 1926.

Boucé, Paul-Gabriel. "Imagination, Pregnant Women, and Monsters in Eighteenth-Century France." In *Sexual Underworlds of the Enlightenment*, edited by G. S. Rousseau and Roy Porter, 86–100. Chapel Hill: University of North Carolina Press, 1988.

Butler, Judith. "Commentary on Joseph Flay's 'Hegel, Derrida, and Bataille's Laughter.' " In *Hegel and His Critics: Philosophy in the Aftermath of Hegel*, edited by William Desmond, 174–78. Albany: State University of New York Press, 1989.

———. *Gender Trouble: Feminism and the Subversion of Identity*. New York: Routledge, 1990.

———. *Subjects of Desire: Hegelian Reflections in Twentieth-Century France*. New York: Columbia University Press, 1987.

De Man, Paul. "Sign and Symbol in Hegel's *Aesthetics*." *Critical Inquiry* 8 (1982): 761–75.

Derrida, Jacques. *Glas*. Translated by John P. Leavey Jr. and Richard Rand. Lincoln: University of Nebraska Press, 1986.

———. "The Pit and The Pyramid: Introduction to Hegel's Semiology." In *Margins of Philosophy*, translated by Alan Bass, 69–108. Chicago: University of Chicago Press, 1982.

Descartes, René. *Oeuvres Philosophiques*. Edited by Charles Adam and Paul Tannery. 11 vols. Paris: Libraire Philosophique, 1964–75.

Eagleton, Terry. *The Ideology of the Aesthetic*. Oxford: Basil Blackwell, 1990.

Engelhardt, Dietrich von. "Mesmer in der Naturforschung und Medizin in der Romantik." In *Franz Anton Mesmer und die Geschichte des Mesmerismus*, edited by Heinz Schott, 88–107. Stuttgart: Franz Steiner, 1985.

Frevert, Ute. *Women in German History from Bourgeois Emancipation to Sexual Liberation*. Translated by Stuart McKinnen-Evans with Terry Bond and Barbara Norden. New York: Berg, 1989.

Friedman, Susan Stanford. "Creativity and the Childbirth Metaphor: Gender Difference in Literary Discourse." In *Speaking of Gender*, edited by Elaine Showalter, 73–100. New York: Routledge, 1989.

Gasché, Rodolphe. "Hegel's Orient or the End of Romanticism." In *History and Mimesis*, edited by Irving J. Massey and Sung-Won Lee, 17–29. Buffalo: State University of New York Press, 1983.

Gilman, Sander L. "Hegel, Schopenhauer and Nietzsche See the Black." *Hegel-Studien* 16(1981): 163–88.

Goux, Jean-Joseph. *Symbolic Economies: After Marx and Freud.* Translated by Jennifer Curtiss Gage. Ithaca: Cornell University Press, 1990.

Grimshaw, Jean. *Philosophy and Feminist Thinking.* Minneapolis: University of Minnesota Press, 1986.

Hegel, Georg Wilhelm Friedrich. *Aesthetics: Lectures on Fine Art.* Translated by T. M. Knox. 2 vols. Oxford: Clarendon, 1975.

———. *Hegel: The Letters.* Translated by Clark Butler and Christiane Seiler, with commentary by Clark Butler. Bloomington: Indiana University Press, 1984.

———. *Hegel's Philosophy of Subjective Spirit.* Translated and edited by M. J. Petry. 3 vols. Dordrecht: Reidel, 1978.

———. *Phenomenology of Spirit.* Translated by A. V. Miller. Oxford: Oxford University Press, 1977.

———. *Philosophy of Mind.* Translated by William Wallace and A. V. Miller. Oxford: Clarendon, 1971.

———. *Philosophy of Nature.* Translated by A. V. Miller. Oxford: Clarendon, 1970.

———. *Philosophy of Right.* Translated by T. M. Knox. Oxford: Clarendon, 1967.

———. *System of Ethical Life.* Edited and translated by H. S. Harris and T. M. Knox. Albany: State University of New York Press, 1979.

———. *Werke.* Edited by Eva Moldenhauer and Karl Markus Michel. 20 vols. Frankfurt: Suhrkamp Verlag, 1970.

Huet, Marie-Hélène. "Monstrous Imagination: Progeny as Art in French Classicism." *Critical Inquiry* 17 (1991): 718–37.

Irigaray, Luce. "Is the Subject of Science Sexed?" *Hypatia* 2, no. 3 (1987): 65–87.

———. *Speculum of the Other Woman.* Translated by Gillian C. Gill. Ithaca: Cornell University Press, 1985.

Jardine, Alice. *Gynesis: Configurations of Woman and Modernity.* Ithaca: Cornell University Press, 1985.

Jordanova, Ludmilla. *Sexual Visions: Images of Gender in Science and Medicine Between the Eighteenth and Twentieth Centuries.* Madison: University of Wisconsin Press, 1989.

Kristeva, Julia. *Revolution in Poetic Language.* Translated by Margaret Waller. New York: Columbia University Press, 1984.

Lacan, Jacques. *Écrits: A Selection.* Translated by Alan Sheridan. New York: Norton, 1977.

Laqueur, Thomas. *Making Sex: Body and Gender from the Greeks to Freud.* Cambridge: Harvard University Press, 1990.

Malebranche, Nicholas. *The Search After Truth.* Translated by Thomas M. Lennon and Paul J. Olscamp. Columbus: Ohio State University Press, 1980.

Marx, Karl. "Economic and Philosophical Manuscripts." *Karl Marx: Selected Writings.* Edited by David McLellan, 75–112. Oxford: Oxford University Press, 1977.

Park, Kathleen, and Lorraine Daston. "Unnatural Conceptions: The Study of Monsters in Sixteenth-Century France and England." *Past and Present* 92 (1981): 20–54.

Schiebinger, Londa. *The Mind Has No Sex? Women in the Origins of Modern Science.* Cambridge: Harvard University Press, 1989.

Schor, Naomi. *Reading in Detail: Aesthetics and the Feminine.* New York: Methuen, 1987.

Scott, Joan Wallach. " 'L'ouvrière! Mot impie, sordide...': Women Workers in the Discourse of French Political Economy, 1840–1860." In her *Gender and the Politics of History,* 139–63. New York: Columbia University Press, 1988.

Spivak, Gayatri Chakravorty. "Displacement and the Discourse of Woman." In *Displacement: Derrida and After,* edited by Mark Krupnick, 169–95. Bloomington: Indiana University Press, 1987.

———. "French Feminism in an International Frame." In her *In Other Worlds: Essays in Cultural Politics*, 134–53. New York: Routledge, 1988.

Stanton, Domna C. "Difference on Trial: A Critique of the Maternal Metaphor in Cixous, Irigaray, and Kristeva." In *The Thinking Muse: Feminism and Modern French Philosophy*, edited by Jeffner Allen and Iris Marion Young, 156–79. Bloomington: Indiana University Press, 1989.

Tuana, Nancy. "The Weaker Seed: The Sexist Bias of Reproductive Theory." *Hypatia* 3, no. 1 (1988): 35–59.

8

Hegel:
Man, Physiology, and Fate

Mary O'Brien

There have been few intellects in the history of Western thought quite so subtle and sapient as that of G. W. F. Hegel. The general problems associated with critique and exegesis of the man's work are notorious. On the most superficial level, the effort to simply understand what he is saying, to come to terms with a formidable syntax and his neological language demands quite a bit of concentrated attention: one must cope with the deadly serious gleefulness with which he cossets the ambiguities of language, for this is an integral methodological component of his attempt to uncover the ultimate moving complexities of Reason. Wres-

The original unabridged version of this article appeared in mimeographed form as "Group for Research on Women Paper no. 12," Ontario Institute for Studies in Education, 1977.

tling with these preliminaries constitutes only a sort of dry run at the most accessible rung of the Hegelian ladder which mounts dizzily upward to the living, moving heart of what may well be the most ambitious philosophical system the Western world has produced.

Hegel has been accused, among other things, of thinking God's thoughts. This man claims to have grasped the significance of Absolute Knowledge in a dialectical unity of thought and action, thereby lowering the curtain on the historical development of Reason. In so doing, he excites about equally the wrath of traditional metaphysicians and the indifference of modern empiricists. Hegel is not, however, an intellectual megalomaniac nor an unrepentant gnostic. He is a man attempting to correct the empiricist fallacies of the Enlightenment, with its crude and unconsciously abstract notion of History as Progress, in order to restore to philosophy the difficult but vital task of resolving the problems uncovered by the metaphysical pioneers of classical antiquity.

The systematic and formal wholeness of Hegel's work presents a further bedevilment for critical analysis. This raises the question of the relation of parts to whole, which is an absurd question if viewed from Hegel's own totally unified perspective.

He irritated his friends by what they saw as his dilatoriness in publishing, a tardiness that even in 1807 evidently had serious effects on academic careers. It does not appear to have been the case that Hegel did not want to publish until he had *something* to say, but that he did not want to publish until he could say *everything*.[1] It is an interesting historical coincidence that not so far away in place and time, though eons away in philosophical understanding, Jeremy Bentham was driving his friends to distraction with the same sort of tardiness. Bentham had an adequate private income, however, which Hegel did not. Both men seem to have felt that language was no longer capable of expressing clearly what they wanted to say. Bentham tackled this problem by writing—execrably—in French, Hegel by torturing the German language into an oddly ebullient submissiveness. The resultant systems cannot be approached critically, however, in the same way. Effective critique of Bentham's inductive/synthetic Principle of Utility is effective critique of the Utilitarian system. To attack Hegel's fundamental postulate that Reason is real is to do more than criticize Hegel: it is to undermine the possibility of philosophical knowledge itself.

Despite Hegel's own insistence on wholeness, it is possible and perhaps even necessary to isolate parts of his system for critical analysis; such

partial endeavors are legion in the stormy history of Hegelian interpretation. For example, Hegel's parable of the struggle for Mastery, the
famous "Master and Slave" episode, has by itself generated a great deal
of exegetical heat. On the conceptual, or, as some would claim, the
ideological level, the battles between young and old Hegelians, Left and
Right Hegelians are a matter of record. Members of these schools
have variously retained Hegel's metaphysics but rejected his dialectics,
launched desperate tirades against the Universality of Reason itself, or
retained the dialectics and rejected the idealism. The position of Hegel's
greatest successor, Karl Marx, does not fit into any of these schools.
Engels is a straightforward member of the anti-idealism school, but Marx
did much more than simply privilege Hegel's sense of the historical
significance of human labor and the confrontation of Master and Slave
as an idealized paradigm of class struggle. Marx's own rather ambiguous
claim to have turned Hegel upside down confuses rather than clarifies
the relationship between the two thinkers. This turning upside down is
usually construed in a simplistic way. Crudely, it is argued that Hegel
says the world is constituted by Ideas and Marx says that Ideas are
constituted by the world. This chicken-and-egg view vulgarizes the
dialectical enterprise of both thinkers, an enterprise that attempts to
comprehend theoretically the human struggle to synthesize rational
thought about the world with the course of actual, active human history.
Perhaps we can grasp more adequately the fundamental unity and
cleavage between the two men if we consider the turning upside down in
terms of the major preoccupation of both thinkers, *history itself*. For
Hegel, history is complete. For Marx, truly human history has not
yet started.

It is precisely at this point that a specifically feminist critique of Hegel
can enter the interpretive fray. Such a critique certainly encounters all
the difficulties that have been sketched above, plus a few peculiar to the
feminist perspective. It is not proposed here to offer a critique of the
whole system, but it is not proposed either to suggest that the shooting
down of a part triumphantly entails the destruction of the whole. In
fact, it is argued that there is one important sense in which Hegel's
system is a "whole," a sense in which it does mark a break in history's
hitherto unfaltering stride. The system is the most ambitious attempt
ever made to define humanity as masculine, to celebrate the transformation of real people to the abstract concept of Universal Man. From this
perspective, Hegel and Marx are *both* correct in a very important

dialectical sense. History *has* stopped insofar as the long tenure of male dominance is crumbling. Truly *human* history has not yet started, and can start only in a rational and free association of men and women.[2]

This perspective on the Hegelian System still does not solve the operational problem of a critical approach, but it does suggest that Hegel's thought is of great importance to feminist thought. We shall be dealing here, in a preliminary way, with what Hegel actually has to say about reproductive relations and the family, not in the congealed prejudice of his mature work but in the struggle for generic understanding in his early works. A critique of Hegel from a feminist perspective cannot consist merely of an anthology of proofs that Hegel is a male chauvinist. This would be a simple task: a skip through part 3 of the *Philosophy of Right* would provide an arsenal of polemical ammunition. What we shall do is approach Hegel more constructively, for we can in fact derive from his work a dynamic model of generic antagonisms that is both dialectical and potentially historical, a model that can in turn serve as a theoretical base for an understanding of generic history that transcends Hegel's own particularist vision. Thus, we shall be partial critics, leaving out any consideration of huge and important tracts of the Absolute system. At the same time, we can demonstrate that the unity of the Absolute in Hegel is *not* complete, and that one important reason for this is that he never does resolve the opposition male/female except in "spirit." We shall, however, still be obliged to offer, for purposes of clarification, a few interpretive abstracts of some of Hegel's more general propositions. This is a daunting task, and anathema to all Hegelians, but one cannot assume that all of one's readers are Hegelian partisans: Hegel is a representative of that kind of male-stressing thought that many feminists feel is dickied-up patriarchal ideology. Further, Hegel is peculiarly resistant to digestion and translation into a less esoteric vocabulary, and to any enraged Hegelian purists I can only say that I am not concerned with Hegel so that I may offer another "interpretation." Rather, I look at his work as a serious building block in Western ideologies of patriarchy that has to be understood if the *universal* fact of patriarchal theory and practice is to be negated.

As far as his analyses of reproduction and human regeneration are concerned, Hegel stopped the clock of history, but he stopped it at the dawn of history rather than the end where his "completion" of philosophy is immodestly asserted. He understood that the *process* of human reproduction is dialectical, and that the social relations of reproduction (i.e., forms of family) change historically. He did not understand that the *reproductive process itself* is not reducible to "nature." The reasons why the clock has to be stopped are twofold: Hegel negated the conscious constitutive powers of women's real reproductive labor in favor of the reflective prowess of the *Idea* of paternity. Yet he did not grasp quite fully the implications of the fact that paternity fundamentally and intransigently is a *conceptualized* experience, a claim inherent in the interesting old "concept" of carnal *knowledge*. The second consideration is itself historical: Hegel could not, any more than Malthus or Marx, or millions of unwilling mothers, anticipate a rational ordering of the social relations of reproduction: such a notion had to await the highly problematic transformation of human reproductive experience by contraceptive technology. This contemporary technology materially transforms the *process* of human reproduction, for within that process the crude materiality of the biological event is inseparable from human consciousness; Hegel showed this in only a one-sided way in that the forms of consciousness he analyzes are crudely sexist in their understanding of who knows what is going on. The ideology of male supremacy has generally insisted on the absolute contingency of reproduction, perceived as an uninteresting animal affair that somehow obliterates human consciousness in anything but a crude reflexive sense. Hegel was more perceptive: he not only recognized a synthesizing parental consciousness of the child as responsibility and potentiality, but also he was, at least in his youth, much concerned about the relation of self-consciousness and sexuality. His perspective on the consciousness question is nonetheless one-sidedly masculine and thus itself still only an *abstract* consciousness.

As a young thinker, Hegel pondered very seriously upon the emotionally and physically synthetic powers of sexuality. In 1797–98 he held the view that human love was a miraculous and ultimately incomprehensible affair. This view may well have been derived from his reverent study of classical antiquity, where it is present, for example, in Plato's obscure discussion of "the nuptial number," and evidently formed an important aspect of the doings of the male Mystery cults.[3] As Hegel's synthesizing ambitions developed, it became quite clear to him that the aspirant to the goal of unification of all contradiction could not bow before the most commonplace opposition of all, the generic differentiation of the species. In an early paper, evidently developed from his 1802–3 lectures, Hegel attempts to deal systematically with the anthropological foundations of history, "anthropological" meaning to Hegel the pre-conscious, pre-rational, and therefore pre-historical forms of human spirit.[4] For an Idealist history of Reason, objective biology offers a very balky starting point, yet without the biological person there is no mundane mansion in which Reason can be at home. Hegel must therefore discover the nature of a movement from biological being to rational, ethical, and spiritual being, from unawakened non-differentiation to self-awareness. He must chart the necessary alienation of rational humanity from its own organic origins while preserving these origins. Self-awareness is, in its awakening form, the potential mediation of rational being and brute world, which in due course will transform abstract naturalness to concrete social history. The biological, prehistorical opposition of male/female, is never an absolute but merely a relative opposition, and as such is indifferent to the mediative prowess of Reason. There is clearly some kind of synthesis at work in the creation of a new life, but life itself, prior to consciousness, is mere negativity, devoid of the ethical reality which marks Reason's debut in the world. Mere life *knows* no opposition, though it will come to grasp death's significance, and has only the dimmest and most negative conception of the reality of the Other: "The other . . . [is] Evil, a being-in-itself, the subterranean principle, the thing which knows what lies in daylight and witnesses how it brings about its own decline, or is in such active opposition that, on the contrary, it substitutes negativity for its own being, for its own self-preservation."[5]

This rather romantic notion of a "dark principle" haunting the struggling consciousness of primordial humanity owes much to Schelling, but for both men it also clearly owes quite a bit to the arboreal antics of Eve and her serpentine paramour. More important, it is this principle of mere life that Hegel, abandoning poesy for a more rigorous philosophical vocabulary, calls "natural" *Particularity.*

Hegel's dialectic always involves an opposition between a Universal and a Particular, and it is therefore important to know what in general Hegel means by these terms if we are to understand the significance of woman's Particularity. For Hegel, a Universal is a unity of conceptualization and reality in which the Concept is the creative essence. The forms which Reason takes in the course of history vary, but the importance of the Concept and the source of its universality and wholeness is that, unlike ordinary understanding, which is of particular knowledge, the Concept is universal in the sense that it creates itself, it determines what it is, generates its own rational reality and wholeness. Its reality is

Reason so that each of its particular creations becomes both rational and real. The Concept is not an empty abstraction, but a living and active reality that determines its own content and its own being.[6] When the Concept has synthesized itself with itself, as it were, unified its universal form and the particular content that it has itself generated, it becomes *Idea*,[7] a synthesis of the object of thought and the creative thinker that Hegel likes to call "concrete." This is a confusing use of "concrete"; it does not only mean objectively present, but embraces an empirical content that remains essentially "abstract" if it is not enfolded and unified with thought. Mind therefore is in constant motion; it is creating and re-creating itself in a world that it is thus actually "making" in its own image. The analogy Hegel frequently uses for the objectification of the Concept in the world is an organic one; the tree is potential in the seed. We may note that he shares with male-stream thought in general a tremendous yearning to create a form of auto-regeneration that is superior to biological *procreation*, but unlike many of his predecessors and successors he does not propose a principle of continuity that is independent from biology and therefore "abstracted" from the real.

The important thing about the Concept, for us, is that it *creates* the particular; in fact it creates a whole series of particulars that stand in contrast as *content* of the Concept, which is a *form*. The Idea is the synthesis of form and content. The Concept becomes in effect the core of reality and the inner life of anything that is real. As woman remains particular and man is the "tool" of the Concept, the logical conclusion is that *man makes woman* in a sense that transcends the merely biological mode in which women indubitably "make" men. Hegel never says this in a forthright way, but Hegel has no interest in the forthright, which lies in the realm of the particular as opposed to universal knowledge. It is, however, something a little more than implicit in his analysis; we find in the *Phenomenology* that man's need to invert biological reproduction to spiritual regeneration entails the constant "suppression" of women. Male supremacy is not established, as it were, in a "one-shot" deal. It has to be worked at. Clearly, men *have* historically "made" women. This is the basic premise of Simone de Beauvoir's analysis of feminine Otherness.[8] Beauvoir herself, who shares an intellectual indebtedness to Hegel with existentialism in general, accepts without reservation the masculine ontological denigration of biological reproduction in a way rather more absolute than Hegel's own.

Hegel's dialectic of thought and reality is something more than a new epistemological model to solve the ancient dualism of subject and object, and Universality is something more than the unity of Reason and History. This is because, for Hegel, Reason itself is something more than the sum of the workings of particular human minds. It is a little difficult to say quite what this "something more" is. It has distinctly theological overtones, and the traditional notion of God comes nearest to Hegel's concept of the Idea. But the parallel is misleading, for Reason objectifies itself in the world, *continuously* concretizing itself in history in all that has been created in and by history. God's objectification of himself in his Son *was* a "one-shot" affair.[9]

In this mobile dialectical model, Universal and Particular stand opposed to one another, and Universal strives at all times to annul and absorb the Particular it has realized so that it might in turn be transformed to a "higher" (i.e., more rational) reality: this model of process is retained by Marx in a more practical and more easily understood way. For Marx, the important particular/universal opposition is that of the active individual and historically created society. The internal tension of the capitalist mode of production is both creative and doomed by virtue of the opposition of *individual* ownership and *social* labor, an opposition concretized in class struggle. For both Marx and Hegel, Particularity is given a negative evaluation; of itself it is both abstract and irrational. It is scheduled for negation, by self-universalizing Reason for Hegel, by historical class action for Marx. Marx's prediction of the burial of the individual bourgeois capitalist, or rather the capitalist's self-interment in his self-dug grave, is not a prospect that necessarily disturbs the majority of people, who don't happen to own the means of production. Those who do give no public credence to the analysis, but work hard to ameliorate the nastier aspects of capitalism in the hopes of affecting the dialectic. Hegel's position is more important for feminists. While the Concept creates and annuls a long series of Particularities, women are the *Principle* of Particularity from Hegel's early work right through to the *Philosophy of Right*. Similarly, we remain objectively affixed in the domestic sphere of Particularity (the private realm) from prehistory until the arrival of the universal and homogeneous State, which Hegel sees as Reason's ultimate social arrangement. The argument that this is actually what happens, that men have "negated" women and re-created them to suit their needs, is *not* Hegel's argument. His woman is *infinitely* particular precisely because there *can be no absolute "negation"* of her necessary reproductive function. We are, as it were, a practically non-negatable reproductive function. As negation is the process by which history becomes rational, we are clearly unable to "make history."

Woman is Particular because she represents mere life as opposed to creative life. Here, Hegel has not advanced much beyond Plato's *Symposium*, where the rejection of the vitality of procreation in favor of the greater creativity of male intellectual intercourse is put into the mouth of a woman, Diotima. However, neither Plato nor Hegel, for obvious reasons, is proposing an all-male universe. The male desire for an all-male universe is not often expressed out loud, but John Milton, whom some misguided feminists in his own time and ours have thought of as a friend of woman because of his early advocacy of divorce by consent, gives the yearning to Adam:

> Oh! why did God
> Creator wise, that peopled highest heaven
> With spirits masculine, create at last
> This novelty on earth, this fair defect
> Of nature, and not fill the earth at once
> With men as angels without feminine,
> Or find some other way to generate
> Mankind?
> (*Paradise Lost*, Book X, 888–95)

For Hegel, women are rescued from prehistory (as indeed are men) by the development of a moral sense, a limited ethical life that involves, in its natural manifestation, the conscious sacrifice of one's own desires in the interests of dependent infants. This is a generically shared task, with the crucial difference being that women are arrested at this level. Men, for reasons that Hegel never quite clarifies, develop also a *social* consciousness, and in doing so start upon their real history, though not, as we shall see, without a struggle. *Before* men embark on their history, the family is established as the first "natural" moral institution, and it is a *patriarchal* family, a circumstance Hegel appears at first glance to have thoughtlessly deduced from the *subsequent* course of patriarchal history. The important point is that the family, while it is established prehistorically, changes and reforms and in fact is eroded in the course of history, but in all these transformations one aspect of the family is curiously resistant to the revolutionary potential of the Concept in action.

Patriarchy remains constant, and women remain satisfied (with a few distressing historical aberrations and the happily natural guidance of brothers) within the nonconflictual, loving, and spiritual ambience of the family.

Men, on the other hand, transcend the particularist limitations of the family, for they must constitute their own self-consciousness, in effect create themselves. The conditions of the birth of the self-constituted self, the self-made man, are the *recognition* of death and of other men. However, other men too desire to be recognized, and this conflict of desires, which is a desire of each for the desire of the Other, must be fought out in mortal combat. The risk of life necessary to this combat comes about because male consciousness has recognized the nature of the Universal Negative, death itself. For men, the actualization of the self is at the same time the recognition of the Negative within and inseparable from the self, hence the desire for external recognition of one's actuality. The price of recognition is a willingness to confront Negation, namely, to risk one's life in struggle with an Other's similar desire for a recognition of self-negation. Hegel's protagonists do not in fact fight to the lethal finish, for one man decides that he values mere life above the struggle for self-conscious life and its chilling embracement of finitude. This Other (though Hegel does *not* say this specifically) becomes *effeminate,* in that he values mere life, his particular life, and eschews the Universalizing potentiality of the struggle to overcome and master Nature.

This epic confrontation is Hegel's celebrated myth of the Master and Slave, for he who chooses Particularity is enslaved by he who confronts death in a free act of potential self-alienation.[10] Neither Hegel nor Beauvoir notice the crucial form of *immediate recognition* that biology denies to man, namely recognition of his particular paternity. Neither do they note that women do not need to create a *principle* of continuity, for they create continuity *concretely* by reproductive labor. But then, neither even addresses the possibility of a *reproductive consciousness.* The myth is essential to Hegel's view of history, for it moves mankind from nondifferentiation, heretofore present only in a relative and abstract way in generic opposition, to a differentiated reality, a new Particularity, a creative and potent particularity that is already reaching out to the negation of its own finitude, and the negation of mere death in creative history. In effect, human continuity is removed from *biological continuity,* which women actively affirm in reproductive labor but from which men are alienated, to an *artificial continuity* in which men who have succeeded in "making themselves" proceed to make historical continuity. Hegel's great merit is to see and acknowledge that the condition of man-made history is to suppress without actual negation the reality of reproductive process. Birth therefore remains privatized and takes place within time but outside of history, which of course goes public. The separation of public and private life becomes a condition of *history*, rather than, as it actually is, a working structure of patriarchal hegemony.

Hegel's Master and Slave parable has many implications, but our interest is a limited one, which is no doubt symptomatic of the particularism of feminist consciousness. Hegel's myth is spun in support of the very reasonable claim that human history is the history of human mastery of the world by means of a unification of rational consciousness and creative activity. This mastery is not, however, simple mastery of the natural environment: Adam the patriarch had already started this process with his little spade. It is mastery of other men, and is the root of the *inevitability* of class divisions that persist up to and beyond the end of history, which Hegel ultimately realizes in the modern State. But at least general class antagonism in its primordial particularity is established *historically*. Male supremacy over women is established *prior* to the dawn of history, and is therefore presumably "natural." It is also rational, for Nature for Hegel is rational. Unfortunately for woman, Nature is also *impotent (Ohnmacht)* in Hegel's system, and is capable of rational and transformative vitality only when she is synthesized with thought in the Concept. The Concept and the sperm appear to have functional similarities, with the sperm's swim outside of history into the cavernous womb made inevitable by its impotence. Having detached this tiresome artifact, men can achieve potency in the making of history.

What Hegel is doing is creating a form of continuity that transcends genetic continuity. There is, of course, nothing wrong with such an enterprise. We are not launching a plea for the regression of life to the biological level. The effort of humanity to come to terms with the natural environment is and has been a struggle, a struggle in which indeed humanity has shaped and defined itself in concrete ways. It is futile to complain to history for being what it has been. It is imperative, though, as Hegel sees so clearly, to *understand* what it has been, and for women that understanding must embrace the historical phenomenon of actual male supremacy. For Hegel, the nonhistoricity of women rests squarely on her Particularity, which in turn rests on the fact that as the bearers of life, women are principles *only* of life, and are hostile to the risk of the lives that they have so hardly borne. They will not risk their lives like those who master slaves. The fact that women do risk life in childbirth does not interest Hegel, perhaps because childbearing was not a rational choice in the precontraceptive age.[11] As the bearers of life, women have no contradiction between themselves and Nature to negate and re-create, and just as Nature is impotent in terms of the creation of concepts, women are impotent in terms of the active creation of history. Women's actuality in its unity with birth is of course negated by death, but this is a negation they do not and evidently need not negate by creating for themselves, as men do, a *second* and transcendent nature. The "second" nature which women create is a *new* life, not their own life, and a life, moreover, that by virtue of its own self-creative powers, will break away from dependence to independence.

Ironically, this transformation from dependence to independence makes women occasionally resistant to their natural impotence. Women, for example, are credited by Hegel with the destruction of the pagan world, an uppityness that presumably justifies their suppression by and incarceration in the domestic realm as rigorous as that practiced in the Athenian polis (*Phen.*, VI.A.a.b.c.). These ancient women asserted the primacy of life in opposition to man's first Universalizing task force, the death-dealing Homeric heroes. In effeminizing these splendid creatures, women destroyed them. Likewise, Hegel becomes cross with the Romans for permitting women to own property, setting up a dialectical relation with the objective world that permitted women to take action in that created world, thus further eroding the natural ethical functions of the family. Despite these historical outbreaks, women remain for Hegel limited creatures who do not share the thrust to Universality. Hegelian Universality is essentially a *Brotherhood*, united in the creation of a community and in the annulment of the natural, in whose sphere women may chafe only impotently. Hegel never gets around to the historical persecution of witches, a very masterful chunk of negation indeed.

What happened in prehistory, like the drama in the Garden, thus required a woman concerned only with carnal reality and abstract species continuity, which she couldn't comprehend beyond one small baby. It also required a man with at least a flickering sense of a wider ethical and rational mission. The mastery of beasts and women, which God gave to

Adam, Hegel bestows on pre-self-conscious man: it is a precondition of his awakening to self-consciousness and his coincident discovery of his finitude. This is all very biblical, except that Cain does not slay Abel but enslaves him. In effect, too, patriarchy becomes man's first political office, political not only in the crude sense of power over others, but in the human sense of being able to *rationalize* that power. Hegel nowhere argues, as might well be argued within his theoretical scenario, that this control over women, which he does not in fact see as control but as a relation of unity, constitutes a primordial taste of mastery for prehistoric man that dictates that his subsequent relations with nature and other men will necessarily take the form of power relations, relations of *force*. This is because of his ahistorical and nondialectical belief that the essence of the relation of men to women, unlike the mastery of men over men, does not entail an act of will that lays existence itself on the line. In terms of consciousness, paternity appears for Hegel to be immediately apprehended. Mastery over nature for productive purposes must be mediated in thought and action, for man's separation from nature is here *absolute,* as is his differentiation from other men. In reproductive process, the only separation is *relative,* the male/female opposition. It does not need to be mediated by individual consciousness, but is mediated by a *potential* consciousness, that of the child.

Hegel sees that the child is a human product in the objective sense, but the labor that produces the child is not unified with rational thought and it is not, strangely, the authentic parturitional sweat of the mother. It is the joint "labor" of copulation.[12] This odd view of sexual intercourse as an aspect of human work in general arises from Hegel's view of the baby as a "tool" of Reason, for Reason must have a living carrier in biological man before it can objectify its metaphysical destiny in human history. The making of the child is not itself a particularly rational business and, indeed, Hegel owns that "it is more rational to make a tool than a child" (*System,* 421). Further, the baby itself is only pure intuition, a bundle of needs absolute only in its dependent Identity with "life." This "Identity" is complete, for the baby in its primordial being annuls distinction between desire and reason and also annuls the sexual differentiation of the parents, a point to which we shall return in a moment. In a limited sense, the baby is the *Concept* of biological reproduction, created and *potentially* self-creating, but in its first appearance able only to manage a particular, abstract, and prerational self-actualization.

The baby, however, is conceptually related as a tool of Reason to all of Adam's other tool-making activities, and in this sense the "making" of this tool in the "work" of copulation is related to the general tool-making activity that Adam takes on to serve his divine sentence of perpetual labor, but this particular activity he shares equally with his woman. Here, of course, young Hegel is developing one of his most brilliant insights, the fact that human labor is the creative alienation that mediates between man and his world. Labor is the activity that in the *Phenomenology* will eventually negate the negation of the slave's freedom, and the factor that will become the linchpin of Marx's creative Materialism. At this moment, however, we are still contemplating Adam's baby and his role in his father's struggle to raise himself from the merely emotional universality of sexuality and reproduction of the human wherewithal to meet Reason's need for worldly continuity. For Adam, this is a "satisfaction" without as yet the conceptualization of nonimmediate gratification, which he develops in the *productive* realm where, like Prometheus, he discovers foresight. At this stage, man has not yet developed the specifically human tool of mediation, which he will create in language. We need not go on to this higher state, for somewhere in the lower state woman has been left behind in the practical realm of dumb intuitive intelligence whose only claim to Universality is the sentimentality of family relations, with one side of her reality in indifference and the other in Particularity. In one sense, men and women are equal, for each has intelligence and each "works" at the creation of the child, but this is undifferentiated equality:

> Labor, subsumed under this intuition, is a one-sided subsumption, since in this very process the subsumption itself is superseded.

> (This supersession is the objective unification of intuitions and parental intelligence . . . the child.)[13]

> The labor [which produces intelligence] is a totality and with this totality the first and second levels are now posited together.

> (These first two levels are the inorganic and the organic, now being completed with the addition of intelligence.)

Man is a power-level, universality, for his other, but so is his other for him.

(At this point, men and women are alike and equal in having the power to create and the intelligence to know they are creating a new intelligence. However, this unity and equality cannot persist, for it returns the protagonists to non-differentiation, albeit on a higher level.)

> and so *he* makes *his* reality, *his* own particular being, *his* effectiveness in reality into an adoption into indifference, and *he* is now the universal in contrast to the first level. (*System* 424, 425; my emphasis)

Thus people are, in the work of creating a child, capable of knowing themselves as both Particular individual and Universal, sensuous as well as sentient, singular as well as social. The man and the woman "desire" one another but this desire itself is not self-determining, it remains the intuitive desire of each for the other's body:

> This supreme organic polarity in the most complete individuality of each pole is the supreme unity which nature can produce. For it cannot get past this point: that difference is not real but is absolutely ideal.

(By this Hegel appears to mean that it can only be felt, not thought, and in any case its middle term, the child, is a separate intelligence, at least potentially.)

> The *sexes* are plainly in a relation to one another, one the universal, the other the particular: they are not absolutely equal. Thus their union is not that of the absolute concept but, because it is perfect, that of undifferentiated feeling. (*System*, 425)

What Hegel is saying here is that in the first instance men and women are each to the other and for each self both universal and particular, and thus in danger of collapsing into absolute nondifferentiation. This nondifferentiation is "Love," but it is emotional rather than consciously ethical, and it cannot become ethical until a new opposition develops out of this indeterminacy. That "opposition" is the child's potential intelligence, mediated in the first place by the child's absolute dependence. What Hegel is *not* saying is why this new but old differentiation into opposition posits the male as Universal and the female as Particular.[14] He never does tell us this, and it can, of course, be written off as mere masculine prejudice. Nonetheless, we can hardly ignore the fact that men have constituted themselves as universal: this is underscored in the linguistic affirmation of pseudogeneric "Man," to say nothing of the historical record of male dominance. We shall therefore pursue Hegel's conceptualization of reproduction a little further, to see if any more light can be shed on the matter of man's *primordial* Universality, already present in biological paternity.

In an earlier fragment, *On Love,* Hegel had addressed the question of sexuality with a little less composure, for the piece was written amidst the political excitements of the 1790s and, presumably, Hegel's own maturing sexuality. Sexuality, which young Hegel decorously refers to as "love," is clearly a problematic and still somewhat mysterious affair. Nonetheless, Hegel recognizes the dialectical form of reproductive process, though the Negation at work here is not the Absolute of death but the partiality of passion. Sexual feeling sweeps the lover into a unity with an Other, a unity that negates the sense ("his" sense, but perhaps hers too) of individuality and annuls the consciousness of self: "the individual cannot bear to think of himself in this nullity." Hegel is here giving expression to a proposition central to his own epistemology and also to that of Marx: human consciousness *resists alienation* and is *forced* into mediative action. Oddly enough, Hegel probably is being *generic* in this part of his analysis when in fact a little more rigor would require a *genderic* differentiation. Both lovers may indeed "lose" their sense of identity, but the male loses something much more concrete. He loses his seed. Hegel does not go into this: "Nothing carries the root of its own being in itself. . . . True union consists only between living things which are alike in power" (*Love,* 307) This idea of "alikeness in power" will be modified by Hegel and by history as the years pass. Here, Hegel is concerned with the simple reality that these objects each carry a seed, and the "root of being" is the unity of these seeds from separate entities unified in the act of copulation. Love, that is, sexual love, annuls not only the distinction between the two lovers, but the further distinction between the lover as lover and the lover as physical organism. In Hegel's view, then, sexuality not only negates lovers as distinct individuals, but annuls the distinction between emotional and physical life: "All distinction is annulled" (Love, 305). This state of universal nondifferentiation is not apparently negated by its mere transience, at least at this stage of Hegel's development.[15] The lover is submerged in the brute and undifferentiated biological unity and continuity of the human race: "The mortal element, the body, has lost the character of separability, and a living child, a seed of immorality, of the eternal self-developing and self-generative race . . . [is] this unity . . . [but] is only an undifferentiated unity" (Love, 305).

The process of human regeneration, then, is a process of "unity, separated opposites, re-union" (Love, 307). In other words, it is a dialectical process at its most fundamental level, though it is clearly not at this point a Universal, for the Concept is not operative, and only an external and as yet merely potentially intelligent mediation is available, the promise of the living child. Hegel is correct: the process of reproduction is dialectical. What is less convincing is, in the first instance, the absolute bodily separation from the process, for this is simply not true for women. Further, this important dialectical perspicacity on Hegel's part is tied to an opposing historical opacity. This is because Hegel cannot break out of an emotionalized organic shell: there is no struggle for recognition going on here, with all its creative potential. In fact, the whole analysis presents a problem for an idealist theory of consciousness rooted in the primacy of the Concept, for reproductive process is formally dialectical prior to its conception in thought; it has however nothing concrete to contribute to the expansion of self-consciousness, but only to the creation of the potential consciousness embedded in the child. The dialectical moments are going on, as it were, behind the back of the beast with two backs.

Hegel appears to have been dissatisfied with his analysis. At some unknown moment he added to his manuscript the words: "The child is the parents themselves." Perhaps seeing the problem created then in the constitution of a self-consciousness for the living "tool" of Reason without a conflict with both parents, Hegel scores out this phrase and lets his original youthful statement stand: the child is the embodied unity of separated parents (Love, 307).

The consciousness that attends reproduction is finally a reflexive consciousness, not a creative consciousness, in Hegel's analysis. Both parents recognize their child, but the child is ultimately the product of action without thought. The fact that the process of reproduction is dialectical in form prior to the bestowal of the formal blessing of the Concept may be the reason why Hegel creates the family prehistorically, but this still cannot explain why this form of the family is already patri-archal.

The family cannot ultimately further the ethical development of Man, for its unity with the organic is fixed in a mute and unchangeable historical presence. The form—family—persists in time, indeed its *essence* is in a sense temporal. It provides the formal biological continuity of the tools of Reason, but is in its Particular content constantly negated. As the children grow, each particular family duly decays. Historically, the expansion of needs and desires created by the Universalizing advance of Reason in its objective manifestations erodes the family, which is incapable of responding to the needs and desires as they become ethical projects of man as *citizen,* striving for the common good of the community.

Man's heroic task of shouldering the burdens of historical process does not go unrewarded. He has "satisfaction," the true creative satisfaction dug up like treasure by Adam's shovel, and he has Mastery, of which more in a moment. On a more prosaic level, he becomes the guardian of the family property. He also has recognition, the respect of his neighbors and the *persona* awarded by the legal systems he develops. When Hegel first talks of ownership in his *System* he speaks of "abstract" ownership, in the sense of the need for means of production still undifferentiated from the preservation of the laborer and his immediate family. Concrete ownership appears with the development of a social surplus and the possibility of exchange. Exchange is motion and action, a motion that takes man beyond the family into relations with others, relations that negate the pure abstract freedom enjoyed by man at work in providing for his own self-maintenance. Ownership now moves from the abstract Universal of kin-shared property to particular ownership, with all the consequent panoply of Law that realizes the otherwise abstract "right" to property.[16]

Hegel's development of the property theme interests us here for its influence on the young lover coping with his self-annulment. The romantic ardor of the sexual engagement is somewhat mitigated by the lovers' sense of bourgeois propriety, in both senses of the word. A "dead world of external objects" intrudes upon the consciousness of the young lovers, in the form of the families' property holdings. In opposing a lover, each lover is opposed also to his or her possessions and those of the other lover. Clearly, things would be simpler if only one lover was a property owner, which may account for Hegel's dislike of Roman activities in the field of property law. Thanks to this ancient resistance to the rational, the women of Hegel's time evidently appeared to him to have traveled a long way from the propertyless perfection of Antigone, even though their position in relation to property looks grim enough to contemporary feminists. Women could have property willed to them by testamentary disposition, an ownership limited to their own life span. Even this limited ownership of property comes between the lovers; according to Hegel, the possibility of sharing property is not a practical one. The embodied unity that the child represents in the process of reproduction is evidently not accessible to the parents' property relations. Property embodies the alienated labor of the individual superseded by the "pure infinity" of legal right invested in the thing—Hegel's way of expressing the idea of *value*.[17] For "things," in this case property, no relation is possible, according to Hegel, except mastery of the object. Clearly with Plato in mind, Hegel argues that the possibility of shared goods is illusory, for "community of goods is still only the right of one or the other to the thing" (*Love*, 307). There seems to be little doubt in Hegel's mind as to *which* one: "Since possession and property make up an important part of *men's* lives even lovers cannot refrain from reflection on this aspect of their relations" (*Love*, 307; my emphasis).

Now we must ask, what is the meaning of all this? There is no doubt at all that Hegel is defending male supremacy, and that the categorization of Female as Particular and Male as Universal has arbitrary (i.e., nondialectical) components. The effects upon Hegel in his maturity are predictable. The creation of communities emergent from the Concept of exchange, itself made possible by the labor of the mastered slave, depends upon humanity's capacity to overcome particularity. This is correct in an important sense. The question is why only male particularity is negated, because of course this is the apologist root for the identification of our species as "mankind." Particularity is not of course *destroyed*, but merely annulled, negated in one form to reappear in another that subsumes but does not obliterate it. Nothing is obliterated in Hegel's view of history. The negation of the individual will is the condition of the ethical community, but the life-giving particularity of women is also necessary to the community, for children are determinate moments in the advance of Reason. The transformed, higher form of community spirit that transcends family is Law, a developed concrete

Universal, and Hegel says of law that it "in its efficient operation in general is the manhood of the community" (*Phen.*, 496). Among these Laws, of course, are those that realize what Hegel understands as the "spiritual essence" of marriage, but they also "realize" the *abstract* nature of paternity, a point that Hegel seems to be hinting at obliquely. The notion of a spiritual essence for marriage neatly evades the actuality of the uncertainty of paternity, which Hegel does not name as a "determinant moment" in reproductive process. His analyses of reproductive process as resistant to constitutive conceptualization pussyfoots around man's efforts to mediate his estrangement from his seed. Knowledge of paternity in general stands opposed to the uncertainty of particular paternity. Thus Law is indeed the efficient objectification of "manhood." Hegel at times seems to come close to this underlying reality only to shy away again. Thus, it is production and exchange that become the only basis for the necessary move to sociability beyond kinship. Hegel does not see, or does not consider important, the fact that the uncertainty of paternity *commands* cooperation between men as a class: lay off my woman and I'll lay off of yours.

Hegel's opposition of life and livelihood is a profound and original understanding of the fact that the relation between the social forms of reproduction and the social forms of production is a dialectical opposition, a point that rather generally eludes Marx's understanding. Yet even this more complex opposition within and between the processes of production and reproduction is for Hegel curiously noncreative: it is *irritant* squabble rather than heroic confrontation, and is dealt with in a most curious way. Men deal with the tension of life and livelihood, of individual and society, not by struggling with women, but by becoming soldiers.

Woman, the representative of "the everlasting irony in the life of the community," "turns to ridicule the grave wisdom of maturity . . . ; she makes this wisdom [a] laughing-stock" and thus teaches her children a lack of respect for men and their philosophies (*Phen.*, 496). Woman cares only, Hegel says, for the "force of youth" and elevates her personal relationships with son, husband, brother to a position that disregards the wider good of the community. The community deals with this, as both Plato and Machiavelli dealt with it, by turning this high-spirited individualist youth into a soldier. This is not simply an expedient way of correcting the baleful effects of feminine influence on young men; the community *must* have soldiers anyway: "War is the spirit and form in which the essential moment of ethical substance, the absolute freedom of ethical self-consciousness from all and every kind of existence, is manifestly confirmed and realized" (*Phen.*, 497).

War destroys property and even the lives of individuals, but this destructive force "stands out as that which preserves the community." At the same time, it keeps "the individual who provides pleasure to women" employed (*Phen.*, 497). War in its destructive aspect, dependent as it is upon *physical* strength, is, like women, immediately related to nature. Yet there is clearly a difference between women and soldiers, for the soldier is serving Universality, even though he does not know he is doing this. This may be a fair example of what Hegel means when he talks of the *cunning* of Reason. Women do not even do this sort of ignorant service. The Universal component of their Being is simply the continuity of the human race, and the care of the individual keeps them "constantly dissolved in the fluent continuum of their own nature" (*Phen.*, 496). War is clearly the universal version of the master and slave dialectic, the ethics of life-risking writ large, but there is no need for this kind of battle between men and women. To be sure, the community must suppress "the spirit of individualism," and "suppress it as a hostile principle" (*Phen.*, 497). The objective form of this principle, woman, must clearly simply be tolerated as a necessary irritant for the sake of creating a concrete community at all.

We may be angry at this show of prejudice or we may even, as Hegel accuses us of doing, mock the comic overtones in this version of ourselves. More constructively, we may look systematically at the moments of Hegel's analysis of reproductive process, which, whatever it does to objective idealism, makes an important contribution to a materialist epistemology; a feminist epistemology must be materialist, for women *have* a material relationship with nature that is particularly feminine. Male denigration of this relationship has left some women intolerant of it, and left in some feminine hearts a yearning to escape from their involvement in reproduction, which is as one-sided and pathetic as the male urge to get back in. In general terms, we may note that the most primitive human functions—eating and giving birth—are dialectically structured. Marx has shown us that this is also the case with "pure" labor (*Capital*, I.3.VII.1). This being so, it may be argued that the structure of human consciousness is dialectical, and that this structure guarantees that humanity will remain restless, creative, and struggling. The structure, however, does not emerge from some metaphysical essence in the Ideal Form of Reason, but it does not emerge solely from material productive relations either. It emerges from humanity's early and immediate experience of *necessity*, and necessity has *two* poles, eating and production on the one hand, copulating and reproducing on the other. A feminist epistemology must take both into account, for male-stream thought has not overtly done so.[18] Of course, the two are only formally similar. In the most obvious case, the *relation* between production and eating is clear and immediate while that between copulating and giving birth is not: it is precisely here that Hegel first goes a little astray. Producing and eating are not *necessarily* social: even where physiological paternity is not understood, reproduction involves at the very least a dyad, mother and child. Women are in fact fundamentally cut off from mere particularity rather than enmeshed in it amorphously and infinitely. We need no act of derring-do to develop a sense of the unity and separation of another human. We recognize our own children.

What Hegel does not ever come right out and say is that *paternity is necessarily a Concept.* This is the unwritten reality underlying his analysis and distorting it. Paternity must be conceptualized because it is not immediate, but is shot through with an intransigent uncertainty, an uncertainty contingent upon the alienation of the male seed. For men, physiology is fate. It is as the custodian of his estranged seed that man experiences woman as oppressive. When Hegel tells us that in the raptures of love the body loses its character of separability, he does not note that the character of separability itself is generically differentiated. The seed separates from the father, while the "undifferentiated" unity embodied in the child separates only from the mother. Further, this undifferentiated unity that "breaks free" from the original unity does not simply break free; it is not, as Hegel claims, "a self-generating entity." It is brought into the world by the mother's *labor.* Hegel's bizarre attempt to give to copulation rather than to parturition the character of labor consciously or unconsciously turns the gestational clock back to a constitutive moment *prior* to the alienation of the male seed, thus evading the very real separation of men from genetic continuity. Man in fact has a double finitude: the individual finitude he shares with all living creatures, and the general finitude in which his participation in the human race is abrupted at the moment of ejaculation. This is why he sees the human race as "self-developing and self-generative." It is nothing of the kind. It is developed and sustained by women's labor, a labor, moreover, of which women are *conscious*. Consciousness is an integral part of reproduction, though it has been customary to imply that because women cannot help what they are doing in childbirth they do not know what they are doing. What woman is doing as she labors is mediating her separation from the child, canceling by life-risking activity the self-alienation of *her* seed in the certain conceptualization of the child who is born as hers. She is establishing a living *continuity* that men must establish *artificially*.

Hegel does not pay attention to the fact that the male alienation of the seed and the female alienation of the child are *temporally* separated, which does more than exacerbate the uncertainty of paternity. The poets are wiser: "Between the conception and the creation" writes T. S. Eliot, "falls the shadow." This is the shadow of uncertainty inseparable from lapsed and discontinuous time. The significance of this for male and female time consciousness is considerable and almost totally unstudied in an age when temporality and finitude are acute and often melancholy concerns of philosophical thought. Time is not only an enemy of man because of his particular death, but because he "dies" genetically with the alienation of his seed.[19]

Hegel's Idealist conception of history, like all such conceptions, takes off from the world of reality, but at least Hegel tries to get back. Nonetheless, the demonstrable male partiality for separating thought from reality and imputing "reality" to somewhere other than the world has a material base in male reproductive experience, for men are naturally abrupted from *genetic time*, which has its necessary substructure in the process of reproduction and its human objectification in history. Hegel is concerned to make thought temporal and reproduction ahistorical. Yet reproductive process, as soon as the relation between copulation and childbirth is discovered (and we simply do not know when that happened—there are those who consider it part of man's innate equipment, gifted, no doubt, by a patriarchal deity); as soon as this connection is made man is forced to conceptualize paternity, for the relation is susceptible only to rational comprehension. It is not as *lover* that man is annulled; it is as *parent*. If he is to restore himself to genetic unity, indeed, if he is ever to make any sense at all of the notion of a Universality for men, a species-being, he *must* act to negate nature's negation of his temporal unity with his species.

It is this nullity, the negation of paternity that stands in absolute opposition to the concept of paternity, which history shows us very clearly that men *cannot bear*. Despite Hegel's spiritualization of marriage, it simply does not make sense to say that man is concerned about the loss of himself in sexual rapture, for rapture is *always* transitory, for the married or unmarried, for men and for women. Nature cares not at all for orgasmic or conjugal bliss. Men have constructed historically a huge institutional edifice designed to ameliorate the uncertainty of paternity, an edifice that is a true *Idee*, embracing the ideological and actual aspects of men's response to what is perceived as a natural injustice. But the fundamental response, the paradigmatic mediation on which this edifice is constructed, is man's relation to the child. Hegel is correct *for men*; the separated child is the middle term between himself and biological universality, but the middle term *for women* is their active labor.

The relation between male subjective preoccupation with death and man's objective history of wanton killing is not easy to establish. Men do murder and destroy the children of women but this is not because philosophers have said that death is the ultimate human reality. Thomas Hobbes perceived the capacity to kill as the only true equality, and an important causal factor in the urge to create contractual limitations that would transform the equality of the killing capacity to the fragile legal obligation not to exercise this equal capacity haphazardly.[20] Hegel is much concerned with death, and in his *System* spends quite some time in the analysis of the differentiated moral content of different kinds of killing (449–60).

Men do kill for many reasons, or for no discernible reason at all. A feminist perspective, however, cannot indulge in the abstract contemplation of death as the Universal Negative. Nor can we dismiss the historical record that shows a dialectical unity between a consistent mesmerized philosophical infatuation with death and an objective record of the irrational destruction of life. Women must show that their particularity, far from being a dehumanizing and pre-ethical preoccupation with "mere" life, is both more rational and more ethical than the unholy conventicles of those masculine angels of death who have hitherto appropriated "their" particular children while they slaughtered young and old "Tools of Reason" with universal abandon. Men have seen the heroic defiance of the reality of death as their most momentous triumph over Nature, a conceptual, spiritual, and ideological triumph touted as a real one. Its relation to the actual "triumph" over nature's perceived injustice in the realm of birth has not been even contemplated in a serious way by anyone but Hegel. Yet for Hegel, too, it is not by birth that man acquires a historical reality, but by death, an inversion that women must find in the first instance simply weird. Death is, for Hegel, the Great Negation, the negative within life that is, in Harris's words, "the link between the natural and ethical levels of the rational individual's existence."[21] Thus, while the discovery of physiological paternity is ignored as a historical event, rational man discovers death "historically." The reason that this event signals the transcendence of the natural by the ethical is presumably that having discovered his potentiality as killer, man may choose not to exercise it, or to exercise it "impersonally," as in war, or as a tool in the development of the Concept of Legality, as in the trial by combat (Harris, *Hegel's Development*, 62). We have already seen that killing in defense of the community is supremely ethical, and presumably the threat to the community in the first place is an aspect of the essential drive to cancel alienation in mastery. Murder, on the other hand, is in the first instance pre-ethical for it is fixed in the negative aspect of mere life and hence in Particularity. It is the taking of a particular life, and as such, is the essence of *family* killing, the *lex talionis* of the natural justice of revenge. Family killing is not so much unethical as simply insignificant in ethical terms. Murder is not that important to the family, Hegel argues, for family life goes on despite the death of one individual who has only a "formal" as opposed to an ethical existence to negate, and can be satisfactorily balanced by another death taken in exchange. Life itself continues. The important death for Hegel is the "personal" death, the death inflicted on a *known* other in single combat over a point of "honor." This is important because here "justice" is involved, and Justice is an ethical concept. "Honor" is the urge to subsume, to gain mastery, as Hegel says bluntly, and in family war (that is, between, not within, families) the only question is, Who is to dominate? or, Who is to seize the ethical honor of dominating?

Hegel's analysis is extremely difficult to follow. For our present purposes, while it is not quite clear how Hegel gets where he is going, it is quite clear where the terminus of his journey lies. It lies in the polis, in political life, which Hegel sees as the realization of the "absolute ethical life," which subsumes the natural ethical life, which is the best that the family can do. The mediation of this transcendent move lies in negativity, the negation of the individual and his rebirth as citizen, but also negativity that transforms the particularist notion of death by the creation of negotiated rules of war.[22] As Harris remarks, Hegel's analysis is worked out more logically at the Conceptual level, where an orderly transition of the Concept of ethical relations from one stage to another is relatively clear and continuous (*Hegel's Development*, 54). There is less continuity between actual family life and political life, where there is no mediation, but simply a play of nondefined "negativity," and the abrupt replacement of family by polity. Despite the opacities, it is quite clear that Hegel is saying that there is no place in the orbit of family life for the exercise of man's need to master. Here, as we have seen, Hegel is simply wrong, but the result is a very curious one. Man's lust to conquer, to overcome negation, to be willing to die and to kill—all of these leave the family, heretofore limited in its preoccupation with the regeneration and sustenance of *life*, hermetically sealed in the eternal flow of death. Women, the agents of life, become the passive servants of the gods of death whom men transcend.

Women won't kill, and thereby deprive themselves of the creative power of negation and conscious self-alienation. This refusal to risk life, one's own or another's, means that women have no need of a higher ethical system, a timorousness for which Hegel clearly despises us. This lack is also a lack of the desire to command the desire for recognition that the Other flourishes in challenging opposition to self-consciousness. The result is that women can have meaningful relations only with the dead, who have in their negativity presumably universalized the passive life (*Phen.*, 471–72). This necromantic dalliance means that the woman's status as daughter and sister, the genealogical line with dead ancestors, is ethically more important than her status as wife or mother, in which her particularity is invaded without resistance and the genealogical purity of the ancestors is continually diluted. The household of the *Phenomenology*, as opposed to the now developed political realm, exists primarily as the arena of death, a conclusion that is cogent enough if, like Hegel, one draws one's historical data primarily from the Classical drama. Death is the "Lord and Master" of family life. This inversion of the existence of women in the continuity of reproductive and productive life to existential immersion in passive death is dialectical of course, for it moves from the particularity of individual life to the universal inevitability of death, but the dialectical logic in question, however impeccable, owes more to the real-life activities of male supremacists than to the unfolding of Reason. The inversion leads to yet another travesty of biological reality, subsumed with a vengeance in a particular Concept of paternity: "In a household of the ethical kind [i.e., patriarchal marriage] a woman's relationships are not based on a reference to this particular husband, this particular child, but to *a* husband, to children in *general*" (*Phen.*, 476). This is not dialectical opposition but ideological inversion, for it is, of course, *men* who are related to "children in general" and to a particular woman—the legal wife—a truly dialectical opposition mediated by marriage. The freedoms to sire and seduce are not the rewards for ethical effort, but an artificial superstructure mounted on a substructure of biological reality and sexual incontinence. Men are compelled to mediate their "freedom" of choice in paternity (whether or not to "own" the child) with the uncertainty of actual paternity. The inversion of women from the agents of life to the custodianship of the dead is matched by Hegel's inversion of the mediated synthesis of each particular woman with her particular child to a general relationship with undifferentiated children. To be sure, parturitive labor does synthesize women with the genetic reality of the species, but not in her nonlaboring particularity as some man's daughter and some man's son's sister, but specifically as mother.

It is at this point that Hegel has nothing more to teach us on the subject of generic opposition, except, perhaps, what we already suspect: that even the most exalted male intellects cannot make male dominance a *rational* phenomenon. Hegel held among his philosophical aims that of abolishing the Kantian distinction between phenomena and noumena, and his objective idealism is an important step in the vital task of demythologizing worldly reality. But the noumenal Concept of paternity escapes ultimately from his analytical rigor. Though it would be extravagant to claim that the necessarily *abstract* male reproductive experience at the biological root of history guarantees the ultimate metaphysical form of the Hegelian and, indeed, all Idealist systems, it would be fair to claim that any system of thought that grounds itself in an ahistorical and idealized version of human reproduction is doomed to go through its most elaborate conceptual hoops somewhere beyond the reality of actual human experience. Hegel finally gives up on the puzzle of sexuality and regresses to the Antigone fetish, a cult of Sisterhood so extravagant and absurd that it embarrasses his most committed devotees:

> The brother . . . is in the eyes of the sister a being whose nature is unperturbed by desire and is ethically like her own. . . . The brother is the member of the family in whom its spirit becomes individualized, and enabled thereby to turn towards another sphere. . . . The brother leaves this immediate, rudimentary,

> and, therefore, strictly speaking, negative ethical life of the
> family, in order to acquire and produce the concrete ethical order
> which is conscious of itself. (*Phen.*, 477)

The sister stays home to mind the household gods. She is not, of course,
separate from her brother's lawmaking activities; indeed, they include
arrangements to stop her falling into the destructive and chaotic behavior
patterns by which she had put an end to the ancient world. She is not
conscious, however, of this role being hacked out for her in the real world
by her loving brother; she only *feels love*, and as a mother will provide
the feeling of love for her children. The brother, meanwhile, is acquiring
in the public realm the "rights of desire," which apparently serve to keep
his sexual ardor in check, for in acquiring these rights, "he keeps himself
at the same time in detachment from [desire]" (*Phen.*, 477).

One cannot help reflecting that in the same year that Hegel published
this affirmation of man's capacity to transcend sexual desire in the
pursuit of the ethics of Universality, his own illegitimate son was born.
In fairness to Hegel, it should be added that he brought the boy into the
"natural ethical community" of his own household with, he claimed,
the full acquiescence of his wife.[23] The fact that Hegel's own relationship
with desire was less detached than his analytical intelligence suggests is
less important, however, than the realities which he inverts rather than
mediates. Male consciousness, however certain of itself as Man, is
uncertain of itself as father, and no amount of ethical sincerity can
annul this uncertainty in spiritual rectitude. In an oblique way, Hegel
perhaps recognizes this, though he still directs the lack of recognition to
the female parent:

> Just as the individual divine man [the historical Christ] has an
> implied father and only an actual mother, in like manner the
> universal divine man, the spiritual communion, has as its father
> its own proper action and knowledge, while its mother is external
> Love, which it merely *feels*, but does not behold in its conscious-
> ness as an actual immediate object. (*Phen.*, 784)

Thus the mother is etherialized and the father objectified, and the
struggle against nature's tiresome negation of paternal certitude is complete . . .

Hegel's is probably the greatest and most sustained attempt to rationalize and perfect the tradition of male-stream thought and to justify the definition of creative humanity as "Man." Yet even Hegel cannot resolve men's reproductive dilemma, and he only abstractly resolves their existential one, created by the definition of the human historical task as being that of mastering and possessing Nature rather than rationally and lovingly nurturing a balanced unity with "Her." Nonetheless, Hegel is not just a historical monument or a stuffed Owl. He has taught us that reproductive process is dialectical. He has shown us, sometimes by default, the structure of man's struggle to weld his potency with his purpose in his struggle with alienation, uncertainty, and nonrecognition. He has shown us that there is a dialectical opposition between the social realities of production and reproduction, an insight Marx unfortunately missed. He has shown us why Life yields to Death as the primordial male experience. In doing these things, he offers us a historical ground and a philosophical foundation for a new transcendent philosophy of Birth and Life that must be the theoretical component of the feminist praxis that history now commands us to develop.

Notes

1. G. W. F. Hegel, *The Phenomenology of Mind,* trans. J. B. Baillie (New York: Harper and Row, 1967 [1807]). Hereafter referred to as *Phen.*

The following abbreviations are used in this paper for Hegel's other works:

"Love"; G. W. F. Hegel, "On Love," in *Early Theological Writings,* trans. T. M. Knox (Chicago: University of Chicago Press, 1948).

"System"; G. W. F. Hegel, "The System of Ethical Life," trans. T. M. Knox and H. S. Harris, unpublished, 1975.

P. of R.; G. W. F. Hegel, *Hegel's Philosophy of Right,* trans. T. M. Knox (New York: Oxford University Press, 1967 [1821]).

I thank Professor Harris for permission to make use of his translation, and also his invaluable unpublished essay, "Introductory Essay to Hegel's 'The System of Ethical Life' " (1975). Like all students of Hegel's early writings, I also owe an immeasurable debt to Harris for his work in this heretofore rather misty area: H. S. Harris, *Hegel's Development: Toward the Sunlight* (Oxford: Clarendon Press, 1972).

2. Whether Marxist theory is an adequate ground for such praxis is too large a question to be tacked on to a discussion of Hegel. However, it should be noted in passing that Marx does not transcend Hegel's generic one-sidedness, and may not, indeed, have so clear a notion of the dialectical structure of reproduction as Hegel has. Marx's theory is a prodigious exercise in the logic of necessity, but necessity has two poles, production and reproduction, and Marx conflates them.

3. Plato's discussion is in *The Republic,* bk. VIII, S546. For a discussion of the role of rites of "marriage" (*telete*) in the all-male mystery cults, see George Thomson, *Aeschylus and Athens* (New York: Haskell House Publishers, 1967), 127 and passim.

4. Hegel finally dealt more broadly with the *Philosophy of Nature*, in which a more developed misogyny is historicized in a romantic vision of prehistory. A more elaborate feminist critique of his work on reproduction that centers on this work is my *The Politics of Reproduction*.

5. The quotation is from the 1805–6 lectures, which are not translated. It is quoted by George Armstrong Kelly, "Notes on Hegel's Lordship and Bondage" in *Hegel*, ed. Alistair MacIntyre (New York: Anchor Books, 1972), 198.

6. T. M. Knox's explication of these terms cannot be improved upon. I have borrowed freely from it, but in a compressed way. See Knox's "Introduction" to *P. of R.*, especially vii–x.

7. *Idee*, to be distinguished from *Vorstellung*, which is idea in the sense of what one is thinking about—there is no such distinction in English.

8. Simone de Beauvoir, *The Second Sex*, trans. H. M. Parshley (New York: Knopf, 1961 [1949]), esp. 59 et. seq. where Beauvoir argues that the Master and Slave argument applies much better to the relation of man and woman. Beauvoir notes correctly that Hegel's discussion of sexuality argues from significance to necessity instead of the other way round (4). Beauvoir's own error is to argue from *sexuality* to significance, neglecting the formal unity of reproductive process in which sexuality is but one aspect of the whole. See also 16 infra.

9. Ultimately, there is a curious dialectical structure to Hegel's Universal notion of paternity, which is too obscure and extensive to be worked out here. Briefly, there is a suggestion of some kind of ideological inversion going on between the Concepts of Divine and mere biological paternity. In this process, Religion becomes Concrete, a unity of spiritual and actual, whereas human marriage becomes essentially spiritual. It is very difficult to "prove" textually that this is what happens; such a demonstration requires a theological sophistication and knowledge of Hegel's religious writings that I cannot claim to possess.

10. *Phen.*, B.IV.A. Beauvoir's argument (12) that the Master and Slave parable would be more apt in a male/female context than in man and man, is, I think, a misunderstanding, for women are already "mastered," and without a struggle. They have no "separability" from the Other to negate, for their tie to others (kin) is complete and their Universality in this limited sphere Conceptually complete (Beauvoir, *The Second Sex*, 49 et. seq.).

11. Of course, modes of contraception have existed for a long time, and many feminists have argued that these have been deliberately suppressed by men. In Hegelian terminology, these have been particular modes of contraception, but contemporary technology can realize "universal" contraception, a fact that profoundly transforms the social relations of reproduction.

12. See Harris, *Hegel's Development*, 34–35, for a clearer account of Hegel's very opaque discussion of the structure of need as opposed to desire. Mere need, immediate gratification, is a subsumption of intuition under the Concept, logically and developmentally prior to the release of the intelligently directed labor which includes foresight as to future needs in productive terms. Reproductively, men and women are "equal" at the animal, intuitive state, but they are not "absolutely equal" (*System*, 425). It is never really clear just why.

13. The interjections in parentheses are mine. The textual interpolations in brackets are the translator's.

14. Men, of course, are not wholly Universal in their Particularity, which includes biological needs, and is concerned and ultimately socialized in Civil Society, existing with but transcended by political society, which is the realization of Man's Universality.

15. This is not the case in *P. of R.* (112), where a distinction is made between ethical (married) lovers and mere philanderers, whose "physical passion sinks to the level of a physical moment, destined to vanish in its very satisfaction. On the other hand, the spiritual bond of union secures its rights as the substance of marriage, and thus rises, inherently indissoluble, to a plane above the transience of passion and the transience of particular caprice."

16. *System*, 437, 438. See also Harris, *Hegel's Development*, 9. Possessions are realized, of course, by virtue of the alienated labor which is their essential content.

17. "The pure infinity of legal right, its inseparability, reflected in the thing, i.e., in the particular itself, is the thing's *equality* with other things, and the abstraction of this equality of one thing with another, concrete unity and legal right, is *value*; . . . but the actually found and empirical measure is the *price*" (*System*, 437).

18. That this reality is a covert substratum to male-stream thought even at its most recondite levels, as well as its more overt manifestations in myth and literature, constitutes an uncovering challenge to feminist scholarship.

19. The very long history of an association between the male ejaculation and death appears to have been of interest mainly to psychoanalysis. Philip Slater, for example, is astonished that such a pervading literary and cultic theme should be rooted in such a "trivial" reality. Slater does not recognize himself as the heir to centuries of alienation. See Philip Slater, *The Glory of Hera: Greek Mythology and the Greek Family* (Boston: Beacon, 1971). Apart from this brief opacity, this book is a very valuable study for students of the ideology of male supremacy.

20. Thomas Hobbes, *Leviathan* (Harmondsworth: Penguin Books, 1968 [1651]), I.XIII.

21. Harris, *Hegel's Development*, 50. In the interests of lucidity, I follow Harris's interpretive essay here, though in a simplified and perhaps oversimplified way. Harris notes some of the difficulties and ambiguities of Hegel's analysis, including the opacity that attends the emphasis put on single combat when Hegel appears to have already moved from the level of the family to that of society.

22. Strictly, havoc is the second form: the first is individual combat, trial by combat in the *System*. In the *Phenomenology*, of course, it is our friends the Master and Slave.

23. The young man does not appear to have been very happy, and died, with chilling appropriateness, a soldier's death from fever.

9

Hegel, Marriage, and the Standpoint of Contract

Carole Pateman

Hegel is usually presented as one of the foremost critics of theories of an original contract. He rejects the idea that the state is (or can be seen as if it is) based on a contract, and he is a profound critic of contractual arguments more generally. But Hegel also shares important ground with the classical contract theorists. This area of agreement goes unnoticed for five related reasons. First, conceptions of masculinity and femininity and of relations between the sexes are assumed by most contemporary political theorists to be peripheral to, or irrelevant to, their major concerns. Therefore, no significance is given to the fact that Hegel, like the contract theorists,[1] claims that women lack men's birthright of freedom and, by nature, lack the capacities required for participation in public life, including its constitutive practice of contract.

Second, standard discussions of Hegel and the classic contract theorists pay little attention to their arguments about the marriage contract, and completely ignore the history of feminist argument about marriage. Thus the major question is never asked of why, if women are held to be lacking in the attributes required to make contracts, they are nonetheless always assumed to be capable of entering into the marriage contract. And why does the marriage contract form part of the arguments of both the classic contract theorists and Hegel?

Third, there is a general failure to distinguish marriage from the family. They are, of course, closely related, but they are not the same. Many theoretical moves and sleights of hand, and many aspects of women's relations to men, go unnoticed when marriage is subsumed into the family. Marriage is the contractual "origin" of the family, and forms one of the three great institutional bonds of modern society—family, employment, citizenship—that have, or are said to have, their genesis in contract.

Fourth, discussions of the idea of an original contract invariably assume that it is synonymous with the familiar social contract, and treat contract as the antithesis of patriarchy. However, the social contract is only one dimension of theories of an original contract, and students of political theory learn only half the story. They are told the tale of the genesis of political right in the sense of the government of the state, but they hear nothing about the other dimension of the original pact: the sexual contract. The original contract is also the genesis of political right in the sense of modern patriarchal right, or men's government over women that is, in large part, maintained through contract.[2]

Fifth, contract theory is all too often assumed to be the same as liberalism, and synonymous with consent or free agreement more generally. On the contrary, contract, as Hegel makes clear, is a specific theoretical viewpoint. Contract hinges upon the idea of the individual as the owner of property in the person. The individual stands to this personal property in exactly the same external relation as to material property such as a car or a house. Property in the person can, therefore, be subject to contract, just like any other property, if it is to the advantage of the owner to sell it or contract it out for use.

Hegel's criticism of contract and the contract theorists does not extend to the sexual contract; he endorses it as firmly as Rousseau. The general failure to notice that the contract theorists and Hegel are agreed on this crucial matter means that some curious features of Hegel's argument are glossed over in the standard discussions. No answer is provided, therefore, to the following puzzle: Why does Hegel, on the one hand, claim that it is "shameful" to see marriage as a purely contractual institution; yet, on the other hand, insist that marriage originates in a contract, albeit one that "is precisely a contract to transcend the standpoint of contract"?[3]

Kant was the contract theorist who provoked Hegel's comment about the shamefulness of marriage "degraded to the level of a contract for reciprocal use" (PR, §75 and addition to §161). Kant saw marriage as "the Union of two Persons of different sex for life-long reciprocal possession of their sexual faculties."[4] Such a conception of marriage is an example of strict adherence to the standpoint of contract. Both Kant and Hegel rejected the conception of the individual as owner, and this rejection not only deepens the puzzle about why Hegel clung to the marriage contract, but also raises another difficulty: Why does Kant treat marriage as a contract for use of sexual property?

Little attention has been paid to Kant's tortuous and contradictory account of the marriage contract. The familiar picture of Kant is of a philosopher whose arguments rest on the premise that, by virtue of being human, everyone has reason and so possesses the capacity to act according to universal moral laws and to participate in civil life. But Kant also upheld the sexual contract and thus saw human capacity as sexually differentiated. His "universalism" does not extend to women, who, he claims, lack political or civil reason.

For Kant, men are governed by reason and are their own masters. Self-mastery is demonstrated in the way a man gains his livelihood; when social circumstances require a man to be another's servant or labor at the behest of another, he lacks the requirement for possession of a "civil personality" and must be excluded from citizenship. Men do not lose the potential for self-mastery, but accidents of fortune and circumstance disqualify some as civil personalities. The case of women is quite different. All women lack self-mastery and are disqualified from citizenship. Kant states that "women in general . . . have no civil personality, and their existence is, so to speak, purely inherent."[5] Women must thus be mastered by men, in particular by their husbands; Kant's marriage contract establishes the patriarchal right of the husband. But if women have no civil personality, how can they be party to the marriage contract? Kant also wants to claim that the spouses are equal. He rejects the suspicion—a suspicion voiced very loudly from a variety of quarters by the 1790s, when the *Philosophy of Law* appeared—that there is something contradictory about postulating both equality and legal recognition of the husband as master. He states that the husband's power over his wife "cannot be regarded as contrary to the natural Equality of a human pair, if such legal Supremacy is based only upon the natural superiority of the faculties of the Husband compared with the Wife, in the effectuation of the common interest of the household; and if the Right to command is based merely upon this fact" (*PL*, §26, 111–12).

Kant's account of marriage both denies and presupposes women's lack of civil personality, and the same difficulty arises with individuals as owners of property in their persons. Kant asks: "Can [the sexes] sell themselves or let themselves out on hire, or by some other contract allow use to be made of their sexual faculties?"[6] He answers that such use is not permissible because property in the person cannot be separated from the individual owner. To acquire "part of the human organism"—to take possession only of the sexual property of another individual—is to acquire the individual as property (*PL*, §25, 111). Indeed, Kant argues that it is impossible to use only part of a person "without having at the same time a right of disposal over the whole person, for each part of a person is integrally bound up with the whole." Kant concludes that "the sole condition on which we are free to make use of our sexual desire depends upon the right to dispose over the person as a whole—over the welfare and happiness and generally over all the circumstances of that person."[7]

In an unconvincing theoretical move, Kant offers an account of the marriage contract in terms of "personal right," or "the Right to the *possession* of an external object as a Thing and the *use* of it as a Person."[8] The only reason that Kant does not simply argue that two persons enter into the marriage contract is that women, lacking a civil personality, are not persons, or individuals, who can make contracts. Women can only remain as things, as property, if the sexual contract is not to be disturbed. In amplifying his notion of personal right, Kant uses the revealing example of the difference between pointing to someone and saying "this is my father," which means only that I have a father and here he is, and pointing to someone and saying "this is my wife." To point to a wife is to refer to "a special juridical relation of a possessor to an object viewed as a thing, although in this case it is a person."[9] Kant notes that personal right is distinct from possessing a slave, a man who has lost his civil personality—but to possess a wife is to possess someone who, naturally, has no civil personality, although she is not called a slave.

Hegel's charge that a contractual view of marriage is shameful is directed at only one element of Kant's argument. He agreed with Kant that the sexual contract and the patriarchal right of husbands must be secured, and so he reenacts the contradictions of Kant's account of marriage and of women's standing as individuals. Hegel regards it as shameful to substitute the individual as owner for the complexity of human personality and ethical life. The individual as owner and contract-maker is what Hegel calls an "immediate self-subsistent person," and although this is one element, or "moment," in the individual personality and in social life, it is not and cannot be the whole (PR, §75). To see marriage as a contract entered into by owners of the sexual property in their persons is completely to misunderstand marriage and its place in modern civil life. Purely as contract, marriage is open to the contingency, the whim and caprice, of sexual inclination. The marriage ceremony becomes merely the means to avoid unauthorized use of bodies. On the contrary, for Hegel, marriage is a distinct form of ethical life—part of the universal social whole of family/civil society/state—constituted by a principle of association far removed from contract.

The marriage contract, according to Hegel, stands on its own; indeed, it transcends contract. From the standpoint of contract, two individuals who contract together recognize each other as property owners and mutually will that they should use each other's property. The owner is related externally to his property and so, as it were, stands outside the contract and is unchanged by it. The unity of will of the two parties is sheer coincidence. In contrast, Hegel's marriage contract creates a rational, ethical bond that unites the spouses internally in their association and not externally as property owners. The consciousness and standing of the man and woman who marry is changed, and a public, duly authorized ceremony is thus essential to marriage. A husband and wife cease to be "self-subsistent" individuals. Hegel writes that, in marrying, the spouses "consent to make themselves one person, to renounce their natural and individual personality to this unity of one with the other. From this point of view, their union is a self-restriction, but in fact it is their liberation, because in it they attain their substantive self-consciousness" (PR, §162).

But this is true only for the husband. He gains the right of patriarchal government in the home and a position from which he can move out into the economy and the state. When a man becomes a husband, for Hegel no less than for Kant and the other contract theorists, he becomes the "one person" who represents the couple in civil life. The wife disappears as a civil personality. Hegel's marriage conforms to the (English common) law of coverture, that Sir William Blackstone explained as follows: "By marriage, the husband and wife are as one person in law: that is, the very being, or legal existence of the woman is suspended during the marriage, or at least is incorporated and consolidated into that of the husband."[10]

The end of marriage, for Hegel, is not mutual sexual use; sexual passion is merely one moment of marriage, a moment that disappears as it is satisfied. The marriage contract creates a substantive relation constituted by "love, trust, and common sharing of their entire existence as individuals." A husband and wife are bound together neither by contract, nor sexual inclination, nor even by love as usually understood. They are incorporated by "ethico-legal love" which transcends the fickleness of ordinary, romantic love (PR, §163 and addition to §161). Hegel states that love is "the most tremendous contradiction" (PR, addition to §158). The contradiction comes about because the lovers' first impulse is to obliterate their individuality in total unification with the loved one. However, in opposition to this desire, they also discover that their sense of themselves as autonomous beings is strengthened through the relationship with the beloved. The gulf between obliteration and enhancement of self can be overcome by the mutual recognition of the two lovers, through which each gains a deeper sense of unity with the other and sense of autonomy of the self. Love (in Hegel's sense) both unifies and differentiates. Thus marriage offers a glimpse of the differentiation and particularity of civil (economic) society and the unity and universality necessary to membership in the state.

Hegel's criticism of the marriage contract goes far beyond the reduction of conjugal relations to a contract of mutual use. If marriage were merely contractual, civil society would be undermined; the necessary, private foundation for public life would be lacking. The idea of the individual as owner is fundamental to contract, but if ownership is exhaustive of the human personality, then, ironically, the necessary social condition for contract is eliminated. Any example of contract presupposes that contracts must be kept; that is to say, trust and mutual fidelity are presupposed. Individuals understand what "to contract" means only because any single contract is part of the wider practice of contracting, and the practice is constituted by the understanding that contracts are binding.

The conception of the individual as owner of the property in his person at once eliminates yet relies upon the intersubjective understanding of what it means to enter into a contract. As Durkheim argued sometime later, "a contract supposes something other than itself."[11] Contract must form part of wider noncontractual social institutions. Contracts can be entered into precisely because consciousness is developed and informed within arenas that are noncontractual. If individuals were merely owners they could enter into no contracts at all; strictly, "contract" would be meaningless to them. Hegel argues that contract has an appropriate place in the economic sphere—the sphere that he calls civil society—but if contract is extended beyond its own realm, social order is threatened. Contract on its own is an incoherent basis for social life.

Hegel, echoing Kant, argues that marriage is an ethical duty: "marriage . . . is one of the absolute principles on which the ethical life of a community depends" (PR, §167). Ethical life depends upon marriage because marriage is the origin of the family. In the family, children learn, and adults are continually reminded of, what it means to be a member of a small association based on love and trust; in the private dimension of ethical life they gain experience of a noncontractual association and so are prepared—or, rather, men are prepared—for participation in the universal public sphere of the state.

In the Philosophy of Right, Hegel criticizes Rousseau's contract theory as well as Kant's marriage contract, but he follows Rousseau closely in his patriarchal understanding of masculinity and femininity. Hegel argues that sexual difference has political significance (rational expression); only men are endowed with the (masculine) capacity to enter civil society and participate in political life, and only the husband has the "prerogative to go out and work for [the family's] living, to attend to its needs, and to control and administer its capital" (PR, §171). Like Rousseau, Hegel sees women as naturally politically subversive; if "women hold the helm of government, the state is at once in jeopardy."[12]

But women play a substantive part in Hegel's argument. For Hegel, as for the classic contract theorists, marriage and the family provide the natural foundation for civil life, but Hegel goes much further. He also implies that, through their love, husbands and wives play out, in a manner suited to the "immediate" ethical sphere, the dialectic of mutual acknowledgment that characterizes relations among men as makers of contracts in civil society and as citizens in the state. Through contract, men recognize each other as property owners, enjoying an equal standing; as citizens they also mutually recognize their civil equality. Hegel's account of love within marriage suggests that the same process of recognition takes place between husband and wife, through the dialectic of autonomy and unity. But one party to the marriage contract is a woman; therefore conjugal relations cannot take the same form as civil relations between men. Sexual difference is political difference, the difference between mastery and subjection, so how can there be mutual acknowledgment by husband and wife as, at one and the same time, particular and universal beings? And if such recognition is impossible, how can marriage and the family constitute a moment of Hegel's social whole of family/civil society/state?

The answer to the last question lies in an appreciation of the different forms of recognition required in relations between men and between husband and wife. Marriage is indeed a crucial moment in Hegel's political theory, but it has a rather different place than is usually suggested. The distinctive contribution of marriage and the marriage contract can be seen by comparing the recognition given to each other by men, as spelt out in Hegel's famous dialectic of mastery and slavery, and that required by a husband from his wife, or men from women in general. Hegel argues that mutual acknowledgment and confirmation of self is possible only if two selves have an equal status. The master cannot see his independence reflected back in the self of the slave; all he finds is servility. Self-consciousness must receive acknowledgment from another self of the same kind, and so the master-slave relation must be transcended. The master and slave can, as it were, move through the moments of Hegel's great story and eventually meet as equals in the civil society of the *Philosophy of Right*. The men's story can be completed once the original pact is sealed and civil society and the modern state brought into being. In the fraternity of public life each man can obtain self-confirmation and acknowledgment of his equality in the brotherhood. But this is not quite the end of the story.

Men's self-consciousness is not purely the consciousness of free civil equals (the story of the social contract); it is also the consciousness of patriarchal masters (the story of the sexual contract). The ostensible universalism of Hegel's public world, just like that of the classic contract theorists, gains its meaning when men look from the public world to the private domestic sphere and the subjection of wives. Marriage (private) and civil society/state (public) are both separate and inseparable. As a husband, a man cannot receive acknowledgment as an equal from his wife. But a husband is not engaged in relations with other men, his equals: he is married to a woman, his natural subordinate. Patriarchal right requires that women's acknowledgment of men cannot be the same as men's acknowledgment of their fellow men. Hegel's political order demands a sexually differentiated consciousness (his discussion of ethico-legal love notwithstanding) so that relations between men and women remain those of masters and subordinates. The recognition that a husband obtains from a wife is precisely what is required: recognition as a patriarchal master, which only a woman can provide.

The rational basis that Hegel finds for women's subordination to men brings us back to the two puzzles with which I began this chapter. Natural subordinates lack the capacities of free men who make contracts—so why, then, does Hegel insist that women are able to enter the marriage contract, and, moreover, insist on retaining the marriage contract when he rejects the standpoint of contract? Other forms of noncontractual agreement exist, to which Hegel could turn. Or, more logically, given the patriarchal construction of masculinity and femininity that Hegel shares with the classic contract theorists, the marriage ceremony could provide more than adequate confirmation of the natural subordination of women when they become wives.

The answer to the puzzles is that Hegel cannot exclude the marriage contract from his political theory without contradicting his claim to have explicated the rationality of a free political order. The reason that women must enter the marriage contract is that they must be incorporated into that order. The political order can be presented as *free* only when free relations extend to all spheres. Hegel retains contract as one essential element of freedom. Unless women are to remain outside the free order, marriage must originate in a contract.

Men interact in civil society (the economy) through the "particularity" that characterizes makers of contracts, and women, as parties to the marriage contract, must thus share in the attribute of particularity. Women are incorporated into the political order through the marriage contract, and are incorporated on the same basis as men; parties to contracts enjoy equal standing. Only if women, too, enter into a contract, can Hegel argue that the dialectic of love is a moment in the wider dialectic of family/civil society/state. Yet the marriage contract also has to be a unique contract. Hegel has to make this claim if the requisite form of consciousness is to obtain within marriage. He rejects the abstraction of the standpoint of contract because even the bond of mutual use cannot exist over time without the trust and faith that the standpoint of contract eliminates. Hegel's special marriage contract must thus transcend the standpoint of contract—but, nevertheless, it cannot transcend the sexual contract.

Hegel's marriage contract must also be different from other contracts because *women* are involved. Hegel claims that his political theory encompasses universal freedom; women, therefore, must share in that freedom, and they do so by entering into the marriage contract. At the same time, the marriage contract confirms patriarchal right and women's (natural) lack of freedom. Women both enter into a contract as free beings and are incorporated into the political order as "women," as subordinates. Men can receive acknowledgment of their patriarchal right only if women's subjection is institutionalized. The difference between the marriage contract and other contracts has always been indicated plainly enough in the vow of obedience, although it is not always now included in the speech acts of the marriage ceremony. Only the marriage contract includes the explicit commitment to obey. The promise of universal freedom, heralded by the story of an original contract, will appear fraudulent from the start if women do not take part in contract. But if men's civil status as equals and patriarchal masters is to be maintained, the contract into which women enter must be separated from other contracts. A woman contracts to obey her husband when she becomes a wife; what better way of giving public affirmation to patriarchal right?[13]

Hegel was not alone in regarding the marriage contract as a unique contract. From at least the early nineteenth century, feminists have criticized the marriage contract on the grounds that it is not a proper contract. The critics take a contract to be an agreement between two equal parties who negotiate until they arrive at terms that are to their mutual advantage. In contrast, the marriage contract gives all the advantages to one party, the terms cannot be altered, and women have little choice but to enter into it. As William Thompson declared in 1825:

> A contract! where are any of the attributes of contracts, of equal and just contracts, to be found in this transaction? A contract implies the voluntary assent of both the contracting parties. Can even both the parties, man and woman, by agreement alter the

terms, as to *indissolubility* and *inequality*, of this pretended contract? No. Can any individual man divest himself, were he even
so inclined, of his power of despotic control? He cannot. Have
women been consulted as to the terms of this pretended contract?[14]

Despite the many reforms of marriage law since 1825, including provision
for divorce, feminist critics in the 1970s and early 1980s once again
emphasized how far the marriage contract diverged from other contracts.[15] For example, a married couple cannot determine the terms of
the marriage contract to suit their own circumstances. There is not even
a choice available between several different contracts; there is only *the*
marriage contract. A married couple cannot contract to change the
essentials of marriage, which are seen as "the husband's duty to support
his wife, and the wife's duty to serve her husband."[16] Feminist critics
have also pointed out that the marriage contract does not exist as a
written document that is read and then signed by the contracting parties.
Generally, a contract is valid only if the parties have read and understood
its terms before they commit themselves. The fact that most marriages
lack any such document, illustrates one of the most striking features of
the marriage contract. There is no paper headed "The Marriage Contract" to be signed. Instead, the unwritten contract of marriage, to
which a man and a woman are bound when they become husband and
wife, is codified in the law governing marriage and family life.

There is another reason, too, why there is usually no written document. A man and a woman do not become husband and wife by putting
their signatures on a contract. Marriage is constituted through two
different acts. First, a prescribed ceremony is performed during the
course of which the couple undertake a speech act. The man and woman
each say the words "I do." These words are a "performative utterance";
that is to say, by virtue of saying the words, the standing of the man and
woman is transformed. In the act of saying "I do," a man becomes a
husband and a woman becomes a wife; bachelors and spinsters are turned
into married couples by uttering certain words. But the marriage can still
be invalidated unless a second act is performed: the marriage must also
be "consummated" through sexual intercourse. Kant was emphatic
about this: "The Contract of Marriage is completed only by conjugal
cohabitation. A Contract of two Persons of different sex, with the secret
understanding either to abstain from conjugal cohabitation or with the

consciousness on either side of incapacity for it, is a *simulated Contract*; it does not constitute a marriage."[17] The story of the sexual contract explains why a signature, or even a speech act, is insufficient for a valid marriage. The act that is required, the act that seals the contract, is (significantly) called *the sex act*. Not until a husband has exercised his conjugal right is the marriage contract complete.

One conclusion to be drawn from such arguments is that, as many feminists have argued, the marriage contract should become a proper contract. But what are the implications of this demand? On the one hand, it may be that "contract" is being used to suggest no more than that the patriarchal arrangement called marriage should be replaced by an equitable agreement between spouses. On the other hand, it may mean that the standpoint of contract should be brought to bear on marriage, so that marriage would become a contract for mutual sexual use. In that case, Hegel's criticisms of contract become relevant. Hegel's endorsement of the sexual contract invites feminists to disregard his insights into contract, but the temptation should be resisted.

Consider, for example, Hegel's argument that a marriage must lead to a family; that is, a husband and wife must become parents. Hegel argues that the unity of the spouses is only "inward" unless there are children; "it is only in children that the unity itself exists externally, objectively, and explicitly as a unity." The love of the spouses for each other is "objectified for them in the child" (*PR*, §173 and addition). Although Hegel does not make this point, from the standpoint of contract there is no good reason to become a parent since an infant can only be seen as an encumbrance. A contract for mutual sexual use can accommodate physical genesis without difficulty. The problem arises with the long-term commitment as a parent required for human development. To make such a commitment will put the parties to the contract at a disadvantage since they will not be able to take up other contracts that offer greater advantages. Hegel did not rule out divorce—although the "ethical dissolution" of the family takes place when grown children became husbands and wives (*PR*, §177)—but divorce is a different matter from the elimination of marriage (and the family) entailed by the logic of contract.

One of Hegel's objections to marriage as a contract is that it leaves the relationship at the mercy of the whims and capricious wills of the contractors. Similarly, Durkheim emphasized that the bond created by contract is both external and of short duration; it leads to "transient relations and passing associations."[18] Contemporary writers have stressed that one advantage of a proper marriage contract is that its term can be limited, running for, say, five years. But why, from the standpoint of contract, should any arrangement that resembles marriage be maintained? Parties to contracts should always be available for new and better transactions. The logic of a contract of mutual sexual use is that "marriage" and "divorce" should be eliminated in favor of an endless series of very short-term contracts to use another's body as and when required. Other services provided at present within marriage could also be contracted for in the market, including care for infants and children. A universal market in bodies and services would replace marriage (and the family). The logic of the standpoint of contract is that marriage would be supplanted by contracts for access to sexual property. Marriage would give way to *universal prostitution.*

Taken to this logical conclusion, the standpoint of contract also entails that "women" and "men" disappear. All that would remain would be individual owners contracting out sexual property for use; sexual difference would be meaningless in these transactions. Contemporary feminist critics have highlighted another defect of the marriage contract that points in the same direction. Unlike other contracts, the marriage contract cannot be entered into by any two (or more) sane adults, but is restricted to two parties, one of whom must be a man and the other a woman (and who must not be related in certain prescribed ways). Not only does a husband obtain a certain power over his wife whether or not he wishes to have it, but the marriage contract is sexually ascriptive. A man is always a "husband" and a woman is always a "wife." Earlier feminists would be quite startled by this criticism; they objected to the status of a *wife,* but they had no quarrel with the fact that only *women* became wives.

What follows from criticism of the sexually ascriptive character of marriage depends upon whether the critics are arguing from the standpoint of contract. There are two other problems with this standpoint. First, that the idea of the person as no more than a collection of pieces of property that can be contracted out for use without detriment to the owner is, as Hegel saw, a fiction. There are, it is true, some parts of the self that are detachable and can be sold as commodities. A trade has developed in, for example, sperm, ova and (more covertly) kidneys. But, in general, the body, self, and capabilities have to be used, or put to use, along with the "property" in question if the buyer is to get what he paid for (consider, e.g., employment, prostitution, or so-called surrogate motherhood).[19]

Second, the owner is not a sexually neutral figure. The logic of the standpoint of contract eliminates sexual difference only in the sense that sexuality would be subsumed under the patriarchal model of "the sex act." A distinctive feminine sexuality, or femininity more generally, would disappear. The triumph of contract is not over patriarchy but over women. The standpoint of contract relies on and reinforces the very unitary, closed view of "individuals" (or "subjects") that recent feminist scholarship has taken such pains to deconstruct and destabilize.

The criticism that only women can be "wives" need not, however, be based on the standpoint of contract. At the close of the twentieth century, marriage as traditionally understood can neither accommodate an equal relationship between a man and woman nor form the basis for the variety of forms of familial households and homosexual unions now so common in most Western countries. A new mode of association is required, but that does not mean a new contractual relationship. The mistaken assumption that "contract" is synonymous with free agreement is a major barrier to new thinking about the transformation of marriage. Once the standpoint of contract is distinguished from promising and other ways of agreeing and making commitments, and the idea of the individual as owner is relinquished, the way is opened up for the creation of genuinely equitable unions between autonomous partners.

Notes

1. Hobbes is the exception. He starts from the radical premise that women and men are equal in the state of nature, but the significance of Hobbes's claim remains unexamined by his commentators; see C. Pateman, " 'God Hath Ordained to Man a Helper': Hobbes, Patriarchy and Conjugal Right," in *The Disorder of Women: Democracy, Feminism and Political Theory* (Stanford: Stanford University Press, 1989).

2. I have excavated the full story of the original contract in *The Sexual Contract* (Stanford: Stanford University Press, 1988). In chapter 4, I also noted that, ironically, although this is a story of origins, the fact that only half the tale is told means that the "true origin" of political right in men's sex-right, or, more narrowly, conjugal right, remains in obscurity. I filled in the missing portion, the "logic," of the story, but, curiously, I have sometimes been taken as presenting my own view!

3. G. W. F. Hegel, *Philosophy of Right*, trans. T. M. Knox (Oxford: Clarendon Press, 1952), §163; hereafter cited as PR.

4. I. Kant, *The Philosophy of Law*, trans. W. Hastie (Edinburgh: T. and T. Clark, 1887), §24, 110; hereafter cited as PL.

5. I. Kant, *Political Writings*, ed. H. Reiss (Cambridge: Cambridge University Press, 1970),

139. This edition of Kant's writings is very widely used, and the book provides interesting confirmation that conjugal right is still seen as outside the "public" matters properly discussed by political theorists: sections dealing with "private right," including marriage, are omitted from the extracts from *The Metaphysics of Morals* (*The Philosophy of Law*), whereas sections on "public right" are included.

6. I. Kant, *Lectures on Ethics*, trans. L. Infield (New York: Harper and Row, 1963), 164.

7. Kant, *Lectures on Ethics*, 166–67.

8. Kant, *PL*, chap. 2, §3, 22, p. 108.

9. Ibid., "Supplementary Explanations of the Principles of Right," 238 n. 1.

10. Sir William Blackstone, *Commentaries on the Laws of England*, 4th ed., ed. J. DeWitt Andrews (Chicago: Callaghan, 1899), bk. I, chap. 15, §111, 442.

11. E. Durkheim, *The Division of Labor in Society* (New York: Free Press, 1964), 381. On these points see also C. Pateman, *The Problem of Political Obligation*, 2d ed. (Berkeley and Los Angeles: University of California Press, 1985).

12. *PR*, addition to §166. On Rousseau's views see C. Pateman, "The Disorder of Women," in *The Disorder of Women: Democracy, Feminism and Political Theory*, and *The Sexual Contract*.

13. There is also another way; prostitution (the prostitution contract) also provides public affirmation of men's sexual mastery; see *The Sexual Contract*, chap. 7.

14. W. Thompson, *Appeal of One Half the Human Race, Women, Against the Pretensions of the Other Half, Men, to Retain them in Political, and Thence in Civil and Domestic Slavery* (New York: Source Book Press, 1970 [first published 1825]), 55–56. Other early feminist arguments are discussed in *The Sexual Contract*, chap. 6.

15. For example, see M. M. Shultz, "Contractual Ordering of Marriage: A New Model for State Policy," *California Law Review* 70, no. 2 (1982); L. J. Weitzman, *The Marriage Contract: Spouses, Lovers, and the Law* (New York: Free Press, 1981); S. A. Ketchum, "Liberalism and Marriage Law," in *Feminism and Philosophy*, ed. M. Vetterling-Braggin, F. A. Elliston and J. English (Totowa, N.J.: Littlefield, Adams, 1977); and D. L. Barker, "The Regulation of Marriage: Repressive Benevolence," in *Power and the State*, ed. G. Littlejohn, B. Smart, J. Wakeford and N. Yuval-Davis (London: Croom Helm, 1978).

16. Weitzman, *The Marriage Contract*, 338.

17. Kant, *PL*, chap. 2, §27, 113.

18. Durkheim, *Division of Labor*, 204.

19. These examples are discussed in detail in *The Sexual Contract*, chaps. 5 and 7.

10

Has Hegel Anything to Say to Feminists?

Heidi M. Ravven

In this paper I argue that the Hegelian philosophy offers insights that are particularly important for feminists: (1) a descriptive analysis of the historic family as a social system whose inherent oppressiveness needs to be transcended; and (2) a model of intrapsychic and social liberation and harmony as precisely the true path of emergence from and rational transformation of the family. Although a clear advocate of the traditional bourgeois family, Hegel, perhaps paradoxically, also took a critical posture toward the family, identifying and formulating theoretically the nature of its oppressiveness and the—or, at least, a—route toward its transcendence. This paper offers, first, a new angle from which to view Hegel's concepts of woman and the family,[1] and, second, draws some implications for a contemporary understanding of women and the family from Hegel's theory of (male) human liberation as the transcendence of the unindividuated harmonious communities of the family and the Greek city.

I conclude that, on Hegelian philosophical grounds, women and the family ought to be seen as capable of inner development through a process of dialectical self-criticism—this despite the obvious criticism that Hegel denied precisely this point. I show that Hegel conceived of the family and the Greek polis as fundamentally parallel and analogous social systems. The fate of Greek society was to transcend its natural, unexamined, and subjective harmony through inner conflict. The ultimate result was the emergence of the rational articulation of freedom— the reconciliation of individual expression and common purposes—in the modern bourgeois state. Although the man of the Hellenic polis, according to Hegel, could and did travel the highway of despair toward personal freedom and just, egalitarian community, the woman of the family, the polis's smaller parallel, could and did not. Woman's static fate was due, according to him, to her purportedly "natural" lack of full rational potential.

Yet, if the nature of woman were to be deemed fully human and rational—a position Hegel could hardly escape in the late twentieth century—the Hegelian parallel between the Greek polis and the family would suggest that the latter's potential and fate can and ought to mirror that of the former as Hegel portrays it. Woman ought to transcend the family and the family ought to be transformed beyond its traditional form as an unreflective, prerational social system, just as man has transcended both the immediate harmony of the Greek city through the dialectic of history and also that of the family through civil society and the political life of the modern state. In this chapter, I set out Hegel's position regarding the family and the Greek polis and then follow out some of the implications of this parallel for a feminist theory of human personal and social liberation, on the one hand, and of the family, on the other.

In *The Phenomenology of Spirit*, Hegel offers a description of womankind and the family in the context of the Greek city and its breakdown. Yet, what he says here[2] about women—and nowhere else in the *Phenomenology* does he address the topic of woman and the family—seems to be valid for him regardless of the historical context in which he places it. According to Jean Hyppolite, "Hegel's dialectic of the family and much of his dialectic of the city retain for him a validity independent of the historical moment at which they appeared in their most adequate form."[3] For Hegel, the Greek polis and the family, in large part, represent the same ethical phenomenon. Each is an immediate social whole, an "immaculate world, unsullied by internal dissension."[4] In both, the particular person is merely a "shadowy unreality."[5] The two laws of family and society are mutually necessary and, in theory, mutually compatible. It is only when they must be acted upon that the two realms are brought into conflict.[6] Moreover, "neither power has any advantage over the other that would make it a more essential moment of that substance."[7] They stand and fall together.[8]

Woman, for Hegel, embodies the law of the family, man the law of the city. Hegel's purpose in describing classical Athens at this point in the *Phenomenology* is to explicate a state of consciousness which Jacob Loewenberg terms, "the ingenuous society."[9] Hegel describes a society at the level of what he calls "ethical immediacy." It is a society in which the individual's ethical personality is completely identified with membership in the social whole. No legitimate differentiation or conflict between the individual and the group has yet developed because no rationally developed individuation of personality and activity are yet possible. The individual lives within the social whole in the peace and harmony of Eden. The individual feels fully at home as him- or herself in the institutions of society—political and familial. He or she adopts no critical posture regarding them. This is a "natural"[10] sort of freedom which Hegel calls in *The Philosophy of History*[11] the "joy" of "youthful freshness, of spiritual vitality." This is a state in which custom prevails:

> when this Reason which Spirit *has* is intuited by Spirit as Reason that *exists*, or as Reason that is *actual* in Spirit and is its world, then Spirit exists in truth; it *is* Spirit, the *ethical* essence that has an *actual* existence.
>
> Spirit is the *ethical life* of a nation in so far as it is the *immediate truth*—the individual that is a world.[12]

Hegel calls this stage "the beauty of ethical life."[13]

The beautiful free life of ethical wholeness—intrapsychic and social— presents itself in two forms: the human and the divine law.[14] This constitutes a "natural allocation of the two laws to the two sexes" but in each prevails "an undivided attitude toward the law" and therefore each "remains within the sphere of natural immediacy."[15] In each area the individual is completely and immediately identified with the group. The human law is the public realm of the polis in which the free man identifies himself fully as the citizen. This is the Athenian democracy.

> The main point in Democracy is moral disposition. *Virtue* is the basis of Democracy, remarks Montesquieu. . . . The Substance, [the Principle] of Justice, the common weal, the general interest, is the main consideration; but it is so only as Custom, in the form of Objective Will, so that morality properly so called—subjective conviction and intention—has not yet manifested itself. Law exists, and is in point of substance, the law of Freedom—rational [in its form and purport,] and valid *because it is Law*, i.e., without ulterior sanction. As in Beauty the Natural element—its sensuous coefficient—remains, so also in this customary morality, laws assume the form of a necessity of Nature.[16]
> . . . The interests of the community may, therefore, continue to be intrusted to the will and resolve of the citizens—and this must be the basis of the Greek constitution; for no principle has as yet manifested itself, which can contravene such Choice conditioned by Custom, and hinder its realizing itself in action. The Democratic constitution is here the only possible one. . . . Of the Greeks in the first and genuine form of their freedom, we may assert, that they have no conscience; the habit of living for their country without further [analysis or] reflection was the principle dominant among them.[17]

The divine law, on the other hand, is the *private*,[18] inchoate realm of the family.[19] The human law is characterized, according to Hegel, by knowledge. It is law and custom explicitly known, conscious of itself and its origins, apparent in the light of day.[20] But the divine law is an inner truth whose origin is in a murky past and an otherworldly realm. It manifests itself not in public institutions but implicitly and "unconsciously" within the customs and relations of the family. The woman in the family "does not attain to *consciousness* of it, to the objective existence of it, because the law of the Family is an implicit, inner essence which is not exposed to the daylight of consciousness, but remains an inner feeling and the divine element that is exempt from an existence in the real world."[21]

At this point, the parallel between the two laws is not complete according to Hegel, for "masculine" law is universal, whereas "feminine" law is particular.[22] The family *"stands over against* that order which shapes and maintains itself by working for the *universal;* the Penates stand *opposed to the universal Spirit."*[23] Hegel therefore maintains that the law of the community is "the superior law whose validity is openly apparent,"[24] while the family is "the rebellious principle of pure individuality."[25] That is to say, the scope of the common purposes and group identity of the human law is the society as a whole. That is the social "universality" which Hegel consistently discusses. The scope of the family is, of course, as a *subgroup*. Its limitation is its circumscribed scope. But, not only that, a society consists of many such component subgroups, each functioning as a centrifugal or "individualist" force in opposition to the unifying direct democracy of the Athenian polis.[26]

Yet, according to Hegel, woman is not mere nature nor man mere nurture. Both the family and the law of the polis contain much arbitrariness and contingency, that is, unmediated naturalness. The human law is still predominantly unexamined custom and the Greek citizens' relationship to it is habitual—immediate and, therefore, "natural." The family is compared here to a government and society in its—albeit, idyllic, but still—infancy. Moreover, the family is ethical precisely because it successfully spiritualized—as far as it goes—the natural. Hegel is very clear on this point in the *Phenomenology:*

> However, although the Family is *immediately* determined as an ethical being, it is within itself an *ethical* entity only so far as it is *not* the natural relationship of its members, or so far as their connection is an *immediate* connection of separate acting individuals; for the ethical principle is intrinsically universal, and this natural relationship is just as much a spiritual one, and it is only as a spiritual entity that it is ethical.[27]

Hegel goes on to clarify what he means by the family's mediation and spiritualization of the natural: "the ethical connection between the members of the Family is not that of feeling or the relationship of love."[28] Hegel does not mean by this that family members do not love each other. Rather, his point is that it is not the arbitrary unpredictable feelings of one particular individual for another that constitute the ethical substance of the family. Instead, the family is an ethical whole, and an immediate ethical whole, because each member of it has the family as his or her end. The family is a unity of purpose and its members define their identity and end in terms of it: "It seems, then, that the ethical principle must be placed in the relation of the *individual* member of the Family to the *whole* Family, as the Substance, so that the End and content of what he does and actually is, is solely the Family."[29] The spiritual purpose of the family is the symbolic transcendence of death and the creation of historical continuity. The memories of dead family members are perpetuated by the family cult of remembrance of the dead.[30] As the human law of the polis presides over the life of the citizen, the divine law of the family presides over his death.

I have dwelt on the ethical dimension of the family in order to emphasize the marked symmetry between the polis and the family. Here woman, as the embodiment of the family, is an ethical being. She mediates merely natural relations: biological continuity, impulsiveness, arbitrariness of emotion, the particularity of personality. She is very much like her counterpart, the man who is a free citizen of the polis. Her individuality is completely and unreflectively absorbed in the good for her social group as his is in his.[31] The scope of hers is more limited and natural (because it is defined, in part, by biology) and therefore is ethically inferior to some extent. Woman, like man, is a socially constructed personality. At this stage of history man and woman are, to a large extent, at similar stages of ethical development and social life.

The near equality of men and women at this stage in history and consciousness is illustrated by Hegel in his recounting of Sophocles' drama *Antigone*. *Antigone* portrays the classical Greek world as depending for its harmonious existence upon the precarious and spontaneous balance of its two equally valid principles and communities: the family and the government. The power of Antigone's claim precisely matches that of Creon's. The inevitable clash of male and female realms, society and family, respectively, necessarily brings down the whole society—that is its destiny.[32] Hegel argues that this downfall occurs precisely because the ethical claims of each realm do not override those of the other. Moreover, the two are interdependent.[33] At the same time, they are mutually exclusive!

Woman is powerful precisely only within and as the power of the family. In fact, as embodying a rival and basically equal and parallel domain to man's, woman is a corrupting force, a perpetual underminer of the larger society. The power of woman is corrosive to the body politic.[34]

> Since the community only gets an existence through its interfer-
> ence with the happiness of the Family, and by dissolving (individ-
> ual) self-consciousness in the universal, it creates for itself in
> what it suppresses and what is at the same time essential to it
> an internal enemy—womankind in general. Womankind—the
> everlasting irony [in the life] of the community—changes by
> intrigue the universal end of the government into a private end;
> transforms its universal activity into a work of some particular
> individual and perverts the universal property of the state into a
> possession and ornament of the Family. Woman in this way turns
> to ridicule the earnest wisdom of mature age.[35]

Although it would be easy to claim that in this passage Hegel is damning
womankind as a sort of societal Lilith, upon deeper examination this
does not seem to be the case. The family is clearly necessary according
to Hegel as both an ethical educator and as a religious institution.
Moreover, its corruptive force stems not from its inherent evil but from
the suppression of it by the (unmediated) universality of the state. The
polis, unlike the modern bourgeois state, did not have civil society,
according to Hegel, to act as mediator between the family and the
government. In civil society, according to Hegel, the individuation
impossible in the family could be fully developed and partly reconciled
with social purposes and the general good.[36]

Here again, then, in his seeming attack upon woman as a corruptive
force, Hegel emphasizes the equality and balance of power between
women and men in Greek society. In relation to Antigone, Hegel dwells
on the ethical heroism of women. Her heroism in upholding the divine
law of the family and taking full responsibility for thereby violating
human law, is, according to Hegel, exactly parallel to the heroism of
Oedipus.[37] The latter in upholding his responsibility to the state does
not deny his guilt toward the familial law, however unknowingly he
violated it.[38] Both Antigone and Oedipus take full responsibility for the
guilt unavoidably incurred in fulfilling one's own duty to one's own group
and thereby violating the opposing ethical realm. Neither disclaims
responsibility by invoking ignorance as a defense, on the one hand, or a
clash of principles beyond one's control, on the other. Hegel portrays
Antigone's acknowledgment of her guilt for her crime against the state
in fulfilling her obligation to the family as the quintessential heroic pose.
Her words typify for him heroic responsibility: "Because we suffer we
acknowledge we have erred."[39]

Antigone takes responsibility for the unintended as well as intended—or perhaps conscious and unconscious—effects of her actions. If Antigone's heroism is to be distinguished at all from Oedipus's it is so in her favor, for Antigone acts in full knowledge and Oedipus unknowingly. Hence, she takes greater responsibility and guilt upon herself than he.

> It can be that the right which lay in wait is not present in its own proper shape to the *consciousness* of the doer, but is present only implicitly in the inner guilt of the resolve and the action. But the ethical consciousness is more complete, its guilt more inexcusable, if it knows *beforehand* the law and the power which it opposes, if it takes them to be violence and wrong, to be ethical merely by accident, and like Antigone, knowingly commits the crime.[40]

Hegel, in his lectures on Greek philosophy, called Antigone "that noblest of figures that ever appeared on earth."

Clearly, the Greek woman did not stand as significantly—if at all—inferior to the Greek man even though the arena of her activity was the limited scope of the biological family and her law subterranean rather than public, in Hegel's view. On the other hand, the modern bourgeois woman, according to Hegel's account in *The Philosophy of Right*, in contrast to her Greek counterpart, is markedly inferior to the modern bourgeois man. As evidence one need only cite Hegel's outrageous statement in §166, *Zusatz*:

> Women may have happy ideas, taste and elegance, but they cannot attain to the ideal. The difference between men and women is like the difference between animals and plants. Men correspond to animals, while women correspond to plants because their development is more placid and the principle that underlies it is the rather vague unity of feeling.

The problem with women, according to Hegel, is due to nature or physiology. They possess a lesser form of rationality than men.[41]

In his denial of the full rationality of women, granting to women a merely partially rational psyche—which necessitates a limited ethical and intellectual life—Hegel follows Aristotle in the *Politics*.[42] Aristotle's argument justifies slavery and the patriarchal domination of women on allegedly natural grounds. It is astonishing that while Hegel would view such an argument for slavery as scandalous and pre-Christian—a product of a state of mind not yet aware of the potentially infinite subjectivity and therefore equality of all *men*—he adopts precisely the naturalistic explanation of the inferiority of women!

If the difference between men and women is, according to Hegel, essentially physiological, why do women fare so much better in comparison with men in the *Phenomenology* than in the *Philosophy of Right,* in Greek society than in the modern European state? Can this difference be explained simply because it is an older, perhaps more conservative Hegel who writes the latter? I believe that there is a better explanation and one that reconciles the two texts. The *Phenomenology* compares the woman with the man of the Hellenic polis. That man lives in a society in which in Hyppolite's words, the "universal and specific do not yet stand opposed."[43] The bourgeois man, in contrast to the Greek, has, in Hegel's words, undergone "self-diremption into explicit personal self-subsistence and the knowledge and volition of free universality, i.e., the self-consciousness of conceptual thought and the volition of the objective final end."[44]

The bourgeois man is he who "only out of his diremption . . . fights his way to self-subsistent unity with himself."[45] In other words, the bourgeois man has undergone the great and arduous process of *Bildung*— the labor of personal and historical development through stages of self-transcendence, self-assertion, self-alienation, and self-expansion through reincorporation of the lost self. Man, as bearer of historical society, has manifested himself politically, culturally, religiously, and ethically in a variety of forms which he has come to acknowledge as his own (past) and also to develop beyond. Woman, on the other hand, has remained the same throughout the ages. Thus, when Hegel cites Sophocles' *Antigone* here in the *Phenomenology*[46] and compares the (Greek and universal) woman with the male citizen of the modern state, the contrast between them is stark. Men are "powerful and active"; women, "passive and subjective." Yet, Hegel's characterization of woman, here, as "mind maintaining itself in unity as knowledge and volition of the substantive," would fit the Greek man of the polis as well as "timeless" woman.

The bourgeois man, on the other hand, Hegel believes, has transcended his immediacy in infinite subjectivity and the higher rational unification of self and other, particular and universal, as a member of the modern Protestant state. The Greek man and all women fail to have a developed sense and embodiment of their own individuality along with their unity with the social whole. The familial harmony and freedom are thus impulsive and lack a rational basis, a secure foundation, and "constitutional" guarantees. The bourgeois man, as a Protestant, knows the potential universality of his particular subjectivity—that is, he knows that it can encompass, in principle, all other selves. He develops his individuality in the capitalist and other enterprises of civil society. His seemingly anarchic purposes and behavior are socialized and reconciled with those of others immediately in the family and rationally, according to Hegel, in the corporation and by the government.

Athens was a glorious memory of a free society in which the I and the We were in perfect (albeit, fragile) harmony. Yet Athens could not be reconstructed in its original form in modernity.[47] Antigone, however, is as much a present ideal as a figure of the past! Neither woman's ideal nor her social reality, Hegel seemed to observe, had changed from the Greeks to the nineteenth century. Hegel, a descriptive philosopher attempting to find the essential in the empirical social world and in history, concluded that the difference between women and men must be a stunting of women's rational, universalizing capacity. A phenomenology of *woman's* consciousness would, for Hegel, stop with Antigone, that is, with woman as the quintessential spirit of the ever selfsame family.

According to Hegel, the "piety of the hearth is itself a profoundly subjective state of feeling."[48] The immediate and undifferentiated reconciliation of self and other in feeling that characterized the family is precisely similar to the customary harmonious political life of the ancients as Hegel describes it in *The Philosophy of History*. In the latter, Hegel lauds the reconciliation of the individual and the group manifested in the political life of the ancients. Yet, at the same time, he reminds us that this ancient reconciliation was only partial. Its partiality consisted precisely in its one-sided subjectivity.[49] The freedom that the modern state, in principle, makes possible, is not merely the *perception* of harmony between part and whole and the *feeling* of justice—a result of an unexamined identification of the individual with the social whole— but rather it necessitates the full and actual development of individuality and differences and their subsequent mediation and channelling toward common purposes. It accomplishes this end through (purportedly) fair and neutral institutional mechanisms which embody the principle of equality, the coincidence of rights and duties. The rational articulation of freedom in both its universal and particular aspects is possible only in modernity.

Consequently, the ancient city, at its *best*, was very much like the family—not, of course, in scope, but in the subjective and one-sided identification of individual and group and in its lack of a critical moment in which individuality could be developed. The modern state, however, transcends this unexamined harmony. Men's real individual personalities are not submerged for the alleged good of the whole. The modern state is, in principle, if not yet in fact, a reconciliation of the fully manifested purposes and conflicts of (male) individuals and subgroups. Such an expression of individual self-determination destroyed the ancient Greek political harmony and would destroy any family. The limited and one-sided reconciliation of the family is transcended, not in time, like the ancient Greek constitution, but in space, so to speak: It is transcended in and by the public realm. The family is superseded by civil society and government, as is also, therefore, an undeveloping, confined, one-sided, immediate woman by a rational, differentiated, universal man.[50]

The modern state alone can contain and channel the destructive and self-destructive yet creative power of spirit—its anarchic particularization in competing wills and embodiments and their potential harmonization and underlying agreement. Since its only full and adequate manifestation in social life is in the public realm, spirit bypasses women, except vicariously. The confinement and fulfillment of women in the family necessitates that a different experience form them: a natural and harmonious, peaceful growth rather than the tumultuousness of spiritual development.[51]

Although idyllic in its alleged harmony and lack of struggle, the natural limitations of family life preclude the realization within it of true freedom. Freedom is only possible within a social system that consciously and constitutionally mediates individual and group. Freedom is only possible for one who has undergone a process of being born in initial unexamined harmony (the family), develops individuality through a process of self-alienation from the initial paradise (civil society) and in "submitting [him]self to physical needs and the chain of these external necessities, and so imposing on itself this barrier and this finitude"[52] regains an ethical relationship to the group. But the social whole thus regained is not the family but the modern state—that is the full human being's true home, in which the full human potential for both self-development and a just common life can be realized.

In a sense, of course, all of history and nature, according to Hegel, led to this real possibility of freedom—a freedom only capable of being fully embodied by Protestant, bourgeois men. Yet women's perpetual confinement in and definition by the family were clear and necessary bases for the realization and continuation of Hegel's bourgeois political ideal. No wonder, then, that Hegel conceived of women's very nature, and not merely their imposed social condition, to be defined by the limiting natural and social purposes of the family: reproduction, the moral education of children, the selfless sacrifice for the good of the whole.

Hegel defines the family as the "mutual self-renunciation" and the "mutual surrender of individual personality" to form "a (corporate) single person."[53] Even if the "surrender" and "self-renunciation" were as "mutual" as Hegel claims—and Findlay's comment on para. 457 of the *Phenomenology* seems to suggest that Hegel saw women as making most of the sacrifices and men as reaping most of the benefits[54]—women were precisely defined by this altruism in which the lost self was never regained. Men had the vital area of civil society in which to regain their lost selves and then membership (at least indirectly) in political life to forge a reconciliation between private desires, corporate needs, and public good. Women, by nature, seemed to have no such (potentially) individuated selves to either regain or socialize. Women *are* their ethical roles. As mothers and wives, if not as sisters, women, according to Hegel, were in fact, interchangeable![55]

However beautiful the life of the polis and the family, the modern man has necessarily renounced them as his ideals. They represent his history: his cultural and personal infancy, respectively. One can be nostalgic about one's own and the human time of innocence but one cannot turn the clock back. That would be to renounce adulthood in favor of perpetual childhood. Yet that is precisely woman's inevitable fate:

> The idea that the state of nature is one of innocence and that there is a simplicity of manners in uncivilized people, implies treating education [*Bildung*] as something purely external, the ally of corruption. . . . The end of reason . . . is to banish natural

simplicity, whether the passivity which is the absence of the self, or the crude type of knowing and willing, i.e., immediacy and the singularity, in which mind is absorbed. . . . The final purpose of education, therefore is liberation and the struggle for a higher liberation still; *education is the absolute transition from an ethical substantiality which is immediate and natural to the one which is intellectual and so both infinitely subjective and lofty enough to have attained universality of form.*[56]

Thus, it is precisely woman and the family—as well as his own impulsiveness—that man must escape in order to reach maturity and freedom. It is both woman's great virtue and her great tragedy that she eternally expresses—albeit within a limited scope—the Hellenic ideal: The immediate, unreflective freedom and harmony (really, merger) of self and other, mind and body, real and ideal. The paragraph quoted above is equally applicable to the family and the Greek polis: they are both the "ethical substantiality which is immediate and natural" to be left behind in favor of a community that is "intellectual," "infinitely subjective," and universal, that is, the modern state.

The family is the first and vital educator of the citizen. Its commonness of purpose prefigures, in rudimentary and limited form, the goal and purpose of the education of the bourgeois citizen: that is, living and asserting one's unity of purpose with society as a whole. The male child experiences the unity of the family and develops "self-consciousness of one's individuality within this unity as the absolute essence of oneself, with the result that one is in it not as an independent person but as a member."[57] He thus experiences a community so tightly woven that Hegel designates it as "one person." The young man can hark back to this initial experience when, later, he strives to reconcile his initially frenzied pursuit of selfish ends in civil society with the political demands of citizenship. He must break the bonds of the family in which he is a mere part of an unmediated whole and grow to become an individual part of that rational, mediated, quintessential "individual," the state.[58] Hence Hegel claims that the two ethical roots of the state are the family and the corporation.[59]

The Hellenic ideal stands, from the point of culture, exactly in the same relation to the bourgeois citizen as the family does from the point of experience. Both represent actually embodied past ideals to be transcended but also to be transformed and reinstated—both in life and in thought—in new adult, rationally articulated forms. The transcendence of Greek society is (logically) possible and necessitated, from a developmental standpoint, by the male universal rational capacity. Man pushes on to fuller individuation, self-reflection, and critical assent to the social forms in which he lives. He creates a less arbitrary legal system and government and religion and values than those emerging from mere custom.

Hegel portrays the breakdown of Greek society to have occurred as the result of the anarchic individualism that resulted from the war between Antigone and Creon, woman and man, family and public. Once Greek men and women recognize that their actions are bound to bring the clash of ethical laws and communities, the immediate embeddedness—that is, secure sense of values—of males and females in their own respective groups breaks down. A rudimentary sense arises of the relativity of values and hence of being an individual apart from either ethic. Hegel identifies this phenomenon as the sophistic and Socratic critical posture that brought into question the givennesses of Greek society.[60] It is clear that Greek society could not contain the war between men and women since it had no mechanisms for mediating the rival claims. Hence the stability of bourgeois society is not due merely to its allowance for the full exercise of individual inclination in civil society. It is also due to its mediation and purported reconciliation of the two potentially rival and different natures and *communities* of men and women. The history of consciousness is exclusively the history of the male transcendence of Creon but the female perpetuation of Antigone.[61]

The past ideal as foreshadowing a future hope is essential to Hegel's theory. One relives past memories and ideals—personal and cultural—in new and ever deeper, expanding, and truer ways. For the future to be the basis for human activity it must bear the fruits of the past and be creatively and ever more authentically expressive of the ideal through a process of the dialectical emergence of implicit conflicts and their higher resolutions. A critically restorative posture in relation to cultural tradition and personal memory is, for Hegel, the source of any worthwhile present and future. Yet such a critical posture in relation to their social context, the family, was precisely what was unavailable to women, according to Hegel. Women could only relive tradition and memory repetitively, never creatively. At their best, they could aspire only to the unreflective, "natural" nobility of Antigone. They could neither be developed individuals nor express conflict openly but only unconsciously and destructively as irony. They could neither transcend nor transform the family substance.

The experience of embodied ideals at the origins of life—cultural and biological—as the bases for finding potential ideals to be developed in every empirical present perhaps led Hegel to idealize the family along the lines that he idealized in the Hellenic culture. Both were, clearly, the idealized images that moved him in his youth. This need did not prevent him, however, from adopting a critical posture in relation both to the limitations of the customary, habitual harmony of the polis and to the social purposes of the family insofar as they constituted clear limitations for *men!* Apparently, regarding women, however, Hegel's sentimentality and/or prejudice inhibited his critical judgment and grasp of the truth.

It is interesting that Hegel was critical enough of these idealized social forms that he recognized and tried to resolve theoretically the submerged conflicts between the community and the individual in both Greek society and the family. He was not at all oblivious to the threat of oppressiveness that the family posed to its men and boys; that is, that it would submerge their creativity and bend it to group needs. It, like the polis, had to be transcended in the interest of freedom and development. It was a tragic flaw in his thinking that he could not envision women in such fully human terms.[62] Yet, at the same time, it seems that in Hegel's analysis lie the seeds of a more honest and liberating vision, if the critical posture were only to be extended as rightfully women's own as well as men's. In fact, an explication of the present development of feminism along these Hegelian lines could perhaps be defined as the next stage in the dialectic of history.

Hegel's state cannot be maintained as resolving the conflict either between men and women or between the individual and society if women are conceived as having the same human nature and potential as men, for in that case women are denied the right to self-development and freedom. Yet, at a more basic level, nothing in the Hegelian philosophic approach would seem to necessitate this extraordinary lapse in the empathic understanding of women.[63] Hegel's failure to conceive of the full humanity of women enabled him to deny and rationalize the subordination of women's selves to the family and the state. The recognition of such pure exploitation of women by and for their communities he failed to perceive. In fact, the acknowledgment of such instrumentalization of some for the (alleged) good of others would precisely explode as a self-serving illusion the Hegelian concept of the purported equal attainment of freedom, in principle, in the modern state. In fact, such an acknowledgment would seem necessarily to point to the dialectical development of women and the family along the lines of the growth of male consciousness and its expression in social life from Oedipus to, perhaps, Hegel himself.[64]

The acknowledgment of women's suppression by the family and social structure would have, one would speculate, necessarily altered Hegel's assessment of the modern liberal state. He would perhaps have concluded that while the (male) civil society and state were suffering from a rampant asocial individualism, women and the family were suffering from a self-destructive communalism—a lack of adequate individuation. It is interesting to conjecture in which direction this acknowledgment might have led him. Would he have advocated the entrance of women into civil society and government? Would Hegel have even conceived of the family as capable of development as a social system?

Would he have, perhaps, changed his view of the family as a collective owner of property? Hegel argued for the necessity of private property for the full expression of personality.[65] Since he identified the family as one corporate person, the communal nature of the family property did not appear to him to contradict his position. Property remained in the individual hands of men in the family, although its use, he believed, ought to be legally limited for the benefit of the family as a whole. When it came, however, to the Platonic ideal of communal property for the guardians of the ideal state, Hegel took strong issue with Plato.[66] He held that any communal organization of property among independent adults necessitates mutual coercion rather than freeing all alike from economic dependence. Hegel's argument seems to suggest that common ownership of property is, at the most, appropriate only regarding children but not regarding equal adults.

Thus, if we look at what (purportedly) constitutes the male transcendence of the Greek polis and the family both intrapsychically and socially-politically, Hegel would seem to offer feminists some suggestive directions for further thought. I have tried to show that the Hegelian philosophy illuminates our present situation as a moment in the dialectical process toward freedom and just community. It offers good reasons to believe in, for example, the reclaiming of conflict against the social whole—familial and public—as creative of new possibilities; in the rights to develop individuality and personality, and to own property, and that these rights are in need of being exercised at the present time; in the possibility of reworking—not merely abandoning—past (social) ideals and forms; in the identification of reason as precisely the source both of a critical posture regarding nature, the givenness of culture, and the social substance and of the confidence in the possibility of social harmony and justice.[67]

Perhaps one of the most instructive aspects of the Hegelian philosophy for feminists is Hegel's formulation of the problem of justice as a question of the reconciliation of family and public, of male and female groups, identifications, and ethics, and not only of the individual and society. Even if some feminists might have serious reservations about the precise terms of this reconciliation, to have identified it in this way, and not merely as a question of the public good, on the one hand, or as a question of interpersonal ethics writ large, on the other, is to have addressed a society that includes both men and women, the needs of biology and familial continuity as well as the larger public welfare and individual desire. The Hegelian model of society as a body of conflicting claims, subgroups, and identifications, on the face of it, would seem to be very appealing as a description of the ethical demands of contemporary women's and men's lives.

Finally, the reading of the Hegelian position regarding women that I have offered here seems to suggest that the family, as we have known it, as a subjective harmony and an unexamined, undifferentiated social system cannot survive a feminist critique, as the polis could not survive (as such) the philosophic critique. From an extension of Hegel's critique of the Greek polis could be derived a Hegelian critique of the family. The family constitutes at best an unconscious reconciliation of people. It provides neither mechanisms nor values that can mediate the emergence of differences and individuation. The latter is excluded from it and its expression is potentially revolutionary. The family, like the Athenian democracy, would seem to operate effectively only as long as the spirit of the group is young and unexamined. Only then is the perception of the common good given automatic precedence over individual considerations.

The development of rational self-conscious individuation from the group's subjectivity and purposes results in a critical evaluation of both (1) the fairness of its submergence of the individual in the group and (2) the appropriateness of its historic purposes to present social realities. Are all members called upon to make equivalent sacrifices? Even if women, as men, enter civil society and government and therefore have an arena for self-expression, why need (and how can) the family remain an undifferentiated group solidarity? How can it (and ought it to) retain its biological and commemorative foci when its adult members have fully defined culturally-based roles in civil society? To what model of community are we then to turn in the search for reconstituting family life on a more just and egalitarian basis, on the one hand, and one which reflects the presence within it of adults who seek personal development within the family as well as beyond it, on the other?

I have tried to show that Hegel addressed precisely this problem in his explication of the Greek city and its aftermath. Hegel's conclusion was that true freedom and a just community demand a more complex process and social structure for the reconciliation of the self and its other than custom and the feeling of solidarity with the group can provide. Does Hegel's political theory, then, have anything to offer the feminist philosopher in search of new models and ethics for the family? Clearly, the Hegelian philosophy provides a mode of discourse about the individual and the group, if nothing else. We must, indeed, ask ourselves whether the languages of phenomenological development (e.g., self-knowledge, self-transcendence, individuation, conflict, the mediation of the natural, finding oneself at home in the social world) and political insights (e.g., freedom, equality, the reconciliation of group interests, the conjunction of rights and duties) are not potentially more generative than the language of biology, love, psychic, and economic merger. Hegel offers a model of human development toward freedom that is fostered by the social and political context. It ought not to be ignored.

Postscript

It is interesting and important to note that the contemporary temptation to read Hegel's account of woman and man and the family in terms of the dialectic of lordship and bondage is not true to Hegel's intention. It is surely tempting to simply reify lordship and bondage as an absolute depiction of freedom (or the possibility of freedom) and then attribute it to women because in contemporary society women have been recognized as occupying a servant status, and then apply it to what Hegel says of women elsewhere. We today might say that lordship and bondage has some important lessons for women, but they are not lessons that Hegel thought applied to women.

It is neither legitimate to identify women with the slave nor to conclude that women emerge from the dialectic of the family with the potential for development, while men, as masters, are ever thereby stymied. This suggests the possibility of a rather intriguing utopian re-reading of Hegel wherein women rather than men become the bearers of a history that emerges from the transcendence of the family rather than from the transcendence of ancient Greece.

For Hegel, however, it is consciousness, Spirit, that progresses and that is the subject of the *Phenomenology*, not any individual actor on the stage who then progresses to the next stage. The stage of lordship and bondage makes possible the replay of lordship and bondage in more sophisticated (and internalized) ways in the stages that follow: stoicism, skepticism, the unhappy consciousness. The slave has not developed; rather, consciousness has undergone a development through having learned from its own experience of lordship and bondage. (In *Phen.*, para. 202, for example, Hegel makes explicit that stoicism and skepticism are developments of the entire configuration of lordship and bondage, and not mere developments of one character and the loss of the other.) Moreover, lordship and bondage is a stage prior to the development of society, one in which self-consciousness has merely doubled itself and is the mere anticipation (but not yet the real appearance) of social life (para. 177). Hence, it cannot offer an adequate social analysis of the institutions of the public and the family in ancient Greece.

When we turn to the textual evidence, a careful reading of the passages under discussion on the ethical world (on men, women, the polis, and the family) makes it clear that the interpretation of them in terms of the lordship of men and the slavery of women is untenable. For example, as Hegel writes (*Phen.*, para. 472), "neither power [namely, that of man and that of woman] has any advantage over the other that would make it a more essential moment of that substance."

> The ethical realm is in this way in its enduring existence an immaculate world, *a world unsullied by any internal dissension.* Similarly, its process is a *tranquil transition* of one of its powers into the other, in such a way that *each preserves and brings forth the other.* We do indeed see it divide itself in two essences and

their reality; but *their antithesis is rather the authentication of one through the other,* and where they come into direct contact with each other as real opposites, their middle term and common element is their *immediate interpenetration.* The one extreme, the universal self-conscious Spirit, becomes, through the individuality of the man, *united,* with its other extreme, its force and element, with *unconscious* Spirit. On the other hand, the divine law has its individualization—or the *unconscious* Spirit of the individual its real existence—in the woman, through whom, as the *middle term,* the unconscious Spirit rises out of its unreality into actual existence, out of a state in which it is unknowing and unconscious into the realm of conscious Spirit. *The union of man and woman* constitutes the active middle term of the whole and the element which sunders itself into these extremes of divine and human law. *It is equally their immediate union which converts those first two syllogisms into one and the same syllogism, and unites into one process the opposite moments:* one from actuality down to unreality, the downward movement of human law, organized into independent members, *to the danger and trial of death;* and the other, the upward movement of the law of the nether world to the actuality of the light of day and to conscious existence. Of these movements, the former falls to man, the latter to woman. (my emphasis)

Now when we look carefully at this passage, we do not find, as some have argued,[68] that Hegel is claiming that women have become the slaves of men—and therefore (according to another false inference) women will be precisely those who rise to freedom in the end. Rather, Hegel informs us repeatedly that it is the "tranquil" "union" of men and women in marriage and the family with which he is concerned here. Moreover, this union, far from being a war between the sexes, is what Hegel calls, "a world unsullied by any internal dissension"! Divine and human laws are united through the union of man and woman. That means each feels a sense of responsibility toward the other's law as well as an identification with his or her own.

It is this union, not the particular characters—men and women, respectively—of this stage, that then undergoes a development which begins with the breaking apart of this fragile and too natural and arbitrary type of unity. The conflict that will arise between the male and female realms is quite different from the conflict of lordship and bondage, which is a battle for recognition between unequal individuals. Here, each is united with the other; they each share guilt for the violation of *either* realm. That is precisely Antigone's tragedy.

In addition, the "danger and trial of death" is not between the two realms but is stated by Hegel in this passage to be a danger inherent in only the male realm because the unity of a man with the family as a member of it as well as of the polis precipitates in him an internal conflict of values. Hegel is suggesting here that the family is an individualistic force in the lives of Greek men, eroding from within men's full identification with public citizenship. Therefore, the danger arises that *individual men are set against other men*, each as a member of a different family. The kind of immediate ethical harmony represented by both the family and the Greek polis falls apart as a stage because this fragile harmony cannot withstand such *internal* conflicts. Hegel does not say, however, that the family is in the same kind of danger from men as the public world of men is from women. Women constitute more of a danger to the male public world, apparently, than vice versa, at this stage. So much for the alleged slavery of women at this stage!

This stage is superseded by a stage of rampant individualism. This next stage is "personified," so to speak, by ancient Rome (Roman men, that is, not women). At the same time, that does not mean that historically there is no one left at the former stage of development. While Spirit may have a dialectical progression in the *Phenomenology*, in historical life societies occupy various stages at any given period and may even deteriorate.

Hence, *Spirit* progresses beyond immediate ethical harmony as a social system. Neither Greek men nor women (nor slaves) are the subjects of this progress of Spirit. Spirit now finds its subjects elsewhere, in ancient Roman law and then beyond. Women, however, as expressive of a particular social configuration and consciousness, are no more likely than ancient Romans and Greeks to progress to Absolute Spirit. Spirit as such is neither Greek nor feminine.

Nor can modern women as depicted in the *Philosophy of Right* be seen to have progressed. Here Hegel offers a theory of the state in which full social freedom is manifest as one form of the fulfillment of the actual universality of the absolute. In this context Hegel maintains that (modern) women are "mind maintaining itself in unity as knowledge and volition of the substantive," a description that aptly fits as well the familially defined and absorbed woman of the *Phenomenology*. Spirit has indeed progressed but its instantiation in women's consciousness and women's lives, according to Hegel, appears to have remained the same from the time of the ancient Greeks.

It certainly would have been more "politically correct" by contemporary standards if Hegel had indeed recognized—as we do today—that historically women have undergone, and to a large extent continue to undergo, a type of bondage from the experience of which a full humanity can begin to proceed. Contemporary thinkers (most notably Luce Irigaray) have applied eloquently and brilliantly the Hegelian lordship and bondage motif, as an interpretive principle, to women's plight and to the male-female relationship. The power of the motif surely transcends even the wonderful use Hegel makes of it; it has had a rich history external to the Hegelian text.

Unfortunately, when we read the data fairly and honestly it is clear that Hegel himself did not apply the motif to women nor did he use it as a tool of analysis of the *internal* structure of the family. Would that he had! Would that Hegel had understood that it is women's social condition and not their nature that has stunted their growth. Surely, he would have had to conclude that women must be capable of intellectual and ethical development in modernity and of a social embodiment expressive of this internal development!

Still, what is valuable about Hegel's analysis of the family is its honesty and lack of (cynical) sentimentality. Hegel tells us what the family really is as a social system and what it does to its members: it educates male children to a primitive ethical level but not to full human ethical capacity and it does so at the (temporary but necessary) expense of the full expression of their creativity and individuality—and at the permanent sacrifice of women's development had they any possibility of that.

Hegel tells us the truth about what confinement within the family means for adults: they have to have half a brain and be merged (and submerged) into their spouse and their children to survive it.[69] If Hegel had recognized that women were fully rational human beings, he could not, at the same time, have consistently maintained that they could legitimately be confined within the family and sacrificed to its purposes. That would have been to advocate the willful slavery of some for the benefit of others—and that would belie what Hegel regarded as the very principles of modernity: equality and freedom.

Notes

1. For other treatments of Hegel's concepts of women and the family, see the Select Bibliography.

2. G. W. F. Hegel, *Phenomenology of Spirit*, trans. A. V. Miller (Oxford: Clarendon, 1977), para. 438–76; see also para. 745. Hereafter cited as *Phen.* with Miller's paragraph numbering.

3. Jean Hyppolite, *Genesis and Structure of Hegel's "Phenomenology of Spirit,"* trans. Samuel Cherniak and John Heckman (Evanston: Northwestern University Press, 1974), 364.

4. *Phen.*, para. 463.

5. *Phen.*, para. 464; see also para. 468.

6. *Phen.*, para. 464.

7. *Phen.*, para. 472.

8. *Phen.*, para. 472: "Only in the downfall of both sides alike is absolute right accomplished, and the ethical substance as the negative power which engulfs both sides, that is, omnipotent and righteous Destiny, steps on the scene."

9. Jacob Loewenberg, *Hegel's "Phenomenology": Dialogues on the Life of the Mind* (La Salle, Ill.: Open Court, 1965), 189ff.

10. For Hegel, the term *natural* has two meanings, a literal and a figurative. The literal refers to biological, physiological, etc. nature. The figurative involves the uncritical acceptance of the given state(s) of things. The latter meaning is thus relative to circumstance and not absolute. Regarding the figurative meaning, see the lengthy quotation below (see notes 16 and 17) and also, for example, Hegel, *Philosophy of Right* (hereafter cited as PR), §187. For the literal meaning see, for example, G. W. F. Hegel, *Philosophy of History* (hereafter cited as PH), rev. ed., with prefaces by Charles Hegel and the translator, J. Sibree (London: Colonial, 1900), 55. This point about the word "natural" cannot be overemphasized. Moreover, if one ignores it, Hegel's philosophy cannot be grasped as a logical progression of stages from the natural—in the literal sense—to the spiritual. Each stage stands as progressively embodied spirit to a prior, more "natural" one: as matter formed to matter unformed, as culture to nature, as freedom to adherence to unexamined authority. Numerous contexts bear out this interpretation. In the following passage, for example, the first referent of the word "natural" is the biological, but in the second Hegel offers the definition of his figurative use of the term, the automatic, uncritical acceptance of the given habits and mores of a specific social context: "the ethical action contains the moment of crime, because it does not do away with the *natural* allocation of the two laws to the two sexes, but rather, *being an undivided attitude towards the law, remains within the sphere of natural immediacy*" (*Phen.*, para. 468; my emphasis in the last phrase). Hegel is indebted to the Neoplatonic tradition for his hierarchical structure of being, i.e., the idea that forms of life form a ladder in which each step higher is "form" to each lower "matter." (The goal of Hegel's system, however, unlike the Neoplatonic, is the full *embodiment* of form and the full spiritualization of matter—not progressive disembodiment.) This hierarchical fulfillment of being expresses itself even on the human level; for the fulfillment of the absolute requires only that the modern Protestant bourgeois state produce some male Hegelian philosophers who can speculatively comprehend the absolute (or at least truly experience and incorporate the absolute through Protestant worship and dogma).

11. PH, 223.

12. *Phen.*, para. 440–41.

13. *Phen.*, para. 441. H. S. Harris in *Hegel's Development: Toward the Sunlight, 1770–1801* (Oxford, Clarendon, 1972), 157, describes Hegel's Hellenic ideal as a *Volksleben* in which "all human capacities were fully and freely and harmoniously expressed; artistic and religious

spontaneity always went hand in hand with political freedom. In the polis freedom was the feeling of one's stake in the whole and being prepared to sacrifice oneself for it when called to do so."

14. *Phen.*, para. 445.

15. *Phen.*, para. 468.

16. The polis, not only the family, is "natural" in the figurative Hegelian sense. Of course, the family, as a biological unity, is also natural in the literal sense. Patricia Mills's account in "Hegel and 'The Woman Question,' " 81, is flawed by her misunderstanding of precisely this point.

17. *PH*, 251–53.

18. Not "individual" in a Hobbesian sense of self-interest, as Mills seems to suggest. Mills gives a mistaken Hobbesian reading of Hegel when she suggests that, in the *Phenomenology*, "man seeks recognition of his own particular self from all men; he seeks universal recognition of his particularity. . . . And universality . . . is 'concrete' or universal individuality" ("Hegel's *Antigone*," 131). The latter is precisely domination and must, according to Hegel, be transcended. Landes (14) commits the same error as Mills. Rather, it is the case that Hegel's concept of the human project is that of the overcoming—the socialization—of mere particularity and selfishness through the "negation" of the self, or self-transcendence, which is the essence of mind or thought. Negation in its final stage involves the capacity to know and will the *universal in its reconciliation with and inclusion of the particular*. Whether Hegel's bourgeois capitalist state (or the traditional family) can in fact achieve the ethical education of the citizen toward the reconciliation of impulsive and personal aims with communal purposes is another matter. Hegel diagnosed his own time as suffering from uncontrollable individualism (see, for example, the many sections in his *Lectures on the Philosophy of Religion* where he discusses the post-Enlightenment ethos). This sorry state of affairs was not due, according to Hegel, to implicit principles within modernity, but rather to the failure of modernity to live up to its potential in his day.

19. *Phen.*, para. 463.

20. *Phen.*, para. 448.

21. *Phen.*, para. 457.

22. I maintain here that the particularity of the family has little to do with any fulfillment of (true) individuality on the part of its members. John N. Findlay's interpretation supports my view as does Luce Irigaray's (in *Speculum of the Other Woman* [Ithaca: Cornell University Press, 1985]). Findlay writes in his commentary (552) on *Phen.*, para 451: "In the Family natural relations carry universal ethical meanings. The individual in the Family is primarily related to the Family as a whole, and not by ties of love and sentiment to its particular members. *The Family, further, is not concerned to promote the well-being of its individual members.* . . . It is concerned with individuality raised out of the unrest and change of life into the universality of death, i.e. the Family exists to promote the cult of the dead" (my emphasis). As mentioned above, Mills and Landes disagree with this position. It is appropriate to recall in this context too that for Hegel the quintessential "individual" is the group—the social substance—of which the particular person is a mere accident. See, for example, *Phen.*, para 441: "Spirit is the *ethical life* of a nation in so far as it is the *immediate truth*—the individual that is a world."

23. *Phen.*, para. 450; my emphasis.

24. *Phen.*, para. 455.

25. *Phen.*, para. 474.

26. Another reason why Hegel calls the family an "individual(ity)" when it is clearly unindividuated community according to him, may be that Hegel, in part, means by the family's individuality its existence, in part, for the sake of particularity (as such), i.e.,

biological and natural impulses. On the level of human purpose the family is primitive. Mills claims, "The question of exactly how woman can represent the sphere of particularity while never knowing herself to be this particular self is a question never addressed by Hegel" ("Hegel's *Antigone*," 139). I believe that this is not a problem for Hegel at all. Just as Mills glosses over the different meanings—literal and figurative—of "natural" for Hegel, so she also glosses over the different meanings of "particular." At the level of the family all human beings are subject to particular and arbitrary impulses—and therefore they are "particular" and "natural" in a literal sense. The "particularity" of natural impulsiveness is mediated by the family. When men have undergone the rational process of *Bildung*, their "particularity," or rather, "individuality," which is the rational and developed expression of self, flourishes in civil society and is mediated by the corporation and fully reconciled with the common good by the modern state. But women never achieve this rational individuation and are always particular only at an impulsive level which is at the same time consistent with their total submergence in the family. For Hegel all such one-sided submergence entails an anarchic, unreconciled particularity outside the unity (and community)—hence the fall of Greek society: its defeat by the principle of (male) individuality and (female) comedy. Hegel's position may hark back to Aristotle's concept of matter. The latter is, at the same time, paradoxically, the basis of both empirical particularization and a total lack of characterization.

27. *Phen.*, para. 451.

28. *Phen.*, para. 451.

29. *Phen.*, para. 451.

30. *Phen.*, para. 451.

31. See Judith Shklar, *Freedom and Independence: A Study of the Political Ideas of Hegel's "Phenomenology of Mind"* (Cambridge: Cambridge University Press, 1976), 76ff., for an analysis of Hegel's concept of Greek society as a "struggle between two social claims."

32. See, for example, *Phen.*, para. 464.

33. *Phen.*, para. 463.

34. Irigaray, in *Speculum of the Other Woman*, offers a daring—and almost midrashic—interpretation of Hegel's concept of woman in the *Phenomenology*. Woman is the Unconscious; man is the conscious self. Woman's domination by man is therefore both social and intrapsychic—both men and women repress the female as a person and within themselves. Thus men and women are both alienated from each other and self-alienated. In this way, Irigaray also uses Hegel's "lordship and bondage" motif as a principle of the interpretation of the male/female relation as Hegel portrays it. Woman has the corrosive power of the repressed parts of the self. Hence, according to Irigaray, "she becomes the voice, the accomplice of the people, the slaves, those who only whisper their revolt against their masters secretly" (218). As the "voice" of the unconscious, however, her tragedy is that she has no articulate speech with which to state her case. Like the slave, she recognizes herself in the master (male) but not in her. Irigaray makes no mention here of any moment of dialectical reversal for the slave/woman. "Her own will is shattered, so afraid is she of the master, so aware of her inner nothingness. And her work in the service of another, of that male Other, ensures the ineffectiveness of any desire that is specifically hers. . . . She is merely the passage that serves to transform the inessential whims of a still sensible and material nature into universal will" (225). Irigaray notes that for Hegel woman can have no development, no self-consciousness, no self-transcendence, no *history*, no subjectivity, no individuation. Yet the lordship and bondage motif would suggest that women have the true hidden strengths; perhaps even the future lies with them. The slave, not the master, has encountered a universal outside the self and has labored to embody it. Labor, for Hegel, is not construed narrowly as the production of goods, but is all-inclusive. The slave has encountered the ongoing threat of death by the master and, as a result, has become aware of the finitude of all empirical things and life forms.

If the master must necessarily—due to his limitations—absolutize the finite (self) and use the slave in the enterprise, then the slave, on the other hand, has the potential for true self-transcendence, acting on behalf of the concrete universality that includes both self and other. (Ironically, this Hegelian analysis would suggest that men, not women, are incapable of living and conceiving the concrete universal, that is, the reconciliation of self and other, because of the lord's incapacity of any actual or sustained self-transcendence.) See Jean Baker Miller, *Toward a New Psychology of Women* (Boston: Beacon, 1976) for an analysis of the (especially ethical) strengths of women precisely due to their servitude. Clearly, Hegel did not draw these conclusions about women, but he realized the revolutionary potential of women in his designation of them as the "eternal irony of the community." Irigaray interprets Hegel as siding decisively with the suppression and repression of women as the price of (male) society. She interprets Hegel's absolute as the ultimate disembodiment of (male) ego-mind from its (female) rootedness in reality, materiality (see 226, last paragraph). I would not be so hard on Hegel. I would emphasize Hegel's more radical tendencies and liberal intentions as well as his more conservative side. For example, the purported justice of the modern state rests, in part, for Hegel, on its having given women true fulfillment and freedom (according to their alleged capacity) in the family and having given the family a legally protected position in society. Moreover, the fulfillment of the Hegelian absolute can occur only in and through its *embodiment*, its concrete reconciliation of particular and universal; and the accomplishment of *Bildung* as self-related otherness can occur only through the incorporation in life and self-consciousness—through the explication in thought—not the denial, of empirical reality, of conflict, and of the implicit intentionality of the empirical. It is clearly not Hegel's aim to dissolve either the empirical or the other, but to demonstrate that the reconciliation of the real and the ideal, the self and the other, is the truth of each. Yet, he surely believes that language can adequately capture empirical existence.

35. *Phen.*, para. 475.

36. Hegel believed in a modified "hidden hand" theory—self-interest necessitated a common life but the true common weal could only be guaranteed by government intervention as well.

37. *Phen.*, para. 469.

38. *Phen.*, para. 469.

39. *Phen.*, para. 470.

40. *Phen.*, para. 470.

41. Hegel, *PR*, trans. T. M. Knox (Oxford: Clarendon, 1952), 263–64, §166, *Zusatz*: "Women are capable of education, but they are not made for activities which demand a universal faculty such as the more advanced sciences, philosophy, and certain forms of artistic production. . . . When women hold the helm of government, the state is at once in jeopardy, because women regulate their actions not by the demands of universality but by arbitrary inclinations and opinions. . . . The status of manhood, on the other hand, is attained only by the stress of thought and much technical exertion."

42. Aristotle, *The Politics*, translated with an introduction, notes, and appendices by Ernest Barker (New York: Oxford University Press, 1958), 35: "The slave is entirely without the faculty of deliberation; the female indeed possesses it, but in a form which remains inconclusive; and if children also possess it, it is only in an immature form. . . . What is true [of their possessing the different parts of the soul] must similarly be held to be true of their possessing mortal goodness: they must all share in it, but not in the same way—each sharing only to the extent required for the discharge of his or her function" (1260a, i.e., bk. 1, chap. 13, §7–8).

43. Hyppolite, 346.

44. *PR*, 114, §166.

45. *PR*, 114, §166.

46. *PR*, 114, §166.

47. See, for example, Shklar, 95: "The *Phenomenology* is not given over to prophecy. It is a work of elegaic remembering, a reintegrating of the past into the present and that in a mood of profound sadness. But the 'perhaps not yet' had its function: it was the spiritual magnet that drew reason onward in its still very incomplete journey toward practical knowledge. To say that free people could be thought of as 'perhaps not yet' made it possible to assign an aim to that voyage."

48. *PH*, 43.

49. *PH*, 43: "We have considered two aspects of Freedom—the objective and the subjective; if, therefore, Freedom is asserted to consist in the individuals of a State all agreeing in its arrangements, it is evident that only the subjective aspect is regarded." See also 48: "The subjective will is a merely formal determination—a *carte blanche*—not including what it is that is willed. Only the *rational* will is that universal principle which independently determines and unfolds its own being, and develops its successive elemental phases as organic members. Of this Gothic-cathedral architecture the ancients knew nothing."

50. *PH*, 59: "*Natural*, and at the same time *religious* morality, is the piety of the *family*. In this social relation, morality consists in the members behaving toward each other *not as individuals*—possessing an independent will; not as persons. The Family therefore, is excluded from that process of development in which History takes its rise. . . . Freedom is nothing but the recognition and adoption of such universal substantial objects as Right and Law, and the production of a reality that is accordant with them—the State."

51. *PH*, 55.

52. *PR*, 125, §187.

53. *PH*, 42.

54. Findlay speaks of the wife's "unequal relation to her husband in which she has duties where he mainly has pleasures" (553). Yet Findlay does not say precisely where and how Hegel makes this point, if it is indeed Hegel's and not Findlay's own.

55. See, for example, *Phen.*, para. 457.

56. *PR*, 125, §187; my emphasis.

57. *PR*, 110, §158.

58. Ironically, an explication of the family in terms of the "lordship and bondage" motif suggests that the male child does not learn self-renunciation from the family but, on the contrary, lordship, that is, the universalization of the finite self (see note 34 above). Interestingly, although Hegel realizes that men and women belong to two rival societies and embody conflicting ethics, he fails to see that phenomenon as arising in the social structure of the family and not beyond it. While he acknowledges that the rights and duties of family members do not coincide, he does not discuss these relations in detail.

59. *PR*, 154, §255.

60. See, for example, *PR*, 8, preface; 92, §138.

61. Antigone is just as much the female ideal of bourgeois woman as of the Greek. Yet, since male nature undergoes development and female nature does not, according to Hegel, it would be ludicrous for a bourgeois citizen to be a modern Creon. Hegel clearly sided with the moderns against the ancients in the contemporary debate over their respective value: "nothing is so absurd as to look to Greeks, Romans, or Orientals, for models for the political arrangements of our time" (*PH*, 47).

62. In a sense, Simone de Beauvoir is correct when she accuses Hegel in *The Second Sex*, 9 and 26, of casting woman as the quintessential and irreducible Other, who can never be understood empathically. Yet, at the same time, this portrayal of woman by Hegel is not an adequate fulfillment of the system but a mark of its failure on its own terms. When it came to women, Hegel's mind met a barrier it could not overcome. The woman's otherness could not

be reconciled with the man's self, but only subjugated, and with that subjugation obscured from view. The true community of freedom and mutuality was built on the instrumentalization of women and the family as the Greek polis had been on that of its slaves. But this is not so by intention, as Beauvoir suggests, but by default.

63. Yet, it must be recalled that Hegel's system reaches fulfilled embodiment and spiritualization in and through a hierarchical course of development. Partial embodiments always must coexist with the full embodiment and spiritual self-return of the absolute in and through knowledge. Only some male Protestant philosophers and citizens of a bourgeois state reach the absolute and thereby make actual the self-return of the absolute. (Hegel's self-return of the absolute can be accomplished conceptually even if its social embodiment is partial.) The limitations of other people and life forms are either their natural or historic contexts. For women, however, it was not their historic context, as it was for all men, that limited their achievement of the absolute, but like natural forms of life, their partial humanity/rationality—like plants, Hegel suggests.

64. This is not to say that there were not other similar lapses in Hegel's vision; for example, the Marxist critique that civil society, rather than freeing all, instrumentalizes some for the sake of others. If one understands civil society and the corporation as failing to overcome rampant individualism (competition) and hierarchy in an egalitarian community of purpose, then the reconciliation of male and female communities and ethics is still more problematic. The woman who has submerged herself in and for the good of the family is then confronted by a male whose ethic is predominantly competitiveness and hierarchy: mastery toward those below him in the corporate structure and subservience toward his "betters." The democratic and egalitarian ideal harmony of Athens is hardly repeated in the capitalist marketplace. Yet the opening of the Hegelian philosophy to such critiques that reveal its lapses from adhering to its own principles makes it self-correcting and therefore dynamic and developing rather than static and final.

65. PR, 236, §46, Zusatz: "In property my will is the will of a person; but a person is a unit and so property becomes the personality of this unitary will. Since property is the means whereby I give my will an embodiment, property must also have the character of being 'this' or 'mine'. This is the important doctrine of the necessity of private property. While the state may cancel private ownership in exceptional cases, it is nevertheless only the state that can do this . . . no community has so good a right to property as a person has" (my emphasis).

66. PR, 42–43, §46: "The general principle that underlies Plato's ideal state violates the right of personality by forbidding the holding of private property. The idea of a pious or friendly and even a compulsory brotherhood of men holding their goods in common and rejecting the principle of private property may readily present itself to the disposition which mistakes the true nature of the freedom of mind and right and fails to apprehend it in its determinate moments. As for the moral or religious view behind this idea, when Epicurus's friends proposed to form such an association holding goods in common, he forbade them, precisely on the ground that their proposal betrayed distrust and that those who distrusted each other were not friends."

67. Feminists who renounce reason as a male trait and embrace femaleness as embodied naturalness ought to take Hegel's counterarguments very seriously. So ought Beauvoir, who rejects Hegel's concept of dialectical reason as necessarily involving a moment of conflict.

68. See, e.g., Stuart Swindle, "Why Feminists Should Take the Phenomenology of Spirit Seriously," The Owl of Minerva 24, no. 1 (fall 1992): 41–54. See there also my response to Swindle (parts of which are reproduced here) and that of Patricia Jagentowicz Mills.

69. This is not a prescriptive conclusion but an intellectual one. Yet, in the Hegelian philosophy praxis surely emerges from, as well as serves as the basis of, embedded understandings made explicit.

11

Critical Relations in Hegel: Woman, Family, and the Divine

Shari Neller Starrett

Without breakthroughs in women-identified spirituality, the "women's movement" would be a non-movement—hopelessly dead and deadening.
—Mary Daly, *Beyond God the Father*

Like so many other feminists I approach the traditionally loaded concepts of "family" and "divinity" with suspicion, so what I am about to argue here surprises me as much as anyone. My position is that there is a positive gain for feminists in the story that Hegel tells (in the *Sittlichkeit* section of the *Phenomenology of Spirit*) about women being bound by what he calls the divine law of the family. This is certainly not an unmitigated gain, but it is important to acknowledge the positive potential of Hegel's linking of women, family, and the divine.

I shall support my reading of Hegel in two ways. First I shall argue that Hegel has a radical and potentially empowering notion of women in the realm of the family. Second, that this unusual notion of women and the family is aligned with the goals and strategies of feminists like

Mary Daly who see the value of placing the women's movement within a spiritual context. I shall argue that in Hegel's story women are seen as embodying a lawlike divine perspective or powerful spiritual voice that calls the immanent-transcendent and the private-public distinctions into question. Women are also seen as involved in an ethical context of what I call *Hegelian critical relations*, which is my characterization of Hegel's strategy for gaining insight into human experience. "Critical" is meant in the sense of being confrontational, questioning, and crucial. Illustrating that a confrontational, questioning demand for legitimation is crucial, is Hegel's remarkable nuance on our academic (philosophical) use of the term "critical."[1] For Hegel, a crisis is precipitated when relations cease to be critical. Hegel also insists that a critical response must be relationally counterbalanced. That is, his confrontational, questioning exchanges between persons are not only seen as crucial; they emphasize the importance of viable, challenging opponents who engage each other and resist (at least for a significant time) being converted or subverted. For Hegel, all relations are not critical, but it is significant that some are, and those that are are the subject of his analysis.

Relations between people are not only critical and noncritical, they are familial and nonfamilial.[2] In the *Sittlichkeit* section of the *Phenomenology of Spirit*, Hegel illustrates how family relations can be critical relations. Some of us don't need to have this demonstrated. Still, it is important to note that Hegel is singular in his development of the critical perspective of women within the family. He does this by linking women's legitimation, defining principle, or source of value to a divine law that represents the family, and by linking men's legitimation to a public law that represents citizens of a community. In general terms, the community and its laws are supposed to value the family; in specific terms, family members are uniquely valued for who and what they are only through women as representatives of the force that binds the family together. On the face of it this sounds like a very romanticized notion of the family, and a thinly disguised attempt to tie women to domestic roles. But it is much more than this.

Women in the Family: Sometimes a Radical Notion

In one important way Hegel's notion of the family deviates radically from the standard notion. Although he calls the family "a natural ethical community,"[3] and begins his assessment by focusing on the husband-wife, parent-child, and brother-sister relationships, he is not just describing or spiritualizing what we typically think of as "immediate" or even "extended" family. Hegel's notion of family is cross-generational in the most dramatic way. The law of the family is tied to the dead as well as living members of the family.[4]

The force that binds the family together is not sentiment, as some would suspect: "the ethical connection between members of the family is not that of feeling, or the relationship of love" (PS, para. 451). Rather, the family is bound together by a connection that extends backward to "the dead," not just in acknowledgment of the ancestral bloodline, but in a way that revitalizes the spirit or voice of past family members. For Hegel, the "immediate" family includes the dead, who live on and make their presence felt through women. It is women who sustain "the relation of the individual member of the family to the *whole* Family" (PS, para. 451; emphasis in original). This unusual view of the family is developed at length and illustrated by reference to Sophocles' *Antigone*.

The explanatory force of Hegel's focus on *Antigone* in understanding his discussion of women and the family has been well developed by Patricia Jagentowicz Mills.[5] Building her case with substantial textual detail Mills draws our attention to the negative consequences for women in Hegel's treatment of Antigone's actions in regard to her dead brother. According to Mills, some of the bleak consequences of Hegel's story are women's recognition of a seriously blocked path to active participation in public life as defined by men, and inattention to the importance of relationships between women, both of which contribute to preventing women from being able to develop as "fully human" individuals.

Mills is entirely correct in calling Hegel on these counts. In *Sittlichkeit* women are consistently defined as outsiders in relation to public or political action; insofar as they are consistently insiders in relation to private or familial action, even the most traditional woman-woman relation of mother to daughter is all but ignored. It is also the case that insofar as social individuality or individual political status is the basis for full humanity, Hegel makes it impossible for women to achieve it.

Additionally, Hegel is guilty of describing women's bond to familial relations in terms of bloodline ties (explicitly to males, living and dead; if there is a bond to dead female relatives it is only implicit or perhaps patrilineally derivative). But it is also the case that Hegel explicitly describes women as empowered with, for, by, or through her cross-temporal family relations, to the extent that she acts as an effective, viable, and even threatening critical opponent to those who are currently empowered through public laws of their own devising. Women (as represented by Antigone) can force men, who are personally identified with and by the laws they create and defend, to recognize their limitations. Women can demonstrate how men's laws fail to support the people they claim to support, especially when those people are not considered as complicated relational beings—beings who do not experience harms and benefits singularly, but along with the people they are connected to.

Hegel didn't but should have developed a fuller appreciation of the variety of familial relations. He should have discussed fully vertical or diachronic genealogical relationships between the living and those who previously struggled to make their lives possible, regardless of gender. He should have considered fully lateral or synchronic relationships between living contemporaries whose support and connection energize each other's lives. He should have extended the notion of family beyond blood relations to include, say, adoptive relationships that are not necessarily legally formalized, but are tacitly accepted between the people involved. He should have included committed sexual relations between persons that are not defined in terms of reproduction. Hegel did not do these things. But he did alter the notion of family in a way that seems to license these fuller understandings of a family.

According to Hegel, "Blood-Relationship supplements, then, the abstract natural process by adding to it the movement of consciousness . . . [and] it comes about that the dead . . . becomes a being that has returned into itself." He then adds: "being-for-itself, or the powerless, simply isolated individual has been raised to universal individuality" in the family; that is, when women represent them. A "dead individual, by having liberated his *being* from his *action*" (emphasis in original) could easily be dishonored, or become "merely a *passive* being-for-another" (my emphasis); that is, merely a memory which is easily tainted. But instead, "the family keeps away the dead from the dishonoring of him . . . and makes him a member of the community" (PS, para. 452) by the woman assuming a role which could be called *co-active* being-with-another.

It might be objected that Hegel describes women as merely an "instrument" in this process: "The dead whose right is denied knows therefore how to find instruments of vengeance" (*PS*, para. 474). But there is not a ranking of the male over the female who is instrumental in bringing those who have died back into the community, for in this same passage Hegel says of the instruments[6] that they are "*equally effective and powerful* as the power which has injured [the dead]" (*PS*, para. 474; my emphasis).

If (and this is a substantial and heavy "if") we can read Hegel's notion of family as implicitly opening up onto those, living or dead, with whom we feel real (but not necessarily genetic) sisterhood, brotherhood, parent-child ties, or a "marriage" of minds, bodies, spirits, wills, or desires, then we can read Hegel's analysis of women empowered by the force of family ties as introducing a powerful critical position for women. But even in Hegel's less open but expanded view of the family, women's critical position is one of being able to use their wide-ranging familial, relational power to challenge those who are empowered by laws that distance them from the reality of particular human relations. So, Hegel's dangerously essentialist view of the sexes as tied to deep, defining laws, ironically establishes women as a constant and critical voice that at one and the same time has the ongoing potential to speak both for and beyond "individual citizens." That is, women, who speak from a relational being-in-the-world toward a recognition of this reality, stand effectively opposed to men whose sex presumably ensures that they can speak only from an individual being-in-the-world toward a community legitimation of their stand.

I believe that Hegel's development of women in *Sittlichkeit* can be read as establishing essential, necessary tension between the sexes, but can also be read as illustrating how women who have historically and socially become bound by immediate family connections can give voice to a connection-based alternative that poses a critical challenge to men who have become historically and socially bound to the creation and protection of abstract rights or laws applicable to hypothetical individuals who they assume are singularly like themselves. Women can be seen as having spoken out for an alternative way of organizing human action and human rights in terms of a co-active, connective (and spiritual) being-with-others as opposed to individual being-for-self.[7] I think that the Hegelian text licenses this reading, even if it does not explicitly advise and consent to it. I do not deny or recommend forgetting the passages that have essentialist, and negative consequences for women, but I offer the following additional textual references in order to build my claim that the text can be mined for positive readings of women's historical, present, and future critical potential.

In the subsection of the *Phenomenology* entitled "The ethical world. Human and Divine Law: Man and Woman," Hegel writes: "the human law . . . is the known law, and the prevailing custom . . . it is the actual certainty of itself in the individual as such. . . . Its truth is the authority which is openly accepted and manifest to all" (*PS*, para. 448). Here, the "truth" of man's law amounts to the open acceptance of the authority of law based on custom and on an unquestioned sense of the status or integrity of the individual. In other words, this law is true until it is effectively and openly challenged, and/or the integrity of the individuals it is supposedly based on is called into question. Hegel goes on to say that "confronting this clearly manifest ethical power there is, however, another power, the Divine Law . . . the simple and immediate essence of the ethical sphere" (*PS*, para. 449).

Here we see Hegel acknowledging that a force is in place that opposes the integrity of human law. The simple immediacy of this oppositional force is then used to establish the family unit (the whole and its parts) as a basic being, with natural ethical integrity: "the ethical sphere in this element of immediacy or [simple] being, or which is an immediate consciousness of itself, both as essence and as this particular self, in an 'other', i.e. as a *natural* ethical community—this is the family" (*PS*, para. 450).

The family unit is then defined as having a cohesive spiritual ethical base: "The family . . . their connection is an immediate connection of separate, actual individuals . . . and this natural relationship is just as much a spiritual one, and it is only as a spiritual entity that it is ethical" (*PS*, para. 451). Hegel then develops the radical, cross-temporal character of the family, embeds it in an experiential context, and clarifies its deep cross-temporal source of legitimation: "The family . . . weds the blood-relation to the bosom of the earth. . . . The family makes [the dead individual] a member of the community [*PS*, para. 452]. . . . [and] the divine right and law has for its content and power the individual who is beyond the real world" (*PS*, para. 453).

Women (described relationally) are then named as the spokespersons and protectors of the "divine" relational integrity of the family: "the sister becomes, or the wife remains, the head of the household and the guardian of the divine law" (*PS*, para. 459). And the difficult, diplomatic connection between temporalities and sensitivities is indicated when Hegel distinguishes "the law valid on earth [the human law] from that of the nether world [the divine law], the conscious from the unconscious, *mediation from immediacy*" (PS, para. 460; my emphasis).

"Movements" associated with men and the human law, and women and the divine law[8] are then described in opposition to each other, the former involving confrontational being-toward-death (risking death in order to achieve independence), the latter as being-toward-conscious experience (breaking through from death or unconsciousness to life, or mediating between death and conscious experience). Hegel then describes how the two movements come together when

> their immediate union . . . unites into one process the opposite movements: one from actuality down to unreality, the downward movement of the human law, organized into independent members, to the danger and trial of death; and the other, the upward movement of the law of the netherworld to the actuality of the light of day and to conscious existence. Of these movements, the former falls to man, the latter to woman. (PS, para. 463)

We are then made aware of the undeniable force behind both the human and divine positions. The implication is that neither of the two movements will fail to be represented: "Nature, not the accident of circumstances or choice, assigns one sex to one law, the other to the other law; or conversely, the two ethical powers give themselves an individual existence and actualize themselves in the two sexes" (PS, para. 465).

Hegel then aptly characterizes the rationale and strategy of the movement of men's public law. Human law by and for citizens attempts to preserve itself by associating itself with virility (or life force), and by attempting to overwhelm and obscure significant relationships other than relationships to the law or its manly representatives: "Human Law . . . is the manhood of the community . . . and maintains itself by consuming and absorbing into itself . . . the separation of independent families presided over by womankind" (PS, para. 475).

In this story that Hegel tells about the confrontation of the divine and human laws there is a period of time in which the opposition of these perspectives works tranquilly to authenticate each of these laws, and the sexes that are defined by them. But eventually, "a dreadful fate

. . . engulfs . . . divine and human law alike" (PS, para. 464), and what follows is "a soulless community . . . a mere multiplicity of individuals" (PS, para. 477). That is, an especially legalistic or detached form of "individual being-for-self" (largely attributable to men insofar as they remain in charge of "public" law) inevitably absorbs whatever inclinations survive a confrontation between people who took their defining laws so personally that they understood their gender identities in terms of them. Men are left stranded in a "soulless" legal arena, and women are left stranded in a soulless family life.

In *Sittlichkeit* women live, breathe, and act for and from their family relations (and understand themselves as having no alternative), and men live, breathe, and act for and from their identity as individual citizens who build and defend laws concerning citizens in general (and understand these efforts as mandatory). What neither women nor men realize in this ethical community is the degree to which their self-definitions interpenetrate. Both are self-righteous about following and affirming their natures, to the point where they either become internal enemies within the social order they have attempted to define, or they are forced into actions that make a relationship between them self-defeating, because they assume as conditions of success the very things that eventually bring about the failure of their relationship, namely, opposing natures and mutually exclusive perspectives. Given some time and reflection, and contexts in which they disagree, each sex sees the other as irredeemably limited. In Hegel's words: "Since it sees right only on one side and wrong on the other, the consciousness which belongs to the divine law sees in the other side only the violence of human caprice, while that which holds to the human law sees in the other only the self-will and disobedience of the individual who insists on being his own authority" (PS, para. 466). Both sexes end up characterizing each other uncharitably: women see men as wantonly destructive and insensitive, and men see women as shallow and unwilling to acknowledge the authority of anything more than their own immediate experience. Both come to an understanding of the other that fails to appreciate what they have understood themselves to be about: men having understood themselves as being about a righteous struggle for the integrity of the individual, and women having understood themselves as being about a righteous struggle for the integrity of close human connections that defy physical death and outlive the grave.

If the description of Hegel's story in the preceding paragraph did not sound familiar or ring true to your sense of the not so distant past in regard to the relations between the sexes, then I have not managed to characterize selected elements of this story well enough. It is important to note that in Hegel's mind what follows this story is a "soulless" condition. While the divine-human confrontation was at work, a strong spiritual element infused their interaction through the family and through women. But when the confrontation ceases to be critically counterbalanced and the positions are trivialized, the spiritual element is lost along with the purported tranquillity that once surrounded the relationships between men and women.

Historically, of course, women have often been seen as responsible and have accepted the responsibility for bringing an appreciation of religious or spiritual elements into the life of the family and the community, or for establishing an atmosphere of tranquil piety in the home. In fact what Miller translates as the "dutiful reverence" that obtains in the family between its members is, in German, *Pietät* or piety. I am not suggesting that Miller's translation is not apt, but that the religious tone present in the notion of piety (which Miller attempts to capture with the word "reverence") is important in understanding the tenor of the law that women embody. Women's association with the spiritual status of the household is established through several references to "the Penates" (*Der Penaten*) or the deities presiding over the household (e.g., *PS*, paras. 457 and 475). And of course, it is often pointed out that Hegel was raised in the Pietist tradition, a movement dating from the seventeenth-century Lutheran Church in Germany, which advocated an emphasis on and revival of piety or religious duty.

Our examination of the text allows us to conclude that when Hegel claims that the family is an "ethical entity" (*sittliches Wesen*) only insofar as it is a "spiritual entity" (*geistiges Wesen*) (*PS*, para. 451), he is claiming that the integrity of the family lies in acknowledging the spiritual being or presence of the "whole" family. This spiritual presence is made manifest in women. So we can then conclude that the intangible is made tangible in the presence of women. Put another way, that which transcends the here and now of experience is made immanent, or brought into the here and now in the sensibilities and actions of women who speak in the present and affirm a vital connection and duty to those who have gone before. Women in their very being (insofar as that being is defined in terms of Hegel's wide-ranging notion of the family) call the transcendent-immanent distinction into question. In the *Antigone*, for example, Antigone does not just speak for her dead brother Polyneices, but in her presence embodies his presence,[9] albeit in a futile confrontation with the public law.

The example of Antigone's tragic confrontation with the public law of men as presided over by Creon, along with our attention to other previously cited passages of the *Phenomenology*, allows us to reach a second conclusion concerning the spiritual presence (*geistiges Wesen*) of women in *Sittlichkeit*. Not only does women's very being in this context call the immanent-transcendent distinction into question, it also stands in a critical relation to the public-private distinction.

As Mills points out in *Woman, Nature, and Psyche*, "Antigone transcends woman's place in Hegel's framework because she breaks out of the confines of her assigned sphere. . . . Antigone becomes . . . a participant in both spheres" (35). Antigone does not just speak in a voice which is (privately, immanently) both hers and her dead brother's; she (publicly, with a presence which is at once hers, and more than her own) speaks against the legal authority, and stands against Creon who claims to be its protector and singular voice. Mills quite correctly points out that "Sophocles does not create Antigone and Creon as ethical equals" (29). She adds that Hegel does not adequately appreciate this imbalance, nor does he properly attend to the fact that in Sophocles' story Creon's unchosen living death (after his loved ones commit suicide in the wake of his actions in regard to Antigone) is meant to compare and contrast to the harsh "justice" that Antigone chooses for herself when she commits suicide rather than bow to Creon's verdict which would have had her buried alive. But even if he does not appreciate the salient features and imbalances of Sophocles's *Antigone*, Hegel does bring the character of Antigone into the public sphere, and call the integrity of both characters and both spheres into question.

Antigone's very presence in the public sphere problematizes the distinction between "public" and "private." Her private (internal) experience of speaking (externally) with and for her brother, is itself an odd sort of privacy. Even if we take her multiple internal experiences to be equivalent to private and singular family matters, the heart of the matters themselves involve public law, and when the matters are made public the privacy of the family is compromised. Also, when Antigone challenges Creon and takes the law into her own hands by defying its authority, her defiance is a public act as well as a private resolution. It can also be argued that suicide is the most intensely public and private act imaginable. Even though Hegel does not comment on Antigone's suicidal defiance of the integrity of the public sphere, he does praise the moral force of her story. Hegel's analysis of Sophocles' *Antigone* is insufficient. But insofar as he does relay Antigone's actions in and against the public sphere, and insofar as he does describe the collapse of the tranquilly counterpoised critical relationship between the two spheres, he does demonstrate that women can be the causally effective agents in undermining the separate integrity of both the public and private spheres.

Feminism and Spirituality: Sometimes a Hegelian Notion

The "spiritual entity" of the family and women's embodiment of that spiritual presence meet a tragic end in Hegel's *Sittlichkeit*. But some contemporary feminists hold high hopes for a successful form of "women-identified spirituality" in the quest for human integrity. Charlene Spretnak, for example, hopes that an "interfaith cross-cultural approach to reclaiming spiritual treasures that have been marginalized by modern culture"[10] will revitalize spiritual practices and interconnections. Spretnak's version of feminist spirituality is reminiscent of Hegel in its focus on what she calls "the fullness of being," and "the being-in relation." Consider the following passage in which Spretnak strikes a Hegelian chord: "the core teachings and practices of the wisdom-traditions—regardless of what sorts of institutional forms may have grown up around them—are thoroughly subversive of the monstrous reduction of the fullness of *being* . . . and the supposedly pragmatic destruction of a being-in relation" (9; emphasis in original).

In *States of Grace*, the combined insights that Spretnak culls from the wisdom traditions[11] result in an "ecofeminist orientation."[12] With special emphasis on women's part in effecting connections, this orientation stands in a critical relation to "the politics of separateness" (245) and "protective autonomy" (246). These systematic forms of organizing life are said to have brought about the destruction of the interrelationship between humans and their environment. In order to address this destruction Spretnak develops an ancient but contested and largely forgotten tradition, "which honored the bountiful dynamics of the natural world as the female process of periodicity and procreation writ large."[13]

I contend that Hegel's *Sittlichkeit* can also be seen as the process of spiritual procreation writ large, with women in the role of spiritual guides. While Hegel does not focus on female periodicity, or cyclical fertility and renewal, he does develop a notion of women as periodically offering fertile ground for the spiritual renewal of life. With Hegel's women in the family, what goes around comes around. That is, Hegelian women offer rebirth and regeneration to people (dead or alive), just as the seasons offer rebirth and regeneration of the earth as a whole and in its parts.

Spretnak's version of "ecofeminism" is a form of what is sometimes called "Goddess" spirituality. This kind of spirituality does not attempt to stand in for god-based religions; it is not "Yahweh in a skirt," as Spretnak said in a recent article in Ms. magazine (March–April 1993). Instead (in part) it holds that (1) "the divine is immanent"; (2) there is an "empowerment experienced by people as they come to grasp their heritage and presence"; and (3) there is a "perceptual shift from the death-based sense of existence that underlies patriarchal culture to a regeneration-based awareness, an embrace of life as a cycle of creative rebirths" (136–37). All three of these aspects of a feminist sense of spirituality are reminiscent of Hegel. Women embody the "divine"; they are empowered through their genealogical connections; and the being-toward-life of Hegelian women makes them powerful instruments[14] of relational rebirth as they provide a critical alternative to the being-toward-death that is associated with men (cf. master-slave relations, and PS, para. 463).

Spretnak's use of the term "grace" in developing her spiritual position also resonates with Hegel's claims about women in the family. She says: "When we experience consciousness of the unity in which we are embedded, the sacred whole that is in and around us, we exist in a state of grace." She adds that the term "grace" names "unitive experiences," sometimes called "revelatory experiences," which are a variety of mysti-cal[15] spiritual experience. Unitive mystical experience consists either of "a sense of unity in multiplicity ('extroverted' mysticism) or unity devoid of all multiplicity ('introverted' mysticism)."[16] Spretnak claims that grace or unitive experiences are primary, and that they are widely reported cross-cultural experiences. She also suggests that (the renown of male mystics notwithstanding) women have had, and continue to have these experiences in a way that is only deepened and critically honed by reflection on their physical experience.[17]

Using the language suggested in the previous paragraph, Hegel could be said to be describing women's familial lives as a form of "extroverted" mystical experience that falls under the version of feminist spirituality developed by Spretnak. That is, when women speak for and with "the natural ethical community" of the family, they embody a sense of "unity in multiplicity," and they live a sort of being-toward unitive experience when they act to bring past members of the "whole" family into the present context of human relations.

It is also important to note that Spretnak says of the unitive experience of grace that it "may be extraordinary, but it is not *super*natural. It would be more accurately labeled ultranatural"—an experience in which "perceptual boundaries between 'inner' and 'outer' dissolve" (208). The feminist spirituality that Spretnak describes bears a strong resemblance to Hegel's position in its claim to challenge distinctions between such things as inner and outer (private and public, immanence and transcendence), in its appreciation of lessons from religious tradition, and especially in the similarity of unitive experience or grace to Hegel's description of women's experience of the "divine" law of the family.[18]

Mary Daly's influential insights regarding women-identified spirituality surely deserve more extensive treatment than space affords here. It should be noted, in contrast to my use of her in connection with a reading of Hegel, that Daly speaks passionately against using male writers to give legitimacy to women's spirituality. Nonetheless, in *Beyond God the Father* (perhaps her most widely read book, although all of them have an enviable audience), she offers a bridge from traditional, male-oriented spiritual perspectives to women's spirituality that helps to illuminate the bridge I am attempting to construct between Hegel and feminist spirituality.

Daly effects the bridge to women-identified spirituality in part by having serious fun reinventing the language of and about religious and political traditions. I shall briefly discuss the relevance to my project of three of her intentionally loaded terms, "stag-nation," "biophilic bonding," and "webster work."[19] Perhaps the term "stag-nation" needs no explanation. Like many of her terms it hyphenates a word in common usage to make a critical point about something conveyed in the whole or the parts of the term, in this case both. The term "biophilic" is an example of creating a new word that plays on the existence of a current word, in this case, the word "necrophilic," illustrating a previously unquestioned prejudice in the language (i.e., naming a love of death but not a love of life). The term "webster" is an example of extending the meaning of a word that already carries multiple connotations, in this case, an allusion to the "Webster" of dictionary fame, and a root reference to weavers, or makers of webs. Daly's websters, of course, are women—whose work is weaving life and language.

Consider the similarities to Spretnak in the following quote: "Websters weaving beyond god the father veto, ban and forbid . . . the mindless devastation wrought by stag-nations."[20] Both writers are concerned with the destruction wrought by the attempt to achieve human integrity as organized and overseen by men, and both writers see women as being in a position to offer a critical alternative. For Daly, women's critical relation to men is effective in its active critique of language, as well as in its critique of a male-oriented (god the father) religious perspective.

I contend that Daly's notion of "stag-nation" can be compared to Hegel's "human law" of men. It is obvious that the "nation" in *Sittlichkeit* is male-defined, and that women as guardians of the family stand in critical opposition to it. "The Family," says Hegel, "stands opposed to the nation itself . . . it stands over and against that order which shapes and maintains itself" (*PS*, para. 450). For Hegel, men's human law (what Daly calls "stag-nation") is a self-perpetuating legitimation structure that protects those individuals who identify with the authority of the laws or prevailing customs—laws and customs which in turn recognize and ensure that these same individuals (i.e., men) continue to have primary value. Daly points out that the people and laws that have been perpetuated in this manner are, at best, stagnant.

Daly's sense of the positive, critical, and spiritual alternative that women are in a position to offer is further developed by her concept of "biophilic bonding." She sees positive possibilities with "a shifting of the focus of hope away from unredeemable structures to the Selves of women and other biophilic creatures" (xx) and contends that as the polluted context "becomes ever more vile and violent, women . . . reweave faith and hope in our power of Presence" (xxiii). Women, that is, can develop a sense of power in their combined presence. This is accomplished through an "independent 'bonding' with each other" (59) that allows them to effectively reject the threat of guilt or co-optation when the critical presence of women is finally felt in the "public realm," "human law," or "stagnation." In contrast to Spretnak, Daly does not utilize mysticism to bridge the distance between what Daly sees as the stagnant spiritual legacy of men and the vital spiritual capacity of women. Daly suggests that some women, presumably the critical mass, simply have it in them to be "biophilic" and to "bond." She dismisses or denies the critical value of those women who (like Ismene, Antigone's sister in Sophocles' play) identify with patriarchal structures and policies; she affirms and even assumes women's essential or unquestionable capacity to resist co-optation into men's laws by means of guilt or subordination.[21]

In Hegel's treatment of the *Antigone,* we see that Antigone will not be co-opted by the public law of men, but we also see a tragic outcome. Hegel closes off two of the most important options for the success of a woman's voice with his use of the *Antigone:* first, with his suggestion that her challenge to the public law compromises both the integrity of that law and of her own moral law; and second, by his excision of the character of Ismene (and the potential for supportive sisterhood, albeit with primarily male-identified women, which the character of Ismene introduced). In contrast, Daly claims that a positive result is possible when (women-identified) women do bond together: "The positive refusal of cooptation means in effect the becoming of the sisterhood of women, which is necessary to overcome paralysis, self-hatred extended to women as a caste, self-deprecation, and emotional dependence upon men for a feeling of self-esteem" (59). In other words, what is missing from Hegel's version of the Antigone story, as Patricia Mills has pointed out, is the potential affirmation of a strong sisterhood. But it is also the case that insofar as Hegel's use of the *Antigone* does send us back to the original work, as it has sent Mills, myself, and others, Hegel (whether he would have liked it or not) provides the occasion for us to rethink the character of Ismene, and to see how long the potential for some form of supportive sisterhood has been a part of our cultural tradition.

I suggest that although Hegel does not develop the notion of the power implicit in sisterhood, he does give us some provocative opportunities to see a radical and extended notion of women in family-type relations. We can then take a lesson from Hegel and see that, as is the case with Antigone's relationship with her dead brother, we are in a position to use women's wide sense of family connections to extend and politicize the concepts and powerful metaphors of family and sisterhood. To the extent that we appreciate the critical power of vital connections with our biological and nonbiological sisters and all of those to whom we feel deeply related, whether they are in our past, our present, or our future, we may find our selves more able to move from where we are toward a political context that underwrites the "relatedness" of people. I contend that Hegel, like Daly, makes radical suggestions concerning the positive empowerment of women through their relational connections, and that these relational connections take on additional significance and potential when we take Hegel seriously about his claims regarding the vital relationship of women to specific people in the past who continue to have an empowering and meaningful impact on their lives.[22]

A Great Notion?

I am not unaware of the danger in the reading of Hegel that I have been arguing for, or of the controversy concerning any argument that perpetuates the notion of women being tied to the "family." In part this is why I have gone to the lengths that I have in developing this positive reading of a philosopher who *has* been used to justify retrogressive women's roles. Even if there are positive lessons to be gained from Hegel's views about women in the family, just how beneficial is a focus on these positive lessons? This remains a real question in my own mind.

In her recent book *Women and the History of Philosophy*, Nancy Tuana argues and develops a powerful schema for "a form of critical reading with an emphasis on gender issues," which she calls "reading as a woman" (she adds that "the ability to read as a woman is a strategy open to men and women alike").[23] Tuana applies this strategy to reading a number of important philosophers, including Hegel. After an illuminating and textually well supported discussion of Hegel, which includes an exegesis of the *Sittlichkeit* section of the *Phenomenology*, a summary of Hegel's views on the importance of men's and women's "natural" active versus passive biological characteristics, and a discussion of Hegel's claims about man's "natural" authority in regard to property, Tuana (in part) concludes that "man's rule within the family, further reinforces woman's passivity" (104); although the family is important in relation to the "public realm," it nevertheless remains static in Hegel's work.

I do not advocate a reading of Hegel contrary to one like Tuana's, which results from systematically and critically "reading as a woman." Rather, I would add another step after Tuana's critical analysis is done and the limitations and dangers of the author's position have been revealed. After doing this important critical work, we can then go beyond the obvious sexism of the work we are analyzing and ask: What can women find in this writer's position to further our liberation? We can give writers the benefit of the doubt about their partially liberating intentions, or look for loopholes in a position that seems to be overwhelmingly sexist. It is my contention that there are many resources yet to be mined in positions that many of us (myself included) have initially been anxious to distance ourselves from. In this essay I have indicated such resources in Hegel's depiction of women, which can be read as a provocative source of thinking critically about women, and what Hegel assumes is women's "nature." Those of us who are inclined to reject Hegel's essentialism (and who may be inclined to reject *any* essentialism about the sexes) are not forced into dismissing all of Hegel's thoughts about women, any more than we are forced into rejecting Daly's many insights because of her essentialist assumptions about women's nature. In both cases we are at liberty to highlight those elements of their visions that open possibilities for us, and question those that do not.

So, to Nancy Tuana's claim that in Hegel, "family life precludes woman from developing full rationality or achieving true freedom" (*Woman and the History of Philosophy*, 106), I add the qualification that this is true only insofar as full rationality and true freedom are defined by Hegel as tied to a realm of "public" laws, and laws affirming family relatedness are seen as irrational and confining. The nation/state/civil society and the "public" law that Hegel describes may indeed constitute, as Daly suggests, a "stag-nation," and so reveal itself to be confining and irrational. And Hegel does seem to suggest that this state and its laws do become stagnant, indeed, to the point where he believes war becomes a necessity for vitality. But such a state also has the logical potential to be modified to a society that could identify and affirm women's relational rationality, even if Hegel does not follow through on this possibility. That is, the basic values of the community of citizens (i.e., the abstract "public" law protection of any individual's rights) that Hegel describes can be seen as criteria for achieving "full rationality" and "true freedom," but they need not be seen as the only criteria.

It is possible, and provocative, to think that Hegel, along with those feminists who see the value of providing the women's movement with a spiritual context, offers us an opportunity to see an alternative (relational) set of criteria that stand in critical opposition to those (strictly individualistic) criteria that are frequently recognized as authoritative, albeit flawed. And we need not see Hegel's notion of the family as static and retrograde; it can also challenge us to extend our notion of family in the radical cross-temporal way that Hegel and some feminists suggest, as well as in an empowering nonbloodline way that some feminists but not Hegel have been inclined to promote.

I have suggested that the critical voice of women that I have attributed to Hegel emerges in his words, but also that it emerges only in part, and in a way that women readers may be inclined to fill out. Whether or not Hegel foresaw this option is an open question. Nora Ephron's film *Sleepless in Seattle* plays on a long-standing claim and joke among women that there are stories with implications that men don't seem entirely to get—even when they write and produce them, as in the case of the film *An Affair to Remember*, which illustrates this very point in Ephron's film.[24] Hegel's story about women in the *Phenomenology of Spirit* may be another case in point.

Notes

1. Of course, popular use of the term "critical" appreciates this nuance, as in "it's critical that you show up on time," suggesting that a crisis of some sort hangs in the balance.

2. The critical relation of women in the family to men in the citizenry is my focus in this essay, but my larger claim is that the master-slave relationship is a critical nonfamilial relation (where life and death hang in the balance in a context of direct physical assault), and that the man (qua husband, father, brother, son)–woman (qua wife, mother, sister, daughter) relationship is a potentially critical familial relation (where ongoing human integrity and the potential for life hangs in the balance). Examples of noncritical nonfamilial relationships would be those between "like-minded" masters, or between "like-minded" slaves, or those who are allied, for some measurable time, in any cultural or pre-cultural context (e.g., Mrs. Hale and Mrs. Peters in Susan Glaspell's "A Jury of Her Peers"). Noncritical familial relations can occur when family relations are not constrained by roles or forces in competition with or external to the family; say, before sisters or brothers establish "adult" roles outside of what Patricia Mills calls their "family of origin" (e.g., the March sisters in Alcott's *Little Women*).

3. G. W. F. Hegel, *Phenomenology of Spirit*, trans. A. V. Miller (Oxford: Oxford University Press, 1977), para. 450, p. 268; hereafter cited as *PS*.

4. Here again, there is a way in which the popular notion of family encompasses the dead (i.e., ancestors; great-great-grandparents are, of course, family). But in our ordinary sense of the family we are immediately tied to and responsible for only living relations. We may think we owe something to the memory of our dead grandmother, but, outside of some feminist sensibilities (and perhaps some Native American and Asian traditions; I am unaware of other cultural practices which may be of this sort) we have rarely felt that we are immediately connected to her as a spokesperson. I shall offer more on this point later.

5. Patricia Jagentowicz Mills, *Woman, Nature, and Psyche* (New Haven: Yale University Press, 1987), esp. 17–49. Mills's work on Hegel and women has deeply influenced my thinking since I began working on my dissertation "Hegel and Nietzsche: The Master/Slave and Man/Woman Relationships," (1989). Her comments on this article have been a continuing source of stimulation.

6. The German word Hegel uses for "instruments" is *Werkzeuge*, a word that helps to make my case for the term "co-active" as descriptive of women's instrumental role. The prefix *Werk-* means act, action, or deed, while *-zeug* carries the meaning of stuff, material, or equipment. *Werkzeug* names a tool or passive agent, but its root meaning consists of more vital stuff. That is, the word *Werkzeuge* itself calls the passive/active distinction into question. One could argue that only in action is a tool an effective force, but on its own it has little force (Wittgenstein suggested something like this about language). Similarly, the picture Hegel paints of woman is one in which she is seen as powerless taken as an individual, but effective and powerful when at work in her relational, familial capacity.

7. This alternative can as well be called a "second nature" acquired through socialization as "natural." The immediacy of conditioned and unconditioned responses is indiscernible.

8. Such "movements" can be understood in terms of a variety of sociopolitical movements: for example, military movements associated with the defense of men's laws (such as slavery and antislavery in the Civil War), or legal movements that take the form of consciousness raising (the women's movement, the arguments for enfranchisement). In my dissertation I also argue that the language of this passage (*PS*, para. 463) is reminiscent of the traditional description of sexual positions and movements that men and women take in physical intercourse: for example, the "missionary" position is taken to be the optimal position for receiving and revivifying the "spirit." It represents the man forcing the issue; the woman, later, in the same position (at least according to male-dominated medical practice), issuing forth.

9. Note that this story also problematizes the reality of the female-male distinction. I hold that the story told in the *Sittlichkeit* section of the *PS* is pivotal in Hegel's attempt to call all binary oppositions into question by demonstrating that confrontational "logic" or schema always breaks down and inevitably leads us to a recognition of the simultaneity and interpenetration of differentiated experience. But this is a far larger claim than can be examined in this essay.

10. Charlene Spretnak, *States of Grace: The Recovery of Meaning in the Postmodern Age* (San Francisco: Harper, 1991), 8. All references to Spretnak are to this work.

11. In addition to what are often called the world's "great" religions, this term is meant to embrace native spiritual traditions and some forms of Buddhism that do not neatly fit under the Western understanding of the term "religion."

12. Spretnak, 5, and throughout *States of Grace*. Spretnak is a major force in both the Green Party and in the feminist spirituality movement. See, for example, her books *Green Politics*, and *The Politics of Women's Spirituality*. I had the pleasure of meeting her (and Mary Daly) when she participated in a symposium that the Philosophy Department at California State University at Fullerton sponsored on "Rationality and Spirituality" in March 1993. I am indebted to conversations with Spretnak, Daly, and others (especially to the student reading group that I facilitated which responded to a paper by Emily Culpepper) at this symposium and to my department for sponsoring this event. Many of my thoughts for this essay were formed in this rich context.

13. Spretnak, *States of Grace*, 245. It should be noted that by invoking the mystical Spretnak walks a delicate line between biological essentialism and affirmation of the insights of women's historical/spiritual traditions. My understanding of her work is that this ambiguity is intentional, that she tries to develop a position that simultaneously celebrates the profundity of the biological experience of women and the complicity of religious or spiritual traditions in this experience, and that she sees a context of meaning issuing from this connection.

14. Keep in mind my comments in note 6 regarding Hegel's use of the word "instrument."

15. "Mystical" is said to contrast to "numinous" spiritual experience, which involves "awareness of a holy presence apart from the self" (Spretnak, *States of Grace*, 209). I am

indebted to Lou Reich for pointing out to me that the terms Spretnak introduces in this paragraph are widely acknowledged among scholars in the philosophy of religion, and were developed by such writers as Walter Stace, Rudolf Otto, and Ninian Smart. (Ninian Smart was also part of the symposium previously mentioned in note 15.)

16. Spretnak, *States of Grace*, 207–9. In a conversation with Spretnak she also told me that in an as yet unpublished paper she uses the term "radical non-duality" to paraphrase "grace" for philosophical audiences. This seems to me to be an apt way of characterizing Hegel's position, and it underscores the radical potential of "unitive" and Hegelian thinking.

17. For discussion of a wide variety of contemporary examples of such experiences see "Earthbody and Personal Body as Sacred," in Spretnak, *States of Grace*, 133–49.

18. Since unitive experience is said to be singular and momentous, there may be objections to the suggestion that women can "live" a unitive way of life in embodying what I have called "co-active being-for another." But I am not claiming that women, so conceived, continuously live a unitive experience, only that they can have a "being-toward" this sort of experience, that they can understand themselves as being in some way "primed" for it. My sense is that Hegel's description of women's co-active experience with dead family members is meant to be of great moment for the women, and analogous to what has been described as the form of grace called "extroverted" unitive experience. What the "ground" of this experience is, is another matter. Both Hegel and Spretnak, I believe, wax ambiguous and paradoxical on this issue, but rely on "natural" descriptions that open themselves up to charges of biological determinism. But I support readings of both of these writers, whether they intend them or not, that are more concerned with motivating radical *and varied* understandings of women's critical positions than with worries about essentialism. My larger claim (which can only be hinted at here) is that we can read Hegel as indicating that in all contexts of meaning, the "ground" is constantly shifting, so much so that it is always impossible to isolate what is "natural," even while we see ourselves as acting "naturally" or as "embedded" in this illusive ground. It is my position that Hegel gives us our first glimpse of finding meaning in varied and challenging critical positions, rather than from a "solid" or "natural" ground.

19. Daly's critical reworking of language is so extensive that, along with Jane Caputo, she has published *Websters' First New Intergalactic Wickedary of the English Language* (Boston: Beacon, 1987). The terms that I discuss here are listed in this "Wickedary" and are used in many of her other works.

20. Daly, *Beyond God the Father: Toward a Philosophy of Women's Liberation* (Boston: Beacon, 1973), from the "Original Reintroduction" in the 1985 edition), xxvi. References in text to Daly are to this work.

21. Daly's essentialism is, to my mind, deeper than Hegel's. It celebrates women and offers deep hope that women are an undeniable force, spiritually and politically, but the price for this hope is a high one. One of the harsh positions that her notion of the bonding of "biophilic" women implies is that women who do not primarily identify with and support other women have been fatally co-opted. Paradoxically, this makes the women on the other side of any contested issue impossible to bond with. Thus, the women on the two sides of the abortion debate remain fatally divided. Daly in fact does reverse the vocabulary on this issue, making pro-choice advocates "pro-life" (biophilic, "being-toward-life" as implied in the full support of women) and anti-choice advocates "pro-death" (the being-toward-death that is implied in male-oriented positions, which aim to control and subordinate). While some divisions between women may seem insurmountable, accepting a position that necessitates deep difference seems to entail a surgical manipulation of gender sensibilities that cuts off parts of women's body politic. Hegel, I believe, at least leaves open the possibility of women reinterpreting their own experience in light of a wide variety of critical options, while Daly's essentialism ironically seems to underwrite our critical voice by silencing diversity or dissent among women.

22. As Kathryn Pyne Addelson has argued, the moral and revolutionary spirit of some of our nineteenth-century sisters like Sarah Grimké, Lucy Stone, and Sojourner Truth empower us today in a very direct way. Addelson credits Nietzsche with being the first to appreciate the category and impact of moral revolutionaries (as opposed to moral reformers) and she suggests that Grimké, Stone, and Truth are exemplars of this Nietzschean category. This is a controversial (but I think correct) interpretation of Nietzsche, given that his writings about women, like Hegel's, are frequently charged with being retrogressive or misogynist. Addelson's reading of Nietzsche has been an important influence on my readings of both Nietzsche and Hegel. See esp. her *Impure Thoughts* (Philadelphia: Temple University Press, 1991), 12–34.

23. Nancy Tuana, *Woman and the History of Philosophy* (New York: Paragon House, 1992), 5. Tuana's reading strategy is a real jewel. I recommend that everyone carefully consider her development of it in this book. I have found it so valuable, that I hope to motivate others to think further about it by presuming to offer the following *oversimplification* of this strategy. I take Tuana to be recommending that the reader reveal the author's gender assumptions and their impact by (1) examining the way the implicit or explicit conception of women's (moral, rational, spiritual, physical) nature is constructed in the text, and examining the conception of women's abilities, roles, and characteristics as they compare to men's; (2) keeping in mind the cultural or historical gender bias (instead of dismissing it), and looking for the effect of the bias on the overall position of the authors, especially in regard to how it undermines their universal claims; and (3) asking the following questions: (a) can you place yourself in the text? (b) if there is a sexist, racist, or classist bias, whom do you identify with, and what are the consequences of this identification? (c) does the woman reader experience tension in the form of alienation, or in seeing herself as "the other" in the text; that is, does she feel she is being spoken about, but not to?

24. Nora Ephron's 1993 film *Sleepless in Seattle* is an interesting romantic comedy in which the man and woman protagonists are separated and allowed to develop their supposed gender sensibilities in a manner that allows the viewer to see the man and woman as having parallel and opposing self-understandings even though these characters both respond to the profundity of important relational connections in a similar way. They both exemplify emotional awareness of a "magic" fit between people that overrides conventional explanation, and defies ordinary limitations. But the female lead openly expresses her emotions when she recognizes a case in point (i.e., the relationship between the couple in the film *An Affair to Remember*), while the male lead (either insincerely or self-deceptively) implies that such a display of emotion is silly and unjustified. Leo McCarey's 1957 film *An Affair to Remember* is a romantic drama in which a man and woman make an unavoidable connection in a brief shipboard relationship and then defy all of the contingencies which contribute to a situation that, given the conventions of the time, would ordinarily have ensured that they both ended up alone, or at least partially frustrated. Ephron's film suggests that women understand the earlier film's point that relationships can transcend conventional constraints when the connection between people is profoundly felt, and that women are openly moved by this possibility, while men either attempt to minimize this point and women's response to it, or fail to get the point entirely.

12

Let's Spit on Hegel

Carla Lonzi

Translated by Giovanna Bellesia and Elaine Maclachlan

Nothing or nothing any good has been recorded about the historical presence of women: it is up to us to rediscover our past and learn the truth.

The master-slave dialectic is a settling of accounts carried out by groups of men: such a dialectic does not envision the liberation of women, who are the main target of oppression in patriarchal civilization.

The strength of men lies in their identity with culture; ours, in our denial of it.
—*Manifesto Rivolta Femminile*, 1970

The woman question means the relationship between every woman—without power, history, culture, or self-defined role—and every man—his power, his history, his culture, his absolute role.

The woman question casts doubt upon everything that absolute man has done and thought: that man who has no awareness of woman as a human being on his own level.

This is an abridged, cross-cultural translation of Carla Lonzi's classic text *Sputiamo su Hegel* first published in 1970; the text was reprinted in 1974 and 1977 in a collection of her writings entitled *Sputiamo su Hegel: La donna clitoridea e la donna vaginale, e altri scritti* (Milan: Scritti di Rivolta Femminile). By cross-cultural translation we mean to emphasize our efforts to produce an English

.   .   .

We asked for equality in the eighteenth century, and Olympe de Gouges was sent to the gallows for her *Declaration of the Rights of Woman*.[1] The demand of women for equal rights with men coincides historically with the assertion of the equality of men among themselves. Such a demand was appropriate at that time. Today women are conscious that we ourselves are posing a question.

The oppression of woman does not begin in historical time, but is hidden in the darkness of our origins. The oppression of woman cannot be solved through the killing of men. It cannot be solved through equality; rather, it proceeds in equality. It cannot be solved through revolution; rather, it proceeds in revolution. The world of alternatives is a fortress of male superiority: in it there is no room for woman.

The equality available to us today is not philosophical, but political: should we, after thousands of years, knowingly desire to become part of a world planned by others? Do we consider it gratifying to participate in the great defeat of humankind?

By the equality of woman was meant her right to participate in the exercise of power in society through the recognition that her capabilities were equal to those of men. But in the last few years, women's experience has been most true and clearsighted in unveiling a process of the global devaluation of the world of men. We have come to realize that, as far as the exercise of power is concerned, it is not capabilities that are required, but a special form of extremely effective alienation. The position we take does not imply a participation in male power, but a reevaluation of the very concept of power. It is to ward off this attack on the concept of power by women that we are now being taken on as equals.

Equality is a juridical principle: it speaks to the common denominator present in every human being, guaranteeing justice to all. Difference, however, is an existential principle concerning the modes of being human, the peculiarities of our experiences, our ends, our possibilities, our sense of existence in a variety of situations, whether given or desired.

---

text that is not necessarily word-perfect but conveys above all the spirit of Lonzi's work. Such a translation was the only way to meet the challenge of the complexity and ambiguity of Lonzi's prose.

The difference between woman and man is the fundamental difference of humankind.

Black men are equal to white men, black women are equal to white women.

What makes all women different is that they have been absent from history for thousands of years. Let us take advantage of the difference: if women were to become equal members of society, who knows how many thousands of years it would take to shake off this new yoke? We cannot relegate to others the task of overthrowing the order of the patriarchal structure. Equality is what is offered to the victims of colonization on the level of laws and rights. And what is imposed on them on the level of culture. It is the principle by which those who exercise hegemony continue to condition those who do not.

The world of equality is the world of the legalized abuse of power, of one-dimensionality; the world of difference is the world where terrorism throws down its weapons and the abuse of power gives way to respect for the variety and multiplicity of life. We realize now that "equality between the sexes" is what is used today to mask the inferiority of women.

This is the conclusion reached by those who, being different, intend to enact a global change in the civilization that has imprisoned them.

We women have discovered not only the facts of our oppression but the alienation produced in the world by our having been kept prisoners. Women do not have one reason, not one single reason any more, to endorse the objectives of men.

In this new stage of awareness women reject, as a dilemma imposed by male power, both equality and difference, and affirm that no human being and no group ought to define itself or be defined on the basis of another human being or another group.

The oppression of women is the result of thousands of years of history. Capitalism inherited it; it did not produce it. The rise of private property is the expression of the need for power every man claimed over every woman. It institutionalized the imbalance between the sexes at the same time as men were defining the power relationships among themselves. If we give an economic interpretation to the destiny that has always accompanied us, we resort to a mechanism without knowing its real origins. We know that by nature human beings aim for instinctual satisfaction, which they may or may not achieve, in their contacts with the opposite sex. Historical materialism has been blind to this emotional aspect that is the key that determined the passage to private property. But that is where we must return to rediscover the archetype of property itself, the first object conceived by man: the sexual object. Women, by removing themselves as the original prey of man's unconscious, unblock the primal knots of the pathology of possessiveness.

Women are aware of the political connection that exists between Marxist-Leninist ideology and their own suffering, needs, and aspirations. But they do not believe that women's liberation will come about as a consequence of the revolution. They will not allow their own cause to be considered subordinate to the issue of class. They cannot accept a battle plan and a vision that leave them out.

Marxism-Leninism needs to equalize the two sexes, but a settling of accounts carried out by collectives of men can only produce a paternalistic granting of their own male values to women . . .

Hegel's master-slave relationship is a relationship internal to the male human world, and this dialectic is perfectly suited to it in terms precisely deduced from the presuppositions of the seizure of power. But the conflict of woman versus man is not perceived as a dilemma: no solution is foreseen for it insofar as patriarchal culture does not consider it a human problem, but rather a natural phenomenon. It is seen as a consequence of the hierarchy between the sexes, whose essence is considered the result of their opposition: thus a definition of superior and inferior conceals the origin of a conqueror and a conquered. The male vision of the world has found its justification within the limits of its own unilateral experience. But the origin of the opposition between the sexes still remains unclear to women, and they search in the causes of their primordial defeat for the evidence of the crisis of the male spirit.

Forcing the woman question into a master-slave concept of struggle, such as the class struggle, is a historical mistake. That particular concept grew out of a culture that ignored the essential form of discrimination of humankind—the absolute privilege of man over woman—and approached the issue of humanity in terms of a male problematics; that is, it set up the terms of the debate solely in terms of relations between men.

If women subordinate themselves to an interpretation based on class, they are accepting terms borrowed from a type of slavery different from their own, terms that are the most convincing evidence of a mistaken analysis. Woman is oppressed as woman, on all social levels: at the level not of class, but of sex. This lacuna in Marxism did not come about by chance, nor can it be filled by broadening the concept of class to make room for the female masses, the new class. Why has the relationship between woman and production not been seen in the light of her activity in the reproduction of the workforce in the family? Why has her exploitation within the family not been seen as a function essential to the system of the accumulation of capital? By entrusting the revolutionary future to the working class, Marxism has ignored woman as oppressed and as bearer of the future; it has produced a revolutionary theory from the matrix of a patriarchal culture.

Let us examine the relationship between man and woman in Hegel, the philosopher who saw in the slave the motor-force of history. Hegel, more insidiously than others, rationalized patriarchal power in the dialectic between a divine feminine principle and a human male principle. The first principle presides over the family, the second over the community. "Since the community only gets an existence through its interference with the happiness of the Family, and by dissolving [individual] self-consciousness into the universal, it creates for itself in what it suppresses and what is at the same time essential to it an internal enemy—womankind in general."[2]

Woman in Hegel does not go beyond the stage of subjectivity: recognizing herself in her legal and blood relatives, she remains unconsciously universal; she lacks the basis to cut herself off from the family ethos and cannot achieve the self-conscious force of universality through which man becomes citizen. Woman's condition, which is the result of her oppression, is viewed by Hegel as its cause. The difference between the sexes becomes the natural metaphysical basis both for their opposition and for their reunification. Hegel locates in the feminine principle the a priori of a passivity in which the evidence of male domination is made to disappear. Patriarchal authority has kept woman in subjugation, and her only value is then identified as her conformity to it as if it were her very nature.

Consistent with the tradition of Western thought, Hegel regards woman as confined by nature to a stage that he considers to have great worth, but it is such that any man would prefer not to have been born rather than consider it for himself.

Nevertheless, the feminine, "the eternal irony of the community," mocks man the thinker who, as he ages, becomes indifferent to pleasure, while the universe becomes his only thought and concern; woman turns to the young man to find an accomplice in her contempt of him. Beyond the divine law she embodies, beyond her duty toward the household gods, beyond the noble gestures of Greek tragedy with which she ascends from the nether world toward the light of existence, woman reveals an attitude that only her weakness has rendered more bizarre than threatening: her recoil from mature men and her predilection for young men. But Hegel's identification with the values of patriarchal civilization makes him find in this attitude a purely instrumental meaning. Indeed, woman's valorization of youthful males, or virility, is seen by Hegel as the stimulus within the community that brings into focus the element needed for activity toward the outside: war. But in fact, through this gesture of the woman, the power the patriarch exercises over her and over the young man becomes transparent. Her aim is directed simultaneously against the family and against society wherever they embody the power that dominates both women and youth. Mockery is used to point to the historical figure of the oppressor from whom liberation is sought. But he is the one who, as leader, can manipulate and exploit every move the woman and the young man may make. The young man, spurred on by woman's attention, thus becomes a valiant warrior for the preservation of the community.

In the manifestation of woman as the "eternal irony of the community," we acknowledge the presence of feminist issues through all time.

In Hegel two positions coexist: one that sees the destiny of woman connected to the principle of femininity, and another that recognizes in the slave not an unchangeable principle, an essence, but the human condition that realizes in history the evangelical message: "The last shall be the first." If Hegel had recognized the human origin of the oppression of woman, as he recognized the human origin of the oppression of the slave, he would have had to apply the master-slave dialectic to her case, too. And in so doing he would have run into a serious obstacle: in fact, although the revolutionary method of the dialectic can identify the movement of social dynamics, there is no doubt that women's liberation does not fit into the same pattern. On the level of the man-woman relationship there is no solution that eliminates the other, hence *the seizure of power as a conclusive act becomes irrelevant.*

The irrelevance of the seizure of power as a conclusive act is the element that distinguishes the struggle against the patriarchal system as the next phase, a phase that is also concurrent with the dialectical struggle of master and slave.

The Hegelian axiom that everything that is rational is real reflects the conviction that the cunning of reason will not fail to find a way to reach an agreement with power. Such an accommodation is always made possible through the mechanism of the dialectic itself. In a way of life not dominated by patriarchy the triadic construction of the dialectic loses its grip on the human psyche.

The *Phenomenology of Spirit* is a phenomenology of the patriarchal spirit, the incarnation of the monotheistic divinity in time. The image of woman here appears as a signifier in someone else's hypothesis.

History is the result of patriarchal actions.

Christ represents the irreversibility of the sense of guilt on which the power of the Father rests. Following his path to the end the Son attains the certainty that, through his self-sacrifice, he will be carrying out the will of the Father. And he will thus redeem the community to the greater glory of the Father.

The two colossal refutations of Hegel's analysis are within our power: women in their rejection of the family, young men in their rejection of war.

* * *

Young men grasp intuitively that the ancient right of life and death of the father over his children was the expression of a wish rather than the legitimation of a practice. The young man thus comes to see war as a subconscious expedient to kill him, a conspiracy against him . . .

Behind his anguish about becoming a member of society, the young man is actually hiding a conflict with the patriarchal model. This conflict becomes manifest in moments of anarchy in which a global "no" is expressed, a "no" without alternatives: youth's virility here refuses to be paternalistic and a form of blackmail. But without the presence of his historical ally, woman, the anarchical experience of the young man is undermined and he gives in to the lure of organized class conflict. The Marxist-Leninist ideology gives a constructive character to his rebellion as he joins the struggle of the proletariat to which his liberation is entrusted. But in so doing he is sucked back into the dialectic as expected by patriarchal culture, the culture of the seizure of power. Since he thinks he shares with the proletariat a common enemy in capitalism, he abandons his personal fight against the patriarchal system. He places all his trust in the proletariat as the bearer of the revolution: he wants to arouse the proletariat when he finds it lulled by the successes of trade unions and the tactics of political parties, but he never doubts that the proletariat is the new historical agent. Fighting for others, the young man once again subordinates himself: which is exactly what has always been demanded of him. Women's feminist experience has a two-century advantage, first within the French Revolution, and then within the Russian Revolution. Women have tried to tie their situation to that of men in the political sphere but in the end have found themselves mere adjuncts. *Women now affirm that the proletariat is revolutionary vis-à-vis capitalism, but reformist vis-à-vis the patriarchal system . . .*

In communist countries the socialization of the means of production hardly affected the traditional institution of the family. Quite the contrary: it reinforced it insofar as it reinforced the prestige and role of the patriarchal figure. Revolutionary struggle adopted and expressed typically patriarchal and repressive personalities and values. These had repercussions in the organization of society first as a paternalistic state, then as a truly authoritarian and bureaucratic state. The class concept, and therefore the *exclusion of woman as active participant in the elaboration of the issues of socialism,* turned this revolutionary theory into an inevitably patricentric theory. Sexual phobia, moralism, conformity, and terrorism tightened their grasp on social roles. Hence these suffocating roles were not eliminated, as for centuries people had hoped they would be, as an obvious consequence of the elimination of private property. The family is the cornerstone of the patriarchal order: it is founded not only on economic interests but on the psychic mechanisms of men who in every epoch have kept women as objects of domination and as the foundation for their own higher achievements. Marx himself lived his life as a traditional husband, absorbed in his work as scholar and theorist while siring many children, including one born to his maid . . .

The resumption of the struggle for women's liberation did not take place in socialist countries, where the social structure assumed a severity typical of the Dark Ages through the authoritarian imposition of patriarchal myths reinstated by the revolution. Instead, it reemerged in the bourgeois states where the collapse of traditional values can happen only through the intervention of women. Such a collapse is, in fact, the collapse of the very idea of patriarchal reality: in its aftermath is evident the corrosion not only of the middle classes but also of a certain kind of male civilization. Marxism dealt with the master-slave dialectic as the fundamental contradiction in the development of bourgeois society, and articulated this dialectic in terms of class struggle. But the dictatorship of the proletariat has sufficiently demonstrated that it is not the bearer of the dissolution of social roles: it maintained and consolidated the family as the central social institution continuously duplicating a human structure incompatible with any substantial change in values. The Communist Revolution developed out of a male cultural-political foundation, *out of the repression and exploitation of feminism,* and must now face the revolt against those male values, a revolt that women will carry to the end, beyond the dialectic of class struggle within the patriarchal system.

Even at the peak of the struggle for the dictatorship of the proletariat, feminism directly confronted the situation of women with extraordinarily creative insights and methods. But it was precisely at that point that communist women were called back to what the authorities deemed the "real" problems and a nondeviational approach. This created the frustration that drove women to self-immolation . . .

No revolutionary ideology will ever again convince us that there are duties and solutions for women and young men in class struggle, work, sublimation, and sport. Such ideology is merely the means for adult men to perpetuate the privilege of their domination.

Women have traditionally been apolitical. In this we see their spontaneous reaction to a universe of ideologies and causes in which their problems are barely allowed to surface—and this only when, from the heights of paternalism, women are deployed as a force that can be manipulated.

While young men are working for a sociopolitical revolution that will prevent them from wasting their lives in the administration of a society ultimately alien to them, there are those who count on the neophyte enthusiasm of women to buffer the crisis of male society: women are allowed to fill men's roles, and this maneuver is made to appear as their compensation for having been excluded from society since the beginning of time, and as a victory of the feminist movement . . .

Motherhood, although distorted by the conflict between the sexes, by the impersonal myth of the continuation of the species, and by the forced dedication of a woman's life, has been a reservoir of thoughts and feelings, the locus of a special initiation. It is not the having of children that turns us into slaves: it is not the son that enslaves us, but the father.

Before seeing the mother-son relationship as a setback for humankind, we should remember the chain that has always oppressed them both: the authority of the father. It is against this authority that women and young men have become allies.

Let them not ask us what we think of marriage or its historical antidote, divorce. The institutions created to secure the privilege of men reflect an organization of the relationships between the sexes that can no longer be tolerated. We are going to blow everything up, all the instruments of torture used against women . . .

The family is the institution that expresses the taboos adult men have always used to inhibit free relationships between adult women and young men. Psychoanalysis has reformulated this situation, but still in terms of tragedy, as originally asserted in antiquity.

Tragedy is a male projection because in the instant when man is pushed by his life cycles toward new sexual objects, he cannot stand for women to display their own kinds of desires, causing repercussions to occur in the realm of his possessions.

The myth of maternal love crumbles in the moment when women, living their lives at the fullest, find in the natural exchange with the young that authentic sense of delight, pleasure, and enjoyment that the taboos of patriarchal organization had allowed them to realize only in their own children.

Behind the Oedipus complex lies not the incest taboo but rather the exploitation of this taboo on the part of the father for his own protection.

A significant image from the past comes to mind: on the one hand, stairs and a man proudly climbing up; on the other, stairs and a woman tiredly climbing down. The little bit of pride that she is permitted to have in the maternal stage of her life is not enough to sustain her till the end of it . . .

From culture to ideology to codes to institutions to rites to customs there exists a vicious circle of male superstitions about women: every private situation is polluted by this prejudice, from which men continue to feed their presumption and their arrogance.

Young men are oppressed by the patriarchal system, but at the same time they present themselves as candidates for the position of oppressor; the outburst of intolerance of young men is thus characterized by an inherent ambiguity.

Even the movement of youth rebellion is distorted by patriarchal culture. By interpreting the hippie movement as a religious movement, politically committed students are using a politically disreputable label to act paternalistically. From the heights of their ideological certainties they state: the hippie movement is merely a notable episode, a nondialectic moment of society. But this is exactly what makes us appreciate its value as a form of disgusted escape from the patriarchal system: it signifies the abandonment of the culture of the seizure of power and of male-organized political models. Hippies no longer separate life into private and public moments, but turn their lives into a mixture of the feminine and the masculine.

But what of the young woman who withdraws in frustration from student political organizations or agrees in frustration to comply with the culturally revolutionary behavior of her comrades? She finds herself stuck in a situation whose options have been defined by collectives of men: men who continue to keep for themselves what has always been their area of operation. A global view of problems will be a fiction as long as men maintain their monopoly not only of bourgeois culture but also of revolutionary and socialist culture. Hippies—young men and women— have been the first to judge this hierarchy ridiculous. They have created a nonmasculine kind of community, built on the discarded ruins of aggression and violence, the inheritance of their fathers' war-mongering, a belligerence their fathers had always justified in the name of reason and for the purpose of modifying the world to their liking. The forced absence of women from every moment in the life of the community magnified men's abnormal behavior in their struggle for a way of living and thinking. The reappearance of women launched the signal for a voluntary dropping-out of young people that in every possible way— destructive but nonviolent—manifests their conviction that they must begin again from ground zero. The fact that hippies may be reabsorbed by the establishment, as many prophesy or hope, does not diminish the turmoil that their sudden and unexpected appearance has caused in the world . . .

The whole structure of civilization, like a single hunting party, pushes its prey toward the places where it will be captured: marriage is the conclusive moment in which women's captivity takes place. While governments allow divorce and the Catholic Church fights to deny it, women reveal their maturity by being the first to denounce the absurdity of the ways the relationships between the sexes are regulated. The crisis of men is evident in their attachment to formulas, because formulas provide a seal of approval for their superiority.

All their lives women must depend economically first on their fathers and then on their husbands. Their liberation, however, does not consist in reaching economic independence, but rather in demolishing that institution that has enslaved them longer than slaves were enslaved.

Every thinker who has studied the human situation as a whole has reiterated the inferiority of women from his own point of view. Freud, too, located his theory of women's damnation in their assumed desire for a completeness that was identified with the penis. We, however, are bewildered by the psychoanalytic dogma that attributes to little girls a feeling that they are losers from the beginning, because of a metaphysical anguish caused by their difference.

In every family the little boy's penis is a kind of "son in the son," which is alluded to with pride and pleasure and without inhibition. A little girl's sexual apparatus is ignored: it has no name, no term of endearment, no character, no literature. Its physiological secrecy is taken advantage of to maintain silence about its existence: the relationship between male and female is thus not a relationship between two sexes, but between one sex and the lack of another.

In a letter from Freud to his fiancée we read:
"Precious darling,
     While you are taking such pleasure in the activities and management of the household, I am at the moment tempted by the desire to solve the riddle of the structure of the brain."[3]

Let us inquire into the private lives of great men: the presence at their side of a human being they have coldly deemed inferior has turned all their simplest gestures into aberrant behavior.

From our personal and direct observation we see neither geniuses nor individuals who have reached everywhere and on all fronts a correct position. No one has been able to compensate for the failures of human nature.

We live in this moment, and this moment of our struggle is unprecedented. But we want the future to be unpredictable rather than unprecedented.

*   *   *

It is immensely important to us that women safeguard that exceptional spurt of emotional self-confidence that is part of the vital period of youth and that is the basis of the creativity that will shape their lives. One error a young woman can make is to think that she can reclaim later in life a psychological experience she missed out on in her youth. The emancipated woman is a sterile model because it suggests that a personality whose spurts of growth have not occurred at the right times can be readjusted.

Looking back, we recognize ourselves in the high points of creativity that women have reached by chance in history, but above all we recognize ourselves in the forced waste of our intelligence and in the monotony of our everyday lives throughout time. On such a bloodbath idealism has continued to build the myths of femininity.

We do not wish to make a distinction between women who are worse or better because what interests us is the most intimate place within each of us that is common to every woman and that every woman finds as alive as it is painful.

The feminist movement is not international; it is planetary.

The Marxist split between the economic base and the superstructure has sanctioned a law according to which the changes in humankind have always been and will always be changes in the economic base: according to this theory the superstructure has reflected and will reflect those changes. This is the patriarchal point of view. But we no longer believe in this theory of reflection. *The mode of action we choose is the shedding of our culture.* It is not a cultural revolution that follows and integrates the economic revolution; it is not based on the verification at all levels of an ideology but on the lack of ideological necessity. Woman has opposed to the constructions of man only her existential dimension: she has not had generals, thinkers, and scientists. Instead she has had energy, thoughts, courage, dedication, attentiveness, common sense, and madness. The traces of all of this have disappeared because they were not destined to remain, but our strength lies in our refusal to create myths out of facts: action is not confined to any one group, but it becomes so when it addresses a specific form of power. Men have mastered this mechanism using culture as a justification. Giving the lie to culture means giving the lie to an evaluation of facts on the basis of power.

Motherhood is the moment when, reliving the initial stages of life in emotional symbiosis with her child, a woman separates herself from culture. She sees the world as a product extraneous to the primary demands of the existence she is reliving. Motherhood is her "trip." The consciousness of a woman spontaneously returns to the origins of life and she questions herself.

Male thought has sanctioned the mechanism that makes war, generals, heroism, and the generation gap appear necessary. The male unconscious is a receptacle of blood and fear. Since we recognize that the world is populated by these spirits of death and we see pity as a role imposed on women, we abandon man so that he can reach the bottom of his loneliness.

For Hegel "war preserves the ethical health of peoples in their indifference to specific institutions, preserves it from habituation to such institutions and their hardening. Just as the blowing of the winds preserves lake waters from the foulness which would result from a continual calm, so also corruption would result for peoples under continual or indeed 'perpetual' peace. . . . Whatever is by nature negative must remain negative and may not become fixed."[4]

Even the most recent sociological and psychoanalytic analyses of the origins and reasons for the institution of war accept the submission of woman to man as a natural law of the human race. The behaviors of individuals and of primitive and contemporary groups are studied within the framework of the patriarchal absolute, without recognizing the domination of woman by man as the circumstance of oppression in which an already altered psychic course is manifested. The father and the mother are continually referred to as subject and object of processes of projection that invest and deform what might be a normal elaboration of the elements of reality. Yet they are not two primary entities, but the product of a dishonesty between the sexes that has found its niche in the family.

* * *

Unless we start from these premises, it is an illusion to think we can remove the psychic causes of the threat of atomic warfare. This cannot be done either by hypothesizing a return to private values, as in the denial of the sovereignty of the State, or by promoting institutions that outlaw war as an individual crime. If one were to do so, one would be forgetting first that private values are family values and that it is precisely the family that has sanctioned the unconditional surrender of woman to male power. The family thus consolidates the mechanism of pathological anxiety and its related defenses that have generated the delegation of individual responsibility to the community. And second, one would be forgetting that the mental illness of humankind cannot of itself choose its own salvation in an authoritarian form and then abide by its choice . . .

In Hegel's conception Work and Struggle are the starting points of the human world as the history of men. The study of primitive peoples offers, instead, the realization that work is a feminine attribute, whereas war is the specific task of man. So much so, that when a man is deprived of war or, as a captive, is put to work, he says he does not feel himself a man any more, he says he feels as if he were transformed into a woman. War therefore appears from its beginning to be strictly connected to the possibility of its having a gender identity. In this way men overcome, through an external test, their internal anxiety concerning the failure of their own virility.

But we ask: what is this anxiety of men that runs gloomily throughout the history of humankind and always brings to a dead end all our efforts to escape the compulsory choice of violence? The male species has expressed itself by killing; the female species has expressed itself by working and protecting life. Psychoanalysis interprets the reasons why man has considered war his special task, but does not tell us anything about the concomitant oppression of woman. And the reasons that brought man to institutionalize war as a safety valve for his internal conflicts lead us to believe that such conflicts are inevitable for man, a "given" of the human condition. But the human condition of women does not manifest the same needs; on the contrary, women mourn the fate of their sons sent to die and, even in the passivity of their *pietàs*, they separate their role from that of men. Today we can now conceive of a solution to war much more realistic than the one offered by the experts. We find it in the destruction of the patriarchal system through women's dismantling of the family as an institution. This may allow that process of the renewal of humankind from the ground up, a process that many people have invoked without knowing what miracle would have to take place to normalize humankind.

Work as Struggle marks the passage to the supremacy of male culture.

Women experience in themselves the atmosphere of tension in the family: this is the start of the tension in community living. Let us claim for ourselves the grandiosity of the historical collapse of an institution that, appearing to be the condemnation only of women, has finally revealed itself as the authentic condemnation of humankind.

We do not want to be described any longer as those who carry on the species. We will not give our children to anyone, neither to man nor to the State. We will give them to themselves and we will give ourselves back to ourselves.

We see in moralism and raison d'état the weapons legitimized to subordinate woman, and we see in sexual phobia the hostility and disdain used to discredit her.

The taboo against women is the first rule from which God's men derive their awareness of being the army of the Father. Celibacy in the Catholic Church represents the critical moment in which men's negative attitude toward women becomes an institution. There is almost no explanation for why women have been abused for centuries through councils, debates, censorship, laws and violence . . .

The constant reiteration of philosophical predictions leads to a universe corresponding to that wisdom: in this fulfillment we find the bitter happiness of the genius as old man. But the relation between man and woman cannot be one of simple correspondence; wisdom is the male paradise of philosophy . . .

Women are not in a dialectic relationship with men. The demands we are trying to make clear imply not an antithesis, but a *moving on another level*. This is the point that will be the most difficult for others to understand, but it is essential that we not fail to insist on it.

•   •   •

Even in socialist revolutions we have observed the continuation of that mechanism of the dysfunction of the human psyche that is politically identified as a legacy of the bourgeois condition. The antidote that is continually proposed is to reflect on the wisdom and realism developed by the Father. In this sense political ideology has replaced theology for the masses.

The corruption of democracy, whether the result of capitalism or communism, consists in the fact that every man studies the kind of paternalism needed for power as if he expected to hold that power himself.

The women's movement is full of political and philanthropic intruders. We warn male observers not to turn us into objects for their study. We are indifferent both to their support and to their polemics. We suggest that it would be more dignified for them if they did not interfere.

We must not accept gratuitous suggestions from those men who encourage us against their own sex. Each of us can discover in her own private experience enough disdain, understanding, and intransigence to find more creative solutions.

Our urgency is characterized by the appropriation of our own selfhood, and its legitimacy is justified by the fact that with every hesitation of ours someone faster than we are has always managed to take us over.

Colleges and universities are not the places where young women are liberated through culture, but places where their repression is perfected, the same repression that is so well cultivated within the family. The education of a young woman consists in slowly injecting her with a poison that paralyzes her just as she is on the verge of the most potentially responsible actions, of the experiences that might increase her self-confidence.

Our specific task lies in looking everywhere, at any event or subject of the past and present, for its relationship to the oppression of woman. We will sabotage every aspect of culture that quietly continues to ignore it.

• • •

It seems to us that, even after the collective atrocities of Nazism, Fascism, and Stalinism, and during the imperialistic atrocities still taking place, men are under the illusion that they can redeem these terrible events in human history. We are always aware of the truth of their reality even though we realize all the work that has been done to circumscribe these phenomena. The true drama of men consists in the fact that they have always seen the reasons for their anxiety in the external world, defining them as evidence of an enemy structure to struggle against. Men are now on the verge of discovering that the essence of the human dilemma lies within themselves, in that rigid psychological structure of theirs that can no longer hold back its destructive cathexis. This is how the sensation of living in an irreversible crisis has established itself in the world, with the only alternative identified as the red flag of socialism.

The self-criticism developed in our culture seems to have taken a path of license and recklessness. Men must leave this path *to put an end to their historical role as protagonist.* This is the change we are advocating.

From the beginning of feminism to today the deeds of the last patriarchs have passed in review under the eyes of women. We refuse to see any others arise. This is the new reality we are living. From this come the ferment, the turmoil, and the issues of a female humanity that has been kept on the outside.

Woman as she is is a complete individual: the transformation must not take place in her, but in how she sees herself within the universe and in how others see her.

We are no longer conscious of the meaning of contradictions in thought: when we make our remarks we do not mean to submit them to the realm of opposites, but progressively one after the other in order to reconstitute the whole out of all the evidence we have found and create our agenda from it. We are totally against consumption, even of the ideas we like, against subsuming them immediately into a dialectic that makes them appetizing.

We intend to perform any subjective operation that will give us space. By this we do not mean to imply a concern with identity: identity has a compulsive male character that cuts down the flowering of an existence and keeps it under the command of a rationality that is used to control dramatically, day after day, its sense of failure or success.

Man is wrapped up in himself, in his past, in his aims, in his culture. He thinks reality is used up; space travel proves this. But woman affirms that life must still begin for her on our planet. She sees where man no longer sees.

The spirit of man entered a definitive crisis when it triggered a mechanism that touched the safety limit of human survival. Woman exits man's guardianship when she recognizes the heart of the danger in the very structure of the patriarch and his culture.

Hegel writes: "Self-consciousness exists in and for itself when and by the fact that it so exists for another; that is, it exists only in being acknowledged. . . . [When one] self-consciousness is faced by another self-consciousness . . . they *recognize* themselves as *mutually recognizing* one another. . . . This presentation is a twofold action . . . [in which] each seeks the death of the other. . . . Thus the relation of the two self-conscious individuals is such that they prove themselves and each other through a life-and-death struggle. They must engage in this struggle, for they must raise their certainty of being *for themselves* to truth, both in the case of the other and in their own case. And it is only through staking one's life that freedom is won. . . . The individual who has not risked his life may well be recognized as a *person*, but he has not attained to the truth of this recognition as an independent self-consciousness. Similarly, just as each stakes his own life, so each must seek the other's death."[5]

The male species has constantly endangered life and is now endangering survival; woman has remained in slavery because she has not agreed to this; she has remained inferior, incapable, and powerless. Woman claims that survival itself is a value.

Man has searched for the meaning of life beyond and against life itself; for woman, life and its meaning constantly overlap. We have had to wait thousands of years for men to stop using their anxiety about our attitude toward life to redefine it as a sign of our inferiority. "Woman is immanence, man transcendence": in this opposition philosophy has idealized the hierarchy of our destinies. Insofar as man was speaking as the transcendent he could not harbor doubts as to the excellence of his action; if the female is immanence, man has to negate her in order to start the process of history. Man, therefore, has won, but only by inventing an opposition necessary to himself.

Woman must simply claim her own transcendence. Philosophers have really talked too much: what was their basis for recognizing the male transcendental act, their basis for denying it to woman? It is when faced with a *fait accompli* that one resorts to transcendence and considers it an act at the origin of things, whereas the same transcendence is denied where there exists no confirmation of it in actual power. But defining transcendence as the confirmation of facts is typical of patriarchal society: as man's absolute civilization, patriarchal society allows itself any and all male alternatives. Woman has been forcibly conditioned by being identified as the principle of immanence, of stasis, and not as a different kind of transcendence that, under the pressure of male transcendence, has remained repressed. Today woman openly judges that culture and that history which imply male transcendence, and she judges that same transcendence. Through every sort of conscious and unconscious trauma, man is also slowly beginning to doubt his role as protagonist. But man's self-criticism does not go so far as to renounce the axiom that everything that is real is rational, and he continues to put himself forward as the revolutionary subject, justifying this as necessary for his form of overcoming [*superamento/Aufhebung*]. Woman has had enough of the ways man has overcome himself by oppressing her and at the same time blaming her immanence. Self-criticism must give way to imagination.

We say to man, to the genius, to the rational visionary, that the world's destiny does not correspond to his idea of always going forward in accordance with his desire for an overcoming. The unexpected destiny of the world consists in starting out anew, on a new path where woman is subject.

Let us acknowledge that we have the ability to turn this attitude into a complete transformation of life. Those who are not part of the master-slave dialectic are coming into consciousness and are introducing into the world the Unexpected Subject.

We reject as an absurdity the myth of the new man. The concept of power is the element of continuity in male thought and therefore of the notion of final solutions. The concept of woman's subordination follows it like a shadow. Any prophecy based on these premises is false.

The woman question is *in and of itself both the means and the end* of the substantive changes of humankind. It needs no future. It makes no distinctions between proletariat, bourgeoisie, tribe, clan, race, age, or culture. It does not come from above, or from below, from the elite or from the masses. It is not to be directed, organized, diffused, or publicized. A new subject pronounces a new word and in that pronouncement is confident of its diffusion. Action becomes simple and elementary.

There is no goal, only the present. We are the dark past of the world. We are accomplishing the present.

Notes

1. Olympe de Gouges, "Declaration of the Rights of Woman" (1791) in *Women in Revolutionary Paris, 1789–1795: Selected Documents,* ed. and trans. Darline Gay Levy, Harriet Branson Applewhite, and Mary Durham Johnson (Urbana: University of Illinois Press, 1979), 87–96.
2. G. W. F. Hegel, *Phenomenology of Spirit,* trans. A. V. Miller (New York: Oxford University Press, 1977), 288, para. 475.
3. Letter 65 (Vienna, May 17, 1885), *Letters of Sigmund Freud.* Selected and edited by Ernst L. Freud. Trans. Tania and James Stern (New York: Basic Books, 1960), 145.
4. G. W. F. Hegel, *Natural Law* [1802], trans. T. M. Knox (Philadelphia: University of Pennsylvania Press, 1975), 93–94; translation amended.
5. G. W. F. Hegel, *Phenomenology of Spirit,* 111–15, paras. 178–89. This quote from the *Phenomenology* replaces but gives the substance of a quote from Lonzi that could not be located because it was not adequately referenced. The quote in Italian reads as follows: "Ciascuno deve-necessariamente conoscere se l'altro sia una coscienza assoluta; deve-necessariamente porsi nei confronti dell'altro in una relazione tale che ciò pervenga alla luce; deve offenderlo. E ciascuno può sapere se l'altro sia totalità solo costringendolo a spingersi sino alla morte; e, allo stesso modo, ciascuno si dimostra a sé medesimo come totalità solo spingendosi sino alla morte. Se si ferma in se stesso al di qua della morte . . . allora è per l'altro, in maniera-immediata, una non-totalità . . . diventa schiavo dell'altro. . . . Tale riconoscimento dei particolari è dunque in se stesso contraddizione assoluta: il riconoscimento non è altro che l'essere-dato della Coscienza, come totalità, in un'altra Coscienza; ma in quanto la prima Coscienza diventa oggettivamente reale, essa sopprime dialetticamente l'altra Coscienza: per tal modo il riconoscimento si sopprime dialetticamente da sé. Esso non si realizza, ma cessa al contrario di essere in quanto è. E nondimeno la Coscienza non è in pari tempo che come

atto-d'esser-riconosciuto da un altro e non è in pari tempo Coscienza che come unità numerica assoluta, e deve-necessariamente esser riconosciuta come tale; ma ciò significa che deve-necessariamente avere come scopo la morte dell'altro e la propria, e che essa è solo nella realtà oggettiva della morte."

13

Hegelian Silences and the Politics of Communication: A Feminist Appropriation

Alison L. Brown

Hegel's implicit theory of communication—both from self to same-self (internal communication) and from self to other (external communication)—can help us better to understand the conflicts feminists feel within ourselves and in our "groups" or "communities" as feminists. That is, even though Hegel can be said to have helped to canonize an exclusion of women from certain sorts of communications, a reconstructed account of his manner of viewing communication can help us through what some have called the conflicts of feminism[1] by showing that the nature and place of our conflicts are theoretically resolvable.

This essay is dedicated to Anne L'Ecuyer. Patricia Jagentowicz Mills's comments were invaluable. I thank Joe Boles, Tamsin Lorraine, and David Sherry for helpful readings.

Hegel theorizes these "communications" in ways that can help us understand how better to construct and reconstruct ourselves and what real possibilities exist for the future.

Feminists have long considered internal and external communication important. Internal communication of one's needs, desires, aspirations within one's many selves, or subject positions, is seen as a necessary step to empowerment by such diverse feminists as Gilligan[2] and Irigaray.[3] Communication from self to other, breaking the silence so to speak, is seen as the impulse behind much feminist writing.[4] Not speaking, not attempting to occupy the social positions that have been denied us, prolongs and exacerbates silence about the concerns many of us have. Silence here is conceptually straightforward: it is the articulate but unspoken space and time before socially recognized and sanctioned communication. The more primal silence is never articulate in itself, but it is a necessary precondition for any linguistic function. It can be described as the mute desire for sense.

The account of these silences is latent in Hegel's texts; my reconstruction of that repressed account of communication must occur around the sine qua non of communication: language. Part of what makes Hegel's conceptual scheme interesting and fruitful in this context is his attention to the necessary linguistic foundations of both internal or external communication. Hegel's insight into silences (the inarticulate speech) depends on his contention that inner consciousness and external communication are not formally identical processes. That is, thinking is not strictly parallel either to speech or writing. He shows that we are not always in control of the process that transforms thinking into writing. For one, there are times during which sense cannot be made. Other times, the transformation necessarily places the speaker in a position she or he did not choose. At the level of inner communication, silence is the requisite for meaning because it is through this silence that we acquire the sense-certain position vis-à-vis objects that allows us to express objects through thoughts. External communication is possible only because of the desire present in our articulate silences: the desire to overcome the object-ness of the other with whom we come in contact and to whom we wish to communicate. Silence, and its attendant desire for meaning and exchange, is as necessary to language as is sound.

When writing and speaking come effortlessly and meaningfully, Hegel points out, we are brought in close proximity to pointlessness and meaninglessness, in part because our words do not yet have meaning-for-us. Using reason to examine these moments is part of meaning, language creation and language re-creation. This pre-Freudian discussion of meaning-creation presupposes an alterior space that cannot be systematized—a linguistic possibility that cannot be assimilated. The first words of Hegel's phenomenology of consciousness are: "The knowledge or knowing which is at the start or is immediately our object cannot be anything else but immediate knowledge itself, a knowledge of the immediate or of what simply is. Our approach to the object must also be *immediate* or *receptive;* we must alter nothing in the object as it presents itself. In *a*pprehending it, we must refrain from trying to *co*mprehend it" (Hegel 1977, 58, para. 90). It is in this space, that of nonlinguistic or pre-graphematic immediacy, that I suggest inner communications can be examined and affirmed. My reading sees the passages in the *Phenomenology* that describe consciousness as spelling out this meaningful but inarticulate inner silence that is the foreground to inner communication.

Desire comes into play in the first pages of the phenomenology of self-consciousness; desire is immediately for recognition by an other. The silence between a subjectivity and all its others is a second kind of silence. This kind is one that Hegel overlooks in a particularly significant manner for feminists. In the *Phenomenology* he recognizes that the communication between so-called unequal persons (whether they exist in the same corporeal body or not) requires a recognition of radical equality. The inequality of the two is recognized at first (Hegel 1977, 112–13, para. 185), but for anything to happen the two sides must recognize that without the other, nothing can happen, no desire can be fulfilled, no work can be done (Hegel 1977, 112, para. 184). It is interesting to note that this recognition is necessarily one man's of another. There is no way to substitute women or girls in the slave position. If we try to read this passage to allow a female entrance and if that female entrance is a woman or girl as defined by the Hegelian system, then there is no way for mutual recognition to occur. Inequality cannot be dissolved into recognition of the other as *equally* necessary. Indeed, replacing the slave with the "woman" defined by Hegel, freezes subjects into radically unequal but perceivedly necessary social or political positions.

In analyzing the *Antigone* in the *Phenomenology* and in the *Philosophy of Right*, Hegel describes inequality as necessary for the smooth flow from family to public life. In the *Phenomenology*, Hegel argues that women (as wives or sisters) *cannot* be conscious of themselves as actual (1977, 275, para. 458). The dialectic of divine law (which applies to and is understood by women) and human law (the male analogue) cannot solve the problem for women actualizing themselves politically, since the supersession of either law takes place where women are not and cannot be.[5] It might be argued that these passages refer to stages of history and stages of personal development that do not have to do with persons, male or female, in so-called free or modern times. But, then, how can we account for Hegel's similar arguments in *The Philosophy of Right*, where woman are likewise excluded from actuality? The "concrete person" (Hegel 1952, 122, para. 182) of civil society is necessarily a man. Hegel does not seem to notice that this exclusion amounts to denying a self-conscious voice to women. She *chooses* family as he *chooses* civic life.[6] That is, while there is strictly speaking no exclusion on this count, self-consciousness cannot be achieved in abstraction, only in the concrete. Hegel is troubled by the denial of property or right to any person; he fails to notice that strictly speaking the latter is what must be denied to women within his system. That he fails to notice this denial stems from the same blindspot that keeps some persons thinking that texts which exclude some group (often women) are still unproblematically open to the excluded group.

Many philosophical texts fail to have explicit meaning for women readers; that is to say, women, like men, can come to the discourse at the first level of processing data (mere consciousness), which does not force concrete assimilation. Once that process turns to the strictly cognitive level, what Hegel would call a level past self-consciousness, some women can be struck by the absence and denial of women in the discourse by the discourse. Another way to put this is that the structural or formal nature of the text is not going to be inaccessible to women *qua* women; the exclusion comes when the reader realizes that the philosophical system being read *must* exclude some socially determined aspect of herself. For some women, the processing of information doesn't always break through to second-level processing (external communication) because the communication at this level is often closely not *for* us. This is not to say that the material cannot be "learned." It can be processed but not internalized because it does not "match" us.[7] Thus, while there is no immediately necessary prohibition to women reading the text, the process of giving *meaning* to the text, of interpreting the text, brings trouble to some women, sometimes.[8] I am not arguing that any specific woman's reading of a text cannot be immediate to a text that has erased the female. Instead, "female" readings of texts that have erased women's voices cannot be immediate at the level of self-consciousness. "Female" positions with respect to philosophical texts are evolving very rapidly given the fact that female voices that have been persistently silenced and female texts that have been erased are resurfacing with different meanings for us.[9] The nature and extent of the exclusion of female voices from philosophical literature has been and is being described and catalogued. A diversity of women's voices from the margin are deconstructing and challenging the canon. Still, familiarity with this literature does not prepare a woman for the personal realization she will have again and again that the texts she is interpreting do not include women in descriptions of the highest level of human development or in the ruling segments of society, and that her experience is not considered consonant with much of it. But some of us are torn. Many of us want to create and find created texts that pertain to us; however, we do not want to lose the good in those we have read that do *not* pertain to us. We want, in short, to break out of margins but also to call all marginalized entities to presence. If the actual exclusion is at the secondary level, not at the primary one, language itself does not exclude us.[10]

Even though Hegel describes as systemic certain exclusionary paradigms, thereby "legitimating" them with respect to external communications, he can help us understand the manner in which those paradigms work on us. The important thing here is that our reading of Hegel can prepare us to read society in ways that revolutionize it. When a marginalized person comes to an understanding of that marginalization as an arbitrarily coerced restriction, the step to action against those who marginalize her is conceptually made. If the marginalization has the force of reason, or the force of interest, or the force of practicality, such a step is much more difficult. Understanding the exact point where communication excludes by gender, will show us when to speak and which social structures to attack, which to adopt. From the creative perspective, it tells us those places where our voices most need development. Consistently reassessing and reevaluating systems from *both* the inside and the outside makes feminists very good at analyzing social texts and inserting ourselves in positions that demand a respect for the former kind of silence and a cessation of the latter kind. Neither respect nor cessation comes at once—if at all. But feminists are in a singularly powerful position to make the demand for recognition coherent.[11]

After a discussion of these two silences (and their overcoming) I shall argue that feminist political theory can make good use of an appropriation of Hegel in spite of his allegedly totalitarian system.[12] Hegel's theory of communication (the ways in which we can situate our first internal silence and the ways in which the second, more public silence can be broken) shows the way to revolutionizing social categories including those of gender.

Appropriating Self-Consciousness

The silence prior to internal communication, that is, the work we do in constructing and reconstructing ourselves is very difficult to describe. The process of coming to inner communication is important to many and diverse feminists. But the process, too, is elusive, thereby making consciousness-raising problematic. Consciousness-raising is properly not just to the level of another's understanding but also to one's own possibilities. That is, to engage in the sorts of self-conscious communications that elicit change in ourselves through others, we must have some idea of our own permutations, including our capacity for mutation.

Hegel exposes his fear and fascination with language very early in the *Phenomenology* where he says of those persons in sense-certainty emerging into consciousness that

> they speak of the existence of *external* objects, which can be more precisely defined as *actual*, absolutely *singular*, *wholly personal*, *individual* things, each of them absolutely unlike anything else; this existence, they say his absolute certainty and truth. They *mean* "this" bit of paper on which I am writing—or rather have written—"this"; but what they mean is not what they say. If they actually wanted to *say* "this" bit of paper which they mean, if they wanted to *say* it, then this is impossible, because the sensuous This that is meant *cannot be reached* by language, which belongs to consciousness, i.e. to that which is inherently universal. (Hegel 1977, 66, para. 110)

Language is necessary to communication. Language requires a sense of certainty with respect to discrete things. But for any discrete thing that exists, that discrete thing is in a class by itself. Language makes universal categories to classify things thereby taking away the discrete particularity of the object described. Consequently, "what is called the unutterable is nothing else than the untrue, the irrational, what is merely meant, but is not actually expressed" (Hegel 1977, 66, para. 110). For Hegel, sense-certainty is incompatible with meaningful expression because at the stage of sense-certainty, one cannot mean what one says. The self one finds for oneself at this stage perceives sensuous truths but cannot yet express this meaningfully because it is not yet sufficiently self-conscious. To be sure, in the above Hegel is concerned with the subject/object relation. The expression of this certainty to another subject is not yet under discussion. The philosophical puzzle here is only, How is it possible that the subject described by Hegel at this stage can ever pass beyond itself while retaining even Hegel's brand of unity? (That is, sufficient unity to make some sense from one moment to the next.) Another way to put this question is, How will we be able to make the transition to internal communication when the building blocks of our language, coming up from silence, are in the sense described necessarily false? The Hegelian answer is that we can only know the answer to this question in retrospect—from the position of self-consciousness. The movement from sense-certainty to a rudimentary thinking is a necessary step to internal communication which in turn is a necessary step to external communication. This kind of silence, the silence prior to internal communication, cannot be gendered.[13]

This silence is prior to meaning. Still, it is constitutive of meaning. Reading texts involves two separate (but on occasion simultaneous) coming-to-meaning processes: that to internal and external communications. A confusion between these has been the partial cause of supposing that women were barred from language itself. Men and women both suffer, and learn, from the first kind of silence (apparently this part of the process is both chronologically and logically necessary). Sense-certainty's precursor is a silence whose supersession results in internal communication. Hegel's mistake is in making the supersession over-strong—a mistake he repeats repeatedly! This silence, in my reading, must stay with us alongside our various communications.

At the level of mere sense-certainty we do not recognize others as others—or perhaps as anything. We are grappling with coming-to-language. As Judith Butler (1987) points out, only at the later point, that of self-consciousness, "do we become convinced of its [an Other's] existence" (42). Butler describes the subject at this lower stage of development as one who "mistakenly restricts his dependence to the world of natural objects," who "shows no understanding of human embodiment," and who because of the peculiar arrogance attached to ignorance is "swiftly" on the way "toward defeat."[14] Butler's puzzle concerns why Hegel had not introduced the Other earlier in the journey to selfhood: "Why did the journeying subject of the *Phenomenology* begin its journey alone?" (Butler 1987, 46). How does the subject begin its journey as a subject that first distinguishes itself from objects not others? Her answer helps to solve the puzzle about the genesis of language in a subject with as yet no communication(s).

Butler notices that "desire" and "Other" would be impossible in the dialectic if they had not always already been there in some form before their actual appearance. For Hegel, "coming into existence . . . is never . . . a creation *ex nihilo*, but is, rather, a moment in the development of a Concept" (Butler 1987, 47). For Hegel, there can be no reality, nothing at all, without the Other. Consciousness of others presupposes a perception of self that is a pure perception. That is, self-recognition and other-recognition are ultimately simultaneous—so much so that any given consciousness cannot come to know itself without having first performed a mirroring of its experience of the other always already being present to it, by splitting itself in two. "They must engage in this struggle, for they must raise their certainty of being *for themselves*, to truth, both in the case of the other and in their own case" (Hegel 1977, 114, para. 187). The puzzle about the seemingly premature appearance of language is analogous to that about desire. That language is ontologically prior cannot be demonstrated until the proper form of consciousness has been achieved. Language is the construct that makes Hegel's teleological system, with its succession of stages of consciousness, coherent as a totality. As late in the *Phenomenology* as the discussion of "Morality," Hegel states:

> Here again, then, we see language as the existence of Spirit. Language is self-conscious existing *for others*, self-consciousness which *as such* is immediately *present*, and as *this* self-consciousness is universal. It is the self that separates itself from itself, which as pure "I" = "I" becomes objective to itself, which in this objectivity equally preserves itself as *this* self, just as it coalesces directly with other selves and is *their* self-consciousness. It perceives itself

just as it is perceived by others, and the perceiving is just *existence which has become a self.* (Hegel 1977, 395, para. 652)

Absolute Knowing is the communication of the self who knows itself as spirit with all its predecessors: the selves it retains from every stage back through sense-certainty. Hegel has us shed these stages; according to my reading, we retain these stages alongside our supersessions. Thus, Absolute Knowing *is*, as Hegel suggests, a refined and knowledgeable refinement of sense-certainty—a concrete internal communication. How could this communication be possible if we had not retained the primary silence in addition to its "solutions?" Hegel sounds as if he would not be entirely unhappy with this less negativizing reading when he says:

> But recollection, the *inwardizing*, of that experience, has preserved it and is the inner being, and in fact the higher form of the substance. So although this Spirit starts afresh and apparently from its own resources to bring itself to maturity, it is none the less on a higher level that it starts. The realm of the Spirits which is formed in this way in the outer world constitutes a succession in Time in which one Spirit relieved another of its charge and each took over the empire of the world from its predecessor. Their goal is the revelation of the depth of Spirit, and this is *the absolute Notion.* (Hegel 1977, 492, para. 808)

Each stage that Spirit undergoes on its way to knowing itself as itself is preserved in its richness, in "its inner significance."[15] The communication that is the ground of Community requires a language that calls up the richness of shared experience, even if that experience remains unspoken. The context of intersubjectivity necessitates some explicit awareness of something that makes such a context possible: language and its prelinguistic component. People can know of each other that they are significantly alike and hence comprehensible each to each.[16] We are in important respects the same sort of things. We *can* understand one another because conflicts of reality and expression form our many and diverse possibilities. There is no inherent barrier against understanding. I have a motive in finding a philosophical justification for this position. It has seemed philosophically incoherent, while socially clear, that men and women are radically different, perhaps even irreconcilably so. Reading many feminist philosophers of language has given me reason to believe that the creative moment before language is feminine. Through my reading of Hegel, I hope to show that at the level of analysis when inner communication has not logically come into being, "masculine" and "feminine" *cannot* make sense. This tenet is essential to mounting an argument against identity politics. In my view such a stance is not reducible to a totalizing humanism. That is, finding this minimal commonality does not force one to then minimize *every* difference. Instead, what Hegel has theorized, unwittingly, is a nongendered account of silence prior to speech that renders accounts of radical alterity nonsensical. That it does so before actual levels of exclusion, both logical and historical, should be encouraging to many feminists.

The discussion of language at the stage of self-certainty becomes coherent in retrospect. It becomes coherent after communication has been achieved. Language is a necessary precondition for consciousness of sense-certainty even though the existence of language is not known to the subject at this specific point of development. How is it possible that language in its universal aspect turns everything into its opposite? How can it be that the language of self-certainty does not let "what is meant get into words at all?" (Hegel 1977, 6, para. 110). Even a self-conscious "I" = "I" cannot fully express self-consciousness in language. Something in the equation of communication must be constant, and that is the abstract process of overcoming silences. Silence stands outside of the communication process waiting to be transformed. Such transformation is the work of meaning-creation.

As Butler notes, Hegel requires a necessary metaphysical place for each self (Butler 1987, 5). Language, as abstract mediation, establishes this necessity through change. It is thus at once the prime mover of the system and that through which subjects find their necessary metaphysical place. Thereby language does what had seemed impossible; namely, reverse the intentions (meanings) of speakers. When one speaks, one fills a subject position reversing what had been intended: to express oneself. Hegel would part company with me here although I think he is required to stay if he is to remain consistent. I imagine that he would argue that societies' subject positions, like meaning-creation, follow a necessary unfolding of Spirit. However, this entry into Hegel, through the spaces left open by silence, frees up the possibility for a diverse array of gendered subject positions within the system. A Hegel not bound by his gendered prejudices might have seen that as we construct and reconstruct ourselves through language, we are likewise reconstructing, not merely political subject positions, but also the very conditions of what might constitute such subject positions. This is to say, that the exclusion based on nature is the merely prejudicial view and can be overcome by the terms of the properly augmented system. If my reading of Hegel is correct, then the exclusion is necessarily societal; and this conclusion, that said exclusion is social, is not a tautology.

The teleological nature of Hegel's system expresses the position of the "they" that cannot say what they mean. If "they" could already say what they meant, there could be no point in movement. Which is to say, there could be no progression or change from one stage of life or history to the next. If the conflict of reality finds itself bound and begot by language, then every "thing" that can talk is forced into conflict. We can see now that Hegel's concrete person, his Man, while accorded rights in the *Philosophy of Right*, is restricted from being human (strictly speaking) until a mastery of abstraction is achieved as shown in the *Phenomenology*. The self in Hegel who counts as a uniquely human self is a *constructed* self. Feminist appropriations here indicate a knowledge of this silence, the prelinguistic one; and this knowledge by itself, can translate into revolutionary power by finding meaning in nonprescribed social formations that cannot exclude women. For example, while it is unwise to overlook the social nature of said formations, one need not only repeat such formations subversively. One *can* find a nonprescribed social formation when one sees that the same is possible. Once stated, of course, a prescription is implicit. Because texts have the power that they do, such prescriptions are best left tacit. Such appropriation also reveals that a space before talking need not be always already in conflict. The conflict arises in trying to go beyond.

External Communication

Hegel's texts are open to insertion, reinterpretation, and care. It is not inconsistent to see in him the atheist/theist; revolutionary/reactionary; poetical/boorish; autonomous/slavish. The textual-historical silence alongside the texts of Hegel helps save that in Hegel which we should not discard. What we should not discard is that which Hegel, by being oversystematic, showed us (I think unwittingly). Seeing a total system, Hegel believed for a short while that there could be no more history;

instead there could only be a carrying out of the subject positions within this total system. Kojève (1969) so represents Hegel and says that this knowledge was the same as despair for Hegel. But when Kojève describes what happened when Hegel "discovered" that everything was already over, the description sounds like something that could have happened before the "French Revolution," before the "culmination of Protestant- ism." I can imagine so many others besides Hegel thinking those thoughts that Kojève, following Hegel, "knows" to be impossible before Hegel.

> [T]his knowledge cost him dearly. He speaks of a period of total depression that he lived through between the twenty-fifth and thirtieth years of his life: a "Hypochondria" that . . . was so severe as to "paralyze his powers" and that came precisely from the fact that he could not accept the necessary abandonment of Individuality—that is, actually, of humanity—which the idea of absolute knowledge demanded. But finally he surmounted this "Hypochondria." And becoming a wise man by that final accep- tance of death, he published, a few years later the First Part of the "System of Science," entitled "Science of the Phenomenology of the Spirit," in which he definitively reconciles himself with all that is and has been, by declaring that there will never more be anything new on earth. (168)

Kojève's Hegel is rather one-dimensional. He sees the totality of system on a personal and historical level, he understands certain dehumanizing consequences and after a long, mad silence . . . acquiesces. Why not read this moment of self-assessment as having more depth? Hegel *did* acquiesce in certain ways. He keeps the totalizing system, for instance. Still, he does not go back and erase these precommunicative spaces to which I have been calling attention. He has not closed the totalizing system to possible reinsertions and reinterpretations. Spirit retains the depth of its supersessions and its exclusions; Hegel takes pains to remind us of this. Of especial note is his reinsistence on this point in the penultimate paragraph of the *Phenomenology*.[17]

When Hegel writes, his margins can be peopled with men or women. This doubling of margins makes women the second margin to the marginal man—and there is the marginality of the socially constructed male which arises through his guilt at having marginalized, even though in some cases unwittingly, women. To be sure, such redoubling does not indicate a penance. Still, the logging of psychological overtime in the effort to sustain such arbitrary divisions, will erupt not just from the margin, but back to the margin. Teresa Brennan (1992) suggests something similar when she argues:

> In line with this chain of reasoning established thus far, we can suppose that successful masculinity has in some way split affect and representation, and disposed of its hostility, without negative consequences for itself, and secured the attention from outside that maintains its identity, without having to divert its own stream of attention to the same end. The question, of course, was, From whence does it secure this extra attention? There is a strong case being built now for the idea that the surplus of attention in masculinity is extracted from the feminine other, and that femininity, when it is pushed to its pathological limit, is carrying the disordered feeling of the masculine other. (132)

There is no question that women are further marginalized than men. The manner of marginalization is likewise different for each sex, and in the end for each person and its many positionings. The silence that is forced on women's external communications forces an "extra attention" *from* the feminine *for* the masculine blurring the distinction between the kinds of silences. Since the social quickly feels eternal, the social silence is easily mistaken for the necessary silence, not just as process but in its very form (or formlessness). The latter suppressions mimic more primal ones, making it easy for theorists to suppose that a social exclusion is textual. Perhaps when we think of margins we should proliferate not just their loci, but their origins. When we write about Hegel now, there is a new margin: the space for the good Hegel, the Hegel who was trying to talk.

Silence stretches alongside so many texts, both spoken and written, such as Hegel's silence alongside Kojève's, or that of the good Hegel alongside Hegel's articulate silence. And what if we were to read philosophical texts as if alongside each word, each margin, the silence of woman at once bounded it and was bound by it?

What we might see in such imagining is that by excluding women from self-consciousness in the *Phenomenology* and from civil society in *The Philosophy of Right*, Hegel not only silences women in the systems;

he also excludes his own possibilities for sensuous communications. To bear this, he takes up woman's position of silence forcing back on that particular female instantiation the lack of center he had previously felt. This reading does not force pity for Hegel, but legitimate anger at *his* inability to enter the communications from which he (metaphorically) has barred women—exclusion that ironically forces a self-exclusion.

If I allow a generalization from the master/bondsman paradigm to states of interaction not restricted to the ancient world, then the paradigm can be used to expose the double bind of arbitrary exclusions.[18] The master, Hegel tells us, is truly in fact bondsman to the bondsman. The alterior silence, the female other whom Hegel silences, erupts at every point of the text. He can't write away what exists; what exists as thinking thing will speak. He points to this. The transition from thinker to speaker occurs necessarily. If one can go beyond sense-certainty to self-consciousness, one has learned how to think oneself sufficiently to speak to another. If one has existed in a family, one has learned a sufficient amount to engage in civil society. That women have no place in the positions created by the system implies and requires force against us. The silence speaks. Reclaiming the importance of the first silence simultaneously forces the refusal of the second.[19] Rethinking Hegel helps to show us why it is so much more complicated than merely women at the margin of men, or moral society at the margin of civil society, or subjects excluding nonsubjects. Every exclusion redoubles both in the excluding and in the excluded. It must do this because there is unrest at being in the position that is excluded or that is doing the excluding. Such exclusion occurs at every communicative level, and not solely at the level of hegemonic silencing of the many for the one.[20] I believe that this analysis of Hegel's theory of communication as well as a look at how his communications worked on and through him can help us examine our unrest at the positions we are forced to take both in and outside of "margins" . . . or "closets." I turn now to the final section where this application is attempted.

The Application to Feminist Politics

There is nothing described in the Hegelian system that women cannot be. Many of us have felt such affirmation, but the canon that excludes us explicitly at so many levels gives us no fodder for proof. I hope to have shown that in Hegel's case, every exclusion is an exclusion by an arbitrary and irrational use of power—on his own terms. The way to appropriate Hegelian communication is not to argue or fight for an equal share of power in the realm of civil society. Instead, feminists would do well to reject the notion of equality between the sexes by showing that sex itself is no more stable a category than any other. The demand for equality is *not* reasonable.[21] It does not make sense. The demand should be for recognition of gender diversity based on the important features of any given desired social configuration. We must focus our efforts on reconstructing a rights analysis that can accommodate our many gender positions. For example, if we fight for structural equality between the sexes in the workplace, the particular needs of mothers are overlooked. If, in an attempt to ameliorate this situation, we fight for equality between men and women who are not mothers, with provisions to make equal women with children, we risk relegating mothers to one of their roles and hence perhaps to the patronizingly named, but very real, "Mommy track." Perhaps a better way to ask our questions of equity, so that we don't end up with the unhappy results just sketched, is to look at a concrete situation, determine what the real (unspoken in some cases) desires for change are in that situation and try to instantiate the preferred situation through mediation and struggle. This is not to suggest that the method just described is not something we don't already do. But much of the rhetoric and theory that surrounds such actions differs drastically from the practice.

Feminists might consider producing a *Philosophy of Right* that respects the integrity of the *Phenomenology* as we have just re-read it, one that refuses to make *any* bipolar gender divisions at any level.[22] This seems, at first glance, a frightening and unwise move. The advances made by women on behalf of all of us largely relied on debunking the myth of abstract equality by focusing on the socially defined differences between men and women. But sometimes that notion of abstract equality creeps back into our thinking as the ostensible aim of feminist praxis. My point here is that a *Philosophy of Right* that did not assume and enforce definite gender distinctions would allow for a freer explication of actual gendered persons. These texts (manifestos, actions) could serve as guidelines toward power and away from disruptions of external communications. The margins would proliferate until there would be no more need for text. Feminism's endpoints must be as indifferently gendered as are its starting points.

It is crucial here to note the needs of a particular group: mothers. Isn't my request a denial of the real and grueling hardships experienced by them in a society that rarely rewards or values their labor? Furthermore, isn't my request a denial of what Kelly Oliver (1993) asks, namely, that "the logic of the maternal body . . . be spoken. What needs to be spoken is what has been repressed within patriarchal culture and patriarchal theory"? (188). My response to these questions is twofold. First, if we could produce a *Philosophy of Right* that included the now unrepressed silences of the *Phenomenology*, that text would necessarily include the voice and demands of real mothers. My concern to keep the text gender-neutral is, in part, motivated by the erasure women, including mothers, face in the reduction to biology, generalized bipolar gender classifications often force. Bracketing gender divisions that generalize leaves room for richer gender diversity to speak its many tongues. Second, Oliver's concerns cannot be raised within the confines of classical liberalism because classical liberalism always already excludes such questions by categorizing them out of the picture. Oliver's questions have a possibility of being answered only within the sort of political structure I am suggesting here: one that does not predetermine the sorts of answers that can be articulated.

The liberation of starting points shows the many as the necessary originary—and not the One. Our external communications can be grounded in a philosophically tenable nonsolipsism. The amorphous silence of thought before speech must "condense" into new positions. How is one to make sense of Hegel's insistence that his abstractions are all the more concrete for the nature their "condensation" takes? Hegel says that only in speaking of a "recognized" human reality can the term "human" be used to state a truth in the strict and full sense of the term. For only in this case can one reveal a reality in speech. One may reveal a reality only if one is self-consciously (i.e., certainly) nonsolipsistic. Hegel (1977) provides this other-based beginning:

> What still lies ahead for consciousness is the experience of what Spirit is—this absolute substance which is the unity of the different independent self-consciousnesses which, in their opposition, enjoy perfect freedom and independence: "I" that is "We" and "We" that is "I." It is in self-consciousness, in the Notion of

Spirit, that consciousness first finds its turning-point, where it leaves behind it the colourful show of the sensuous here-and-now and the nightlike void of the supersensible beyond, and steps out into the spiritual daylight of the present. (110–11, 177).

The only nonsolipsistic view is one that truly recognizes the other. To achieve this, one must have first *been* other—and once one has *been* other, one will always recognize the new positionings one accommodates or founds as other too. Taking a social position from the prelinguistic position begins the process anew. An example from recent feminist literature shows a Hegelianism made conscious, one where categories supposed to be as specific as "human" start to come apart when one is aware of the silences that impel one toward definition and attempts at self-definition.

Judith Butler, the author of *Subjects of Desire* and to whom this analysis owes so much, provides an example of the sort of political theorizing I am advocating. She asks: "Is sexuality of any kind even possible without that opacity designated by the unconscious, which means simply that the conscious 'I' who would reveal its sexuality is perhaps the last to know the meaning of what it says?" (1991, 15). Sexuality is not necessarily gendered and is "known" in its many moments at the stage of sense-certainty. The "I" of self-consciousness discovers her sexuality only to realize that that aspect was already known in many important respects. When these thoughts have been thought, external communication is in order (is possible?). When speaking of sexual identities, the stepping into a transgressive position reverses the meaning of what was intended: an expression of "I." What is expressed is a multiplicity. Butler continues:

> [T]o claim that this is what I *am* is to suggest a provisional totalization of this "I." But if the "I" can so determine itself, then that which it excludes in order to make that determination remains constitutive of the determination itself. In other words, such a statement presupposes that the "I" exceeds its determination, and even produces that very excess in and by the act which seeks to exhaust the semantic field of that "I." In the act which would disclose the true and full content of that "I," a certain radical *concealment* is thereby produced. (1991, 15)

I argued that Hegel excludes his proper "I" from true speech due to his uneasy sense of having excluded too much. Hegel sacrificed too much in his attempt to find meaning; he reversed too much. The madness Hegel felt when he glimpsed the rapidity of the subject positions he had created, forced a radical concealment of *his* true desire, or identity of that moment: communication with an other. The second level of silence from margin to margin is replicated consciously in Butler when she argues that

> the "being" of the subject is no more self-identical than the "being" of any gender; in fact, coherent gender, achieved through an apparent repetition of the same produces as its *effect* the illusion of a prior and volitional subject. In this sense, gender is not a performance that a prior subject elects to do, but gender is *performative* in the sense that it constitutes as an effect the very subject it appears to express. (1991, 24)

If we can be liberated from rigid subject positionings to performative and provisional identities, we may find that this is what we always already were. So freed, we may find that political paths are open to us that we had not even imagined.[23] Choosing the wrong path as a unitary and solitary entity is to risk making one's new positioning into an irreversible solitude. Hegel felt he was risking madness; some of us with less grandiose attempts at repositioning may sense that it is unethical to break solidarity with our assumed group, or even that we are betraying one of our past "I's."[24] Hegel makes "sense" of that which seems nonsensical: that we want conflicting things, that we are conflicting things, that we need conflicting groups. An understanding of internal communication turns an oppressive silence into an empowering one, for when silence is seen as the possibility of external communications (which in turn can change and rearrange our subject positions), our possibilities for real social change proliferate exponentially.

Notes

1. See for instance, Hirsch and Keller (1990), which addresses both the conflicts women can face within themselves and those we face against and with each other as different kinds of feminists, nonfeminists, and antifeminists.

2. In early work she stresses the need of self-chosen care for women (Gilligan 1982); in

later work it becomes apparent that internal communication remains an important social step for girls and women (Gilligan, Ward, and Taylor 1988).

3. A theme throughout Irigaray's work is that as women, we must find ourselves in the hidden images of maternal multiplicity. The lack of female representation has denied us a proper valorization of the many meanings and functions of the maternal. See especially *Elemental Passions* (1992), 157; *Marine Lover of Friedrich Nietzsche* (1991), 86; and *Speculum of the Other Woman* (1985b), 300–301.

4. The need of women to reach out to other women in discursive space that is not predetermined by the male is evident in the work of Monique Wittig (1992); Andrea Nye (1990); Hélène Cixous and Catherine Clément (1987); and Luce Irigaray (1992). This is of course just a small sampling chosen for the diversity: Wittig theorizes her novels as almost guerilla attempts to open up the language for real communication; Nye critiques the space of logic from a position of alterity; Cixous and Clément write beautifully of the possibility of overcoming a position of alterity without quite abandoning it; and, Irigaray chooses a set of completely radical others to write "herselves" to.

5. Hegel (1977), 284, paras. 470–71. Patricia Jagentowicz Mills convincingly argues that the dialectic cannot "go through" for women. While an *Aufhebung* of divine and human law occurs through Christianity in the modern world for man, a similar *Aufhebung* cannot be found for Hegel's Antigone because Hegel cannot acknowledge (recognize) her as an *acting* being. See Mills (1986).

6. It is important in this regard to note that marriage is not required by rationality. Marriage is "voluntary" for men and women; see Hegel (1952), 115, para. 168.

7. What doesn't match will be different from woman to woman. And certainly there will be material that cannot be internalized by certain men. The important point is that there is a sense of having been shut out that women will encounter when engaging with the bulk of the philosophical canon. For an intelligent discussion of this phenomenon, see Michele Le Doeff (1989), 100–129.

8. For example, readers of the *Apology* read with emotion the directives to live honorably and reflectively; but then for women readers there is the moment where exclusion comes to the surface. Part of what it means to be noble is to always refrain from being womanly. More to the point, readers of the *Philosophy of Right* may become caught up in the movement toward world-historical importance, all the while knowing that they aren't invited to the end of history—or to any history for that matter.

9. See for an insightful manner of reading philosophical texts from gendered positions Tamsin E. Lorraine (1990). For a text that resurrects a female voice from the margin, while pointing out the difficulty of keeping a feminist voice within the canon, see Nancy Paston (1991).

10. A consequence of this is that "phallocentric" is more properly applied to terms such as communication, politics, and social structure than to foundational or ontological categories. The latter categories are eschewed by many of late but perhaps we have given them up overhastily.

11. As are other misrepresented groups. It is no surprise that exciting theories of the last century come primarily from such groups whether the theories' content is overtly racial, ethnic, feminist, queer, or not.

12. Of course, we *need* not appropriate anything at this point. Linda Singer's (1993) argument that it is time for feminists who so desire to theorize without inserting themselves into the "canon" is compelling. Appropriations can after all, come to an end. Still, there are occasions, for instance when organizing against the persistence of poverty or against an imperialist war, when the systematic politics afforded through grand narrative become strategic; and there, Hegel's theories elucidate many feminist concerns.

13. An argument I shall not make here is that every exclusion based on gender is necessarily societal. Arguments against those who gender any precommunicative space easily follow from the analysis presented here.

14. Butler (1987), 42. While expositing Hegel, Butler uses the male pronoun to represent the subject.

15. Hegel (1977), 481, para. 790. Hegel allows apparently invisible preservations. The preservation of silence is strictly analogous to the preservation he explicitly allows.

16. Hegel notes that "self-consciousness found the Thing to be like itself, and itself to be like a Thing; i.e. it is aware that it is *in itself* the objectively real world (1977, 211, para. 347).

17. "The self-knowing Spirit knows not only itself but also the negative of itself or its limit" (Hegel, 1977, 492, para. 807).

18. There is no room to argue here that such a generalization is warranted. At first blush, it is not. Marx, of course, makes the generalization to the relations of production in capitalism. Following him other commentators so generalize. For our purposes here, it is worth noting that Kojève is such a commentator; see especially Kojève (1969), 42–43.

19. If this sounds glib, as if to say, "Just say no to exclusion," I have not made myself clear. One can only overcome the silence of exclusion by reclaiming the first silence and this is not a simple matter of asserting no.

20. While drawing heavily on theoretical constructs crafted by Luce Irigaray, I distance myself from the position that exclusion is primary; see especially Irigaray (1985a). Here she argues that the thread of the philosophical canon that stems from Plato forces women into the position of inferior copy of a copy. She points out that woman is a multiplicity and that the unity of the Forms will necessarily distort the possibilities for women's speech being heard. That "woman" will erupt is also argued. Thus, while women are explicitly excluded from the unifying discourse, their presence is implicitly felt in the womb shape of the cave, for one example.

21. For an analysis of the equality/difference debate see Joan W. Scott's (1990) discussion of the Sears case. Scott's contention is that the simple demand for equality (for example, in hiring) overlooks crucial differences between men and women as they are currently constructed.

22. This call distantly echoes Carole Pateman's (1990) call for a "feminist total critique of the liberal opposition of private and public" (137). I share her sense that such a critique has not yet been properly mounted and agree that finding such a critique is crucial.

23. I have used Judith Butler's *Gender Trouble* (1990) in feminist theory courses, empowering some students to experiment with who and what they are without fear of negating themselves or other women—a real fear that we often have. Still, I should note that the same text can have a chilling effect on women in the same class. Seeing the force of an argument that releases the perceived stability of their "I's" they are more likely to stress repeatedly that they "know" who they are. My point here is that differing perspectives—or stages of development—will receive cognate theories as liberatory or chilling.

24. A theoretical construction of obligations in this new framework is necessary. An application without careful thought on these issues is potentially dangerous. For an excellent analysis of obligation from a feminist perspective see Nancy J. Hirschmann (1992).

Works Cited

Brennan, Teresa. 1992. *The Interpretation of the Flesh: Freud and Femininity.* New York: Routledge.

Butler, Judith. 1987. *Subjects of Desire: Hegelian Reflection on Twentieth-Century France.* New York: Columbia University Press.
———. 1990. *Gender Trouble: Feminism and the Subversion of Identity.* New York: Routledge.
———. 1992. "Imitation and Gender Insubordination." In *inside/out: lesbian theories, gay theories,* edited by Diana Fuss, 13–32. New York: Routledge.
Cixous, Hélène, and Catherine Clément. 1986. *The Newly Born Woman.* Translated by Betsy Wing. Minneapolis: University of Minnesota Press.
Gilligan, Carol. 1982. *In a Different Voice.* Cambridge: Harvard University Press.
Gilligan, Carol, Janie Ward, and Jill Taylor. 1988. *Mapping the Moral Domain.* Cambridge: Harvard University Press.
Hegel, Georg Wilhelm Friedrich. 1952. *Philosophy of Right.* Translated by T. M. Knox. New York: Oxford University Press.
———. 1977. *Phenomenology of Spirit.* Translated by A. V. Miller. Oxford: Clarendon Press.
Hirsch, Marianne, and Evelyn Fox Keller, eds. 1990. *Conflicts in Feminism.* New York: Routledge.
Hirschmann, Nancy J. 1992. *Rethinking Obligation: A Feminist Method for Political Theory.* Ithaca: Cornell University Press.
Irigaray, Luce. 1985a. "Plato's Hysteria." In her *Speculum of the Other Woman,* translated by Gillian C. Gill, 228–364. Ithaca: Cornell University Press.
———. 1985b. *Speculum of the Other Woman.* Translated by Gillian C. Gill. Ithaca: Cornell University Press.
———. 1991. *Marine Lover of Friedrich Nietzsche.* Translated by Gillian C. Gill. New York: Columbia University Press.
———. 1992. *Elemental Passions.* Translated by Joanne Collie and Judith Still. New York: Routledge.
Kojève, Alexandre. 1969. *Introduction to the Reading of Hegel.* Translated by James H. Nichols Jr. Ithaca: Cornell University Press.
Le Doeuff, Michèle. 1989. "Long Hair, Short Ideas." In *The Philosophical Imaginary,* translated by Colin Gordon, 100–129. Stanford: Stanford University Press.
Lorraine, Tamsin E. 1990. *Gender, Identity, and the Production of Meaning.* Boulder, Colo.: Westview.
Mills, Patricia Jagentowicz. 1986. "Hegel's Antigone." *The Owl of Minerva* 17, no. 2 (spring 1986): 131–52. Reprinted with minor revisions as Chapter 3 in this volume.
Nye, Andrea. 1990. *Words of Power.* New York: Routledge.
Oliver, Kelly, 1993. *Reading Kristeva: Unraveling the Double Bind.* New York: Routledge.
Pateman, Carole. 1990. "Feminist Critiques of the Public-Private Distinction." In *Contemporary Political Theory,* edited by Philip Petit, 116–37. New York: Macmillan.
Paxton, Nancy. 1991. *George Eliot and Herbert Spencer: Feminism, Evolutionism, and the Reconstruction of Gender.* Princeton: Princeton University Press.
Scott, Joan W. 1990. "Deconstructing Equality-Versus-Difference: Or, the Uses of Poststructuralist Theory for Feminism." In *Conflicts in Feminism,* edited by Marianne Hirsch and Evelyn Fox Keller, 134–48. New York: Routledge.
Singer, Linda. 1993. "Defusing the Canon: Feminist Rereading and Textual Politics." In her *Erotic Welfare: Sexual Theory and Politics in the Age of Epidemic,* 163–76. New York: Routledge.
Wittig, Monique. 1992. *The Straight Mind.* Boston: Beacon.

Select Bibliography

Aboulafia, Mitchell. "From Domination to Recognition." In *Beyond Domination: New Perspectives on Women and Philosophy*, edited by Carol C. Gould, 175–85. Totowa, N.J.: Rowman and Allanheld, 1984.

Barber, Benjamin R. "Spirit's Phoenix and History's Owl or The Incoherence of Dialectics in Hegel's Account of Women." *Political Theory* 16, no. 1 (February 1988): 5–28.

Beauvoir, Simone de. *The Second Sex*. Translated and edited by H. M. Parshley. New York: Knopf, 1953; New York: Vintage, 1974. See especially the introduction and part 1.

Blum, Lawrence A. "Kant's and Hegel's Moral Rationalism: A Feminist Perspective." *Canadian Journal of Philosophy* 12, no. 2 (June 1982): 287–302.

Brod, Harry. *Hegel's Philosophy of Politics: Idealism, Identity, and Modernity*. Boulder, Colo.: Westview, 1992.

Butler, Clark. "Hegel's Idea of Marriage: Science or Ideology?" In *Hegel: The Letters*, with commentary by Clark Butler, and translations by Clark Butler and Christiane Seiler, 234–52. Bloomington: Indiana University Press, 1984.

Chanter, Tina. "Antigone's Dilemma." In *Re-Reading Levinas*, edited by Robert Bernasconi and Simon Critchley, 130–46. Bloomington: Indiana University Press, 1991. This essay looks at "the question of woman" in the work of Derrida, Levinas, and Sophocles.

Cornell, Drucilla. *Beyond Accomodation: Ethical Feminism, Deconstruction, and the Law*. New York: Routledge, 1991.

———. *The Philosophy of the Limit*. New York: Routledge, 1992. See especially chapter 3.

Dahlstrom, Daniel O. "The Sexual Basis of Moral Life." In *Hermeneutics and the Tradition*. Proceedings of the American Catholic Philosophical Association, 62:202–10. Lancaster, Pa.: Wickersham, 1989.

d'Eaubonne, Françoise. Excerpt from *Feminism or Death*. Translated by Betty Schmitz. In *New French Feminisms*, edited and with introductions by Elaine Marks and Isabelle de Courtivron, 64–67. Amherst: University of Massachusetts Press, 1980. Carla Lonzi's work is central to d'Eaubonne's critique of phallocentrism.

Derrida, Jacques. *Glas*. Translated by J. P. Leavery Jr. and R. Rand. Lincoln: University of Nebraska Press, 1986.

Dietz, Mary. "Citizenship with a Feminist Face: The Problem with Maternal Thinking." *Political Theory* 13 (February 1985): 19–37. This article offers a feminist interpretation of Sophocles' *Antigone*.

Diprose, Rosalyn. *The Bodies of Women: Ethics, Embodiment and Sexual Difference.* New York: Routledge, 1994.

———. "In Excess: The Body and the Habit of Sexual Difference." *Hypatia: Special Issue on Feminism and the Body* 6, no. 3 (1991): 156–71. This essay offers a re-reading of the *Antigone* through a critique of Hegel's account of that story. It goes on to explore a contemporary, post-Hegelian ethics of difference.

Donougho, Martin. "The Woman in White: On the Reception of Hegel's *Antigone.*" *The Owl of Minerva* 21, no. 1 (fall 1989): 65–89.

Douzinas, Costas. "Law's Birth and Antigone's Death: On Ontological and Psychoanalytical Ethics." *Cardozo Law Review* 16, nos. 3–4 (January 1995): 1325–62.

Dunayevskaya, Raya. *Philosophy and Revolution: From Hegel to Sartre, and from Marx to Mao.* New York: Columbia University Press, 1989.

———. *Women's Liberation and the Dialectics of Revolution: Reaching for the Future.* Atlantic Highlands, N.J.: Humanities Press, 1985. See especially the introduction/overview.

Easton, Susan M. "Hegel and Feminism." In *Hegel and Modern Philosophy*, edited by David Lamb, 30–55. New York: Croom Helm, 1987.

Elshtain, Jean Bethke. "Antigone's Daughters." *Democracy* 2 (1982): 46–59. Reprinted as "Antigone's Daughters: Reflections on Female Identity and the State," in *Families, Politics, and Public Policy: A Feminist Dialogue on Women and the State,* edited by Irene Diamond, 147–97. New York: Longmans, 1983.

———. *Public Man, Private Woman: Women in Social and Political Thought.* Princeton: Princeton University Press, 1981. See especially chapter 4.

Feral, Josette. "Antigone or the Irony of the Tribe." Translated by Alice Jardine and Tom Gora. *Diacritics* 8 (fall 1978): 2–14. Feral interprets Irigaray's reading of Antigone in this article.

Ferguson, Kathy E. *The Man Question: Visions of Subjectivity in Feminist Theory.* Berkeley and Los Angeles: University of California Press, 1993. Chapter 2 deals with Hegel.

Fraser, Nancy. "The French Derrideans: Politicizing Deconstruction or Deconstructing the Political?" In her *Unruly Practices: Power, Discourse and Gender in Contemporary Social Theory*, 69–92. Minneapolis: University of Minnesota Press, 1989. This essay makes reference to Hegel and Marx in the context of a discussion of the politics of deconstruction.

Fuchs, Jo-Ann Pilardi. "On the War Path and Beyond: Hegel, Freud, and Feminist Theory." *Women's Studies International Forum* 6, no. 6 (1983): 565–72.

Geller, Jay. "Hegel's Self-Conscious Woman." *Modern Language Quarterly* 53, no. 2 (June 1992): 173–99.

Gould, Carol C. "The Woman Question: Philosophy of Liberation and the Liberation of Philosophy." *Philosophical Forum* 5, nos. 1–2 (fall–winter 1973–74): 5–44. Reprinted in *Philosophy of Woman: An Anthology of Classic and Current Concepts,* 2d ed., edited by Mary Briody Mahowald. Bloomington: Indiana University Press, 1983.

Hodge, Joanna. "Women and the Hegelian State." In *Women and Western Political Philosophy: Kant to Nietzsche*, edited by Ellen Kennedy and Susan Mendus, 127–58. New York: St. Martin's, 1987.

Hoffheimer, Michael H. "The Idea of Law (*Recht*) in Hegel's *Phenomenology of Spirit.*" *Clio* 21, no. 4 (1992): 345–67. See especially 350–52.

Irigaray, Luce. "The Universal as Mediation." Translated by Gillian C. Gill. In *Sexes and Genealogies*, 125–49. New York: Columbia University Press, 1993.

Janssen-Jurreit, Marielouise. *Sexism: The Male Monopoly on History and Thought.* Translated by Verne Moberg. New York: Farrar, Straus and Giroux, 1982. See especially chapter 28.

Lacour, Claudia B. "Austen's *Pride and Prejudice* and Hegel's "Truth in Art": Concept, Reference, and History." *ELH (English Literary History)* 59, no. 3 (fall 1992): 597–623.

Landes, Joan B. "Hegel's Conception of the Family." *Polity* 14, no. 1 (fall 1981): 5–28. Reprinted in *The Family in Political Thought,* edited by Jean Bethke Elshtain, 125–44. Amherst: University of Massachusetts Press, 1982.

Le Doeuff, Michèle. *The Philosophical Imaginary.* Translated by Colin Gordon. Stanford: Stanford University Press, 1989. See especially chapter 6.

——— "Women in Philosophy." Translated by Debbie Pope. *Radical Philosophy* (London, England), no. 17 (summer 1977): 2–11.

Lloyd, Genevieve. *The Man of Reason: "Male" and "Female" in Western Philosophy.* Minneapolis: University of Minnesota Press, 1984. See especially 88–93 on Hegel.

MacGregor, David. *Hegel, Marx, and the English State.* Boulder, Colo.: Westview, 1992. See especially chapter 5, "The Father's Arbitrary Will Within the Family."

Newman, Amy. "Hegel's Theoretical Violence." In *Modern Engendering: Critical Feminist Readings in Modern Western Philosophy,* edited by Bat-Ami Bar On, 155–66. Albany: State University of New York Press, 1994.

Nussbaum, Martha. *The Fragility of Goodness: Luck and Ethics in Greek Tragedy.* Cambridge: Cambridge University Press, 1986. (See especially chapter 3 on Sophocles' *Antigone.*)

Pritchard, Annie. "Antigone's Mirrors: Reflections on Moral Madness." *Hypatia* 7, no. 3 (summer 1992): 77–93.

Ring, Jennifer. *Modern Political Theory and Contemporary Feminism: A Dialectical Analysis.* Albany: State University of New York Press, 1991.

Rosenthal, Abigail. "Feminism Without Contradictions." *The Monist* 57, no. 1 (January 1973): 28–42. Reprinted in *Morality in the Modern World: Ethical Dimensions of Contemporary Human Problems,* edited by Lawrence Habermehl. Encino, Calif.: Dickinson, 1976. This is an originative feminist appropriation of Hegel whose only flaw is the uncritical use of sexist language.

Scholz, Sally J. "Reproductive Labor: The Impact of the Patriarchal Family on Hegel's Phenomenology." *Clio* 22, no. 4 (summer 1993): 357–68.

Siebert, Rudolf J. "Hegel's Concept of Marriage and Family: The Origin of Subjective Freedom." In *Hegel's Social and Political Thought: The Philosophy of Objective Spirit,* edited by D. P. Verene, 177–214. Atlantic Highlands, N.J.: Humanities Press, 1980.

———. *Hegel's Concept of Marriage and the Family.* Lanham, Md.: University Press of America, 1979.

Steiner, George. *Antigones.* New York: Oxford University Press, 1975. This book attempts to give a comprehensive view of the Antigone legend in Western thought but lacks a feminist perspective.

Tuana, Nancy. *Woman and the History of Philosophy.* New York: Paragon House, 1992. See especially 98–111.

Willett, Cynthia. "Hegel, Antigone, and the Possibility of a Woman's Dialectic." In *Modern Engendering: Critical Feminist Readings in Modern Western Philosophy,* edited by Bat-Ami Bar On, 167–81. Albany: State University of New York Press, 1994.

———. "Hegel, Antigone, and the Possibility of Ecstatic Dialogue." *Philosophy and Literature* 14 (1990): 268–83.

————. *Maternal Ethics and Other Slave Moralities: Race, Gender, and Recognition*. New York: Routledge, 1995.

Woolf, Virginia. *Three Guineas*. New York: Penguin Books, 1977. See especially 94 on the *Antigone*.

Zerilli, Linda M. G. "Machiavelli's Sisters: Women and 'the Conversation' of Political Theory." *Political Theory* 19, no. 2 (May 1991): 252–76. This essay focuses on the use of Antigone in Irigary, Elshtain, and Dietz.

Contributors

GIOVANNA BELLESIA teaches in the Italian Department at Smith College. A native of Italy, she received her *Laurea* and a degree in translation in Milan. She also holds a Ph.D. from the University of North Carolina at Chapel Hill. Her research interests are translation theory and modern Italian women writers. She is currently studying family structure and motherhood in twentieth-century Italy.

SEYLA BENHABIB is professor of political theory in the Department of Government at Harvard University. She is the author of *Critique, Norm, and Utopia* (Columbia University Press, 1986) and *Situating the Self* (Routledge, 1992); and is the editor, with Drucilla Cornell, of *Feminism as Critique* (University of Minnesota Press, 1987), and with Fred Dallmayr, of *The Communicative Ethics Controversy* (MIT Press, 1990). Part of her continuing debate with Judith Butler, Drucilla Cornell, and Nancy Fraser has been published in *Feminist Contentions: A Philosophical Exchange* (Routledge, 1995). She is currently completing a book entitled *The Reluctant Modernism of Hannah Arendt*.

ALISON BROWN is assistant professor of philosophy at Northern Arizona University. She works on issues of communication, community, and self in political theory. She is writing two books: one on truth, the other on lying.

ERIC CLARKE is assistant professor in the Department of English at the University of Pittsburgh, where he teaches lesbian and gay studies and nineteenth-century British culture. He is currently working on a study of the interconnections between sexual politics and cultural values in the canonization of the poet Percy Shelley. He is also coediting, with

Chantal Nadeau, a collection of essays on the history of sexuality as a site for critiquing traditional forms of knowledge production.

LUCE IRIGARAY is the director of research in philosophy at the Centre National de la Recherche Scientifique in Paris. She holds doctorates in linguistics and philosophy and is a psychoanalyst in private practice. Her books in English include *Speculum of the Other Woman* (Cornell University Press, 1985), *This Sex Which Is Not One* (Cornell University Press, 1985), *An Ethics of Sexual Difference* (Cornell University Press, 1993), *je, tu, nous: Toward a Culture of Difference* (Routledge, 1993), *Elemental Passions* (Routledge, 1992), *Marine Lover of Friedrich Nietzsche* (Columbia University Press, 1991), *Sexes and Genealogies* (Columbia University Press, 1993), and *thinking the difference: For a Peaceful Revolution* (Routledge, 1994).

DAVID FARRELL KRELL is professor of philosophy at DePaul University in Chicago. He is the author of *Daimon Life: Heidegger and Life-Philosophy* (Indiana University Press, 1992), *Of Memory, Reminiscence, and Writing: On the Verge* (Indiana University Press, 1990), *Postponements: Woman, Sensuality, and Death in Nietzsche* (Indiana University Press, 1986), and *Intimations of Mortality: Time, Truth, and Finitude in Heidegger's Thinking of Being* (Pennsylvania State University Press, 1986; 2d ed., 1991). His most recent book is entitled *Lunar Voices: Of Tragedy, Poetry, Fiction, and Thought.* He is editor and translator of a wide range of books and articles in German and French thought and letters.

CARLA LONZI was an influential Italian feminist until her untimely death in 1982. An art historian by training, she was an art critic until 1970 when she gave up the profession to devote herself to feminism, the Rivolta Femminile group, and its Milan publishing house, Scritti di Rivolta Femminile. Her writings published by Scritti di Rivolta Femminile include *Sputiamo su Hegel* (Let's spit on Hegel) in 1970; *La donna clitoridea e la donna vaginale* (The clitoral woman and the vaginal woman) in 1971; *Taci, anzi parla—diario di una femminista* (Speak not, no, speak—diary of a feminist) in 1978; *Vai pure, dialogo con Pietro Consagra* (Go then, dialogue with Pietro Consagra) in 1980. Works published posthumously by Scritti di Rivolta Femminile include *Scacco Ragionato: Poesie dal '58 al '63* (Poems from 1958 to 1963) edited by Anna Jacquinta and Marta Lonzi (1985), and *Armande sono io!* (Armande is me!), a collection of notes and reflections from Lonzi's research on Les Précieuses, a group of intellectual and literary women in seventeenth-century Paris, edited by Marta Lonzi, Angela De Carlo, and Maria Delfino (1992).

ELAINE MACLACHLAN teaches in the Italian Department at Smith College. Her translations have appeared in the *Atlantic Monthly, Harper's,* the *Paris Review, Daedalus,* and *Metamorphoses.* She is currently writing on sixteenth-century Italian women's lyric poetry, especially that of Chiara Matraini, exploring female narrative voice in sonnet sequences.

PATRICIA JAGENTOWICZ MILLS is associate professor of political theory in the Department of Political Science at the University of Massachusetts at Amherst. She is the author of *Woman, Nature, and Psyche* (Yale University Press, 1987), a study of the relation between the domination of nature and the domination of woman in the dialectical tradition that includes Hegel, Marx, Marcuse, Horkheimer, and Adorno. Her published articles focus on ecofeminism, women and myth, and the critical theory of the first generation of the Frankfurt School. She is currently working on a series of essays for a book tentatively titled *Thinking Differently: Meditations for a Feminist Critical Theory.*

MARY O'BRIEN is professor emeritus of the Department of Sociology of Education at the Ontario Institute for Studies in Education in Toronto, Canada. She is the author of *The Politics of Reproduction* (Routledge and Kegan Paul, 1981) and *Reproducing the World: Essays in Feminist Theory* (Westview, 1989). Before entering the academy, she spent twenty-five years as a midwife and nurse.

FRANCES OLSEN is professor of law at the University of California, Los Angeles, and founder of the feminist caucus of Critical Legal Studies. She has consulted, lectured, and published on five continents on women's rights and feminist legal theory. Her latest work is the two-volume set *Feminist Legal Theory* (Dartmouth University Press, 1995).

CAROLE PATEMAN is professor of political science at the University of California, Los Angeles, and a member of the Center for Social Theory and Comparative History. She was president of the International Political Science Association (1991–94) and a Guggenheim Fellow (1993–94). Her current research is on issues of citizenship and democratic theory.

HEIDI M. RAVVEN is associate professor of religious studies at Hamilton College, where she has been on the faculty since 1983. Her Ph.D.

is from Brandeis University where she studied Jewish Philosophy under Alexander Altmann. She has published articles on Hegel, Jewish feminism, and Spinoza. Her particular areas of interest are Hegel's and Spinoza's moral and social philosophies and their implications for feminist ethics. She is currently working on a book on Spinoza's moral philosophy tentatively titled *Corruptions of Desire: Spinoza and the Moral Problem*.

NAOMI SCHOR is professor of French at Harvard University. She is the author of *Reading in Detail: Aesthetics and the Feminine* (Methuen, 1987), *Breaking the Chain: Women, Theory, and French Realist Fiction* (Columbia University Press, 1985), and *Zola's Crowds* (Johns Hopkins University Press, 1978). Her most recent book is *George Sand and Idealism* (Columbia University Press, 1993). With Elizabeth Weed she co-edits *differences: A Journal of Feminist Cultural Studies*.

SHARI NELLER STARRETT is assistant professor of philosophy at California State University at Fullerton. She has published a number of articles on Nietzsche's writings on women, and is currently working on several articles dealing with Hegel and Nietzsche, and a book tentatively titled *Co-Lateral Attachment: A Path from Hegel and Nietzsche, to Feminist Criticism*.

Index

and marriage contract, 216, 217
men and, 186
and particularity, 72
and paternity, 186
self-consciousness and, 152, 294
and women, 73
reconciliation (*Aufhebung*), 88 n. 26, 172–73 n.
16, 317 n. 5. *See also* dialectics
in bourgeois society, 238
and conflict of the ancient world, 73, 77,
83–84
denial of female difference, 11
of desire and morality, 79
and the detail, 136–38, 143–44
of family and public world, 241
individual and group, 234–35
of male and female groups, 241
of the particular and the universal, 60, 61
of the self and the Other, 242
and transcendence of opposition, 5
as unconvincing, 8, 41
woman's domination and, 22, 84–85, 295
relations, critical. *See* "critical relations"
religion, 206 n. 9. *See also* divine law
and art, 134, 136
and family, 261
remembrance (*Erinnerung*), 56
repression in colleges and universities, 292
reproduction, 3, 15. *See also* birth; genitality;
maternity; reproductive consciousness
as ahistorical, 199
appropriation of, 170
concept of, 15, 151–53, 189
dialectical form of, 16, 192, 193–94, 205
and epistemology, 197–98
equality of, 206 n. 12
and history, 16, 180–81
labor and continuity, 186–87
love and, 80
and paternity, 16, 196
vs. production, 279
and spiritual regeneration, 183, 264
universality of, 190
women and negation, 184–85
reproductive consciousness, 16, 180–207
reproductive organs. *See also* genitality
homology of, 151–54
responsibility. *See also* divine law
brother-sister relationship, 65–66
and consciousness, 232

and divine law/human law, 244
guilt and, 231–32. *See also* crime and guilt
woman/family and, 59–88
revolution
and class inequalities, 2–3
and legacy of bourgeois condition, 292
and liberation, 19, 278
and repression, 282, 283, 284
Reynolds, Joshua, 124–26, 135
Romantic art, 13, 163
and the detail, 122–24, 134–35
Romanticism, 36–38, 111–13
and neoclassicism, 120
Rome
and individualism, 245
and property ownership, 188
Rousseau, Jean-Jacques
family and citizenship, 32
and sexual contract, 210
social contract, 215
Russian Revolution, 282, 283

salaries of women, 109
salons, 36
sameness, 54, 55
"saming," 9, 10
Schelling, Caroline Schlegel, 8, 36–40
Schelling, Friedrich Wilhelm Joseph von, 37,
38, 135
"dark principle," 182
Schiller, Friedrich von, 105 n. 2
Schlegel, August Wilhelm, 37–39, 135
Schlegel, Caroline, 8, 36–40
Schlegel, Friedrich von, 35–36, 37, 105 n. 2,
106 n. 7, 106 nn. 8 and 10, 116 n. 7
Schleiermacher, Friedrich, 37, 103, 106 n. 9
Schor, Naomi, 13–15, 23 n. 13, 119–47
subjectivity, 8
science, aesthetics as, 167. *See also* Encyclopedia
of the Philosophical Sciences
Scott, Joan, 170–71 n. 2, 318 n. 21
sculpture, 13, 122, 123, 126–27
"second nature"
and childbearing, 188
Geist and, 29, 31
polis/political realm, 61, 69
and social universality, 61
seduction, 97, 103, 111, 203
"seed." *See also* semen
alienation of female, 16, 199